Bruce's History Lessons —The First Five Years (2001-2006)

Bruce G. Kauffmann

iUniverse, Inc.
New York   Bloomington

Bruce's History Lessons -
The First Five Years (2001-2006)

Copyright © 2008 by Bruce G. Kauffman

iUniverse books may be ordered through booksellers or by contacting:

iUniverse
1663 Liberty Drive
Bloomington, IN 47403
www.iuniverse.com
1-800-Authors (1-800-288-4677)

ISBN: 978-1-4401-0642-2 (pbk)
ISBN: 978-1-4401-0643-9 (ebk)

Printed in the United States of America

iUniverse rev. date: 11/03/2008

Introduction:

"Trying to plan for the future without a sense of the past is like trying to plant cut flowers."

-Daniel Boorstin, Librarian of Congress

When I launched my short, once-a-week history column, Bruce's History Lessons, in January of 2001, there were two things I did not know. First, how much I was going to enjoy writing it. And second, how hard it was going to be to sell it. With typical foresight and impeccable timing, I was starting a newspaper column just as the newspaper business was going into its death spiral, plagued by falling circulation and advertising due to so many competing sources of news and information. Newspaper editors were dropping columns, not adding them, and they were even dropping columns written by famous journalists, backed by well-known and respected syndicates. By contrast, I was a nobody. I had no syndicate, no agent and no reputation. And I was cold-calling editors, trying to convince them to consider a column that did not deal with current events, did not deal with health matters (human or pet), did not offer advice about relationships (human or pet), and did not dispense tips about saving, or making, money.

Still, I figured since I loved writing the column, I should press on and I managed to pick up some 25 newspapers at my peak. And that taught me one other thing that I had not known — how many thousands of readers there are out in America who love history, who love stories about our shared past, and who love reading about the men and women who shaped our world, or who were, in some very amazing ways, shaped by it.

Which is not to say that I didn't receive letters and e-mails from readers telling me that I was an idiot, or just plain wrong, or a right-wing nut job or a left-wing cornflake. I did, and much more. Sometimes these readers made excellent points, sometimes not, but I was so gratified that they cared enough to read, and write to me, that I made a pledge — which I have always kept — to write back every reader at least once to thank them for writing. And when appropriate, in my response I would acknowledge their point of view when I thought it had merit, or I would defend my own point of view when I thought mine was the better argument. And I would try to answer every question readers asked. Granted, as the years went by and the column grew in popularity and readership, that took up more and more time. But I always thought of my give-and-take with my readers as part of the fun.

And fun is what history is — or can be. History is not only educational and informative, but it can be entertaining as well. Indeed, my love of history stems from the fact that, as the old cliché goes, "You can't make this stuff up." Put the most imaginative Hollywood screenwriter on every mind-expanding drug you can think of, and he (or she) still wouldn't be able to make up stories as crazy, weird and just plain unbelievable as the stuff that actually happened. Truth really is stranger than fiction.

But history must be properly told. Indeed, as my readers constantly remind me, history is *not* about dates, or figures, or statistics or arcane facts that need to be memorized and regurgitated in history tests, only to be promptly forgotten later. History is, as one reader so nicely put it, "about people who are heroic or tragic, who make decisions, often bad ones. People who have hearts and souls."

And history is also about good people who become evil and evil people who are redeemed. And strange people, and funny people, and people who are, to borrow from Shakespeare, born great, or who achieve greatness, or who have greatness thrust upon them. And history is also about people who should have been great but were ignored or overlooked by history through no fault of their own. *These* are the people I like to write about, and these are the people who populate the pages of this book.

Did I say truth is stranger than fiction? Many people know that John Adams, our second president, was the one who chose Thomas Jefferson, our third president, to write our Declaration of Independence, which became official on July 4th, 1776. But how many know that both Adams and Jefferson died on the exact same day, and that the day they died was July 4th, 1826 — the 50th anniversary of our first famous 4th?

Truth is stranger than fiction? Many people know that England's King James I commissioned the writing of a famous bible, the King James Bible. But how many know that, in 1604, James himself wrote a pamphlet titled

"Counterblast to Tobacco," in which he argued that tobacco was "a custom loathsome to the eye, hateful to the nose, harmful to the brain, and dangerous to the lungs." In other words, more than 400 years ago, James I recognized that tobacco was un-cool (loathsome to the eye), gave you bad breath (hateful to the nose), was addictive (harmful to the brain) and caused cancer (dangerous to the lungs). It would be another 350 years before the American Medical Association got around to that conclusion and to this day the tobacco lobby still hasn't figured it out.

Truth *definitely* is stranger than fiction. David Atchison, from Frogtown, Kentucky, was, technically speaking, America's 12th president — for about three minutes.

This book consists of the first five years of my history columns, beginning with the publication of my very first column in the Canton Repository (Canton, Ohio) in mid-January of 2001 (for which I will be forever grateful to the first editor who took a chance on me, Gayle Beck, the Repository's editorial page editor and now a friend). Reading it you will see that I write about people, places and events that are well-known, but also not-so-well known. I write about conventional history, but I also write about cultural and sports history. I write about wars, but also about cars; about great statesmen, but also great artists; about Supreme Court decisions, but also designated hitter rulings; about Communism and Fascism, but also chauvinism and feminism; about evil geniuses, but also useful idiots.

In every one of my history lessons I try to be entertaining as well as educational. The greatest compliment my readers pay me is when they write me that had history been taught in school the way I present it in *Bruce's History Lessons*, class would have been a lot more fun.

But I also try to be educational as well as entertaining. When attempting to convince newspaper editors to run my column, a point I would constantly make to them (almost always in vain) is how ignorant today's Americans are about our shared heritage, and how dangerous that ignorance can be. Daniel Boorstin, one of America's great historians, knew what he was talking about when he uttered the quote that begins this introduction, as did President Ronald Reagan, when, in one of his last speeches, he said, "If we forget what we did, we won't know who we are. I am warning of an eradication of the American memory that could result, ultimately, in an erosion of the American spirit."

I share that concern, which is one reason I began this column, which — while occasionally covering world history — concentrates mostly on America's shared past. I wanted my readers to have a better understanding of "American History," but have fun while they were doing so. I am happy to say that, from the thousands of readers who have e-mailed me to that effect over the years, I seem to be on the right track, but I want to leave you with one of my favorites, from Catherine Marty, who reads my column in the Dubuque Telegraph-Herald:

Dear Mr. Kauffmann, I've been meaning to write to you for some time to tell you that I truly enjoy your column. Within the bulk of paper that arrives at my door on Sunday, only a few articles are a must-read for me. Yours is at the top of the list. I enjoy history, especially American. You have a gift of telling a story that is educational, factual, entertaining, interesting, and concise, all at the same time. You have taught me many tidbits that merged and helped to form our wonderful country and its people. Thank you for being a bright spot within the often dreary world of news.

Or as Pulitzer-prize winning columnist Paul Greenberg once so elegantly wrote, "The American ethos, always in the making and never made, is a dynamic civility — like federalism *and* baseball. It is liberty *and* order. It's the Declaration of Independence *and* the Constitution, Lincoln *and* Lee, Emily Dickinson *and* Walt Whitman, F. Scott Fitzgerald *and* William Faulkner, Washington *and* Henry Ford — a grand Mormon Tabernacle Choir concatenation of seeming opposites producing something always new."

Which, when you think about it, is another way of saying what that great American philosopher, Yogi Berra, said when told that Dublin had elected its first Jewish mayor. "Only in America."

So maybe that "erosion of the American spirit" isn't such a worry after all. Enjoy.

Dedication:

For my wife Judy, my daughters Remy and Joanna, and all the underpaid, overworked history teachers out there who are passionate about what they do.

Author's Note:

I once had lunch with a well-known columnist for *The Washington Post*, and in the course of our lunch he was on the phone a half-dozen times with his research assistant and his three different editors, discussing the language, the fact-checking, the nuances and the possible repercussions of his upcoming column. Granted, his column expresses a usually partisan opinion on often hot-button current events, and he often takes public figures to task, so he has a real interest in getting his facts right. My column, on the other hand is about the past and most of the people who populate it are long dead. But other than a friend who looks at my column when she can for grammar, syntax, and clarity, I'm on my own. I am my own fact checker and editor — and this is a second career, forcing me to research and write the column evenings, weekends and vacation days. As a result, I have made mistakes of fact in the past and will continue to in the future. There may even be a few in this book. If so, I apologize. As I say in my introduction, my approach to history is not dates, or figures, or statistics or arcane facts, but rather the people, good and bad, who are shaped by, and shape, the larger forces of history. I hope that you will read the columns in this book in that spirit.

Contents

Table of Contents by Subject Matter

Race, Sex, Business And Culture

Science

Sports

Crime

The American Revolution and Aftermath

The Old West

The Civil War Years

The World Wars, In Between and After

The Cold War Years

Modern Times

Bruce's History Lessons:
A New Inauguration Day

This week in 1937, one of President-elect George W. Bush's predecessors, Franklin D. Roosevelt, became the first president to be inaugurated in January. Prior to 1937 the president-elect had taken the oath of office on March 4th, which — given the primitive communications, logistics and transportation conditions of our nation's early years — was deemed necessary to allow enough time to count the vote, appoint the electoral college members, record their votes for president (and Veep), and allow the official winners to settle their affairs and travel to the nation's capital in plenty of time to be inaugurated.

By 1920, however, many felt that technology had improved enough that the country could easily shorten the time from the November election to inauguration. Among those believers was a Republican senator from Nebraska, George Norris, who from the mid-1920s on repeatedly attempted to convince Congress to approve a Constitutional Amendment moving the Inauguration date from March to an earlier time. For years his efforts had succeeded in the Senate but failed in the House and, ironically, it was only after the opposition Democrats recaptured the House in 1931 that his campaign met with success.

And why were the Democrats suddenly so keen on shortening the time between election and inauguration? Because in the upcoming election of 1932, they expected that the White House would once again be theirs. The Republican president, Herbert Hoover, was being blamed for the country's worst economic recession (soon to be the Great Depression) in 50 years. The Democratic challenger, Franklin Roosevelt, seemed a shoo-in for president, yet under the old rules, the lame-duck Hoover would still be running the country for four months after his defeat.

Thus did both the House and the Senate approve a Constitutional Amendment shortening the interregnum from election to inauguration by about six weeks — January 20 instead of March 4. They sent it to the states for ratification in early 1932, but alas, when our 20th Amendment was ratified in 1933, it was too late to affect the race between Hoover and Roosevelt. Roosevelt had to wait four months before taking power. However, it did affect all subsequent elections, meaning FDR's successors are inaugurated some six weeks sooner than were his predecessors.

Including George W. Bush, whose inauguration makes him the 43rd president of the United States. For both Bush and Gore supporters this begs an interesting question: Would this election have ended differently if, instead of being under intense pressure to concede in the face of a looming deadline, Al Gore had had an extra six weeks to convince the courts, and the country, that more time was necessary — *and available* — to determine the real winner?

© *Kauffmann 2008*

Bruce's History Lessons:
Take This Job and ...

"I do not propose to be buried until I am actually dead."
–Daniel Webster, turning down the Vice Presidency

For a job that comes with free housing (and a mansion at that), your own airplane (a jumbo jet), the best medical, dental and life insurance available anywhere (also free), a terrific retirement package, a good chance for advancement and a six-figure salary, it is amazing how many people have disdained from applying for it, or have refused to accept it. And their reaction pales in comparison with that of the unfortunate souls who have actually held the job! Which must have the guy who recently took the job wondering: Is being vice president of the United States really so awful?

Actually it depends. From a strictly Constitutional standpoint, the Veep has only two duties. First he (or she) becomes president of the U.S. Senate, where he/she can only vote when a matter before the Senate results in a tie and needs the vice-president to break it. Second, the Veep assumes the presidency should the president be impeached, die or resign — or is unable to perform the duties of office.

And that's it. Which means that the relationship between vice presidents and their bosses is crucial in determining what role they will play and, consequently, how much satisfaction they will get out of the job. In the current case, given George W. Bush's relative youth and inexperience, and Dick Cheney's years of government service, most experts believe that Cheney will have considerable responsibility and power in the Bush administration.

Then again, that's what they said about John Kennedy and Lyndon Johnson. The former was a young, first-time senator. The latter was among

3

the most powerful Senate majority leaders in history. Yet President Kennedy treated Vice President Johnson like a messenger boy, ignoring his advice, shutting him out of the White House inner circle, and sending him on junkets just to get rid of him.

So nothing is set in stone, including the longevity of the president himself. Sure, as Johnson said of the vice presidency, "In the end, the job amounts to nothing." But as he reportedly also admitted to Clare Booth Luce (wife of *Time* magazine founder, Henry Luce) in one of the least spoken but most revealing statements about why anyone would accept the job, "I looked it up and one out of every four presidents has died in office. I'm a gamblin' man and this may be the only chance I got."

As we know, Johnson's gamble "paid off" upon Kennedy's untimely death. Like it or not, that possibility exists in the mind of every Veep, including — you can be sure — the newly installed one.

© *Kauffmann 2008*

Bruce's History Lesson:
The Tet Offensive

Ask your average baby boomer to recall a major Vietnam War battle and those of us whose memories survived the '60s (it was a drug thing; you wouldn't understand — or want to) would probably reply "Tet," which began this week (Jan. 30) in 1968. Tet was *the* turning point of the Vietnam War.

During Tet, which is Vietnam's version of our New Year, the war's two belligerents — North and South Vietnam — traditionally observed a cease-fire, but in '68 the North's leader, Ho Chi Minh, launched a massive surprise attack, using both his regular army troops and his guerrilla troops in South Vietnam, the Vietcong. Little remembered is that before Tet the U.S.-backed South Vietnamese army was at least holding its own on the battlefield. Ho wanted to change the momentum.

Ho also changed tactics by attacking all of the South's provincial capital cities, making Tet the North's first major foray out of the countryside and into an urban battle. When Tet was over it was a decisive military victory.

For the U.S. and the South. Not only did the North lose four times as many regular troops as the South Vietnamese army, but also the Vietcong was almost destroyed. Which begs the question: If the North *lost* the Tet battle, and Tet was *the* turning point of the war, how come the North eventually *won* the war?

Several reasons, starting with the fact that appearance is reality. Prior to Tet, U.S. leaders had told the public that the war was going so well the North was all but finished as a significant threat. Tet, which was a major campaign fought all up and down South Vietnam, exposed that lie. What's more, Tet was fought in the cities, making it easier for the American media to beam back footage of the carnage. If Vietnam was known as America's first "television war," Tet was the first time that the war — in all its gory — was seen in living color, in America's living rooms, night after night.

Which is why in Tet's wake, anti-war sentiment, which *had* been limited to drug-addled, free-love hippies (at least that was the general perception), quickly spread to Middle America. Instead of a fight to "contain Communism," most Americans began to see Vietnam as a costly, chaotic civil war spinning out of control in a far-off land that posed no discernible threat to U.S. security, or discernible boon to U.S. interests.

As a result, the military defeat that the North suffered was more than compensated for by its public relations victory. Tet began the slow unraveling of American public support for the war, which is why it rightly deserves its designation as the war's turning point.

© *Kauffmann 2008*

Bruce's History Lessons:
Joe McCarthy's Wild Ride

It isn't every junior Republican senator from Wisconsin who is accorded an "ism" after his name, but such was the case with Joe McCarthy, who ushered in "McCarthyism" this week (Feb. 9) in 1950 in Wheeling, West Virginia. There, McCarthy gave a speech in which he claimed that 205 members of the Communist Party worked in the State Department. With that statement, "Tail Gunner Joe" (a nickname he gave himself while serving as an airman in WW II) took off on a flight that — when it crash landed four years later with McCarthy's condemnation by the U.S. Senate — left a lot of human debris in its fiery wake. During the McCarthy era he and his acolytes accused hundreds of innocent people of being Communists, which in many cases ruined their careers and destroyed their lives.

And McCarthyism was basically an accident. Having spent an undistinguished four years in the Senate, McCarthy had been looking for an issue to run for re-election on in 1952, and anti-Communism seemed as good as any. But when McCarthy began accusing Democrats of being "soft on Communism," and "harboring Communists" within the government, he never dreamed he would give voice to a widely shared fear that in the uncertain post-war world America faced a grave threat from "the enemy within" — a phalanx of subversives sympathetic to, if not controlled by, the Communist Party. It mattered little that McCarthy never proved his accusations, or that the number (and names) of these so-called Communist subversives changed almost daily. What mattered was that Republicans had an issue with which to regain power, and to the extent that there actually were Communists in the government (and there were — lots of them, in fact), so much the better.

Which in a sense helped ensure McCarthy's downfall. McCarthyism certainly helped Republicans regain control of both the White House and Congress in the 1952 elections, but McCarthy — both drunk with power and (a serious alcoholic) often just plain drunk — somehow failed to notice. He kept up his attacks on "Communists in government," even though his own party now controlled that government. Thus did Republican President Eisenhower join with the Democrats to bring McCarthy's wild ride to an end. Outraged that McCarthy was even accusing the U.S. Army of harboring Communists, Eisenhower encouraged Congress to investigate McCarthy, which it did in April of 1954. When the Army-McCarthy hearings ended in June, McCarthy was shown to be a demagogue and a bully. He never recovered and died of alcoholism three years later.

But his memory lived on. Indeed, for the next half-century, the fear of being branded "soft on Communism" shaped the foreign policy, for good or ill, of every subsequent American president — Democrat *and* Republican.

© Kauffmann 2008

Bruce's History Lessons:
The Survivor

A high-powered rifle with sniper's scope and silencer.
A poisoned cigar. An exploding pen.
An exploding sea shell.
Poisoned toiletries (toothpaste, mouthwash, etc.)
A poisoned scuba diving wet suit. A poisoned drink.
Mind altering drugs. Drugs to make facial and scalp hair fall out.
A car bomb. A house bomb. An atomic bomb.

No, that wasn't Theodore "Unabomber" Kaczynski's Christmas list. At one time or another every one of the above was proposed or discussed by the CIA, the Pentagon, the Justice Department and/or the White House as a way of ending the rule, and life, of Cuba's "Maximum Leader," Fidel Castro. The life began in 1926. The rule began this week (Feb. 17) in 1959 when his rag-tag revolutionary army took power in Havana on the heels of the fleeing former Cuban dictator, Fulgencio Batista.

Interestingly, President Eisenhower's first reaction to Castro was mixed. He was wary of this self-proclaimed revolutionary but gratified to have finally been rid of the pro-American, but extremely corrupt, ruthless, despised (and embarrassing) Batista. As for Castro, at the time he came to power he held no strong ideological convictions. Unlike his fellow revolutionary, Che Guevara, he was not initially a Marxist-Leninist, although like most good Latin Americans he did have a reflexive dislike of the U.S. But many historians have argued that with more patient and flexible diplomacy, Castro might not have wound up in the arms of the Russians and might even have been lured into the American camp.

Perhaps, but several realities get in the way of this hope. First, Castro had made no secret of his intention, once in power, to "nationalize" (confiscate)

9

millions of dollars worth of American owned property — something no U.S. president could shrug off without political consequences. Second, although Castro's conversion to Marxism came late, it was probably inevitable given his obsession with holding on to power. The great thing about being a Marxist-Leninist is that you don't have to hold elections, or seek consensus with rival parties, or worry about public opinion.

In any case, the Soviets couldn't help but see the advantages of embracing an anti-U.S. revolutionary dictator of a country just 90 miles off Florida's coast. Thus began a Soviet-Cuban partnership whose implications for U.S. national security — including the fear (soon-to-be-realized) that Cuba would become a launching pad for Soviet nuclear missiles — led to the assassination proposals listed above.

None successful. In fact, 44 years and 10 American presidents later, Fidel Castro is *still* the Maximum Leader of Cuba. And at this point it looks very much as if he will be so until the day he dies of natural causes. Forget the television show. This guy is the real "Survivor."

© *Kauffmann 2008*

Author's note: In 2008 Castro finally did relinquish power to his brother Raul

Bruce's History Lesson:
The Man Who Would Not Be King

On George Washington's real birthday I want to share the true story of how George refused to become America's first king, prevented a military coup that would have undermined the American Revolution, and saved the country from further bloodshed and eternal ignominy. As Tom Jefferson put it in retrospect, Washington's brave and selfless action "prevented this revolution from being closed, as most others have been, by a subversion of that liberty it was intended to establish."

It was a close call. At the end of the Revolutionary War, most officers in the army were so bitter at the Continental Congress's unwillingness (actually inability) to pay them their back salary that they planned a coup against the government.

The wild card was their leader, Washington himself, but the conspirators hoped that if they offered him the chance to be a real king he would join them. The plan was to persuade Washington that the country was in "turmoil" and needed a strong hand to "stabilize" the situation (a line of reasoning we have heard from dictators throughout history)

Washington was aghast when he heard of this plan, so upon learning the conspirators had planned a strategy meeting, he called his own meeting, believing — rightly — that his officers would at least hear him out.

That hearing came on March 15th, 1783. Washington began by reminding his officers that he too had served beyond the call of duty. He told them their coup would ruin their families. He promised to do all he could to get them their money.

Nothing worked. The soldiers sat sullenly as Washington, in desperation, decided to read aloud a letter he had received from a Congressman stating

11

that Congress had not forgotten its debt to the army. George thought it might help ...

The poet Robert Burns once wrote that the best laid plans of mice and men don't always work the way we hope. Yet sometimes it is the *unplanned* action that turns the tide *for* us. So it was when Washington, realizing he could not read the letter without his spectacles, pulled them out — to the surprise of his soldiers who had never seen him with glasses. To this murmur of surprise, Washington added, "Gentlemen, you will permit me to put on my spectacles, for I have not only gone gray, but almost blind, in the service of my country."

That did it. The soldiers' defiance was gone. Many wept openly, for they finally saw clearly the physical toll that the war had taken on their leader. They realized that his single sacrifice had almost matched theirs collectively. The coup was over and a country "conceived in liberty" was born.

© Kauffmann 2008

Bruce's History Lessons:
The Missouri Compromise

On the long road from the American Revolution to the Civil War there were several detours and one was the Missouri Compromise, which was agreed to this week (March 5) in 1820. What looks at first like an immoral bargain that kept a hideous institution—slavery—in place was, in hindsight, a godsend. As we shall see.

To set the stage, by 1818 the Missouri Territory finally had gained sufficient population to apply for statehood and since its residents were mostly southerners, Missouri petitioned Congress for entrance into the Union as a slave state. But northern congressmen, always sensitive to slavery's expansion, objected, all the more so because in Congress there then existed a delicate balance of 11 slave states and 11 free states. Should that balance be upset by another slave state, political power would shift south. For that reason Congressman James Tallmadge of New York proposed not only banning future imports of slaves into Missouri, but also emancipating the slaves currently in the state. That would shift political power north.

Southern members of Congress naturally spurned Tallmadge's proposal and the matter stood deadlocked until residents of the Maine Territory, which also recently qualified for statehood, similarly petitioned Congress for Union entry. Since Maine would unquestionably enter as a free state, a political deal seemed possible and through the efforts of Henry Clay, then one of America's most influential politicians, a compromise was reached. Maine entered the Union as a free state and Missouri entered as a slave state, thereby preserving the delicate slave-versus-free state balance.

But sensitive to the country's growing anti-slavery sentiment (to say nothing of the monstrous injustice of the institution itself), the Missouri Compromise also stipulated that—Missouri excepted—in all of the territory that then comprised the Louisiana Purchase, slavery was forbidden north of Missouri's southern border. In that way slavery would be confined to the South as the Framers had intended when they wrote the Constitution.

So why was the Missouri Compromise a godsend? Simply put, it postponed the Civil War. In 1820, settling the issue politically instead of militarily meant the country stayed intact and the later "Compromise of 1850," another a political solution over slavery, did the same thing. This virtually ensured that when the Civil War did come—in 1860—the North would win it because from 1820 on, the North's economic, industrial, manufacturing and military might grew exponentially over the South's. The Northern economy, after all, was based on industry and manufacturing. The Southern economy was agrarian.

What is more—no small thing—in 1820 Abe Lincoln was not president, and Lincoln was the only politician in the land who had the fortitude to fight, and win, the Civil War.

© Kauffmann 2008

History Lesson:
The Evil Empire?

"Let us beware that while they preach the supremacy of the state, declare its omnipotence over individual man, and predict its eventual domination over all the peoples of the earth, they are the focus of evil in the modern world."

- R Reagan

This week (March 8) in 1983, Ronald Reagan appeared before the National Association of Evangelicals and gave perhaps his most famous speech, the one in which he called the Soviet Union an "Evil Empire." The media uproar was instantaneous. Reagan was accused of everything from insulting the Soviets to heating up the Cold War.

Should Reagan have used such provocative rhetoric? Alas, I'm not schooled enough in the diplomatic nuances of superpower relations to say. On the other hand, *was* the Soviet Union really an "Evil Empire"? You betcha.

It was certainly an empire. It had the ultimate say over the political, economic and cultural life of every country behind the Iron Curtain, and it proved in Hungary in 1956, in Czechoslovakia in 1968, and in Poland in 1981 that any attempt to alter that arrangement would be met with brutal force.

It was certainly evil. Tens of millions of people disappeared, or were killed, tortured or imprisoned for the simple crime of having displeased the state. Instead of freedom there was state control of all economic output, all property, all opinion and all information (Yakov Smirnoff, the expatriate Russian comedian, joked that there were two channels on Soviet television: Channel 2 was round-the-clock Soviet propaganda and Channel 3 was an angry Red Army General who ordered you to turn back to Channel 2). A

Soviet citizen literally could not move from one place to another without receiving permission from the State.

Instead, there was the gulag, the purges, the pogroms, the Berlin Wall, the Show Trials, the Siberian death camps, the KGB and the interrogation rooms in Lubyanka prison. Instead there was Stalin's forced starvation of the Ukraine, which caused 8 million deaths. And let's not forget the expulsion, incarceration and defection of some of the world's greatest thinkers, scientists and artists, from Andrei Sakharov, to Natan Scharansky, to Lech Walesa, to Alexander Solzhenitsyn, to Vladimir Horowitz.

Instead, there was the almighty "Big Brother" that George Orwell described so well. Black was white, right was wrong, history was false, the truth was lies, and lies were the truth if the government said so.

It *was* an evil empire, and if calling it so *in any way* hastened its demise, then Reagan was right to do it, just as he was right when he predicted in another eerily prophetic speech (mostly ignored by the media) that it would soon be on the ash heap of history.

© *Kauffmann 2008*

Bruce's History Lessons:
James Madison: The Most Underrated Founder

Here are a few things you may or may not know about (my hero) James Madison, Founding Father *extraordinaire*, who was born this week (March 16) in 1751.

He was short — maybe 5' 5" in his stocking feet, prompting his wife, Dolley, to call him "the great little Madison." His nickname, "Jemmy," even *sounds* like someone who is short.

He was shy. He hated large gatherings and loathed the spotlight. At social functions he preferred to retire to the corner of the room and engage in quiet discourse, usually political, with a few trusted friends and advisors.

Fortunately he had a wife who enjoyed being the center of attention and who was one of the great official greeters and hostesses in the history of Washington society. (Dolley Madison is the only First Lady to have served that function for two different presidents. When Madison was secretary of state in the Jefferson administration, President Jefferson, a widower, asked her to be his official hostess.)

He was a life-long hypochondriac. Madison would tell anyone who cared to listen that he was sure to die young. He wound up being the last of the Founding Fathers to die — at the ripe old age of 85 — prompting him to say late in life, tongue firmly in cheek, "Having outlived so many of my contemporaries, I ought not forget that I may be thought to have outlived myself."

He was self-effacing and polite to a fault. He went out of his way to give others credit whether they deserved it or not, and he would concede the merits of an opposing argument regardless of how idiotic it happened to be — which, as historian Joseph Ellis has noted, allowed him to more easily demolish it. "He seemed to lack a personal agenda," Ellis writes, "because he seemed to lack a personality. Yet when the votes were counted, his side almost always won."

Which brings me to the last thing you may or may not know about James Madison. After George Washington, he was the most effective and important of the Founding Fathers.

There are three documents that serve as the foundation on which our nation is built. They are the Declaration of Independence, the Constitution and the Bill of Rights. Madison is chiefly responsible for the last two. He wrote the Virginia Plan on which the Constitution is based — earning him the title "Father of the Constitution" — and he created, and engineered passage of, the Bill of Rights, earning him the title "Chief Architect of the Bill of Rights."

The Constitution is our owner's manual and the Bill of Rights is our warranty (the Declaration, Jefferson's, is our mission statement). Not a bad life's work.

© Kauffmann 2008

Bruce's History Lessons: Magellan's Slave Enrique: Around the World First

Not Columbus, Balboa, Cortez, Cook, Marco Polo, or Magellan himself. The first man to circumnavigate the world — thereby proving it was round — was a slave from a tiny island in the Philippines.

He was, in fact, Magellan's slave and accompanied the great Portuguese seaman on what is arguably the most significant sea voyage ever undertaken — the journey from Sanlucar, Spain, in September of 1519, around the world and back again in 1522. This voyage would take the crew into what Magellan would later name the Pacific Ocean. No one sailing from Europe had ever reached the Pacific before.

It's a story for the ages. Surviving mutiny, desertion, violent storms, freezing temperatures, starvation and the mistaken belief that there was a shortcut — a secret water passageway cutting across South America — Magellan and his crew finally discovered the Pacific Ocean (Magellan named it for its *pacifico* "peaceful" waters) by sailing all the way down and around South America's Southern coast, passing what is now the Magellan Straight.

And at that point the journey got really hard. The cartographers of the day had vastly underestimated the size of this ocean, and Magellan, having no good maps to go by (none had sailed it before), was forced to travel blind, not knowing when he would again sight land.

It would be another four months and a journey of almost 13,000 miles. Food became so scarce the crew was forced to eat leather, and the relentless sun and *pacifico* waters drove many sailors mad. Finally, miraculously, this week (March 25th in 1521, they arrived in the Philippines where friendly natives welcomed them.

Among the islands comprising the Philippine archipelago were the Visayan Islands, where a young man named Enrique had been born sometime in the 1490s, captured and shipped to the island of Malucca, where he was sold as a slave to Magellan himself. From there, Enrique traveled everywhere with Magellan, including to Spain where this historic voyage began. And now, by chance, he was back in his Visayan Island home. It was for him a joyous reunion, but for history it was a hallmark event. A Philippine slave had done what no man had done before — literally traveled around the world.

History records that Magellan's journey, and life, ended in the Philippines when he senselessly involved himself in a local tribal war. His remaining ships and crew continued the journey, but only one ship — the Victoria — would return to Spain, thereby completing the circumnavigation of the globe. Although nearly 300 men who had begun the trip, only 18 completed it. Enrique was not among them, having elected to remain on his Visayan Island home. He had traveled enough.

© *Kauffmann 2008*

Bruce's History Lessons:
Lyndon Johnson: The Flawed Giant

"Flawed Giant," is how historian Robert Halleck describes our 36th president, Lyndon Baines Johnson, and it is hard to imagine a more apt description. That LBJ was flawed, tragically, is undeniable. That he was a giant is beyond question.

When LBJ became president after John Kennedy's assassination, he pledged to carry on Kennedy's legacy and carry out Kennedy's programs, but deep down Johnson believed his destiny was to change the country in ways Kennedy would never have dreamed. Where Kennedy had called for a "New Frontier," Johnson called for a "Great Society." Where Kennedy's presidency had oozed charm, radiated energy, set an inspirational tone — but accomplished little — Johnson's goal was to pass concrete legislation that improved the lot of the less fortunate and leveled the playing field for the disadvantaged. He meant to build a legacy that no president before him had ever achieved, including universal medical coverage (something even Franklin Roosevelt hadn't accomplished), massive federal aid to education, the eradication of poverty, urban renewal and — finally — laws guaranteeing African-Americans the full rights, benefits and opportunities of citizenship.

And he thought he was in a unique position to do it all. Unlike Kennedy, a one-term junior senator from the North, Johnson had been among the Senate's most powerful majority leaders, meaning he knew how to get the votes he needed to pass legislation. Even better, he was a Southerner at a time when the most powerful members of Congress came from that region. As a Texan, he believed he understood not only the ingrained cultural prejudices of Southern politicians, but also the political challenges they faced in changing a system that made blacks second-class citizens and doomed them to poverty and ignorance.

Johnson's was the ultimate "liberal" dream — put the federal government to work re-engineering society — and as such it was doomed to failure. But if Johnson's head wasn't always in the right place, his heart was, and thanks to the Civil Rights Act of 1964, Medicare (1965), the 24th Amendment (abolishing poll taxes), the Voting Rights Act of 1965, and other programs aimed at fighting poverty and guaranteeing equality before the law, America is a different, and in many ways better place than it was.

And thanks to the Vietnam War, America is a different, and in many ways worse place than it was. As we all know, Johnson's hell-bent pursuit of that war was his undoing — his true tragic flaw. The war divided the country, impoverished the government, destroyed Johnson's credibility, undermined his leadership and, this week (March 31) in 1968, caused him to announce that he would not seek re-election for president. By the tiny rock that was Vietnam, the Flawed Giant was brought down.

© Kauffmann 2008

Bruce History Lessons:
The Death of a King

"If a man hasn't discovered something that he will die for, he isn't fit to live."

–Martin Luther King, Jr.

The Reverend Martin Luther King, Jr. discovered something to die for when he was just 26 years old, married with a child, and newly installed as pastor of the Dexter Avenue Baptist Church in Montgomery, Alabama. That is when leadership of America's Civil Rights movement was literally thrust upon him during the 1955 boycott of Montgomery's segregated public transportation system. From that time until his death today in 1968, King was a marked man.

Despite that, or perhaps because of it, King's courage seemed almost recklessly defiant. He led his non-violent movement by example, exposing himself to taunts, threats, arrests, physical attacks and incarceration during marches, sit-ins and demonstrations in some of the most racially charged parts of the Deep South — Birmingham, Alabama; Atlanta, Georgia; Jackson, Mississippi; and in April of 1968, Memphis, Tennessee, where he joined black sanitation workers in a demonstration against their working conditions.

Also in Memphis that April was an unemployed drifter who was, like King, familiar with the inside of a prison cell. But unlike King, James Earl Ray had been arrested for several real crimes, including assault and robbery. Learning that King was in town, Ray rented a room at a nearby rooming house with a clear view of the motel where King was staying, and on April 4th, as King and his entourage left their motel rooms to go to dinner, Ray shot King with a high-powered rifle, shattering his jaw and severing his spinal chord. Bleeding profusely, King was rushed to a nearby hospital where he died at 7:05 p.m.

In the wake of King's death America's inner cities exploded, with nationwide rioting that lasted an entire week and caused millions of dollars in damage. As for Ray, he was later arrested and convicted of King's death, and although he protested his innocence until the day he died, the evidence overwhelmingly points to him as the murderer.

So Dr. Martin Luther King Jr., Nobel Peace Prize Laureate, Civil Rights leader, preacher, husband, father and son, became a martyr, something that he had all but predicted in a sermon he delivered in Memphis the day before he died. "Like anybody, I want to live a long life," he said, "… but I am not concerned about that now. I just want to do God's will. So I am happy tonight. I'm not fearing any man. Mine eyes have seen the glory of the coming of the Lord."

It is said that a man dies well who dies wanting to live. Dr. King died wanting to live and truly fit to live.

© *Kauffmann 2008*

Bruce's History Lessons:
"Houston, We've Had a Problem"

Ignoring superstition is one thing. Mocking it is something else entirely. Developers of high-rise buildings refuse to designate a 13th floor for fear of accidents caused by bad luck, yet the National Aeronautics Space Administration (NASA) gives the name Apollo 13 to one of its lunar missions — an undertaking with, oh, about 5 million more things that can go wrong than building a high-rise hotel.

Bang! Compounding the irony, and folly, of that decision, on April 13, 1970, Apollo 13 — carrying astronauts James Lovell, Fred Haise and Jack Swigert — is jolted by the explosion of one of its oxygen tanks, which knocks out the other tank. Without oxygen, the fuel cells that supply power won't work. Without power, the on-board computers and control systems won't work. Without computers and control systems, the command module won't work. Without the command module, Apollo 13 shuts down, meaning that, as flight commander James Lovell said to Mission Control in Houston, "Houston, we've had a problem."

Talk about heroic understatement. In succession, Mission Control and the astronauts had to shut down the command module and reconfigure the lunar module — whose engines were only designed for a short journey to the moon's surface and back — so that the lunar module could power the whole spaceship the nearly 300,000 miles back to Earth. Then they had to change the ship's course so that it swung around the moon and headed for Earth, rather than go into lunar orbit. Then they had to align the spaceship for re-entry into earth's atmosphere, a process with no margin for error and fatal consequences for failure. Then they had to figure out how to separate the service module, command module and lunar module right before re-entry (which had never been done before), all without the usual on-board computerized data assistance, and using as little power as possible.

25

Meanwhile, the astronauts were without water, so they quickly became dehydrated; without sleep, increasing the likelihood of human error; working in extremely cold temperatures (no power, no heat), making them very uncomfortable; and facing a malfunction of the equipment that removed excess carbon dioxide, threatening to make them sick and disoriented (they eventually repaired it).

And finally, even under optimum conditions, revising a flight plan of this magnitude would normally take about three months. Under the conditions described above, the astronauts and Mission Control had three days.

Despite all of this, the "problem" was solved. When Apollo 13 finally splashed down in the Pacific Ocean on April 17, it was less than four miles from the recovery ship, and all three astronauts were in good spirits and good health. They had beaten odds that can only be described, literally and figuratively, as "astronomical."

© Kauffmann 2008

Bruce's History Lessons:
Tax Day (April Fools)

"Taxes are the price we pay for a civilized society."
-Oliver Wendell Holmes, Supreme Court Justice

"April is the cruelest month."

-T.S. Eliot, Poet

Among the many ways that our beloved Founding Fathers proved their wisdom was their rejection of an income tax, preferring to raise revenue through duties, imposts and other indirect forms of taxation. It took a Constitutional Amendment, our 16th, to produce the madness and "cruelty" that abounds leading up to this week's April 15 filing deadline. And that amendment was the result of a too-clever-by-half strategy by leaders of the Republican Party — a strategy that backfired.

The story begins early in the 20th Century when our nation's "Captains of Industry" (sometimes called robber barons), such as John D. Rockefeller, J.P. Morgan, Andrew Carnegie and others, were amassing obscene fortunes through monopolistic practices that stifled competition and suppressed the wages of the average worker. As a result, the cry went up to "soak the rich" through a direct tax on incomes above a certain level. Sensing a political opportunity, Congressional Democrats introduced a series of income tax bills, only to see them repeatedly defeated by conservative Republicans.

These victories were costly for Republicans, however, because they were soon labeled "the party of the rich" (still are), which bode ill for upcoming elections. As a result, Republicans decided to turn the tables on Democrats by pretending to support a Constitutional Amendment approving a direct federal income tax. GOP leaders reasoned that this "support" would deflect voter anger on the one hand, while on the other hand preserve the status quo because they were convinced the necessary three-fourths of the states would never approve such a controversial amendment. Thus did Republicans, who for years had successfully stymied income tax legislation, join with Democrats to approve an amendment calling for just such a thing. The House vote was 318-14 in favor. The Senate vote was unanimous.

But Republicans badly underestimated the groundswell of public enthusiasm for a "soak the rich" income tax, and to their amazement and horror, state after state quickly voted for ratification until, in 1913, the 16th Amendment was added to the Constitution. It gave Congress the power to "lay and collect taxes on incomes, from whatever source derived ..." A new era had begun.

Alas, if it all looked so innocent in 1913 when only about one percent of the population even earned enough money to *pay* the federal income tax, it doesn't look so innocent now when only about one percent of the population (thanks to the advice they get from their accountants and lawyers) even *understands* the federal income tax.

And guess what, dear reader? They are the same group of people, and neither you nor I belong. Happy Tax Day.

© Kauffmann 2008

Bruce's History Lessons:
Shut Up and Eat

The story goes that at the height of his power as the leader of Fascist Italy during World War II, Benito Mussolini was dining with family and friends when one of his children asked him, "What is Fascism?" Mussolini didn't answer, but the child kept repeating the question until, exasperated, Mussolini finally shouted, "Shut up and eat!" After a pause, he turned to a dinner companion and said, "*That* is Fascism."

That was certainly an apt description of Italy *under* Fascism (from the Italian *fascio*, meaning "bundle," it came from Roman times and symbolized unity). In 1921, when Mussolini took power, Italy was an economic and political mess, which he addressed by taking control of the economy, destroying all political opposition, censoring all free expression and creating a police state that — as was said in admiration — "made the trains ran on time." Shut up, Italians, and eat.

He also allied Italy with Adolf Hitler's Germany to form the Axis Powers that declared war on the U.S. and its allies in 1941. But alas for Italy, Mussolini was the junior partner in this alliance, which forced him to follow Hitler along his path of national suicide, even though Italy's army was pathetic and its leadership incompetent. Indeed, militarily Italy was arguably more of a hindrance to Nazi Germany than to the Allies because Hitler was often forced to pull German troops from crucial battlegrounds in the East and send them to bail out Mussolini's hapless armies in the Mediterranean. Memorably, even Hitler's timetable for invading the Soviet Union was partly delayed by the need to help out an Italian army — a delay that meant the Germans would not be able to complete their invasion before winter set in. Sure enough, Russia's subfreezing temperatures helped stop the German advance 30 miles short of Moscow, changing the entire course of the war.

Eventually, even Mussolini's colleagues tired of the havoc he was wreaking on Italy, and he was deposed. But once again, Hitler's storm troopers rescued him, allowing him to set up a Fascist rump state in northern Italy. By April of 1945, however, Hitler himself was doomed, and seeing the handwriting on the wall, and Allied armies approaching, Mussolini and his mistress tried to flee Italy for Switzerland. This week (April 28) in 1945, near Lake Como, they were caught by Italian partisans and executed. The next day their bodies were dumped in Milan, where a mob of angry Italians strung them up and repeatedly kicked their lifeless bodies.

One woman, refusing to "shut up" any longer, let her gun speak for her by firing five shots into Mussolini, "in revenge for my five sons," who had all fought, and died, in the Italian army.

© Kauffmann 2008

Bruce's History Lessons:
A Day in the Life of a Freedom Rider

This week (May 4) in 1961, in Washington, D.C., in what would later be called "Freedom Summer," black and white college students boarded buses to begin their historic freedom ride through the most segregated areas of America's Deep South. Their intent was to break state laws that prohibited whites and blacks from sitting in the same bus seats on interstate highways, or using the same bathrooms in the bus depots along the way.

To advance their cause, which they hoped would garner national attention, the students were prepared for beatings, arrests and jailings. They got all of that and then some, including the fire bombing of their buses.

But of all the indignities visited upon these freedom riders, perhaps the most memorable happened to a young black man named Frederick Leonard after he and his fellow freedom riders were jailed in Jackson, Mississippi, which at the time was arguably the most racist state in America.

Allowed only one possession, the Bible, the young inmates began praying and singing, which so angered the prison guards that they removed the mattresses in their prison cells, forcing the students to sleep that night on the cold floor.

The next day the mattresses were returned, but when the freedom riders resumed their praying and singing, the guards ordered the mattresses removed again.

"So they came to take our mattresses, and by 'they' I mean the black inmates doing hard time," Leonard recalled. "They did all the guards' dirty work."

Except that Leonard decided he was not going to give up his mattress, and so, holding on to it for dear life, Leonard was dragged out of his cell.

"So they had this one inmate named Pee Wee," Leonard said, "And he was *hard*, man. He was this short, black, muscular guy. And the guards pointed to me and said, 'Get him, Pee Wee!' So Pee Wee came down on my head ... BAM! BAM! He hit me hard.

"But here's the strange thing ... Pee Wee was crying! I mean tears were rolling down his cheeks! And I remembered all those times when my parents would say to me, 'Son, this is going to hurt me more than it hurts you.' Well, it hurt Pee Wee a *lot* more than it hurt me."

No doubt. After all, in Leonard, Pee Wee saw a black kid with more strength in one scrawny finger than he, Pee Wee, had in his entire muscle-bound body. Pee Wee also must have seen, and been saddened by, a vision of a future that he knew he would never be a part of — a future that would include, as one result of Leonard's strength and courage, this past February's annual celebration of black history.

© Kauffmann 2008

Bruce's History Lessons:
Winston Churchill, Prime Minister

Most people listen to music when they take long road trips. I listen to BBC recordings of the war speeches that Winston Churchill delivered from 1939 until 1945. As a result, I know most of them by heart, including the one that he gave this week (May 13) in 1940 after becoming British prime minister in the wake of Hitler's invasion of France and the Low Countries — an invasion that effectively began World War II. Addressing the House of Commons, Churchill spoke as follows:

"Sir, I will say to this House, as I have said to those who have joined the government, I have nothing to offer but blood, toil, tears and sweat! We have before us an ordeal of the most grievous kind. We have before us many, many long months of struggle and suffering. You ask, 'What is our policy?' It is to wage war by sea, land and air with all our might and all of the strength that God can give us. To wage war against a monstrous tyranny, never surpassed in the dark and lamentable catalogue of human crime. That is our policy.

You ask, 'What is our aim?' Sir, I can answer in one word. Victory! Victory at all costs. Victory in spite of all terror. Victory no matter how long and hard the road may be. For without victory there is no survival. (PAUSE) Let that be realized. No survival for the British Empire. No survival for all that the British Empire has stood for. No survival for the urge and impulse of the ages — that mankind may move forward toward its goal.

But I take up my task with buoyancy and hope! I feel sure that our cause shall not be suffered to fail among men. At this time I feel entitled to claim the aid of all and I say, 'Come, then, let us go forward together with our united strength!'"

What is important to understand about Churchill's early war speeches is that they had a two-fold purpose. First, most obvious, they were meant to give hope to the British people, and in that they succeeded brilliantly. But Churchill's second goal was to signal to Hitler that under his leadership there would be no negotiated settlement, no "deal" in which Great Britain and Nazi Germany managed to co-exist. Hitler had thought, not without reason, that the leadership in Britain was so defeatist it would eventually sue for peace, hoping to get the best deal possible, and leaving Hitler master of Europe. But Churchill understood that without total victory, Britain was doomed. His speeches were meant to impress upon Hitler that — for Great Britain and Germany — this was a fight to the finish.

© Kauffmann 2008

Bruce's History Lessons:
History and the Homestead Act

The confluence of forces that shape history are wondrous and varied indeed, as the following example attests. This week (May 20) in 1862, in the midst of the Civil War, President Abraham Lincoln signed into law the Homestead Act, which gave citizens title to 160 acres of western land, provided they settled it and lived on it for five years, at which point (after paying a small filing fee) it was legally theirs.

From a big picture standpoint, this was Manifest Destiny at its finest — the federal government encouraging western migration, with the ultimate objective being the conquering of the continent and an America that stretched from the Atlantic to the Pacific.

But the act was the result of more narrow political objectives as well, for it provided that any new states carved out of this territory would be free states, thus tipping America's longstanding, and precarious, "slave state/free state" balance solidly in favor of the latter. From the Missouri Compromise of 1820 to the Kansas-Nebraska Act of 1854, the fight between slave and free states for political and economic advantage had been tense and often violent, and Lincoln wanted to end the impasse (and eventually destroy slavery) for good. In fact, an act similar to the Homestead Act had been proposed in 1858, but it was killed by Southern congressmen who saw it as the same threat to slavery's expansion that Lincoln did. By 1862, of course, those obstructionist Southerners had left Congress when their states seceded from the Union, so Lincoln could pass this act without their opposition. In doing so he sowed the seeds of a free West and ultimately helped ensure all of America would be free.

Another historic force at play in 1862 was the furthering of an ethnically diverse America, for the Homestead Act was also open to foreigners, provided they became U.S. citizens. Given the overcrowding conditions in Europe compared with the spaciousness of America's heartland, countless thousands of immigrants accepted this offer, most of them experienced farmers who would help make the Midwest and West an economically prosperous area.

Which brings up the final historic force — human ingenuity and initiative let loose by the freedom of American private enterprise. This allowed a young blacksmith named John Deere to invent (and patent) the only plow that could unearth the stubborn soil of America's prairie and literally make farming possible. Without it, the Homestead Act might well have been a failure.

And so, partly as a result of these historic forces all converging, America today stretches across the continent, and is inhabited by an ethnically diverse, freedom loving, prosperous people — about half of whom, or so it sometimes seems, now own a John Deere tractor or lawnmower.

© Kauffmann 2008

Bruce's History Lessons:
The Constitutional Convention

This week in 1787, in Philadelphia, a gathering of truly great men began the work that would forever change America and to some extent change the world. On May 25, George Washington called the Constitutional Convention to order and delegates began debating how to turn the unworkable Articles of Confederation, which had governed America since after the Revolutionary War, into a government of more permanence, effectiveness and strength. Three hot and muggy months later they produced the U.S. Constitution.

Although several issues needed resolving, the Convention's core challenge was to correct the Articles' chief defect — no strong central government. Granted, having recently suffered under a strong "central government" in the form of England's King George III, Americans were justifiably leery of consolidating too much power in one place. But giving most power to the 13 states, as the Articles did, had resulted in a U.S. Congress so weak it could not regulate commerce among the states, or make treaties on behalf of the states, or issue a uniform currency, or collect taxes, or defend the nation's shores, or promote its interests (under the Articles there was no chief executive). As a result, the country had become a fractious group of 13 independent state governments that was heading toward dissolution.

Thus did the new Constitution include a strong federal (central) government with a number of specific, delegated powers, including those outlined above. But bowing to the ever-present fear of vesting too much authority in one place, these powers were spread among three different branches of the government — an Executive, Legislative and Judicial branch — and they all were intended to balance and check one another.

It was, in hindsight, a power-sharing arrangement bordering on genius, but it quickly ran into trouble, first among several delegates, and later among the general population whose ratification was required to make the Constitution binding. Power-phobic to the end, opponents complained that the Constitution failed to spell out specific political rights that the people would always possess in defiance of government power.

But the Constitution's proponents had worked too hard to be thwarted, and having spent the past three months becoming experts at the art of compromise, they came up with another. If opponents would approve the Constitution as is, a Bill of Rights would be added later. And that is what happened. The Constitution was ratified in 1789, amendments to it then were proposed, and the first 10 — the Bill of Rights — were ratified in 1791.

Chief among those rights are freedom of speech and of the press. Or at least that's my opinion, but if you don't agree you are always free to write a letter to the editor of this newspaper and say so.

© Kauffmann 2008

Bruce's History Lesson:
LBJ and Memorial Day

"Gentlemen, we are being killed on the beaches. Let us go inland and be killed."
> -General Norman Cota, Omaha Beach, the
> Normandy invasion, 1944.

In honor of the brave men and women who have died defending their country or fighting in its service, from the Civil War to the present, once a year on the last Monday in May we pay tribute to these veterans by observing Memorial Day, which is now a national holiday.

With that in mind, the following true story about a past Commander-in-Chief is worth telling. It shows that Lyndon Baines Johnson, reviled for his role in the Vietnam War *("Hey! Hey! L-B-J! How many kids did you kill today?")*, had his moments of honor and a better grasp of history than did those students (like me) who cursed and mocked him at countless Vietnam protest rallies. The story goes like this:

In 1966, Charles de Gaulle, leader of the French resistance during World War II and then-president of France, announced that his country was pulling out of the military wing of the North Atlantic Treaty Organization (NATO). De Gaulle's motives were no secret. Worried that France was seen as a second-rate power, he wanted to free France from "American hegemony" and establish a new identity for his country.

In addition to leaving NATO, de Gaulle announced that all American troops on French soil must be evacuated. He wanted no trace of America's military presence in France, even if those soldiers served as part of a NATO force.

This, of course, is the same de Gaulle and the same France that had been liberated during the war by a similar force of American soldiers, many thousands of whom died in the fighting. Which is why when Johnson's secretary of state, Dean Rusk, briefed the president on the plan he would present to de Gaulle — a plan that spelled out how we would move NATO headquarters from Paris to Brussels and remove all American soldiers from France — Johnson had only one comment.

"Ask him about the cemeteries, Dean," Johnson said to Rusk.

Quickly grasping the meaning of Johnson's request, Rusk tried to talk him out of it but Johnson was insistent. "Ask him about the cemeteries, Dean!" he repeated, turning the request into a presidential command.

And so Rusk did. At the end of his meeting with de Gaulle, in which he explained how America would comply with de Gaulle's orders, Rusk asked him whether his demand that all American soldiers be removed from French soil included those thousands of GIs still buried in French cemeteries — GIs who had given their lives so France could once again live as a free and sovereign nation.

In his autobiography Rusk records that de Gaulle, embarrassed, did not reply.

© *Kauffmann 2008*

Bruce's History Lessons:
The D-Day Weatherman

The history books note the incredible pressure on Gen. Dwight Eisenhower as he contemplated ordering the long-awaited cross-channel invasion of France — what will forever be known as "D-Day" — this week (June 6) in 1944.

And rightly so. By June 2, months of planning and unprecedented feats of engineering and logistics were completed. The troops were briefed and on their ships — all 2,700 of them — which were at their debarkation points in the English Channel. The minefields were being cleared, the paratroopers were ready to board their planes and the support personnel were all in place. The largest, most complicated invasion in history was set to begin and upon its success greatly depended the success of WWII.

Everything depended on Eisenhower making the decision to go.

Yet, little known even today, Eisenhower himself depended on the decision of a group captain in the Royal Air Force named James Stagg, whose training had nothing to do with the military. He was a weatherman and he had to tell Eisenhower whether the weather would allow the invasion to proceed. If Stagg determined the weather was not suitable, the entire invasion would have to be postponed for at least two weeks because there were only so many days in a month when the tides and the moon were in alignment for a beach landing on France's Normandy coast.

Talk about pressure. We think today's "meteorologists," with their satellite photographs and "Doppler Radar," are maddeningly unreliable, yet in 1944 weather prediction was just a cut above guesswork, depending mostly on crude radar, weather balloons and airplanes. But Stagg had earned Eisenhower's confidence and so, on June 3, when Stagg reported that the weather on June 5 would be too windy and rainy, and the channel too choppy, for an invasion, Eisenhower ordered D-Day postponed to June 6, the last day the moon and the tides were in alignment.

Then, late on Sunday evening, June 4, with the wind howling and rain pummeling Eisenhower's headquarters, Stagg told Eisenhower and his staff that he thought the weather would improve briefly over the next 48 hours. Heartened, but wary, Eisenhower ordered the group to meet again at 4:30 a.m., and even though it was still pouring when the group reassembled, Stagg now told them it was a certainty — the weather would improve long enough for the invasion to be completed.

On cue, as if by a miracle, the wind and rain suddenly died down. "O.K.," Ike said, "Let's go."

As history records, the weather held, the invasion succeeded and the war was eventually won. Eisenhower went on to even greater glory while Stagg went back to his weather charts, another unsung hero who helped change the course of history.

© Kauffmann 2008

Bruce's History Lessons:
Pioneer 10: From Here to Eternity

This week (June 13) in 1983, the tiny spacecraft Pioneer 10 boldly went where no man, or machine, had ever gone before when it flew out of our solar system. The next day it transmitted back our first-ever, first-hand data from interstellar space. It has been sending us data ever since.

And it has been doing so in defiance of obstacles so diverse, and odds so long, they are incalculable. Since March of 1972, when Pioneer was launched, it has dodged space debris the size of Alaska in the Asteroid Belt, survived the intense radiation of Jupiter (while confirming the planet is mostly liquid), and even righted itself after a course-altering encounter with a mysterious object beyond Pluto. Unperturbed, Pioneer 10 has kept rolling on, increasing our knowledge of our sister planets, our sun and interstellar phenomena such as the Milky Way.

It has even outlived the official end of its mission, in March of 1997, and the threat of a funding cutoff that would have shut down the project and doomed Pioneer to a life of transmitting data that no one would receive. Fortunately, scientists studying the chaos theory incorporated Pioneer's transmissions into their research and the tiny spacecraft survived once again. It is now headed for Aldebaran, a star in the constellation Taurus (The Bull), which it should reach in another two million years.

In fact, Pioneer 10 could still be exploring the galaxy five billion years from now when the sun burns out and makes Earth uninhabitable, at which time, no doubt, the human race will have either destroyed itself, or long before mutated into a different form and/or found a different planetary home. It is also possible that before five billion years is up, other life forms will have encountered Pioneer 10 on its travels, and from it determined the location of our distant solar system and fragile planet. A small plaque on

Pioneer 10, designed in part by the astronomer Carl Sagan, displays a picture of a man and woman, a map showing the location of our sun and the flight path of Pioneer 10. Galactic visitors are welcome.

Most deservedly, in 1999 the U.S. Postal Service honored Pioneer 10 with its own commemorative stamp as part of the "Celebrate the Century" postage stamp series, but not long after earning that distinction Pioneer 10 stopped transmitting, raising fears that its dwindling nuclear-powered battery supply had run out, and it would never be heard from again. Instead, this past April, after a nine-month silence, the plucky, intrepid and stouthearted Pioneer 10 suddenly contacted us again to tell us (in so many words) it still has a date with destiny, and eternity, that it plans to keep.

© Kauffmann 2008

Bruce's History Lesson:
Burning the Flag

This week (June 21) in 1989, in *Texas v. Johnson*, the U.S. Supreme Court handed down one of its more controversial decisions when it ruled that Gregory Johnson could not be convicted for burning an American flag — which he did at the 1984 Republican National Convention — because in so doing he was engaging in a form of political speech, which is protected under the First Amendment's free speech provisions. For millions of Americans it was not the court's finest hour, and although burning the American flag does, and should, arouse passionate feelings of anger and disgust among the vast majority of our citizens, that is precisely why the Founding Fathers wrote a Constitution and created a Bill of Rights. The Founders feared the effect that passion — anger, disgust — could have on good government, good law and social harmony. The Bill of Rights was one of the principal safeguards against such passion.

And the First Amendment was arguably its most important safeguard. Ask yourself what possible reason would someone burn an American flag *other* than to make some kind of statement and you begin to see why the Supreme Court ruled the way it did. Political speech comes in many forms, but whatever its form, it deserves protection.

Even when — make that *especially* when — such political speech is being promulgated by a small minority (such as flag burners) and the political message is expressed in ways unpopular with the majority.

What was paramount in (my hero) James Madison's mind when he created the Bill of Rights was that it should protect the rights of every American, but especially Americans who find themselves in the minority. Majorities by definition don't need protection — they're in the majority — but the power of their numbers should not allow them to stifle the views of those who disagree with them. Such "tyranny of the majority" had been the great fear of the Founding Fathers in the 1780s as they witnessed popular majorities in the various state legislatures pass laws that favored them at the expense of minority rights. The Bill of Rights was, in part, created to protect those minority rights against the passions of an aroused majority.

In *Texas v. Johnson* the U.S. Supreme Court ruled that protecting a symbol — the American flag — is not as important as protecting one of the bedrock constitutional principles that define our nation. Indeed, desecrating our flag — however vile — can be looked at as an affirmation, and a reminder, of our freedom to express our sentiments, popular or unpopular, without fear of government reprisal.

Something to think about given that, at one time or another, all of us have been in the minority, saying and doing things offensive to the majority.

© *Kauffmann 2008*

Bruce's History Lessons:
The 26th Amendment:
"Old Enough to Vote"

"Old enough to fight, old enough to die, old enough to vote."

— '60s slogan

In 1970 the average age of the soldiers fighting in the Vietnam War was 19, yet not one 19-year-old had any say in choosing the political leaders who were sending him into that war. Senator Jennings Randolph of West Virginia thought that was wrong.

Actually he had thought for a long time — since the 1940s — that it was hypocritical to make 18-year-old men eligible to fight in wars, and eligible to work and pay taxes to fund those wars, but not eligible to vote their opinion of those wars until they turned 21. Both during his years as a congressman and during his later years as a senator, Randolph had introduced 10 bills to lower the voting age to 18. All failed, but in 1971 Randolph proposed a Constitutional amendment to lower the voting age, and it unanimously passed in the Senate and overwhelmingly passed in the House. Sent to the states, the amendment took just 100 days to receive the necessary two-thirds majority for ratification, and this week (July 1) in 1971 ratification of the 26th Amendment was completed when North Carolina voted its approval. It states, "The right of citizens of the United States, who are eighteen years of age or older, to vote shall not be denied or abridged by the United States or by any State on account of age."

That the 26th Amendment passed when it did, in the early 1970s, is a testament to Randolph's perseverance and powers of persuasion, because at that time the prospect of adding 11 million new voting teenagers to the ranks was not a cheerful one for many politicians. By 1971 the Vietnam War had polarized the nation, especially America's youth, many of whom hated the war and blamed the status quo politicians for prolonging it. What's more, the growing Civil Rights movement, which was populated mostly by young Americans, had faced opposition not only from angry mobs, but also from establishment political leaders, especially in the South. Thus did some elected officials worry that this new voting bloc of politically active young men and women would threaten their careers.

On the other hand, Randolph's message resonated because it was right and because Randolph himself had gained an eminence based on his years of public service and his unflagging devotion to this cause. Randolph, dubbed the "Father of the 26th Amendment," is one of my unsung heroes of history.

And a hero worth remembering as our young men and women fight in another controversial war, and as another national election looms — one in which my own 18-year-old daughter, Remy, will eagerly and proudly vote.

© Kauffmann 2008

Bruce's History Lessons:
A Bomb and a Bombshell

This week in 1946, in the aftermath of America's detonation of an atomic bomb over the Bikini Atoll islands in the South Pacific, the world expressed shock, outrage and near universal condemnation. Oh, and the bomb blast and atomic radiation that subsequently leaked into the atmosphere caused some concern as well.

For it was on July 5th of 1946 that French clothing designer Louis Reard sent a Parisian "model" (actually a nude dancer) down a Paris runway wearing a bathing suit so skimpy that, as he would later boast, "it could be pulled through a wedding ring." Pressed to name his shocking fashion creation, he recalled the day's headlines, which announced a large atomic bomb had been detonated over the Bikini Atolls. The bikini was born.

It was an instant success and an instant scandal. While Reard got the cash and his "model" got the fame, the governments of many nations, especially in predominantly Catholic countries such as Spain and Italy, got busy condemning the bikini and banning its sale. Which, of course, only intensified interest in the tiny two-piece swath of cloth.

Here in America the reaction was mixed, with many so-called "Decency" organizations pressuring stores not to sell it and demanding that Hollywood refuse to showcase it in films (a quixotic hope, that). Fashion magazines sneered at it as "tacky" and claimed that any woman who wore it was lacking in taste.

America would soon discover just how tasteless its female population was, for bikini-clad women began showing up on beaches from California to the Florida Keys, and while America's churches were soon in high dudgeon, America's male population didn't seem to mind at all.

Interestingly, the bikini — like the bomb that helped name it — was in part the result of the Second World War, which had prompted our federal government to institute nationwide rationing on a number of products necessary for the war effort. One such product, a certain type of cloth fabric, was also used in swimwear, and a government-ordered ten percent reduction of its use for women's bathing suits resulted in the switch from one-piece suits with skirts to two-piece suits that exposed the midriff. This two-piece bathing suit soon caught the attention of the French who, being French, made the bikini the inevitable next step.

Today, of course, the bikini is a fixture at the world's beaches and swimming pools, and to those narrow-minded prudes and overly judgmental throwbacks to the Victorian Age who still have a problem with it, or with women wearing it, I say, lighten up, and remember that the human form is among God's greatest creations.

Not that I would *ever* let my teenage daughters out of the house wearing one.

© *Kauffmann 2008*

Bruce's History Lesson: Storming the Bastille: Myth vs. Reality

This week (July 14) in 1788, in Paris, the Bastille prison was stormed, heralding the French Revolution. If you think "spin doctoring" is an art form today, read on. Their later bloody botch of the revolution aside, the leaders of this rebellion against the French monarchy brilliantly turned the humdrum reality of the storming of the Bastille into a mythical masterpiece of self-serving political propaganda. To wit:

Myth: An undermanned citizen's army defeated the mighty forces of Louis XVI.

Reality: The Bastille's defenders comprised 30 Swiss mercenaries and 80 *invalides*, who were essentially regular army rejects. The attackers outnumbered the Bastille's defenders 9 to 1.

Myth (aided by deliberately distorted paintings of the prison): The Bastille was a monstrosity, with walls and ramparts that only citizen-patriots, flush with the rightness of their cause, could have scaled.

Reality: The Bastille was a run down fortress converted to a prison. Prior to July 14th, people frequented the undefended exterior court, chatting amiably with the gatekeeper or examining the progress of the prison governor's (warden) tomato garden.

Myth: The Bastille was teeming with political prisoners, jailed in brutal retaliation for the slightest criticism of the regime.

Reality: On July 14th, the Bastille held four legally convicted forgers, two certifiable nut cases, and history's poster boy for sexual masochism, the Marquis de Sade (committed by his family).

Myth: The prisoners suffered unspeakable treatment, including torture and starvation.

Reality: The prisoners lived more comfortably than the populace. Their daily ration of bread, cheese and even wine certainly had it over the thin gruel and breadcrumbs being fought over by their half-starved countrymen (food riots sparked the Revolution). Many prisoners received books, mail and visitors, including the aforementioned Marquis de Sade, who in addition to regular visits from his (unbelievably tolerant!) wife, enjoyed the use of a dressing table, hung tapestries, velvet reclining pillows, a full wardrobe and a library. A "torture machine" that the revolutionaries claimed crushed human bones was actually an old printing press.

Talk about spin. Since the reality was of no use to the revolutionary propagandists, it was tossed aside like so many day-old *baguettes*. Instead, the Bastille became, as historian Simon Schama has written, "... much more important in its 'afterlife' than it had ever been as a working institution of the state ... Transformed from a nearly empty, thinly manned anachronism into the seat of the Beast of Despotism, it incorporated all of those rejoicing at its demise into the new community of the Nation."

The myth of the Bastille electrified a citizenry and energized a revolution. But like so many other historic events based on lies and deception, in the end it would all turn out badly.

© *Kauffmann 2008*

Bruce's History Lessons:
A Bold Eagle

The first humans in history walked on ground other than Earth this week (July 20) in 1969, when astronauts Neil Armstrong and Edwin "Buzz" Aldrin left their lunar module "Eagle" to explore the moon.

It's a familiar story, but with a subplot worth retelling — one that proves NASA was right to make combat test pilots its first crop of astronauts. Those are the guys who land jet planes on the flight decks of aircraft carriers in rolling seas in the dead of night, and in terms of skill, endurance, focus and that special brand of courage Ernest Hemingway aptly called "grace under pressure," they are a breed apart from the rest of us.

As Armstrong would prove: On July 20, Eagle separated from the command module "Columbia" and headed for the moon's surface where, at 4:10 p.m. EDT, it began its final descent, controlled by the Automatic Landing Mode (ALM) computers. Suddenly — one after the other — two alarms sounded, indicating two computer overloads, and although Command Center in Houston gave the astronauts the go-ahead to proceed, it was not an auspicious beginning.

And at 2,000 feet, as Armstrong looked out at the lunar surface, he saw that their initial landing area was much too rocky for a safe touchdown. Overriding the ALM computers, Armstrong took manual control of Eagle and began searching for another landing site.

It was 4:16 p.m. and Eagle was less than a football field away from the surface when another warning light flashed, indicating Eagle's engines were kicking up lunar dust, reducing visibility. If that wasn't bad enough, as Armstrong continued his search for a flat surface area, the fuel warning light flashed, telling him he had 90 seconds to land or abort the mission.

At 4:17, Houston tersely warns Armstrong, whose visibility problems have only gotten worse, that he has 30 seconds of fuel left. The world is holding its collective breath, when — at last — Armstrong's calm voice finally announces, "Houston, Tranquility Base here. The Eagle has landed."

Talk about grace under pressure. During the entire harrowing landing, while flying virtually blind, on manual control, dangerously low on fuel, destination uncertain, with hundreds of millions watching, and the possibility of failure, and even death, very real, Armstrong's heartbeat barely registered above normal. Indeed, he was arguably more nervous about what he was supposed to say after stepping on the moon than he was during his moon landing. His historic remark was scripted to be "This is one small step for *a* man, one giant leap for mankind," but in his nervousness, he left out the "a," slightly changing the meaning of the sentence. But in no way changing the significance of the deed.

© Kauffmann 2008

Bruce's History Lessons:
Kellogg-Briand and the End of War

What if they gave a war and nobody came?

— '60s Peace Slogan

Or better yet, what if they made war illegal? What if nations signed an official treaty that made it a crime to start a war?

So wondered U.S. Secretary of State Frank Kellogg in 1928 after France's foreign minister, Aristide Briand, proposed that the two nations outlaw war between them. Kellogg suggested they expand the proposal to include all interested nations, and that year 15 nations signed the Kellogg-Briand Pact, thereby affirming their "renunciation of war as an official instrument of national policy." Fifty other nations soon signed on, making Kellogg-Briand — in terms of *participation* — among the most successful international treaties ever drafted. Its *effectiveness* was another matter.

The Kellogg-Briand Pact, which went into effect this week (July 24) in 1929, was an understandable, if somewhat misguided reaction to the horrors of large-scale war. World War I, which had ended just a decade earlier, had resulted in some 10 million soldiers dead and 21 million wounded, and had cost the belligerents an estimated $200 billion. Small wonder that throughout the 1920s international peace and disarmament conferences sprang up like spring flowers after a good rain. The Kellogg-Briand pact was, so to speak, a rose in full bloom.

But a rose without thorns. The treaty's Achilles heel was the absence of enforcement provisions. The U.S. Congress, for example, ratified the treaty only after inserting a provision that declared America was not obligated to take action against any signatory that broke the treaty — which made K-B essentially toothless. As was the case with the League of Nations, which

America had refused to join in 1919, Congress would not agree to any document that gave an entity other than Congress the power to declare war and send American troops into harm's way. And given that Congress historically consented to such steps only if it thought America's national security or national interests were at stake, it seemed highly unlikely that America would fight under her Kellogg-Briand obligation if, for example, Australia and New Zealand, which were two K-B signatories, attacked each other.

Or Japan and China. In 1931, just two years after Kellogg-Briand was signed, K-B signatory Japan attacked Chinese forces in Manchuria, and in 1935, Italy — another K-B signatory — invaded Ethiopia. In both cases the other Kellogg-Briand signatories did nothing.

And by 1939 when K-B signatory Germany attacked K-B signatory Poland, which caused K-B signatories England and France to declare war on Germany, it was obvious to all that Kellogg-Briand was worthless — a fact made even plainer in 1941 when K-B signatory Japan attacked K-B signatory America at Pearl Harbor. At that point World War II, although technically illegal, was very much a reality.

© Kauffmann 2008

Bruce's History Lesson:
The Whiskey Rebellion

"So who's in a hurry?"

- Robert Benchley, when told that drinking was "slow poison."

This week (August 1) marks the anniversary of the beginning of the "Whiskey Rebellion" in 1794, an episode that offers a few lessons on taxation, political deal-making and the advancement of civilization.

The rebellion began because the federal government under George Washington was seeking a way to pay for its earlier agreement to assume the war debts incurred by the states in the wake of the American Revolution. Washington's treasury secretary, Alexander Hamilton, had brokered this debt agreement, and he decided an excise tax on whiskey was the perfect way to pay for the debt.

Now like all good taxes, a whiskey tax was bound to hurt some more than others, and in this case it was bound to hurt "Westerners" the most (back then the "West" was Western Pennsylvania). Why? Mainly because these Westerners, who were mostly farmers, drank more whiskey than the sophisticated Easterners, whose tastes ran to wine and port. What's more, many more Westerners earned a living making whiskey, while more Easterners earned a living making politics (I leave it to you, dear reader, to decide which poses more long-term health risks). So the combination of a (perceived) lack of political clout on the part of the Westerners, and the fact that the Easterners would pay proportionately less due to their drinking habits and their livelihoods, made a whiskey tax seem ideal—at least to Easterners.

Not so to Westerners, who rebelled against the tax. The rebellion spread swiftly but was no match for George Washington, who raised an army and quickly defeated the rebels' ragtag band. That ended the Whiskey Rebellion, although the excise tax was—unlike the whiskey—later diluted.

This said, there are some interesting similarities between this episode and the fate of cigarettes today. As a reformed smoker, I agree that cigarettes cause myriad health problems, but—let's face it—as we of the "educated class" became more aware of the harm cigarettes cause, and therefore reduced our use of them, we conveniently became more enamored of the idea that taxing the bejabbers out of tobacco was a great way to improve the country's health and raise revenue.

This has angered smokers, although instead of armed rebellion you mostly see letters-to-the-editor, or smokers complaining on TV about losing their "rights," or—increasingly—lawsuits and counter lawsuits.

Call it progress. In 1794 they would have reached for their firearms and started shooting. Today we reach for our lawyers and our lobbyists, our PACs and our PR firms. And most of our shots are verbal. It goes to show (I think) how civilized we have become.

© *Kauffmann 2008*

Bruce's History Lesson: Nagasaki and the End of Nuclear War

The significance of the anniversary of the bombing of the Japanese city of Nagasaki, which this week (Aug. 9) in 1945 became the second city ever destroyed by a nuclear weapon dropped in anger, is simply this:

Nagasaki is also the *last* city destroyed by a nuclear weapon dropped in anger.

Before the U.S. dropped atomic bombs on the Japanese cities of Hiroshima (three days earlier) and Nagasaki at the end of WW II, advances in weaponry had always *expanded* the scope of war's possibility and destruction. The machine gun killed more soldiers in five minutes than the rifle killed in fifteen. The submarine created a new battleground — under water. The tank made the battlefield mobile. The aircraft carrier allowed aerial battles in conjunction with naval ones. The bomber put distant cities in harm's way. In sum, every new invention in the field of weaponry increased the likelihood of war as it increased the number of combatants and casualties. Until the nuclear weapon.

The nuclear weapon crossed a unique threshold because, for the first time in history, a weapon that was more destructive than anything before it became less feasible. In Nagasaki's wake, the U.S. and the Soviet Union built huge nuclear weapon stockpiles, conducted countless nuclear tests, and were joined in the "nuclear club" by a half-dozen other countries, including several dictatorships, some of dubious stability. Yet not once in more than 50 years has a nuclear weapon been used in war. In effect, the ultimate war weapon became the ultimate guarantee that it would not be used. The costs of using nukes so far outweigh the benefits that there literally could be no victor in such a war. So why wage it?

In his book *Now We Know: Rethinking Cold War History*, author John Lewis Gaddis illustrates this point thusly: "Their (nuclear arms) distance from conventional arms — to resort to a football metaphor — was roughly that between getting a new kind of shoe allowing better traction in tackling the other team's players, on the one hand, and on the other, developing a device capable of instantly destroying not only the other team, but also one's own, to say nothing of the playing field, the spectators, the stadium, the parking lot and the television rights."

Which is not to say that someday, somehow, somewhere, a nuclear explosion won't cause massive destruction, either by terrorism or by accident. But that is a different subject. The nuclear genie has been out of the bottle for sometime now and there is no putting him back. My point is simply that with the advent of nuclear weapons a new phenomenon occurred. Their unimaginable power has made using them in war almost equally unimaginable.

© Kauffmann 2008

Bruce' History Lessons:
Nixon to Reagan: "Stonewall!"

"I've made mistakes, but I have learned from them," Richard Nixon once told an interviewer. Well, we'll see about that.

In June of 1973, Nixon's former top lawyer, John Dean, testified before a Congressional Committee investigating the illegal break-in of the Democratic National Convention headquarters at the Watergate complex in Washington, D.C. Dean told the committee that President Nixon knew of, and was involved in, a cover-up of the break-in, which was directed by top White House officials, including Attorney General John Mitchell and key aides John Ehrlichman and Bob Haldeman. Concurrently, Harvard law professor Archibald Cox, who was appointed special prosecutor to investigate Watergate, uncovered other illegal activities allegedly conducted by the Nixon gang, including wiretapping, illegal campaign contributions and political espionage.

A month later it was revealed that Nixon secretly tape-recorded his White House conversations. Cox subpoenaed those tapes, but Nixon, citing "executive privilege," refused to release them, consenting only to release "summaries" of them. Cox, not surprisingly, refused Nixon's offer, so Nixon fired Cox, which caused a nationwide uproar. Nixon's approval ratings plummeted and calls for his impeachment began.

Cox's successor, Leon Jaworski, took up where Cox left off, even going to the Supreme Court, where a unanimous ruling in July of 1974 left Nixon no choice but to release the Watergate tapes. They confirmed what Dean had said about Nixon's involvement, and three days later the House of Representatives Judiciary Committee voted to recommend that Nixon be impeached for several violations of the law, including obstruction of justice and abuse of presidential powers.

On August 9, 1974, Nixon became the first president in American history to resign from office. It was widely acknowledged, later by even Nixon himself, that had he not "stonewalled" and covered-up, had he not stymied the investigation at every turn, the Watergate break-in would have been a minor embarrassment, quickly forgotten.

Fast forward 13 years. This week (Aug. 13) in 1987, ex-President Richard Nixon wrote then-President Ronald Reagan a letter commenting on Reagan's own problems with the law — stemming from an episode called Iran-Contra in which the Reagan White House was alleged to have traded arms with Iran for hostages, while illegally supporting the Contra rebels in Nicaragua. Reagan was accused of covering up his role in this affair.

In his letter, Nixon offered Reagan some simple advice. Stonewall!! "Don't ever comment on the Iran-Contra matter again," Nixon wrote Reagan. "Have instructions issued to all White House staffers and Administration spokesmen that they must never answer any question on or off the record about the issue in the future."

Fortunately for him, Reagan ignored Nixon's advice, survived the Iran-Contra scandal and managed, unlike an older-but-not-much-wiser Nixon, to serve out his term.

© Kauffmann 2008

Bruce's History Lesson:
Lincoln's Letter to Greeley

In the midst of the Civil War, Horace Greeley, the influential editor of *The New York Tribune*, published an editorial rebuking President Abraham Lincoln for vacillating on the issue of emancipating the slaves. An abolitionist and staunch supporter of preserving the "union" — meaning a unified country — Greeley was nevertheless not shy about criticizing Lincoln's conduct of the war.

Lincoln's reply to Greeley, written this week (Aug. 22) in 1862, was perhaps the most famous letter he ever wrote, especially the following excerpt: "My paramount object in this struggle is to save the Union, and is not either to save or to destroy slavery. If I could save the Union without freeing any slave I would do it, if I could save it by freeing all the slaves I would do it; and if I could save it by freeing some and leaving others alone I would also do that."

As it happened, Lincoln had already written a draft of the Emancipation Proclamation that he would issue on January 1, 1863, because he was finally convinced that it would help the North win the war and preserve the union. As his letter makes clear, the nation's preservation was his first priority.

But why? Why was saving the union so paramount that even an issue as morally repugnant as slavery became a secondary concern? The answer is that Lincoln felt he was not only preserving the nation for his generation of Americans, but also for generations not yet born, both in America and around the world.

"The last best hope of earth," he called our country, and he had a point. For one thing, America in 1862 was the world's only successful democratic republic, and attempts to duplicate it in Europe and next door in Latin

America had repeatedly failed. For another, the world's monarchies and dictatorships openly rooted against America's survival and took gleeful delight in the threat to the union (and to democracy) that the Civil War posed. As Lincoln well understood, the success or failure of the "American experiment" would set a global precedent. Should the union fail, then the world would be convinced that "government of the people, by the people and for the people" was not destined to be a fixture on earth. But should it succeed, it would give hope to people everywhere that representative government could work.

Lincoln was willing to countenance slavery during the war because he believed that once the war was won and the union preserved, slavery in America would end. At that point, America would stand as a beacon to freedom and as living proof that "the people" could govern themselves without any help from kings, queens or dictators.

He was, as usual, right.

© Kauffmann 2008

Bruce's History Lessons:
Thar She Blows — and Gushes!

This past winter people in California experienced skyrocketing electricity bills, rolling blackouts, and a near doubling of gasoline prices. And the rest of the country didn't fare much better. It was called an energy crisis, and the approach to solving it became a hotly contested issue. On one side, people such as California Governor Gray Davis called for government intervention in the form of price controls on energy. On the other side were those who said it was a classic supply-and-demand problem. A record-cold winter had pushed up energy demand to the point that it far exceeded available supply, which pushed up prices. Higher prices, these people said, would stimulate the search for new sources of supply, while encouraging conservation, which would eventually bring supply and demand more in balance — and moderate prices.

We have been here before, including in the 1850s when the price of the primary fuel Americans then used to light their lamps and illuminate their homes — whale oil — was in such demand producers couldn't keep up, although they sure did try. Hunting for the sperm whale that supplied this oil was so intense the poor animal was close to extinction. Meanwhile the price of whale oil approached the equivalent of $1.70 a gallon, which was an all-time high.

So what did the government do? Did it put price controls on whale oil? Did it regulate the industry? Did it haul whale oil producers before a congressional committee and demand an explanation? Nope. It sat back and let the market work, figuring that $1.70 a gallon for whale oil was plenty of incentive to solve the problem by finding more supply.

Sure enough, two businessmen named George Bissell and James Townsend saw an opportunity and formed an oil company. They then hired two drilling experts, William Smith and Edwin Drake, and sent them to Titusville, Pennsylvania, where a new kind of oil with great potential had been found floating in a lake. Drake and Smith sunk a well nearby and almost immediately struck oil. The date was August 27, 1859.

The result was an oil boom and the displacement of expensive whale oil by cheap petroleum. Oil wells sprung up all over Pennsylvania, bringing the price down even further, and soon oil wells were gushing in Texas, Oklahoma and Louisiana. A new industry was born that changed the course of history. Oil was cleaner than coal, and cheaper and easier to transport than were any of the available competing fuels.

The moral of the story is that the free market almost always has a better solution to a problem than the government. Just ask the grateful sperm whale, whose chief pursuers these days are whale-watching tourists.

© Kauffmann 2008

Bruce's History Lessons:
Tom Jefferson and Sally Hemings

Did Tom Jefferson, author of the Declaration of Independence and third president of the United States father children by one of his black slaves, Sally Hemings?

Contrary to what you may have read or heard, there is zero, zip, zilch conclusive proof that he did. There *is* conclusive proof — via the DNA of one of Hemings' descendants — that *someone* belonging to the Jefferson family, *perhaps* Tom himself, fathered at least one of Hemings' children. But that is a far cry from certainty.

The accusation first surfaced this week (Sept. 2) in 1802 in *The Richmond Recorder*, a Federalist newspaper that was openly hostile to Jefferson and his Republican Party. What's more, this *Recorder* story was written by James Callendar, an unscrupulous hack-for-hire who had once been paid by Jefferson to malign the Federalists. Angered that President Jefferson had denied him a political appointment, Callendar promptly switched sides and began spreading rumors and gossip for the Federalists. Thus anything that Callendar wrote about Jefferson was of dubious veracity.

And yet there is a body of circumstantial evidence that supports Callendar's charge. Not only was Sally young, attractive and light skinned, but also she was the half-sister of Jefferson's wife Martha (Sally's mom was the slave mistress of Martha's father), who, before she died young, extracted a promise from Jefferson that he would never remarry. Given Jefferson's relative youth and physical robustness, it is possible that he saw a relationship with Sally as a way to "square the circle" of honoring Martha's request, yet still have a "conjugal" relationship with someone close in blood, body and spirit to his dead wife.

But perhaps the most compelling circumstantial evidence centers on the fact that, with almost clock-like regularity, every time Tom returned home to Monticello from one of his many trips, Sally produced a child approximately nine months later. In her book *Thomas Jefferson and Sally Hemings: An American Controversy*, historian Annette Gordon-Reed writes, "Jefferson comes home for six months and leaves. Hemings bears a child four months after he is gone. Jefferson comes home for six weeks. Hemings bears a child eight months after he is gone. Jefferson comes home for two months and leaves. Hemings bears a child eight months after he is gone. This went on for fifteen years and six children. He was there when she conceived and she never conceived when he was not there."

Interesting, even compelling, but to repeat, inconclusive, which is why our present-day obsession with proving Jefferson had children with a slave mistress seems almost obscene. Jefferson *may* have been the father of slaves. He *definitely* was a founding father of the greatest nation on earth. The latter dwarfs the former in importance.

© *Kauffmann 2008*

Bruce's History Lesson:
The Death of The Kingfish

The closest America ever got to a bonafide dictator died this week (Sept. 10) in 1935, having been gunned down two days earlier by an assassin in the Louisiana State capitol building. Huey "The Kingfish" Long, Louisiana's governor from 1928 until 1932, ran his state like a personal fiefdom — and the people loved him for it.

Born poor in a backwoods part of the state, his rise to power fed off America's slide into the Depression. His political slogan to make "every man a King," and his "Share Our Wealth" program, in which high taxes on the rich would guarantee every American an annual income of $2,500 and provide retirement pensions for the elderly, hit a populist nerve. It also made Long a national political phenomenon and convinced him he could beat Franklin Roosevelt in the next presidential election (Roosevelt called Long "one of the two most dangerous men in the country" — the other being General Douglas MacArthur).

That Long was a corrupt demagogue is undeniable. He ran Louisiana on kickbacks, bribes and graft (plus high taxes on the state's oil and natural gas interests). He also drank heavily, womanized brazenly and gambled obsessively, and he allowed nothing to stand in the way of his personal advancement. (About Long's need to double-cross an ally for political advantage, one of his assistants complained, "But Governor, you *promised* him! What am I gonna tell him?!" "Tell him I lied," was Long's blunt answer.) What's more, his "Share Our Wealth" program was economic Socialism, bordering on utopianism.

That said, Long genuinely believed he represented "the little guy" against the greed and cronyism of Wall Street bankers, business conglomerates, Eastern elitists and business-as-usual politicians — FDR included. Having raised living standards in Louisiana by building schools and hospitals and establishing public works programs, Long planned to run for president on a similar program that guaranteed every American a home, a job and a car. And given the national mood, and Roosevelt's failure to pull the country out of the Depression, many political pundits believed he could do it.

In hindsight, that seems preposterous — Long had actually been impeached (although not convicted) on corruption charges in 1929 — but although his assassination made a run for the presidency moot, Long's popularity definitely had an affect on the Roosevelt administration. In fact, many of the programs in Roosevelt's "Second New Deal" were moderate versions of Long's radical proposals, especially the Wealth Tax Act, which mirrored Long's goal of raising taxes on large incomes and corporate profits.

"God don't let me die, I have so much to do!" Long cried before drawing his last breath. Actually, on balance, Long served his purpose, and his colorful death was a fitting end to a very colorful life.

© *Kauffmann 2008*

Bruce's History Lessons:
Day of Infamy 2001

The tragic terrorist attack on New York's World Trade Center and the Pentagon in Washington, D.C., has been called "another Pearl Harbor" and in many ways, rightly so. The "day of infamy" in 1941 was a nefarious sneak attack that brought the United States into a world war, and last Tuesday's attack was equally nefarious and undoubtedly will bring this nation into war again — although exactly what kind of war, and with whom, is at this writing uncertain.

There are also similarities in terms of tragic security lapses. For example, prior to Pearl Harbor, relations between the U.S. and Japan had so seriously deteriorated that war seemed very possible. Certainly, Pearl's naval commanders knew that the Japanese Navy had been behaving unusually. It had changed its call signals twice in one month — twice a year being normal. Japanese aircraft carriers in the Pacific had stopped communicating (to hide their positions), and thanks to an illegal FBI wiretap, U.S. commanders knew that the Japanese consulate in Hawaii had suddenly started burning documents. Thus it was inexcusable that the naval fleet at Pearl was on a peacetime condition of alert, that sailors got weekends off (the attack was on a Sunday), that few anti-aircraft guns were manned and that no anti-torpedo nets were protecting the ships. In Pearl's wake, the commander, Admiral Husband Kimmel, was relieved of command.

In last Tuesday's attack, the fact that four commercial airplanes were simultaneously hijacked, that the command center responsible for U.S. Air Defense was nowhere to be found during the entire attack (how is it possible that it was notified of a hijacking less than ten minutes before the first airplane hit?), and that the Pentagon — a symbol of American defense readiness *at least equal to* Pearl Harbor in 1941 — was hit with impunity raises similar security questions. This is especially true given reports that eavesdrops of recent conversations by Saudi extremist Osama bin Laden — linked to earlier attacks on the World Trade Center and the U.S.S. Cole — reveal him boasting of an imminent attack on America. And while U.S. targets overseas, not the Pentagon or the World Trade Center, were considered the primary objectives, so too were the Philippines, not Pearl Harbor, considered Japan's primary target in 1941.

The point being that a thorough review of America's defenses against this new kind of war is obviously forthcoming, and before it's over — just as at Pearl — many questions will not have completely satisfying answers, and many procedures (and people) will be changed.

And there is another similarity. In 1941, Americans thought the war raging in Europe would never affect them, and before last Tuesday most Americans thought such massive, organized terrorism only happened in the Middle East. "You may not be interested in war," Russian revolutionary Leon Trotsky once wrote. "But war is interested in you."

© Kauffmann 2008

Bruce's History Lessons:
War and Remembrance

The following call for a national day of prayer and remembrance was made the last time American blood was spilled in war, on American soil, by a foreign invader. It was made by the fourth president of the United States, (my hero) James Madison, 189 years before the one just made by our 43rd president, George W. Bush. And although both occasions were in response to national tragedies — the War of 1812 and September 11, 2001 — it is comforting to know, as you will by reading below, that the nation today remains much the same.

America is still a nation of religious belief *and* religious tolerance. It is still deeply patriotic, but aware of its faults. It is still peace loving, but fearsome in war when called to be so. It is still mindful of the need to administer justice, but equally mindful of the need to seek it.

And finally, in times of crisis it still becomes one nation, indivisible, as its enemies throughout history have learned to their sorrow.

"WHEREAS the Congress of the United States, by a joint Resolution of the two Houses, have signified a request, that a day may be recommended, to be observed by the People of the United States, with religious solemnity, as a day of public Humiliation and Prayer: and whereas such a recommendation will enable the several religious denominations and societies so disposed, to offer, at one and the same time, their common vows and adorations to Almighty God, on the solemn occasion produced by the war, in which he has been pleased to permit the injustice of a foreign power to involve these United States; I do therefore recommend the third Thursday in August next, as a convenient day, to be so set apart, for the devout purposes of rendering to the Sovereign of the Universe, and the Benefactor of mankind, the public homage due to his holy attributes; of acknowledging the transgressions which might justly provoke the manifestations of His divine displeasure; of seeking His merciful forgiveness, and His assistance in the great duties of repentance & amendment; and, especially, of offering fervent supplications, that in the present season of calamity and war, he would take the American People under His peculiar care and protection; that He would guide their public councils, animate their patriotism, and bestow His blessing on their arms; that He would inspire all nations with a love of justice & of concord, and with a reverence for the unerring precept of our holy religion, to do to others as they would require that others should do to them; and, finally, that turning the hearts of our enemies from the violence and injustice which sway their councils against us, He would hasten a restoration of the blessings of Peace."

© Kauffmann 2008

Bruce's History Lesson:
Sputnik

Seldom, if ever, has an object the size and shape of a basketball had the impact on politics and international relations as that of the tiny satellite that the Soviets put into orbit this week (Oct. 4) in 1957.   Sputnik, as it was called, not only ushered in the Space Age, it raised to a new level (literally and figuratively) the Cold War competition between America and the Soviet Union.

It also had a profound impact on American education. Shocked that the Soviet Union and not the U.S. had been first in the "race to space," Americans questioned whether our schools were properly teaching math and science, especially since our civilian space program — called Vanguard — had been a dismal failure. Attempting to launch a puny three-pound satellite (Sputnik weighed 180 pounds), the Vanguard rocket kept exploding on the launch pad. Thus, by the early 1960s, we began revising our public school curriculum to emphasize math and the applied sciences.

Yet the irony was that, long before the Russians, America had the technological know-how to put a satellite in orbit — we just refused to acknowledge it because the know-how was developed by that bugaboo of bugaboos, the "military industrial complex." While we poured time, effort and a fortune into the hopeless Vanguard rocket, the Redstone intercontinental ballistic missile (ICBM) — which in the event of war we relied on to send nuclear warheads up into space and then down into Soviet territory — lay idle. Then-President Eisenhower refused to consider putting a satellite on top of a Redstone because it would give "military taint" to our "civilian" space program.

After Sputnik, however, he changed his tune, no doubt helped by a reminder from the Pentagon that Sputnik meant the Soviets now had a greater capability to send nuclear weapons into space and drop them down on us! Ike quickly authorized the Explorer project, based on using Redstone ICBMs to deliver a civilian payload into space. And sure enough, the following year when the Explorer I finally carried a satellite into orbit, the rocket that delivered the goods was a Redstone ICBM.

Only it wasn't called that. Still determined to keep all trace of the "military" out of his civilian program, Eisenhower instructed the Explorer Project leaders to change the name of the Redstone to Jupiter. So while the world watched in wonder as pioneer astronauts such as John Glenn shot into orbit (and history), few realized that the missile they sat on top of was the same one a nuclear warhead sat on top of every other day of the year.

Meanwhile, back in our nation's schools, everyone was studying hard, hoping to turn out scientists and mathematicians as good as the Soviets ...

© Kauffmann 2008

Bruce's History Lessons:
Eleanor Roosevelt (ER)

Eleanor Roosevelt, born this week (Oct. 11) in 1884, is by almost any measure the greatest woman America has produced. Her fame and influence rested partly on her marriage to Franklin Roosevelt, but the opposite is probably just as true. And while the details of their rocky romantic union are well known, politically their partnership was among the most effective ever.

She was his eyes and ears. Crippled by polio, FDR could not travel the country the way most presidents do, so Eleanor went in his stead. During the depths of the Depression she visited coal miners in West Virginia, destitute farmers in California and Oklahoma, poor blacks in the South and city slums, and struggling factory workers in the Northeast — and she reported on all of it to her husband, giving him a feel for the plight of the average American that helped shape his most important social policies.

What's more she was a political Godsend because her appeal to one wing of the Democratic Party — blacks, laborers, women, intellectuals — allowed him to concentrate on the other wing — white Southerners — ensuring his re-election and his party's hold on power. As he said once when she asked him if her liberal activism bothered him, "Oh no, you go right ahead. I can always say, 'Well, that's my wife. I can't do anything about her.'"

Not that they didn't have disagreements. Eleanor drove FDR crazy with her insistence that it was the Federal government's duty to right every social wrong she discovered (and she discovered a lot of them; the joke in Washington held that FDR's bedtime prayer was, "Please, Lord, make Eleanor a little tired."). And as World War II loomed, and FDR went from "Dr. Fix the Country" to "Dr. Win the War," Eleanor and her priorities gave way to new challenges and new advisors (including Winston Churchill; ER and WC barely tolerated each other). But all in all, her influence on his administration, on liberalism, on the Democratic Party, and on America from the 1930s until today has been immeasurable.

In fact, after FDR's death her influence probably increased. Her newspaper column, "My Day," was so popular her syndicate renewed it even after FDR was gone. And until her own death she helped shape, or further, such causes as civil rights, child and labor protection laws, women's equality and creation of a Jewish state — and such organizations as the United Nations, the Red Cross, the AFL-CIO and the NAACP.

Eleanor died in 1962 at age 77. She is buried at the Roosevelt family estate, right next to her husband, allowing them to confer, argue, agree, strategize and reminisce for Eternity. That would be a conversation worth listening in on.

© Kauffmann 2008

Bruce's History Lessons:
Grace Bedell and Abe Lincoln's
Historic Beard

"My opponent has called me two-faced. I ask you, ladies and gentleman, if I had two faces do you think I would have chosen this one?"

-attributed to Abraham Lincoln during the
Lincoln-Douglas debates

Tall, gangly, with a face that he himself described as "homely," Abe Lincoln, our 16th and (I would argue) greatest president, cared little about his personal appearance except as a source of self-deprecating humor. So people became curious when, during his campaign for president in 1860, he suddenly grew a beard, having been clean-shaven all his life.

The idea was not his, but that of a young girl from Westfield, New York, who wrote the Republican candidate a letter this week (Oct. 15) in 1860 suggesting that he would have a better chance of being elected if he grew a beard. The girl's name was Grace Bedell, and having seen pictures of Lincoln on a campaign poster, she thought Lincoln's face was too thin. "All the ladies like whiskers and they would tease their husband's [sic] to vote for you and then you would be President," she advised the candidate, adding that if he grew a beard she would convince her brothers to vote for Lincoln as well.

The letter, which he received at his home in Springfield, Illinois, greatly amused Lincoln, who promptly responded with his own letter. Since he'd never had whiskers, he wrote Grace, wouldn't growing them now seem a "silly affectation?"

Affectation or not, Lincoln began growing a beard soon after, and as it happened, during the journey to Washington to assume the presidency,

Lincoln's train stopped at Westfield for an impromptu rally. Learning that Grace Bedell was in the crowd of well-wishers, the full-bearded Lincoln greeted her by saying, "You see, Grace, I let my whiskers grow for you."

Lincoln kept his beard until the day he died, and it is the bearded Lincoln who graces the five-dollar bill and penny, and who watches over the nation's capital from the Lincoln Memorial. Indeed, thanks to Grace Bedell it is the bearded Lincoln who is the most recognized American political figure in the world.

Which prompts a few musings. First, how styles have changed. No president has had facial hair since William Taft in 1913, and today (Al Gore notwithstanding) it would be considered a political liability. Second, how civil rights have changed. Grace hoped to convince her brothers to vote for Lincoln because she, being female, legally could not. And finally, how postal service has changed. Lincoln's reply to Grace was written on October 19, meaning that — way back in 1860 — her letter, written on the 15th, traveled all the way from New York to Illinois in just four days.

© *Kauffmann 2008*

Bruce's History Lessons:
The Volstead Act: Putting Teeth into Prohibition

The 18th Amendment to the Constitution prohibited the nation from consuming alcoholic beverages, but it said nothing about how to enforce this noble goal or — perish the thought — punish those who might not share it. That task was left to the Volstead Act (after Congressman Andrew Volstead), which passed this week (Oct. 28) in 1919.

Both the amendment and the act were the result of a temperance movement that finally came into its own around the turn of the century. In particular, the Anti-Saloon League and the Women's Christian Temperance Union mobilized thousands of people — mostly women — to fight for passage of a national law banning alcohol. After all, it was women, especially poor women, who had born the brunt of husbands whose paychecks were wasted in after-work saloons and who, in drunken dementia, often beat them and their children when they came home.

Alas for temperance adherents, the Volstead Act was riddled with loopholes that made enforcement difficult. But the real challenge was organized crime, which saw "Prohibition" (the name given this chapter in American history) as a golden opportunity to earn huge profits illegally "bootlegging" liquor from Canada, and other places where it was still legal, to clandestine night clubs, called "Speak-easies," in American cities across the land. In many cities, Chicago foremost among them, payoffs to corrupt police and politicians allowed bootlegging to flourish to the point that there was hardly a need to keep it underground.

What's more, millions of Americans engaged in their own form of "bootlegging" by brewing homemade alcohol such as hard cider and "bathtub gin," which they drank in quantities at least as great as when liquor had been legal. And given the "quality control" of this homemade brew, alcohol-related deaths and diseases actually increased during the years of Prohibition.

And so did crime. In addition to bribes, payoffs and other forms of graft, serious crimes such as murder, burglary and assault increased significantly as rival gangsters such as Al Capone and Bugs Moran battled each other, as well as outmanned and outgunned federal agents, over control of this extremely lucrative trade. As one sociologist put it, "Prohibition destroyed legal jobs, created black-market violence, diverted resources from enforcement of other laws, and increased prices people had to pay for prohibited goods."

In short, Prohibition was a total failure, and was put out of its misery by the 21st Amendment, which repealed the 18th Amendment and overturned the Volstead Act in 1933. The American public had finally come to the (sobering) conclusion that if alcohol was here to stay — and it was — then regulating and taxing its distribution and sale was better left to the government than to the gangsters.

© *Kauffmann 2008*

Bruce's History Lessons:
The Code Talkers

In warfare, the attempts by armies to develop a communication code that no enemy can break have been matched only by their attempts to break their enemy's code. Being able to listen to your enemy's conversations, while knowing that your own communication is inviolate, has made the difference in many military conflicts throughout history.

It certainly made a difference in World War II, especially against the Japanese in the Pacific from 1941 on, where America deployed the only code that the Japanese never deciphered despite a technological wizardry that made them extremely proficient at code breaking. But perhaps Japan's problem had something to do with the fact that this code was developed before there was such a thing as "technology." Indeed, it was developed before there was such a thing as America.

The code was the language of the Navajo Indian tribe, which has no alphabet and a syntax and dialect so complex that it is essentially gibberish to anyone not raised a Navajo, or trained in the language by Navajos. Of the latter there were fewer than 30 people in the world in 1941, and none was Japanese, who had trouble enough with certain English vowels and consonants, let alone a Navajo sound like *debeh-li-zine.*

As a result, a group of volunteer Navajo "code talkers" were trained as Marines and then deployed throughout the Pacific Islands that the U.S. and Japan fought over from 1942 to 1945. At Guadalcanal, Okinawa and Iwo Jima, code talkers relayed messages from one Marine unit to another, so sure that their code was unbreakable that they chatted away on telephones, radios and walkie-talkies. So what if the Japanese were listening? What would they do with a sound like *chay-da-ghi?*

In fact, what made deciphering even harder was that the Navajo language had no words for many military terms, so the Navajos improvised. For example, *besh-lo,* which means "iron fish," became the code for submarine. And because the language has no alphabet, the code talkers often "spelled out" words based on the English alphabet's first letter of an object. Thus "*tsah* (needle) *wol-la-chee* (ant) *ah-keh-di-glini* (victor) *tsah-ah-dzoh* (yucca)" spelled N-A-V-Y.

That the code talkers were invaluable to America's victory in World War II is beyond question. The only question is why — given the shameful history of mistreatment that Native-Americans have suffered since America's birth — these Navajos would display such patriotism on America's behalf. Perhaps the answer to that question will be answered by the new movie about these code talkers that is coming soon to theaters. Starring Nicolas Cage, it should shed some light on this amazing chapter in our history, and accord some long overdue honor to the brave Navajo soldiers who made it happen.

© *Kauffmann 2008*

Bruce's History Lesson: Elizabeth Cady Stanton: The Making of a Feminist

Today's women's movement owes a great debt to many heroic pioneers, but perhaps none was more indispensable than Elizabeth Cady Stanton, who was born this week (Nov. 12) in 1815.

For starters, she was a prime organizer of the Seneca Falls Conference in 1848, which galvanized the women's movement and made it a force to be reckoned with. At that conference she wrote a woman's Declaration of Independence modeled after the original, except that it made *men* the villain in the same way that Tom Jefferson had made England's King George III the villain.

Stanton was also co-founder with Susan B. Anthony of the National Woman Suffrage Association. This organization later joined the American Woman Suffrage Association to become the National American Woman Suffrage Association (whew!). NAWSA was to women's rights what the NRA is to gun ownership, and among its legacies is the 19th Amendment to the Constitution, which gave women the right to vote.

Stanton was a brilliant speaker and talented journalist — she edited the first women's feminist magazine, *Revolution* — *and* she was tireless and even fanatical in her efforts to gain equality for women. As a result, many a historian has examined the forces that shaped Stanton's passion, and although it is generally agreed that her feminist conversion occurred during a stint working in her father's law office — where she saw first-hand the legal discrimination against women — I have my own theory, based on a little-known event in her life.

Elizabeth Cady was born in Johnstown, New York, the seventh of eleven Cady children, and while she was an exceptional child in every way, her oldest brother was the apple of the family's eye — especially Mr. Cady, who doted on the boy. Alas, the lad died in childhood, and Mr. Cady went into a state of grief that deeply affected Elizabeth, who vowed she would fill the void that her brother's death had caused in her father's life. And so she became an exceptional athlete and student. Among other physical pursuits, she was a horsewoman *extraordinaire,* and she excelled in the classroom, winning many academic honors at the Troy Female Seminary, now the Emma Willard School, in Troy, N.Y. (Troy, where I misspent much of my youth, is the home of the real life character on which America's "Uncle Sam" is based).

Then one day she won one of New York state's most prestigious scholastic prizes, and when she showed it to her father she expected that this accomplishment would fill him with parental pride. Instead, he gave out a loud sigh, shook his head and said sadly, "Oh, Elizabeth, if only you had been born a boy!"

My guess is *that* was the beginning of her journey into the women's movement.

© Kauffmann 2008

Bruce's History Lessons:
The Vietnam Memorial

"The parade we never got."

– A Vietnam veteran describing the Vietnam Memorial

It was truly poetic injustice that the National Vietnam Veterans Memorial, dedicated this week (Nov. 13) in 1982, in Washington, D.C., would itself be controversial, considering how controversial was the war it was meant to honor. From the moment the design of a Yale University architecture student named Maya Lin was chosen as the winner of the open competition to create a memorial to Vietnam, the debate raged. Many Vietnam veterans, politicians and civic leaders — to say nothing of contemporary architects — were furious that her winning design contained no statues or stirring quotes, but was simply a black granite wall carved into the earth and inscribed with the names of the 58,183 military personnel who died in Vietnam. Lin was reviled in print and in person, and was forced to defend her design in a number of public hearings in Washington and elsewhere.

Little noticed, or forgotten, was the fact that Lin's design was the unanimous choice of the selection committee, or that she had, with great distinction, met all four design criteria imposed — that an American citizen be chosen, that the memorial be contemplative and harmonious with its surroundings, that it make no political statement, and that it display the names of all who died. In the ensuing outcry, even Lin's ethnic background and patriotism were called into question.

But she prevailed, and from the moment her memorial was dedicated a curious thing happened. Visitors loved it. Or more to the point, they were profoundly moved by it, and it is now the most visited piece of public American artwork created in the 20th century. Today, more than one million people a year walk along "The Wall" to find the name of a friend or loved one, or leave behind a flower or photo, or — if one is a veteran of that war — to remember and reflect. No visitor to this memorial, including this writer, has failed to come away moved, and even changed.

Which evokes a memory of my first time at The Wall. Leaving it, shaken but stirred, I saw ahead of me a rather large man sitting on a park bench. As I got closer I realized that this was a red-bearded giant — maybe 6' 5", 250 pounds — wearing a "Hell's Angels" jacket, several tattoos, biker boots, cut-off T-shirt and blue jeans. On a normal day he would be considered menacing, even dangerous, but not that day. That day he was crying so hard and shaking so uncontrollably that he was beyond caring who saw him.

Another visitor to the Vietnam Veterans memorial, and as good an answer to its critics as you could ever find.

© Kauffmann 2008

Bruce's History Lessons:
Watergate and the 18 ½ Minute Gap

"Time is a slippery thing."

- Sherwood Anderson

The episode in our history known as Watergate went from a crime to the ridiculous this week (November 21) in 1973 when it was revealed that there was a mysterious 18 ½-minute gap in one of President Richard Nixon's subpoenaed White House tape recordings. Earlier in the year, in testimony before a congressional committee investigating Watergate, White House staffer Alexander Butterfield revealed to an astonished nation that President Nixon secretly recorded all conversations in the Oval Office. The clear inference from this revelation was that if Nixon had any involvement in the Watergate burglary and cover-up, he almost certainly would have discussed it with aides, and those discussions would be on those tapes. Immediately, the special prosecutor appointed to investigate Watergate, Archibald Cox, subpoenaed the tapes, which Nixon immediately refused to release.

But cooler heads prevailed and discussions commenced over what information relative to those tapes might be shared with the special prosecutor and Judge John Sirica, who was presiding over the Watergate burglary trial. It was during these discussions that Alexander Haig, the White House chief of staff, admitted to Judge Sirica that "some sinister force" had erased 18 ½ minutes from one of the subpoenaed tapes. In later sworn testimony Haig became more specific, if perhaps not more believable, when he said "devil theories" were being discussed as the possible explanation. Haig added that this was "a source of great distress" to White House lawyers, making it, arguably, the first time in the history of American jurisprudence that defense lawyers experienced "distress" over an inability to provide prosecutors with key evidence in a criminal trial.

Judge Sirica, also distressed, ordered Haig to come up with a more realistic explanation. Casting about, Haig's eyes lit on Nixon's secretary, Rose Mary Woods, whom he promptly blamed for the erasure. Miss Woods admitted that while transcribing the tapes she might have mistakenly hit the "erase" button on her recording machine during a five-minute phone conversation in her office, but that still left 13 ½ minutes to explain. Haig's reply immediately endeared him to the budding feminist movement. "I've known women who think they've talked for five minutes and have talked for an hour," he scoffed.

As it happened, no one ever developed a satisfactory explanation for the entire 18 ½-minute erasure, which didn't matter since other tapes proved Nixon had participated in criminal activity. Facing impeachment, he resigned on August 9, 1974.

As for Rose Mary Woods, she promptly faded into obscurity, while Alexander Haig — perhaps not entirely exorcised of his "sinister forces" and "devil theories" — later became President Reagan's first secretary of state, before resigning over "ideological differences." He lasted about 18 ½ months.

© Kauffmann 2008

Bruce's History Lessons:
Play It Again, Uncle Sam

"Of all the gin joints in all the towns in all the world, she walks into mine."

          – Humphrey Bogart, "Casablanca"

And it's a darn good thing she did because otherwise Casablanca would have been bereft of one of the great love stories of all time and a poignant subplot to the political struggle that drives the action in this classic film set during World War II. And speaking of WW II, Casablanca the movie was timed to open this week (Nov. 26) in 1942 to benefit from the publicity surrounding the just-completed Allied takeover of Casablanca the city. Until November of 1942, this port city in Morocco, which was formerly a part of the French colonial empire, had been under the dual control of Nazi Germany and the Nazi-puppet government in Vichy, France, that the Germans installed after occupying France in 1940.

In Casablanca (the movie), both the Nazis and their French "Vichy" collaborators play prominent roles, especially Captain Louis Renault (played memorably by Claude Rains), the cynical, amoral French police chief whose chief aim is to get rich through graft and gambling at *Rick's Café*, the "gin joint" owned by the equally cynical (but morally principled) Rick Blaine (Bogey).

For its part, the box office success of Casablanca (the movie) focused attention on Casablanca the war conference, which convened in Casablanca (the city) shortly after the movie opened. And as it happened, at Casablanca (the conference) President Roosevelt and Britain's Winston Churchill finally severed their relations with the Nazi-puppet Vichy government and began to consider Charles De Gaulle and his Free French government-in-exile as France's legitimate authority. Similarly, while in Casablanca (the movie) Captain Renault is initially an unsavory opportunist, by the final scene he too has renounced his Vichy connection and joined Rick in a pro-Allied partnership.

If these plot similarities seem like examples of "art imitating life," perhaps it wasn't a total coincidence, for as any aficionado of this classic film knows, the Casablanca script was written from one day to the next, and the screenwriters could easily have searched the day's front-page war headlines for thematic ideas. Indeed, neither Bogart nor Ingrid Bergman, who played his love interest, Ilsa, knew until the last days of shooting whether Ilsa would be leaving Casablanca (the city) with her husband, Victor Lazlo, or staying with Bogey.

In the end she makes the right choice (she leaves), which can only partially be said of the members of the Motion Picture Academy. Although they gave Casablanca (the movie) Oscars for Best Picture, Director and Screenplay, they denied Bergman and Bogey (especially Bogey!) well-deserved Oscars for Best Actress and Actor — a cinematic injustice that has become only slightly more bearable as time goes by.

© Kauffmann 2008

Bruce's History Lessons:
Delaware: Why It's The First State

Delaware became the first state to ratify the Constitution this week (Dec. 7) in 1787, earning it the sobriquet "First in Freedom." Yet a look at *why* Delaware was so quick to join the new United States reveals that "First in Security" might be a more accurate motto.

Recall that during the Constitutional Convention in the summer of 1787 the greatest argument was not — as is often supposed — between slave states and free states over slavery, but between big states and small states over representation in the Senate and House of Representatives. Big states such as Virginia wanted proportional representation in both branches of Congress — i.e., the larger your state's population, the more senators and representatives you got. The smaller states, of which Delaware was decidedly one, wanted *equal* representation in both branches, fearing that they would be dominated by the big states if proportional representation prevailed.

The issue became so heated that the big states threatened to form their own union, thereby freezing out the small states, while the small states threatened to invite a foreign power, or powers, to become their protector — including England. This, needless to say, would have undone the entire aim of the Revolutionary War.

Enter what became known as the "Great Compromise," in which the convention would split the difference. The House of Representatives would have proportional representation, while the Senate would give each state, regardless of size, two senators. While this appealed greatly to the small states, it was still an anathema to the large ones. To them it was as if, to use a modern analogy, Haiti and America had the same representation, and power, in the United Nations Security Council.

Alas for the big states, they were outnumbered by the small states, which meant that when it was time to vote on the Great Compromise, the small states prevailed. As a result, as we all know, the Constitution established that two senators from every state, regardless of size or population, would sit in the United States Senate. With this safeguard established, small states like Delaware saw great advantage in joining a larger body of states in a union that would protect them geographically, militarily and politically. Thus Delaware quickly and unanimously ratified the Constitution. Soon after, other smaller states like New Jersey and Georgia followed suit.

In hindsight, of course, this compromise has worked well, and relations between small and large states during the past 215 years have been very amicable. On the other hand, if you're from a large state it might gall you to know that, even today, only 600,000 people live in Delaware. *Chickens* outnumber people in the state by more than 100 to 1.

© *Kauffmann 2008*

Bruce's History Lessons:
An Affair to Remember: Alexander
Hamilton Comes Clean

That great men are imperfect has long been a given and is certainly proved by Alexander Hamilton, one of our greatest Founding Fathers. Together with James Madison he created, defended and helped ratify the U.S. Constitution, and as our first secretary of the Treasury, he developed the monetary system on which our economy is based even today.

But he had a character flaw typical to so many politicians. In 1791, happily married, a doting father, and at the height of his political powers, he had an affair with Maria Reynolds, a woman 11 years his junior who claimed her husband had deserted her. In reality Maria and her husband James were partners in a scam to blackmail Hamilton for this affair. Trapped, Hamilton paid the Reynolds their "hush money" and, still infatuated with Maria, continued the affair before breaking it off in 1792.

Alas, as is often the case, the affair came to light when James Reynolds was caught in a separate illegal activity and offered his knowledge of the Hamilton affair as a bargaining chip. But Reynolds claimed that Hamilton had also abused the powers of his office, using government funds to pay his hush money, and engaging in general corruption. Thus did three members of Congress confront Hamilton about these charges this week (Dec. 15) in 1792. Hamilton had a choice. Lie, stonewall, or come clean.

He came clean. Inviting the congressmen to his home, he admitted the affair but denied the corruption. He provided voluminous evidence to prove his innocence, including the correspondence between him and the Reynolds, and he offered the congressmen the opportunity to examine his financial records. So impressed were they by his thorough and honest defense, they dropped the matter entirely.

The media, however, had other plans, and a few years later a pamphlet accusing Hamilton of speculation and insider trading gained widespread attention. Again, Hamilton faced a choice. Lie, ignore the charges, or refute them. He chose to refute them in his own pamphlet titled *Observations on Certain Documents ...in Which the Charge of Speculation Against Alexander Hamilton ...is Fully Refuted.* In this pamphlet he completely disproved the charges and laid out the details of his adultery so thoroughly that it was, as one observer put it, "humiliating in the extreme."

But it was so honest, and Hamilton was so cooperative and forthright, that his reputation for public trust, if not marital fidelity, was restored — and remains so to this day. To Hamilton the former was all that mattered, and he would not besmirch it by lying.

A cautionary tale. Would that William Clinton or Gary Condit, just to name the most recent pols, had recalled it when their hour of adulterous travail came 'round.

© *Kauffmann 2008*

Bruce's History Lessons:
Willard Libby Dates Us

Lying about your age got a whole lot harder thanks to the man who was born this week (Dec. 17) in 1908. Willard Libby was a chemist who had worked on the atomic bomb during WW II, but his real claim to fame (relatively speaking) came from his pioneer work in the scientific method of "radiocarbon dating." Today we use radiocarbon dating to determine the ages of everything from ancient Egyptian mummies to the Dead Sea Scrolls. It has proven to be so accurate that it can identify within a few years the ages of objects up to 70 thousand years old.

Libby's forays into radiocarbon dating began at the University of Chicago in 1947, where he conducted experiments on carbon-14, the carbon isotope on which radiocarbon dating is based. Libby's experiments were predicated on several known facts, beginning with the fact that carbon-14 is produced when nitrogen is bombarded by cosmic rays in the atmosphere. It then falls to Earth where it becomes carbon dioxide, which — as we know from our high school biology days — is then absorbed by plants through "photosynthesis." From there, carbon spreads to the animals, such as humans, that eat the plants, and to the other animals (humans included) that eat the animals that eat the plants.

The point, as Libby surmised, is that everything containing carbon, including living organisms, also contains various levels of carbon-14. Or to put it another way, we are all slightly radioactive. What's more, when an organism dies it stops absorbing carbon-14, and instead starts losing it as part of the decaying process. Because carbon-14 decays at a predictable rate — one-half of the original amount disintegrates every 5700 years — Libby concluded that if there was a way to measure how much carbon-14 had been lost, and how much was left in an organism, then one could accurately predict how old that organism was. Using a sophisticated Geiger counter to measure carbon-14 amounts, and a sophisticated scientific formula that is too complicated for me to understand, let alone explain, Libby then tested his radioactive carbon dating method against pieces of wood (once part of a living tree) from an Egyptian tomb whose age was already known. They matched, and radiocarbon dating would subsequently revolutionize such fields as archeology, anthropology and geology. It would also, not surprisingly, spark new debates over religion.

One of those unknown "Men of Science" whose work has profoundly affected modern life and human understanding, Libby received the 1960 Nobel Prize for Chemistry. He died quietly in 1980, and ironically — or perhaps intentionally — Libby ensured that scientists from 70 thousand years in the future would never be able to determine his age. He was cremated and his ashes scattered.

© Kauffmann 2008

Bruce's History Lessons:
Kreating the Ku Klux Klan

The Ku Klux Klan was formed this week (Dec. 24) in 1865 when six former Confederate Army officers met in Pulaski, Tennessee, to create a secret organization dedicated to maintaining white supremacy in the South. In the wake of the Civil War, the northern-controlled U.S. Congress had passed federal laws giving newly freed blacks a number of political and civil rights, which was an anathema to most white southerners.

Originally, the Ku Klux Klan — which comes from the Greek word *kuklos*, meaning "circle" — intended to merely frighten blacks by donning white sheets with hoods and passing themselves off as the "ghosts of dead Confederate soldiers." But beatings, lynchings, mutilations and cross burnings soon followed, and as a result, after a brief post-Civil War "Reconstruction" period in which many blacks began exercising their newly won rights, the South reverted back to the *ante bellum* status quo. Klan activities, abetted by racist "Jim Crow" laws, returned blacks to a state of powerless, segregation and economic subservience.

Its mission essentially accomplished, the Klan subsequently disbanded, but it re-emerged during World War I as an influx of European immigrants — especially Jews and Roman Catholics — were perceived by the Klan as a new threat to the supremacy of white, Anglo-Saxon Protestants. By the early 1920s a rejuvenated Klan had as many as 3 million members and its stepped up campaign of terror, murder and mayhem was again abetted by passage of racist state and local laws.

By the 1930s, however, internal power struggles and a crackdown by the federal government diminished the Klan's power and influence. And as the years went by, and the Civil Rights movement progressed to the point that the South largely put its legacy of segregation and racism behind it, the Klan's power diminished even further. Today it is such a shell of its former self that when the Klan now marches or holds a rally on behalf of some racist cause, more often than not it must first apply for a government permit.

That said, there is an interesting, if imperfect analogy between the Klan of the 1860s and the al Qaeda terrorist network of Osama bin Laden and the Taliban of 2001. In both cases, the struggle was against "infidels" and "outsiders" bent on "destroying our way of life," "perverting our values," "mocking our traditions," "defiling our religion" and even "violating our women."

In truth, of course, the real struggle was, and is, between a racist, xenophobic ideology and a progressive, inclusive one. And as patience, unity, steadfastness and superior power derived from a more advanced society were the key to defeating the Klan, so too are they the key to defeating bin Laden and al Qaeda.

© Kauffmann 2008

Bruce's History Lesson:
The Emancipation Proclamation

On New Years Day (Jan. 1) in 1863 Abe Lincoln issued the Emancipation Proclamation, ringing in the new year in a historic way. For many historians the EP is considered the single greatest act of his presidency. But back then it was considered controversial and even hypocritical. After all, the Proclamation only freed slaves in the *Confederate* states where Lincoln had no power to enforce it. Those slaves in the states that still belonged to the Union, where Lincoln still had presidential power, were not affected. Which begs the question: What was Lincoln thinkin'?

He was thinking about the big picture. At the time he issued the Emancipation Proclamation, Lincoln had major political problems, the first being that many pro-Union border states had sizable slave populations. A blanket emancipation might have driven those states into the Southern camp, to disastrous result.

But more important, Lincoln felt legally bound to uphold the Constitution, which — whether he liked it or not — at that time still protected slavery. Lincoln never wavered in his belief that the South was *still* a part of the Union (even if in rebellion) and therefore still under the protection of the laws of the land. Thus, he felt he had no *civilian* authority to free slaves in either the North *or* the South.

But military authority was another matter. Lincoln believed "military necessity" gave him broad powers as Commander-in-Chief of the armed forces, so he used the Proclamation as a weapon of war. By freeing slaves in the South, which (unlike the North) posed a threat to the Union, Lincoln believed many of them would run away and come north. The result would be two-fold — these free Southern blacks could swell the ranks of the Union army (see the movie *Glory*), and their absence would force Southern soldiers to return to their farms to work the jobs their slaves had abandoned. This would deplete the Southern army.

Lincoln also had geopolitical concerns. England, which imported Southern cotton, was considering recognizing the South's independence, which would have bolstered morale and increased the South's war-making capability. But England also had a sizable abolitionist contingent that hated slavery. Lincoln figured — correctly — that the Proclamation would energize the abolitionists and force England to remain neutral.

That said, the Emancipation Proclamation is not considered a great speech, and the notable absence of the type of stirring rhetoric and inspired phrasing so prevalent in his other major addresses (Gettysburg; both Inaugurals) was probably on purpose. The EP was not a political document; it was basically a military order, born out of military necessity. Yes, Lincoln wanted to free all of the slaves — he hated slavery passionately — but not at the expense of losing the Union.

© *Kauffmann 2008*

Bruce's History Lesson: The U-Boat Attacks Sink... Germany

This week (Jan. 9) in 1917, as World War I raged in Europe, one of the chief belligerents in that war, Germany, made a fateful miscalculation that would ensure it lost the war. Germany decided to renew its U-boat (submarine) attacks against U.S. shipping.

This reversed a decision made at the start of the war by Germany and its main enemy, Great Britain. At that time, both countries decided to refrain from attacking neutral shipping, even shipping intended for the enemy, because they feared such attacks would alienate the neutrals, especially the United States.

But things were different in 1917. After three years of bloody stalemate in the trenches on the Western front, Germany and Britain were both looking for a new strategy to win the war. The Germans re-discovered the U-boat, which they thought could destroy 600 thousand tons of neutral shipping a month and knock Great Britain — an island that depended on imports to survive — out of the war in six months.

The Germans also re-evaluated their fear of U.S. reprisals, wondering why they were denying themselves a war-winner — the U-boat — in deference to a country that was an ocean away and had no army, air force or navy to speak of.

It was a good question. In 1917, the U.S. military was pathetic for the simple reason that it was unnecessary. Protected by oceans to the east and west, one friendly nation to the north and a weak one to the south, America didn't need a large armed force. And given its pervasive isolationism

— President Woodrow Wilson had specifically campaigned on the promise to keep America out of World War I — America didn't *want* a large armed force.

But in deciding to renew their U-boat attacks, and almost certainly force the U.S. to enter the war, the Germans made two mistakes. First, they were unaware of the extent of America's industrial potential, and thus totally underestimated the country's ability to gear up for war.

Second, the Germans hadn't counted on the U.S. greenback dollar. This was significant because, unbeknownst to Germany, in 1917 Britain was near bankruptcy. Indeed, it is arguable (although by no means certain) that the Germans would not have needed *U-boats* to stop neutral shipping from reaching Britain because Britain's *creditors*, by refusing to lend any more money, would have done the job more effectively.

Instead, upon entering the war in retaliation for Germany's resumed U-boat attacks, the U.S. lent Britain and its main ally France billions of dollars, allowing them to continue the war. This, plus the combination of American soldiers and military equipment that began pouring into European ports in 1917, spelled the beginning of the end for the German Kaiser and his crew.

© Kauffmann 2008

Bruce's History Lessons:
John Kennedy's Inaugural Address

Judged by its rhetoric, the inaugural address that President John Kennedy gave in Washington, D.C., this week (Jan. 20) in 1961 is one of the greatest inaugural speeches ever delivered.

It was full of stirring phrases — "We shall pay any price, bear any burden, meet any hardship, support any friend, and oppose any foe, to ensure the survival and the success of liberty." It produced some memorable lines — "Ask not what your country can do for you. Ask what you can do for your country." And it had many evocative images — "The world is very different now, for man holds in his mortal hands the power to abolish all forms of human poverty, and all forms of human life." It also had a theme — it was a clarion call to Americans to prepare themselves for a "long twilight struggle" against the global spread of Communism.

In short, this half-hour address, penned by one of the most talented writers ever to serve in the White House, Ted Sorensen, is an American classic.

But as Kennedy's young aide Harris Wofford realized when he read the speech the night before it was to be given, there was one thing it lacked. It lacked any mention of the other "struggle" that one segment of America was engaged in at the time — the struggle for equality for all Americans regardless of race, creed or color. And that struggle was beginning to gather momentum. On January 19, the same day that Wofford read Kennedy's speech, black students in Richmond, Virginia — just 100 miles away — had demanded service at the segregated lunch counters in two of Richmond's biggest department stores. They were quickly arrested.

After reading the speech, Wofford confronted Kennedy. "There is an equal rights struggle going on here at home," he told the president-elect, "and you have to say something about it."

And so Kennedy made one change to his draft. "Let the word go forth," he intoned on Inauguration Day, "from this time and place, to friend and foe alike, that the torch has been passed to a new generation of Americans, born in this century, tempered by war, disciplined by a hard and bitter peace, proud of our ancient heritage, and unwilling to witness or permit the slow undoing of those human freedoms to which this nation has always been committed, and to which we are committed today — *at home* — and around the world."

Two words — "at home." That was Kennedy's revision and the sum total of his commitment to equality in a speech that challenged Americans to re-make the world. Small wonder that Kennedy was so unprepared for the massive civil rights movement that would soon challenge and bedevil his administration.

© Kauffmann 2008

Bruce's History Lessons:
God Takes A Hero

"I am ready to meet my Maker. Whether my Maker is prepared for the ordeal of meeting me is another matter."

–Winston Churchill, at the end of his life.

My choice for the 20th Century's "Person of the Century" — Winston Leonard Spencer Churchill — went on to his just reward this week (Jan. 24) in 1965. One must presume that for all his sins (which were legion), Churchill's just reward was a place of honor among the angels. And no doubt, Churchill's "Maker" even took time from His busy schedule to grant an audience to the man who, more than any other, saved Europe and the world from the century's original "Evil Empire," Nazi Germany.

When Churchill became British Prime Minister in May of 1940, most of Europe was — in Churchill's memorable phrase — "under the grip of the Gestapo and the odious apparatus of Nazi rule." In a stunning series of diplomatic and military victories, Nazi Germany controlled, or would soon control, Austria, Czechoslovakia, Poland, the Low Countries, Denmark, Norway and France. Italy, the Soviet Union and Japan were German allies. America was isolationist and neutral. England stood alone.

Thus did Churchill face a two-fold task. The first was to quickly build up the British armed forces, which had been badly neglected under the appeasement policies of Churchill's predecessor, Neville Chamberlain. The second was to rally the British people, which he did through a series of speeches and radio broadcasts heard around the world. Every word of every speech he ever gave, Churchill wrote himself (often while dressed in his bathrobe and smoking a fat cigar). "Had Churchill employed a speechwriter, we would all now be speaking German," one British historian quipped and there is much truth to that.

As a result of Churchill's leadership, for nearly two years — until America entered the war after Pearl Harbor and the Soviet Union changed sides after Hitler's disastrous decision to double cross the Soviets and invade the U.S.S.R. — British forces alone managed to fend off the Nazi juggernaut. Meanwhile, the British people, inspired by Churchill's defiant spirit and matchless rhetoric, remained undaunted by Hitler's attempts to invade the island or bomb it into submission. All the while, Churchill pursued a brilliant diplomacy designed to bring England and the United States together in a close working partnership.

We all know the result. The Allies defeated Nazi Germany, thanks in great part to Churchill's courage and statesmanship.

When Sir Winston Churchill died (he was Knighted in 1953), the entire world — including the people of Germany — mourned his passing, and he became the first commoner since the Duke of Wellington to be honored with a state funeral. He is one of my heroes of history.

© Kauffmann 2008

Bruce's History Lessons:
The Order of Succession

President Bush's State of the Union address — given this week in accordance with a longstanding and important tradition — may be, or may have been (depending on when you read this), notable for the absence of Melquiades Rafael Martinez, whose nonattendance *also* would be in accordance with an important tradition.

And who is Melquiades Martinez, you ask, and why might his absence be important?

He is President Bush's secretary of Housing and Urban Development (HUD), which makes him 13th in line to become president of the United States. Because of that, by tradition Martinez — or some other member of Bush's cabinet — will be away from the nation's capital during the State of the Union so that, in case of a catastrophic attack that destroys Washington, one member of the administration could legally assume the duties of president. And given the greater possibility of terrorist attacks since September 11, the presidential succession order has taken on added importance.

As it is, the succession question has long been controversial — so controversial that since the Constitution's creation there have been three laws and two constitutional amendments (the 20th and 25th) dealing with it. The result has been a mish-mash. To give one example, until the 25th Amendment, a vice-president who suddenly became president had no clear, legally established procedure for filling the vice-presidential vacancy that his own promotion had created.

But the real succession controversy begins *after* the vice-president, who at least is mentioned in the Constitution as the president's successor. It was left to Congress to decide who became president after the Veep, and Congress had trouble making up its mind. In 1792, Congress made the Senate's president pro tempore third in line to the presidency and the Speaker of the House fourth. In 1886, Congress removed them both and made members of the president's cabinet — today beginning with the Secretary of State and ending with the Secretary of Veterans Affairs — next in line. Then in 1947 it doubly reversed itself, putting the House Speaker in front of the Senate's president pro tempore and putting them both back in front of the cabinet.

Even then, Congress was not satisfied with the result, which is why the 20th and 25th amendments focus on replacing both the president and vice president quickly — so that the others in line will never be considered.

Which is also why it probably wasn't Melquiades Martinez, but one of the "big three"— Dick Cheney, Colin Powell, or Donald Rumsfeld — who was picked to be the designated absentee during this State of the Union. After all, Mr. Martinez may terrific at running HUD, but in the wake of a devastating terrorist attack that destroys Washington, can you picture him running the country?

© Kauffmann 2008

Bruce's History Lessons: Tippecanoe and the Modern Presidential Campaign

One could argue that the seeds of the modern presidential campaign were first planted by our 9th president, William Henry Harrison, who was born this week (Feb. 9) in 1773. Early in his life Harrison was a true military hero who first defeated the Shawnee Indians at the famous Battle of Tippecanoe, and later won the Battle of the Thames in which the great Shawnee Indian chief Tecumseh was killed. With America's northwest territory, and his own reputation, thus secure, Harrison turned to politics, which culminated in his quest for the presidency in 1840.

A member of the Whig party, Harrison — or "Ol' Tippecanoe" as he was nicknamed — was not the first presidential hopeful to trade on his reputation as a war hero, but he was the first to actively campaign on his own behalf (before him, self-promotion by presidential candidates was considered demeaning). His camp even created a campaign slogan, "Tippecanoe and Tyler, too!" (referring to his running mate, John Tyler), which was the first such slogan in American history. And arguably the schmaltziest.

Harrison was also the first presidential candidate to cultivate the press and personally attend campaign rallies, where — setting another precedent that many modern candidates have followed — he refused to speak a word about, let alone take a position on, the key issues of the day (slavery, tariffs, a central bank).

But his most important "first" was his campaign's orchestrated attempt to paint him as "a man of the people," when in fact he was the patrician son of a wealthy Virginia planter. When an opposition newspaper sarcastically suggested that Harrison be given "a barrel of hard cider ..." and should "sit the remainder of his days in a log cabin …" his campaign advisors seized on the suggestion, and painted Harrison as the "log cabin and hard cider candidate." His opponent, President Martin Van Buren, whose middle-class bonafides were far stronger than Harrison's, was painted as a dandy who drank wine in silver goblets and reclined on pillows in the White House

As a result of all these historic firsts, Harrison helped ensure record voter turnout and was elected president in a landslide. Subsequent presidential candidates took notice of both his campaign tactics and his big victory, and the rest is history.

There was, however, one historic first of Harrison's that no other president has emulated. In his two-hour Inaugural Address, Harrison promised not to run for a second term, a promise that became moot when — as a result of delivering his address in freezing temperatures without a hat or coat — he developed pneumonia and died on April 4th, one month to the day after his Inauguration. His is still the shortest presidency on record.

© *Kauffmann 2008*

Bruce's History Lessons:
Maggie Thatcher — The Iron Lady

In the long history of Great Britain's monarchy, men ruled almost constantly, yet the two most memorable reigns were by women, Elizabeth I and Victoria. Something of the same could be said about the nation's prime ministers. They have all been men, except for one of the most memorable, Margaret "Maggie" Thatcher, who became head of Britain's Conservative Party this week (Feb. 11) in 1975. "The Iron Lady," as she was called, subsequently became the only British prime minister of the 20th Century to be elected to three consecutive terms in office.

As PM, Thatcher's top priority was to end Britain's flirtation with Socialism by privatizing as many state-owned industries as possible, while at the same time reducing the power of Britain's trade unions, which Thatcher believed had prevented Britain from modernizing its economy. She also fought to reduce taxes, cut bureaucratic red tape and encourage home ownership. And last but not least, Thatcher — the daughter of a grocer — worked to hammer the final nail in the coffin of the British class system, which she was convinced stifled the entrepreneurial spirit and prevented talented people, regardless of birth origin, from achieving success.

Thatcher had detractors, especially as unemployment rose in the wake of her privatization plans, and it is probably true that what saved her from being defeated for re-election was Britain's victory in the Falklands War in 1982 — a war in which Thatcher sent British warships to oust Argentine troops from the tiny Falkland Islands that both Britain and Argentina claimed. However, by the end of her second term the British economy had responded to her initiatives, and the British middle class had rallied to her cause. She was overwhelmingly elected to a third term in 1987.

Maggie Thatcher was (like her soul mate, Ronald Reagan) that rarest of political animals, a conviction politician, and, love her or hate her, her unflinching belief in capitalism and democratic government helped her change Britain in truly fundamental ways. Indeed, it says something about Thatcher that, next to the trade unions and other members of the far Left, the group that fought her the hardest during her time in office was the elitist Tory gentry on the far Right (elements of that Tory elite helped oust her from party leadership in 1990). Both groups preferred the status quo, and Thatcher would have none of it.

Today, of all the honors that a still active Maggie Thatcher has accrued, including the title of Baroness, perhaps the one dearest to her heart is the honor of seeing her name attached to an ideology. To this day, "Thatcherism" affects the national life of Great Britain, and it surely will for years to come.

© Kauffmann 2008

Bruce's History Lessons: The Communist Manifesto

This week (Feb. 21) in 1848, Karl Marx published *The Communist Manifesto*, making this date a hallmark in the annals of phony political philosophy and pseudo-economic science. Marx died long before the Manifesto was to make him, alas, one of the most influential philosophers of the 20th Century, with millions of human beings around the globe living — or more accurately suffering — under governments forged by Marxist principles. It is poetic justice that Marx himself died in abject poverty.

There is an argument, and it has merit, that Marxism was so twisted by various ruling parties to fit their own ends that Marx would not recognize his own teachings. Even so, the stuff Marx *would* recognize today as his handiwork was bad enough.

If you ever wondered what the heck the difference was between Socialism and Communism, Marx's manifesto explains it. In Marxist theory the first stage to political and economic nirvana was Socialism, which would then evolve into Communism. Through Socialism, control of a nation's "means of production" — the farms, factories, industries, etc. — would be transferred from the bourgeoisie (the middle-class) to the proletariat (the common laborer). Marx, perhaps history's truest "democrat," believed that political equality was a sham without economic equality. Thus Socialism would redistribute economic power among the masses, reinforcing their emerging political power.

At which point, according to Marx, these "workers of the world" would evolve into Communists, thereby creating an international Communist community that would make unnecessary all national and human individualism. Countries would cease to exist so there would be no nationalism. No nationalism meant no imperialism, so war would also cease.

Humans would, as well, shed their religious beliefs, ethnicity and cultural ties to become one global brotherhood. Central governments would dissolve, as would "bourgeois" market economies. They would be replaced by a system in which goods and services were exchanged, in Marx's famous phrase, "from each according to his ability, to each according to his needs." Where others thought they could change human behavior, Marx thought he could change human nature.

He was wrong. Marx's "scientific man" — a creature governed solely by the immutable laws of economic determinism — would *not* shed his humanity, even when living under the most repressive "Marxist" (military) regimes. Religious beliefs, ethnic ties and cultural identity, and the freedom necessary to express them, all proved impervious to Marxist dogma, as did nationalism and its first cousin, patriotism.

Indeed, history's most successful nation is one in which people of various ethnic, religious and cultural backgrounds are able to both retain those distinctions and assimilate them (willingly) in a "melting pot" society that balances individual freedoms with a respect for the rights of others. That would be the United States of America.

© *Kauffmann 2008*

Bruce's History Lessons: Float Like a Butterfly, Sting Like a Bee

This week (Feb. 25) in 1964, the heavyweight fighter considered the greatest of all time first became heavyweight champ when his opponent, Sonny Liston, called it quits before the seventh round of their historic fight in Miami, Florida. The new champ was Cassius Clay, a 22-year-old African American from Louisville, Kentucky, whose first full day as champion would be his last as Cassius Clay. On February 26th he announced that he had joined the Islamic faith. Not long after, he officially became Muhammad Ali, the name by which the world knows him today.

On fight night, Clay was a seven-to-one underdog, and few expected him to last one round against Liston, a huge, menacing man with a powerful punch that had demolished all previous opponents. Years later, Ali admitted that even he was scared of Liston that night, and this was before he learned that one reporter covering the fight had been instructed by his editors to memorize the route to the nearest hospital so he could be the first reporter there when Clay was rushed into the emergency room.

Yet from the opening round on that muggy Miami night it was clear that Clay was a new kind of fighter. Minutes into the fight Liston thought he had Clay cut off and threw a left jab that should have floored his young opponent — except that Clay wasn't there. He had easily danced way, causing Liston to miss by two feet. Clay countered with a jab to Liston's forehead, repeating the dance-and-jab — what he called his "float like a butterfly, sting like a bee" style — for the next six rounds until Liston, his eyes puffy and his face bloody, couldn't take anymore. "That's it," he told his trainers, ending the fight.

117

Realizing he had won, Clay jumped up, ran around the ring, and then headed for the reporters sitting at ringside. "Eat your words!" he screamed at the assembled media, which had unanimously predicted he would lose. "I am king of the world!"

He would remain king of the fight world for 16 years, becoming the first boxer to gain the heavyweight title three different times. He also would become the only boxer ever to regain his title after first defeating the (Liston-like) U.S. government, which had attempted to jail him, and strip him of his title, for refusing induction into the army on religious grounds. The Supreme Court ruled in Ali's favor in 1971.

Even today, slowed by Parkinson's disease from so many punches, Ali in a very real sense remains "king of the world." His name is arguably the most recognized of any living person on Earth — and it has been 20 years since he last entered the ring.

© *Kauffmann 2008*

Bruce's History Lessons:
Alexander the Great (and Lucky)

This week (March 7) in 1876, Alexander Graham Bell received the patent for a device that would go down in history as one of mankind's greatest inventions (on the other hand, it did lead to the creation of telemarketing). And because Bell applied for his patent for this "telephone" just hours earlier than another inventor named Elisha Gray, Bell and not Gray became rich and famous.

After immigrating to the United States from Scotland, where his father had been a prominent phonetician and teacher, Bell opened a school for the deaf in Boston, later joining the faculty of Boston University as a professor of speech and vocal physiology. But Bell was also a would-be inventor, and he began experimenting with various ideas for relaying sound in ways that might improve communication, especially communication with the deaf. Finally, in 1874, Bell came up with the idea of combining one of his would-be inventions — a device to send several telegraph messages over a single line — with another proposed invention — a machine that recorded sound waves graphically — in hopes of devising a way to "transmit speech telegraphically." This "talking telegraph" would become the telephone.

Meanwhile, Elisha Gray was pursuing an astonishingly similar path. A successful inventor and businessman who had started a company based on his profits from an invention he sold to Western Union, Gray also was working on a device to send simultaneous messages over a telegraph wire, and his solution to the problem of how to transmit and receive these multiple messages would, given enough time, have led to an invention along the same lines as Bell's telephone.

But as it would turn out, time was not on Gray's side. Because Bell filed for the patent first — a mere two hours before Gray — he was credited with inventing the telephone, despite the fact that the device Gray described in his patent application was much more workable than the device described by Bell in his.

No matter, the patent safely registered in his name, Bell eventually perfected his invention, founded Bell Telephone, and became world famous and wealthy beyond imagination.

As a postscript, most of us know that "Watson, come here! I want you!" are the words Bell first transmitted through his invention to his assistant, Mr. Watson, who was listening through a receiver in an adjacent room. Although the words make Bell sound imperious, he was actually crying out in pain, having spilled battery acid on his legs. Fortunately, Bell would soon recover from his wounds.

Not so the increasingly embittered and embattled Elisha Gray, who spent most of his remaining years, and fortune, filing lawsuits in a vain attempt to prove that he, not Bell, really invented the telephone.

© Kauffmann 2008

Bruce's History Lessons: Amerigo! Amerigo! God Shed His Grace on Thee!

Amerigo Vespucci, born this week (March 17) in 1454, is truly a testament to the value of good public relations. Indeed, "America," which is a variation on the first name of this explorer of minor talent — and consequence — has become among the most famous names in history, and it was in large part because Vespucci's written accounts of his travels were more widely distributed and better read than those of that *other* Italian voyager to the New World, Christopher Columbus.

Columbus, as every child knows, was the first European to discover the New World, sighting what is now the Bahamas in October of 1492. Granted, at the time, Columbus thought he had discovered a new trade route to the Asian subcontinent, specifically India, (hence the "Indian" name he gave to the native tribes he made contact with), which had been his goal when he set sail from Spain earlier that year. Vespucci, whose voyages to the New World occurred some eight years later, at least understood that he had found a new landmass separate from Asia. But the fact remains that Columbus, not Vespucci, was the first to reach the two continents that were later to be named *not* North and South "Columbia," but North and South "America."

Interestingly, some historians attribute this to the fact that in his written accounts of his voyages, Vespucci meticulously detailed the lives of the indigenous people he came across, including their sexual habits. Sure enough (some things never change), Vespucci soon had a large and devoted readership back in Europe, and sales of his diaries greatly exceeded those of Columbus, who mostly stuck to describing ship life, the geography, and the flora and fauna.

In any event, one reader of Vespucci's tales of exploration was a German scholar and mapmaker named Martin Waldseemuller, who subsequently published a book that included maps of the two new continents that Vespucci (and Columbus) had visited. Being less familiar with Columbus, Waldseemuller honored Vespucci's voyages by naming both landmasses "America." The name stuck and the rest is history.

Which is not to say that Columbus has been ignored. His name graces a country in South America (Colombia) and countless cities on both continents, including Washington, D.C. And once a year the United States of America celebrates Columbus Day in his honor.

On the other hand, all things being equal, Columbus and his heirs probably would have preferred that once a year the United States of Columbia celebrated Vespucci Day. He, Columbus, was the better sailor, braver voyager, and first Italian explorer to the New World. Vespucci was simply the better known writer. In other words, pop appeal trumps skill and industriousness.

Hmmm … some things really do never change.

© Kauffmann 2008

Bruce's History Lesson: Hogwash!

Thanks to America's technological superiority and the ingenuity of the American farmer, early in the 1960s America's ability to produce food exceeded her ability to consume it and even export it, which led to the classic supply-and-demand problem of over production depressing prices. As a result, many farmers actually lost money on their livestock and crops, which, quite naturally, led to complaints to Congress. Congress, in its infinite wisdom, passed laws paying farmers *not* to grow crops, or raise livestock, in the hopes of bringing supply and demand more into balance. This "agricultural welfare" generated lots of criticism, which took many forms. One of the more humorous was a letter written to Texas Congressman Ed Foreman, this week (March 20) in 1963. This comes from a wonderful collection of American correspondence titled *Letters of a Nation,* edited by Andrew Carroll.

Dear Sir:

My friend over in Terebone Parish received a $1,000 check from the government this year for not raising hogs. So I am going into the not-raising hogs business next year. What I want to know is, in your opinion, what is the best kind of farm not to raise hogs on and the best kind of hogs not to raise? I would prefer not to raise Razorbacks, but if that is not a good breed not to raise, I will just as gladly not raise Berkshires or Durocs.

The hardest work in this business is going to be in keeping an inventory of how many hogs I haven't raised.

My friend is very joyful about the future of his business. He has been raising hogs for more than 20 years and the best he ever made was $400 until this year when he got $1,000 for not raising hogs.

If I can get $1,000 for not raising 50 hogs, then will I get $2,000 for not raising 100 hogs? I plan to operate on a small scale at first, holding myself down to 4,000 hogs, which means I will have $80,000 coming from the federal government.

Now another thing: these hogs I will not raise will not eat 100,000 bushels of corn. I understand that you also pay farmers for not raising corn. So will you pay me anything for not raising 100,000 bushels of corn not to feed the hogs I am not raising? I wanted to get started as soon as possible as this seems to be a good time of year for not raising hogs.

One thing more, can I raise 10 or 20 hogs on the side while I am in the not-raising-hogs business, just enough to get a few sides of bacon to eat?

Very truly yours, J.B. Lee, Jr.

© *Kauffmann 2008*

Bruce's History Lessons:
The China Syndrome

This week (March 28) in 1979, America experienced the worst commercial nuclear power disaster in her history when the Three Mile Island nuclear power plant near Middletown, Pennsylvania, suffered significant damage to its reactor core, nearly causing a "nuclear meltdown," badly scaring the local population, and forcing the evacuation of pregnant women, children, the sick and the infirm.

The cause of the accident is still debated, although human error and equipment failure both contributed to a scenario in which inadequate cooling caused the nuclear fuel to overheat. In particular, a stuck valve caused a misreading of the water level in the primary — the nuclear — power system, incorrectly indicating that there was plenty of water coolant in the system. Thus did a plant operator stop adding water when, in fact, a lack of coolant was causing the overheating problem. This resulted in increased radioactivity, some of which escaped into the environment. It would be several days before the situation was finally brought under control, and by then the entire country was close to panic.

Perhaps not helping matters was the coincidental release of the movie, *The China Syndrome* (starring Jane Fonda and Jack Lemmon), which (talk about *cinema verite*) depicted the near meltdown of the core reactor of a nuclear power plant in California. In one riveting "art-imitates-life" scene, an equipment failure even misled plant operators into taking actions that enhanced the danger rather than mitigating it, but — as at TMI — they realized their error in time. Had it been otherwise, they might have experienced the theoretical "China Syndrome," which refers to what might happen when the exposed nuclear core becomes so hot it burns through earth's core, not stopping until it winds up in China.

Needless to say, the movie was hugely popular, which could no longer be said of nuclear power. Once thought to be the future of American energy, after TMI, nuclear power experienced its own "China Syndrome" in terms of public confidence, experiencing a core meltdown of its image. Since TMI, more than 60 nuclear power plants have been shut down or abandoned, and no new plants have been built for reasons that aren't totally environmentally related. Enhanced safety codes, training, precautions and remedial security safeguards have made building them extremely expensive, and in the wake of September 11, that won't change.

On the other hand, for all its drawbacks, nuclear power is in many ways *the* most "environmentally friendly" energy. It emits zero air pollutants and no greenhouse gases. What's more, as we saw last year in California, America's growing demand for energy is beginning to exceed available supply. So don't be surprised if nuclear power begins to make a comeback. You heard it here first.

© Kauffmann 2008

Bruce's History Lessons:
The Creation of NATO

The North Atlantic Treaty Organization (NATO), the most successful multi-national military alliance in history, came into existence this week (April 4) in 1949. Fifty-two years later it is still in existence, and if its tactical goals and strategies have shifted, its original reason for being — to protect Western Europe against military invasion by the Soviet Union — is still in effect.

Travel back to Europe right after World War II. England is bankrupt, France and the Benelux countries are prostrate, Italy is defeated, Germany is destroyed and cut in half (later becoming East and West Germany), and Eastern Europe is enveloped in an "Iron Curtain" of military control by the Soviet Union. Most American and European leaders believe the Soviets will soon seek to control Western Europe as well.

Which they can do in one of two ways — internally, by supporting newly formed Communist parties, whose path to power will be paved by the poverty and breakdown of social order that exists in these post-war European nations. Or externally, by invading a defenseless Western Europe with the mighty Red Army.

To counter the internal threat, the Truman Administration developed the Marshall Plan — a plan to lend Western Europe billions of dollars in economic assistance to stabilize its economy and make it less susceptible to the (false) promises of Communism. But to counter the external threat, a military alliance was crucial — and one that must include the United States.

Which was controversial in both Europe and America. While the Europeans clearly desired the protection of American power, they worried about being part of an American "empire." What's more, one American condition for joining NATO was that West Germany — which had come under allied control after the war — also be allowed to join, but France and England had deep misgivings about allying themselves with the nation that had fought them bitterly in WW II.

For our part, controversy surrounded NATO's stipulation that "an attack on one NATO member country is considered an attack on all." This implied that a Soviet invasion of Europe would automatically trigger American involvement. Yet the Constitution gives Congress — not an international treaty — authority to involve America in war.

Given these hurdles, and many others, it is a testament to the diplomatic skill of leaders on all sides that NATO was born. A joke at the time said NATO was designed to "keep the Americans in (Europe), keep the Soviets out, and keep the Germans down," but it was true. America realized that its own security was inextricably linked with Western Europe's, while France and Britain realized that a Germany tied to NATO was less of a danger than a Germany excluded from it. In hindsight, both sides were correct.

© Kauffmann 2008

Bruce's History Lessons:
The Man Who Wowed 'Em at Gettysburg

The famous American politician who gave the speech at Gettysburg in 1863 that cast a spell over the audience and earned glowing praise from all observers was born this week (April 11) in 1794. Which may have you thinking to yourself, "Hey, wait a minute, wasn't Abe Lincoln born in February?"

Indeed he was, but Lincoln was not the featured speaker at Gettysburg, nor was his speech considered a critical triumph or even a crowd pleaser. That honor and accomplishment was Edward Everett's, the man with the April 11th birthday.

A renowned scholar, diplomat and politician who had been president of Harvard University and had served as a congressman, senator, governor, and secretary of state, Everett was perhaps most famous of all for his oratorical skills. This made him the natural candidate to give the keynote speech at the ceremony honoring the Gettysburg battlefield and the soldiers from both the North and South who had fought and died there.

What's more, a keynote speech in the 1860s was expected to be entertaining as well as informative; it was supposed to tell a story much as a good book or a feature film would today — and at about the same length. Two hour speeches were the norm back then, giving Everett, who was both a famous scholar and an excellent researcher, sufficient time to describe in intricate detail the three-day battle at Gettysburg, while weaving it into a larger historical theme that reached back as far as the Periclean Age in ancient Greece. And he spoke entirely from memory in a voice so powerful and melodious that the audience was literally spellbound for the entire two hours. Everett then sat down to enthusiastic applause, and in the next day's newspapers the praise was universal. The Boston Journal called it "brilliant" and "the best history of the campaign which this generation will have the privilege of reading."

By contrast, Lincoln's Gettysburg speech — only 272 words long and given in his high-pitched voice — received polite applause and then everyone went home. The next day most papers made scant mention of it.

Six score and 19 years later, of course, we all know which speech has stood the test of time. The Gettysburg Address is considered among the greatest in all of history and has helped make its author a legend.

And, ironically, the one person at Gettysburg who sensed that this might one day be the case was Everett himself. In a note to Lincoln the day after the ceremony, Everett wrote, "I wish that I could flatter myself that I had come as near to the central idea of the occasion in two hours as you did in two minutes."

© Kauffmann 2008

Bruce's History Lessons:
Nixon: Act Two ...

The man who proved F. Scott Fitzgerald wrong died this week (April 22) in 1994 of a stroke. He was 81. Fitzgerald had said, "There are no second acts in American lives." Richard Nixon had more second acts than Shakespeare.

Born to poor Quaker parents in California — his father owned a lemon farm that went bust and then ran a grocery store — the overachieving Nixon managed to graduate with honors both at Whittier College (a Quaker institution) and at Duke Law School, which he attended on a scholarship.

After graduating from Duke he applied to several prestigious east coast law firms and was snubbed by them all, causing him to vow he would never have anything to do with "the Eastern Establishment."

Which he would, but first he returned to California, became partner in a law firm, married his wife Pat, had two daughters, served in the Navy during WWII, mustered out and promptly ran for Congress.

As a Republican. And he won. And he did so by transforming himself from a shy, milquetoast Quaker into a no-holds-barred anti-communist red-baiter, becoming famous in Congress for leading the House Un-American Activities Committee, where he exposed Alger Hiss as a perjurer and probable Soviet spy (later confirmed). Now a "fiery crusader against Communist subversives," he next won a seat in the U.S. Senate — after labeling his opponent "soft on Communism" — and in 1952 was chosen as Dwight Eisenhower's running mate for that year's presidential election. After winning that election, and easily winning re-election, Nixon ran for president in 1960, losing to John Kennedy in one of the closest elections in history. He then went back to California, ran for governor, lost, and announced that his political career was over.

131

Which it was not. He then moved to the heart of "the Eastern Establishment," New York City, where he joined a prestigious law firm and plotted his political comeback. In 1968, the "New Nixon," as he was called, ran for president again, was elected, and in 1972 won re-election, making him the only person ever to twice run for, and win, both the vice presidency and presidency.

And then came Watergate, which made him the only person ever to resign the presidency in disgrace, meaning his career in public life was over.

Which it was not. By 1980, Nixon had reinvented himself again, this time as an elder statesman with vast foreign policy experience. He wrote books, lectured and advised world leaders. When he died, he was even back in the public's favor.

Richard Nixon, the man they called "Tricky Dick," was an American original. But in many ways he was also the quintessential American, where "second acts" are now, literally, a way of life.

© Kauffmann 2008

Bruce's History Lessons:
America's Library

Although they quarreled often in their long lives, on the need to promote education if their new nation was to achieve greatness, our second president, John Adams, and our third, Thomas Jefferson, were always in agreement. To this end, both men played key roles in creating a national library — to be called the Library of Congress — which Adams initiated this week (April 24) in 1800 by approving $5,000 in public funds to spend on books to stock that library. This sum purchased 740 books and three maps.

Upon succeeding Adams as president, Jefferson approved legislation outlining the Library's functions and giving Congress authority to establish its budget, rules and regulations, one of which — Jefferson undoubtedly insisted on it — permitted the president to borrow books from the Library at will. This legislation also created a Librarian of Congress, to be appointed by the president himself.

Jefferson also personally recommended many of the books the Library purchased, and after the British burned much of Washington, including the Library of Congress, in the War of 1812, Jefferson offered to sell his personal book collection to the Library to replace the 3,000 volumes that were lost (this wasn't total munificence; Jefferson was, as usual, deep in debt and needed the money). For $24,000, Jefferson's 6,500 volumes not only doubled the size of the old Library, but also expanded exponentially the variety of its collection. Jefferson, America's first "Renaissance Man," was well read in astronomy, mathematics, literature, philosophy, architecture, botany, several languages, the law and many other subjects. Thanks to him, the Library of Congress became the most comprehensive library in America, and although access to the Library was originally restricted to government officials, it steadily expanded over the years to include Americans from every walk of life. This validated Jefferson's, and Adams', conviction that universal knowledge was the key to the preservation and expansion of democracy.

Today, of course, the Library of Congress is the largest, most comprehensive library in the world, with more than 120 million books, manuscripts, maps, photographs and recordings sitting on about 530 miles of bookshelves. It is also the major research arm of Congress, it houses the U.S. Copyright Office, it is home to our nation's Poet Laureate, and it is a haven for scholars seeking information on every subject under (and above) the sun — in more than 450 languages.

Little known Library facts: Its oldest written material is a cuneiform tablet dating from 2040 B.C. Its largest book is John James Audubon's *Birds of America*, at nearly four feet in length. Its smallest book is an edition of *Old King Cole*, at about the size of the dot on the exclamation point at the end of this sentence!

© Kauffmann 2008

Bruce's History Lessons:
Eva Braun Takes a Husband

"Raise high the roof beam, carpenters. Like Ares comes the bridegroom, taller far than a tall man."

– J.D. Salinger, "Raise High the Roof Beam Carpenters"

This week in 1945, in Germany's capital city of Berlin, Russian soldiers encountered minimal Nazi resistance as they fought their way into Potsdamer Platz (plaza), just blocks from the Reich Chancellery, where deep in an underground bunker the bridegroom contemplated his fate. After five years of war, Nazi Germany was in ruins, its armed forces destroyed, and its citizens prostrate before British and American armies occupying German territory from the West and Russian armies doing likewise from the East.

Finally realizing that no miraculous reversal of the war's fortunes would occur, the bridegroom, who had led Germany for those five years, decided that April 29th would be his wedding day. For nearly a decade he had been married to Germany but that marriage had crumbled. He would now marry his long-suffering companion, Eva Braun, who had stuck by him to the end.

Before the ceremony, the bridegroom dictated a "political testament," in which he blamed the entire war on "international Jewry" and predicted that out of the ashes of the current German nation would arise, Phoenix-like, a new Germany dedicated to the principles of National Socialism. He then named a new leader to succeed him — Grand Admiral Karl Doenitz, the former head of the German navy. As it would turn out, Doenitz's time in his new office would be very short.

Just after midnight on April 29th, the groom finished his official business and exchanged vows with his bride in a ceremony conducted by a Berlin city councilman who had been driven to the bunker in an armored car and ordered to don a Nazi uniform to perform the wedding. Two of the bridegroom's most dedicated followers, Joseph Goebbels and Martin Bormann, were witnesses to the marriage.

With the ceremony completed the bride and groom "celebrated" with staff, drinking champagne, eating sandwiches, reminiscing about past triumphs and periodically bracing themselves against the shock waves from nearby explosions of Russian artillery. Shortly thereafter, the bride and groom retired for the night. Whether they consummated their marriage or had ever engaged in sexual union is not known.

The next day, with Russian troops within hours of capturing the Chancellery, the newlyweds bid their farewells to their friends and followers, retreated into their room and shut the door. Minutes later, Bormann entered the room and found them dead. She had been poisoned. He had shot himself in the head.

As the groom had earlier ordered, the newlyweds were then doused with gasoline and cremated. Eva Braun and her husband, Adolf Hitler, would spend their honeymoon in Hell.

© *Kauffmann 2008*

Bruce's History Lessons:
The Pill Pushers

This week (May 9) in 1960, the Food and Drug Administration approved Enovid-10, the world's first commercially produced birth control pill. This is the very short story of the four very disparate people who made it happen.

Margaret Sanger was one of 11 children. Her father was a radical Irishman whose sexual appetite Margaret blamed for the early death of her mother. Thus did the idea of giving women more reproductive freedom come to Sanger early, and it was certainly reinforced when she moved to New York City and saw so many poor women, saddled with children they could not support, living hopeless, squalid lives. Sanger became the driving force behind creating a convenient, readily available contraceptive for women.

Katherine McCormick became the financier. A wealthy blue-blood who had married Stanley McCormick — his father founded International Harvester — she became involved with Planned Parenthood, where she met and befriended Margaret Sanger. She promised to financially support any research designed to develop an oral contraceptive.

That research was conducted by Gregory "Goody" Pincus, the son of Russian Jews who immigrated to America. A child genius, he majored in biology at Cornell University before teaching at Harvard, where his research won Harvard worldwide acclaim. Denied tenure because he was a maverick, but also because he was a Jew, Pincus went to Clark University in Massachusetts, where he became the leader of a group of independent biochemists doing experimental work in animal reproduction. Learning of his work, Sanger challenged him to develop an oral contraceptive and McCormick promised him funding.

Pincus believed that he could prevent conception by chemically imitating the hormonal condition that occurs during pregnancy when the body naturally blocks ovulation, and in lab experiments the work went surprisingly well — so well that Pincus realized he needed to recruit a medical doctor to join the team. Laboratory research was one thing. Applying it to real people was another.

Dr. John Rock of Harvard Medical School was to Goody Pincus as night was to day. Tall, charming, handsome, and devoutly Catholic, Rock's original reproductive goals were the exact opposite of Pincus'. A gynecologist, he hoped to cure infertility in women.

But Rock became increasingly flexible on birth control and his real-world applications of Pincus' laboratory achievements were the final piece of the puzzle. In tests on poor women in Puerto Rico and Haiti, "the pill," as it was called, was a total success.

And so, what became one of the most life-altering phenomenon of the 20th century, was started by two women — one a radical Irish atheist, the other a wealthy Protestant socialite — and two men — one a short, homely, Jewish lab rat, the other a tall, handsome Catholic physician.

Only in America.

© Kauffmann 2008

Bruce's History Lessons:
The Birth of Israel

Israel's birth, this week (May 14) in 1948 was not auspicious, but it was a harbinger. Hours after its first prime minister, David Ben Gurion, announced Israel's existence at a ceremony in Tel Aviv, armies from Egypt, Transjordan, Syria, Lebanon and Iraq declared war on the new state and attacked. In fierce fighting, Israel prevailed, but in the next 54 years there would be many more Israeli-Arab wars, and as even a glance at today's headlines will attest, relations between Israelis and Arabs in the area called Palestine have not improved.

The dispute goes back to Biblical times when both Arab and Jewish tribes called Palestine home, but its modern origins can be traced to Jewish visionary Theodore Herzl, who, at a Zionist Congress in Switzerland in 1897, argued that establishing a Jewish state in Palestine was the only way to protect Jews from Europe's pervasive anti-Semitism. Herzl asked representatives of the Ottoman Empire, which then controlled Palestine, for permission to settle the area, but he was refused. However, after World War I, when the Ottoman Empire collapsed, Britain took over Palestine and declared its intent to establish a Jewish homeland in the area. At this point Arab opposition to a Jewish presence in Palestine became so widespread, Britain backtracked and actually tried to limit Jewish immigration into Palestine. That became futile after World War II and the murder of 6 million Jews in the Holocaust. By 1945, Jewish desire for a homeland became an obsession.

Unable to resolve the dispute between Jews and Arabs in Palestine, Britain turned the matter over to the newly formed United Nations, which, in 1947, voted to partition Palestine, creating one Israeli state and one Arab state. The Jews accepted their tiny state between the West Bank of the Jordan River and the Mediterranean Sea, but the Arabs did not, and war ensued.

In the years since, conceding that both sides have fanned the flames of hatred in this seemingly intractable conflict, the inescapable fact remains that Israel always was, and still is, willing to live next to Arabs, even Arabs in their own state, provided two conditions are satisfied: Israel must have secure borders and its right to exist must be recognized.

Regarding the first condition, secure borders, that could be resolved if Israel would stop building Israeli settlements on the West Bank. Aside from the provocation, secure borders are impossible if large numbers of Israeli soldiers must continue to defend small numbers of settlers.

Regarding the second condition, Israel's right to exist, that could be resolved if, just for starters, Palestinians would stop publishing maps of "Greater Palestine"— maps their children study in school — in which there is no Israel at all.

© *Kauffmann 2008*

Bruce's History Lesson:
A Bridge Grows in Brooklyn

It is arguably the most famous bridge in the world, totaling 6000 feet in length, making it one of the longest bridges ever built. Its construction was made possible by a special "steel rope" suspension wire, which was invented and manufactured by the engineer, architect and visionary who designed the bridge, John Roebling. He was born in 1806 in Prussia, but he would die before work on the bridge even began — one of some two dozen lives sacrificed to the bridge's creation and completion.

John Roebling was succeeded by his son, Washington Roebling, who also nearly died of the bends while overseeing the bridge's construction, and although the son survived, he was permanently bedridden. As a result, his wife Emily became the *de facto* chief engineer, relaying his instructions (from his sick bed he could see the site) to the crew chiefs, while also supervising the construction, negotiating with local politicians, dealing with the media and even checking the books. Of all of the heroes of the Brooklyn Bridge story, Emily Roebling is the most unsung.

Worker death and injury were not the bridge's only problems. Over the 14 years it took to build it, there were several fires, numerous explosions, and one memorable compressed air blast that destroyed one of the pneumatic caissons that allowed workers to lay the underwater foundations. Fraud was also a problem, with one contractor indicted for supplying substandard cable.

But like its home city of New York, the Brooklyn Bridge thrived on adversity, and finally, this week (May 24) in 1883, it was opened to the public, majestically spanning the East River and connecting Manhattan with Brooklyn. An opening day toll of one penny was charged to the pedestrians and cyclists who crossed the bridge (another 25 years would pass before

Henry Ford's massed-produced autos began clogging its six lanes), which was later increased to three cents and charged until the bridge, which cost $15 million to build (more than $1.5 billion today), was finally paid for.

Today, of course, the Brooklyn Bridge is internationally renowned and an integral part of the lore of New York City. It has starred in films, inspired poets, and served as a backdrop for countless photographs and paintings. It is, in a way, the quintessential American story, designed by an immigrant and built by his native-born son — a vision made into a monument by hard work, sacrifice, pluck and luck.

"They don't make 'em like that anymore," is a familiar refrain in Brooklyn, but the truth is they have never made 'em like the Brooklyn Bridge. It spans a river, but also an era. It connects two city boroughs, but it also connects our present with our past.

© *Kauffmann 2008*

Bruce's History Lessons:
Joan of Arc Burns at the Stake

For a nation as chauvinistic as France, it must be something of an embarrassment that one of its greatest military triumphs — and over the English no less — was led by a woman, actually a teenage girl, named Joan of Arc. Alas, Joan paid dearly for that honor, having later been tried as a heretic by the vengeful English and burned at the stake this week (May 30) in 1431.

It was during the Hundred Years' War between England and France that Joan, a fanatical Catholic, began to hear "celestial voices," which told her to help the young French dauphin, whose coronation as French king was prevented by English control of vast stretches of French territory, including a successful siege of the French city of Orleans. At an arranged meeting, Joan convinced the dauphin that she was on a divine mission to save France, so the dauphin gave her a small French force, which she led to Orleans to relieve French forces trapped there. In fierce fighting, Joan broke the siege and forced the English army to retreat. Over the next month, Joan of Arc and her small French army defeated the English at every turn, finally recapturing the city of Rheims, where the coronation of French kings traditionally took place.

That tradition continued in July of 1429 when the dauphin became King Charles VII. At the coronation, Joan D'Arc was given a place of honor beside him.

As king, however, Charles VII took a curiously pacifist approach to the English, pinning his hopes on diplomacy, so it was without royal support that Joan again took the field against the English occupiers in 1430. Intending to fight them at Compiegne, a city near Paris, Joan was ambushed by forces loyal to the Duke of Burgundy (who had allied himself with England), captured and sold to the English for a large sum.

Bent on revenge, the English put Joan on trial, not for her military exploits — military victories were not punishable by death — but because "hearing voices" proved she was a witch and heretic. Found guilty, Joan was given a lifetime prison sentence, but later, after violating the terms of that sentence, she was condemned to burn at the stake in the English-controlled city of Rouen, in Normandy. With a crucifix in her hands, and repeatedly praising "My Lord, Jesus Christ," Joan at last died. Her ashes were scattered over the Seine River.

But her legend would not die, and five centuries later the "heretic" would become a martyr — and a saint. In 1920, Joan was canonized by Pope Benedict XV, making her among the few people in all of history to have saved both her country and her soul.

© Kauffmann 2008

Bruce's History Lessons:
An Unsung Sailor Saves the Day at Midway

Arguably the most important battle that America fought in World War II was won in large part by an unkempt, mole-like young officer who worked in the windowless basement of a naval building in Pearl Harbor, and whose idea of a military uniform was rumpled khakis, a pair of slippers and a smoking jacket.

His name was Joseph Rochefort. As the Navy's chief cryptoanalyst, his job was to decipher the extremely complex code the Japanese used to send messages — a job that took on added importance in June of 1942 because the Japanese, fresh from its smashing victory at Peal Harbor, hoped to land the knockout punch that would finally put America's badly weakened Pacific fleet out of action. Everyone knew Japan's brilliant naval commander, Isoroku Yamamoto, planned another assault, but no one knew where. Some guessed another attack on Pearl, others guessed the Aleutian Islands, still others guessed California's coast. Wherever it would be, it was imperative that America knew in advance so that it could marshal as many forces as possible against what was sure to be a numerically superior Japanese fleet.

Working around the clock in an attempt to unravel Japan's coded messages, which had suddenly grown in volume (signifying an attack was imminent), Rochefort noticed that Japanese messages increasingly included the phrase "AF," which Rochefort believed was code for Japan's next military target.

Looking at a map of the Pacific, Rochefort's eyes settled on the American-held Midway Islands, which from Japan's standpoint would make an ideal base for raids on the western United States. Believing that "AF" stood for

Midway, Rochefort decided to play a trick. He instructed America's tiny garrison stationed on Midway to radio Pearl Harbor a message — which he expected the Japanese would intercept — warning that the plant that distilled Midway's drinking water had malfunctioned.

Bingo! Two days later Rochefort read an intercepted Japanese cable that said "AF" was running low on drinking water. Midway was Japan's next target.

With that information, U.S. Admiral Chester Nimitz ordered Midway reinforced with fresh troops, planes and antiaircraft weaponry, and he also ordered three additional aircraft carriers to help him defend Midway. In the ensuing battle, which occurred this week (June 4) in 1942, the Americans surprised an overconfident Yamamoto, sinking four of his aircraft carriers and destroying 275 airplanes. Suddenly the relative naval strengths of the two belligerents had almost exactly reversed.

Had Japan won the battle of Midway, America might well have lost the war in the Pacific, and consequently would have been nearly impotent against Nazi Germany's forces in the Atlantic, possibly altering WW II's outcome. Joseph Rochefort is one of those unsung heroes who always seem to make a difference in war.

© Kauffmann 2008

Bruce's History Lessons: Jeanette Rankin, The Pacifist, Suffragette Representative

It is one thing to have voted against America's entry into World War I. Although America had some justification for entering that war — including Germany's sinking of the British ocean liner, *Lusitania*, which resulted in the death of 128 Americans — there was still strong public sentiment for staying out of what looked like another internecine European donnybrook that posed no real threat to isolationist America. And in fact, 50 members of the House of Representatives voted against a declaration of war against Germany when it came up for a vote in April of 1914.

But it is another thing entirely to have voted against America's entry into war against Japan on December 8, 1941, the day after that nation had attacked Pearl Harbor, Hawaii, killing nearly 2,500 Americans, sinking or crippling 18 ships, including four battleships, and nearly destroying America's naval operations in the Pacific. Just one member of either branch of Congress voted against America's entry into what would become World War II, for which she was universally vilified.

Her name was Jeanette Rankin. She was born this week (June 11) in 1880 on a ranch in Montana, which at that time was not yet a state. But when it did become a state, Rankin, who had been a social worker and a leader of the women's suffrage movement, ran successfully for a House seat in 1916, becoming the first women in history to be elected to the U.S. Congress. Her political platform included women's suffrage on a national level, legislation to combat infant mortality, and a demand that America stay out of the war then being waged in Europe by Germany and Austria-Hungary against France, Great Britain and Russia — what became known as WWI. (Her women's suffrage platform was ironic given that she was denied her seat in Congress for an entire month while her male counterparts debated whether a woman could be admitted into the House of Representatives).

After serving one-term in Congress, and recording that memorable anti-WWI vote, Rankin ran unsuccessfully for the U.S. Senate and returned to Montana, where she joined a number of suffrage organizations working for ratification of the 19th Amendment granting women the right to vote. Rankin also stayed active in the pacifist movement, and when the U.S. began drifting toward war in 1940, Montana, then an overwhelmingly pacifist state, sent her back to Congress, where she recorded her historic vote against entering WWII.

Unsurprisingly, given the controversy over that decision, Rankin left the House after one term. She died in 1973, but not before forming the "Jeanette Rankin Brigade" to protest America's involvement in yet another war, the Vietnam War — for which, given its own controversial standing, she was praised as much as vilified.

© Kauffmann 2008

Bruce's History Lessons:
The 1964 Civil Rights Act

"Stronger than all armies is an idea whose time has come."

–Senate Minority Leader Everett Dirksen,
June 10, 1964

This week (June 19) the Senate approved the Civil Rights Act of 1964 after surviving an 83-day filibuster by opponents of the bill — mostly Southerners. It is still the longest filibuster in Senate history. On the filibuster's last day, June 10th, West Virginia Senator Robert Byrd, a leading civil rights opponent, had spoken against the bill for 14 hours straight.

It was not Senator Byrd's finest hour, for when President Lyndon Johnson signed the Civil Rights Act of 1964 in early July, it outlawed racial discrimination in public places, employment, education and voting rights. Rightfully, it is considered the greatest act of Johnson's presidency.

Indeed, it is probable that only Johnson could have achieved this victory. First, he was a Southerner himself with an unblemished record of *opposing* all previous civil rights legislation, which — as was later the case when the rabidly anti-communist Richard Nixon normalized relations with Communist China — helped mute criticism from his Southern brethren. What's more, Johnson had once been among the Senate's most powerful majority leaders, meaning he knew exactly what levers to pull and skids to grease, as well was whom to flatter, whom to threaten and whom to entice with political favors. And to get this legislation passed he was willing to use every trick he knew.

Including invoking the memory of his dead and martyred predecessor, John Kennedy, under whose administration this civil rights legislation had been introduced. By reminding the nation that this was "Kennedy's bill,"

Johnson put political pressure on Democrats to support their fallen leader's goal of a more just society.

He also was helped by nationwide polls showing that America in 1964 was at last ready to support civil rights; in one poll 68 percent of Americans thought additional legislation banning racial discrimination was needed. And finally he was helped by his own moral conversion. Johnson came to understand that denying African-Americans the equal rights they ostensibly had been guaranteed by the 14th Amendment was incompatible with his dream of creating a "Great Society" for all citizens.

The Civil Rights Act of 1964 was hardly the last word in the civil rights movement, but it was an honest start, and given the obstacles it overcame, a historic achievement — one made more so by the courageous act of Senator Clair Engle from California, who, during the vote on ending the filibuster, could not speak because of a brain tumor that would soon kill him. Raising a near-paralyzed arm he pointed to his right eye, thereby signaling "Aye" in the affirmative. By such political courage and physical courage is history sometimes made.

© *Kauffmann 2008*

Bruce's History Lesson:
History's Hapless Chauffeur

"Scratch a fanatic and you will find a wound that never healed."
                                                      - William North Jayme

British Prime Minister Winston Churchill blamed World War I on an incompetent chauffeur. That's an oversimplification, but it's true nevertheless that a chauffeur's wrong turn resulted in the assassination of Austria's Archduke Ferdinand by Serbian nationalists in Sarajevo this week (June 28) in 1914. It was the match that set fire to "The Great War," otherwise known as World War I.

Ferdinand, the heir to the Austria-Hungarian throne, and his wife Sofie were in Sarajevo, then the capital of Bosnia-Herzegovina, in an attempt to improve relations between Austria-Hungary — which had previously annexed Bosnia-Herzegovina — and Serbian nationalists who were infuriated by this annexation because they considered Bosnia-Herzegovina to be part of Serbia (and still do).

Thus in June of 1914, Sarajevo was teeming with Serbian nationalists bent on revenge against any representative of the hated Austria-Hungarian regime. So as Ferdinand and Sofie were driven along a parade route, in an open limo, through Sarajevo's narrow streets, would-be assassins started coming out of the woodwork, throwing a variety of home-made bombs at the limousine and firing crude weapons.

Although these several attempts on his life failed to convince Ferdinand to cancel the parade, they finally convinced him that his and his wife's safety just might be enhanced if they altered the well-advertised route they were traveling. Alas, their chauffeur was unfamiliar with the new route, so at one crucial juncture he took a wrong turn, which put the party in a dead-end alley. As luck would have it, standing there was a young Serbian nationalist named Gavrilo Princip, who had been part of an earlier failed assassination attempt. Scarcely believing his good fortune, Princip hopped on the running board of the archduke's limousine, pulled out a pistol and shot Ferdinand and Sofie as dead as doornails.

The assassination set in motion a complicated, interlocking set of alliances that saw Austria-Hungary and its main ally, Germany, mobilize for war against Serbia and its main ally, Russia. They were soon joined by France, Italy, England and, later, the U.S., making it history's first world war.

But not its last. Although WWI was dubbed "the war to end all wars," it fell considerably short of that goal, due in part to the fact that fanatical nationalism of the kind that killed Archduke Ferdinand and his wife grew stronger in the war's wake, not weaker. For proof of that, just look today at nationalist hatreds among Serbs, Croats, Muslims and others that have recently bloodied the very same Bosnia and its war-torn capital, Sarajevo.

Or consider the fact that in Sarajevo today there *still* stands a statue honoring Gavrilo Princip.

© Kauffmann 2008

Bruce's History Lessons:
The Declaration of Independence:
America's Mission Statement

Technically speaking, America's declaration of independence occurred on June 7, 1776, when Henry Lee of the Continental Congress rose in the Philadelphia State House and declared, "these United Colonies are, and of a right ought to be, free and independent states." Unfortunately (but fortunately for history), the opponents of such a radical break with England managed to delay a vote on Lee's declaration until July, to give Congressional delegates time to sample opinion in their home states.

In the meantime, Congress decided it made sense to prepare a formal document declaring independence, so a committee was appointed to write one. Named to this committee was the young Virginian, Thomas Jefferson, whose service in Congress to that point had been marked mostly by an aversion to participating in the rough-and-tumble of oral debate.

But the printed word was another matter. Jefferson possessed, as John Adams noted, a "felicity of expression" that made him the perfect choice to draft a declaration of this magnitude. And so, alone in his boarding room, Jefferson bent to his task, and even conceding — as has been noted often — that he borrowed from many sources, the eloquence of his handiwork is nonetheless astonishing, especially the passage that begins, "We hold these truths to be self evident; that all men are created equal; that they are endowed by their creator with certain unalienable rights; that among these are life, liberty and the pursuit of happiness; that to secure these rights, governments are instituted among men."

With those 46 words, America had its "Mission Statement," one that has inspired the world and defined our national character ever since, and although many changes were made to Jefferson's draft in the ensuing Congressional debate (which so horrified Jefferson he disavowed the official Declaration for years), not a comma was altered in that passage, arguably the most recognized paragraph in history.

The Declaration of Independence, which would include Henry Lee's official "declaration," was approved by Congress on July 4th, 1776, and in the years since Americans have searched for ways to adequately express its significance to our lives, just as we will this 4th at celebrations across the land.

But only one person really succeeded — that other president who possessed a "felicity of expression," Abraham Lincoln. "All honor to Jefferson," Lincoln wrote years later, "to the man who, in the concrete struggle for national independence, had the coolness, forecaste and capacity to introduce into a merely revolutionary document an abstract truth, and so embalm it there, that today and in all coming days, it shall be a rebuke and a stumbling block to the harbingers of tyranny and oppression."

Words to remember given the new harbingers of tyranny and oppression we face today. Happy 4th of July.

© Kauffmann 2008

Bruce's History Lessons:
America's Most Courageous

What does it take to fly your heavily damaged helicopter directly into enemy fire in order to mark enemy targets, knowing your chances of survival are probably nonexistent. Army Captain Jon Swanson can't answer that question because he didn't survive. His helicopter exploded in flight, over Cambodia during the Vietnam War. He was subsequently awarded the Congressional Medal of Honor, America's highest military decoration, and over the years, Captain Swanson has shared that honor with 3,437 other men and one woman (Mary Walker, an army doctor). Nineteen Americans have won the Medal of Honor multiple times.

When President Abraham Lincoln signed a law creating the U.S. Army Medal of Honor this week (July 12) in 1862 (the Navy Medal was created a year earlier), he said it would be awarded "to such noncommissioned officers and privates as shall distinguish themselves by their gallantry in action, and other soldier-like qualities during the present insurrection." The first soldiers to receive the Medal of Honor in that "insurrection" (to Lincoln the Civil War was nothing more than a rebellion by Southern states) were six members of a Union raiding party that destroyed Confederate communications and supply lines in Tennessee and Georgia. The next year Congress made the Medal of Honor a permanent military decoration, available not only to "noncommissioned officers and privates," but to all officers as well.

Like Captain Swanson, all of the recipients — office and noncom alike — are ordinary people who, at the moment of truth, performed in an extraordinary fashion. In the vast majority of cases, they made the ultimate sacrifice for their country — they gave up their lives.

And sadly, today even the living recipients are rapidly shrinking in number. Only 145 Medal of Honor recipients survive and their average age is 70.

Which may account for the lack of media interest in these American heroes, but it doesn't excuse it. Their stories should be told much more frequently than they are, which is why I encourage all readers to visit the Medal of Honor museum located on the hangar deck of the aircraft carrier *Yorktown*, now stationed at Patriot's Point, S.C. Or, at the least, go to www. cmohs.org and read about them.

On that note, a recent letter to the editor of a local paper complained that when Medal of Honor recipient William Barber died on April 19, not one mention of his passing made it into the newspapers, except on a few obituary pages. Barber's courage saved 8,000 American lives in Korea.

That same week, this letter writer continued, porn star Linda Lovelace, who gained fame in the X-rated movie "Deep Throat," also died, garnering newspaper headlines and in-depth profiles across the land.

© *Kauffmann 2008*

Bruce's History Lesson:
Wilmer McLean and the
Battle of Bull Run

"In my beginning is my end."

- T.S. Eliot

This week (July 21) marks the anniversary of the first Battle of Bull Run (or Battle of Manassas, depending on whether you are a Northerner or Southerner), which was the first major battle of the Civil War. Fought in 1861 near Manassas, Virginia, the battle pitted Union troops under the command of Irvin McDowell against rebellious Confederate troops under General Pierre Beauregard.

For the Union North, the objective was to capture the Confederate South's capital city, Richmond, which McDowell believed would deal the South a mortal blow (until Ulysses S. Grant, no Union general understood that the way to win the war was not to capture Confederate cities, but to defeat Confederate *armies*). Beauregard's job was to stop the Union army and he chose Bull Run as the place to make his stand.

As many readers may recall, the North was so confident of victory that civilians traveled down from Washington, D.C., to watch the battle from the surrounding hillsides. Many brought picnic baskets and blankets in order to make it into a fun outing, and at first this optimism was justified, as the North's forces pushed Southern troops back. However, thanks to the legendary Confederate general, Stonewall Jackson, the tide later turned in the South's favor. At that point it was touch-and-go as to who could run away faster, the terrified civilian onlookers or the panicked Northern soldiers, and the next day the battlefield was littered with a surreal mixture of picnic baskets, union muskets, colorful blankets, regimental backpacks, umbrellas and unused ammunition. If nothing else, Bull Run told the North it was in for a longer haul than its leaders had anticipated.

Bull Run also told Wilmer McLean that it was time to move. An area farmer and southern sympathizer, Wilmer had allowed General Beauregard to use his farmhouse as headquarters, so Wilmer got a close up view of war. Not liking it one bit, Wilmer resolved to move his family far away, to a place where, as he put it, "the sound of battle would never reach them."

Wilmer chose what he thought was the perfect spot — a tiny, remote, sleepy little town located far from Manassas called Appomattox Courthouse, Virginia. It was *not* — as you will surmise — the wisest decision Wilmer ever made because some four years later when the South's Robert E. Lee ended the Civil War by surrendering to the North's General Ulysses Grant, it was at Appomattox Courthouse. To be specific, it was in the parlor of Wilmer McLean's Appomattox home, which made Wilmer and his family the hosts of the opening and the closing battles of the Civil War.

Talk about the circle of life.

© Kauffmann 2008

Bruce's History Lessons:
Joy to the World

Louise Joy Brown's journey from conception to birth was unlike any before her in human history, involving as it did an unprecedented detour. For unlike the other babies born since the beginning of time, Louise's birth was the result of bypassing the Fallopian tubes, which, because of a blockage, had prevented her mother Kelly from becoming pregnant.

Instead, thanks to Dr. Patrick Steptoe, a gynecologist in Oldham, England, and Dr. Robert Edwards, a physiologist from Cambridge University, Louise became the world's first "test tube baby." Her birth in Oldham this week (July 25) in 1978 was made possible because of a technique called "*in vitro* fertilization," in which an egg (ovum) from her mother's ovaries was removed, fertilized with her father's sperm in a glass tube, and then reinserted into her mother's uterus on the other side of the Fallopian tubes.

It was a radical idea, born out of the anguish of millions of infertile women. Before 1978, for pregnancy to occur, a woman's egg first had to travel through the Fallopian tube, after which it is fertilized by sperm, before traveling to the uterus to begin normal development. If the Fallopian tubes were in any way damaged, thereby preventing the egg from passing through, pregnancy was impossible. It is a problem that still causes infertility in one out of five women.

Although Steptoe and Edwards had worked on *in vitro* fertility since 1966, and had fertilized eggs outside of a woman's womb, they had been unable to successfully reinsert the fertilized egg into the woman's uterus. Before 1978, all pregnancies resulting from their *in vitro* procedure had ended prematurely — usually after 10 weeks.

But after reviewing their work, both doctors decided to alter the timing of the reinsertion of the fertilized egg. Instead of waiting four or five days, during which time the eggs had undergone approximately 100 cell divisions (cell division begins right after fertilization), they decided to reinsert the fertilized egg after two-and-a-half days and only 8 cell divisions.

Sure enough, Kelly Brown's pregnancy soon passed 10 weeks, then 20, then 30, and finally, just before midnight on July 25th, the six-pound, blue-eyed, blond-haired Louise Joy Brown was born.

Quite naturally her birth sparked controversy, and to many critics the ethical, moral and even religious questions raised in her birth's wake still have not been satisfactorily answered. But that said, her birth helped give new hope — and new children — to infertile women everywhere, and today *in vitro* fertilization is the world's most practiced artificially assisted reproduction procedure.

As for Louise Joy Brown, she is in excellent health and lives a normal life in England. She is proud to have been a trailblazer.

© Kauffmann 2008

Bruce's History Lesson: JFK and PT-109

You don't have to be a war hero to become president of the United States but it doesn't hurt, as our 35th president, John F. Kennedy, discovered in the wake of the World War II adventure that befell him this week (Aug. 2) in 1943. While commanding a Navy torpedo boat — the PT-109 — in the South Pacific, Lieutenant Kennedy and his crew were returning to base when suddenly they were rammed by a Japanese destroyer, cutting the boat in half, killing two crew members and wounding several others.

Kennedy quickly organized a rescue operation, which necessitated swimming to an island some three miles away. Adding to the burden of a three-mile swim and an injured back that he had sustained during the collision, Kennedy literally had to tow one of the wounded crew behind him -- a tow rope clenched in his teeth as he led his men toward the distant shore. After reaching shore, tending to the wounded and foraging for food, Kennedy began planning their escape and recovery, which was made possible when he and another crew member swam to a nearby island and met two natives who agreed to deliver a rescue message — which Kennedy carved into a coconut — to an Australian coast watcher located in the area. Days later a Navy vessel rescued the entire crew.

And a legend was born. Kennedy was promoted and awarded the Navy and Marine Corps medal, and the story of his heroism was featured in newspapers nationwide, including *The New York Times*.

As for Kennedy, he initially tried to play down the incident, and among experienced Naval officers there was grumbling about the fact that an extremely maneuverable PT boat should easily have avoided a slow-moving destroyer — *unless* the crew had been (if not literally, then figuratively) asleep at the wheel.

But back in the U.S., questions about his seamanship quickly gave way to kudos for his courage, and nearly two decades later when JFK ran for president, the PT-109 story — in true Naval fashion — was brought out of mothballs, given a paint job, and sold to an electorate that was charmed by Kennedy's charisma, but unsure about his depth and strength of character. Songs were written about Kennedy and PT-109, replicas of the boat were handed out at campaign rallies, and the famous Kennedy PR machine promoted the story to every media outlet it could find.

Which is not to say that the PT-109 incident won Kennedy the 1960 election, but it is not to say that it didn't. Kennedy beat Richard Nixon by a mere 100 thousand votes in what is the second closest election in modern times. In politics, every little bit helps.

© *Kauffmann 2008*

Bruce's History Lessons:
Adolf Hitler, Meet Jesse Owens

This week in 1936 should have been an eye-opener for Adolf Hitler, the ruthless, racist megalomaniac who ruled Nazi Germany. His entire political career, from the time he took over the Nazi Party in the early 1920s to the time he plunged Germany and the world into war in 1940, was based on the premise that the Aryan race was superior in every way — culturally, intellectually and most certainly physically.

Indeed, the opportunity to display the physical superiority of Aryans was the reason that Hitler heavily promoted and lavishly supported the 1936 Olympic Games, which had opened the first week in August in Germany's capital, Berlin. Although Hitler had originally opposed hosting the Olympics, which had been awarded to Berlin before he seized power, his propaganda minister, Josef Goebbels, persuaded him that the Games could serve as a global showcase for the superiority of the Nazi system and the invincibility of the Aryan athlete. Soon Hitler was boasting that the 1936 Olympics would be the most spectacular athletic event of the modern era, and when the Games finally opened, banners bearing the Nazi swastika were everywhere.

And then, completely confounding Hitler's theories on race, an African-American member of the U.S. Olympic team named Jesse Owens won four gold medals at the Games, the last coming on August 9 when his 4x100-meter relay team set a world record time of 39.8 seconds. Earlier Owens had won gold in the 100- and 200-meter sprints and the broad jump, setting either Olympic or world records in all three events.

Owens's victories and that of several other black athletes were not exactly what Hitler had come to the Games to see, and although he had publicly pledged to personally congratulate every winner, rather than shake hands with Owens or any of the other African-American medalists, Hitler left the

Olympic stadium before those award ceremonies. Later in a private ceremony, he would honor any victorious German athletes.

When the 1936 Olympic Games finally ended, Germany — with the largest contingent of athletes — had won the most medals, but there was no escaping the fact that in the most popular event, track-and-field, what Hitler called the "*unter-menschen*" (sub humans) had proved to be faster, stronger and abler than most of his "Aryan gods."

Still, Hitler was so pleased with the "triumph" of his Olympic athletes that he pledged to build a 400-thousand-seat stadium in Nuremberg that would hold the Olympics "for all time to come." Alas for *der Fuhrer*, his continued delusion that Aryans would always best other races in any contest — war included — helped ensure his defeat and Germany's total destruction in World War II. Plans for his grand sports stadium at Nuremberg were subsequently shelved.

© Kauffmann 2008

Bruce's History Lesson:
Fulton Speed Ahead!

The critics stood on the riverbank looking disapprovingly at Robert Fulton's new-fangled steam-powered boat, the Clermont, which Fulton hoped to navigate up the Hudson River to Albany, New York. "It'll never start! It'll never start!" they cried in derision, but suddenly the engine did start and the Clermont began steaming up the river. The critics were silent, but only for a moment before running after the boat, waving their arms and shouting, "It'll never stop! It'll never stop!"

Not a true story, although Fulton's Clermont did begin its journey up the Hudson this week (Aug. 17) in 1807. What's more, if those particular critics didn't actually exist, over the years Fulton certainly came up against a number of their real life counterparts. Having already failed as a commercial artist, Fulton turned to engineering during a stay in France, but failed to interest either the French or, later, the British in any of his experimental boat designs.

Finally, he caught the attention of America's ambassador to France, Robert Livingston, who persuaded him to concentrate on designing steamboat engines. Thus did Fulton return to the U.S. where, with Livingston's financial backing, he built and successfully deployed the Clermont.

Contrary to popular belief, Fulton did not invent the steamboat, but he was the one who made the boat a reliable — and therefore commercially viable — mode of transportation, which was to have a tremendous impact on the young United States. Prior to the Fulton steamboat, river navigation — like its ocean counterpart — was at the mercy of capricious winds and currents, meaning predictable, regularly scheduled movement of both passengers and products was impossible. As a result, transporting perishable products to new markets was a gamble, so slower, more expensive land routes were usually used, or the products remained confined to local markets.

Fulton's steamboat changed all that, and as steam-powered technology improved, allowing for bigger, faster and even more reliable boats, it resulted in increased shipping of goods and services, as well as the large-scale navigation of America's rivers and inland waterways. This, in turn, allowed trade to expand rapidly, and paved the way for Americans to explore and settle the Western territories, especially those lands around the mighty Mississippi, which had become part of America under the Louisiana Purchase just a few years earlier.

In his later years Fulton became a nationally recognized expert on steam engines and navigational issues, and, ironically, it was while crossing his beloved Hudson River after giving testimony in Trenton, New Jersey, about repealing laws hindering steam boat operations that he caught a cold which ultimately proved fatal. He died on February 24th, 1815, just as his young country was, literally and figuratively, beginning to gather steam.

© *Kauffmann 2008*

Bruce's History Lessons:
The P.T. Barnum of Baseball

Bill Veeck was the P.T. Barnum of baseball. Better than any baseball owner in history he knew how to put people in the stands. For Veeck no publicity stunt was too bizarre and no promotion was too outlandish.

He also knew how to win. His Milwaukee Brewers — then a minor league team — won three pennants, and when he achieved big league ownership, his Chicago White Sox won a pennant and his Cleveland Indians won a World Series, thanks in part to Larry Doby, whom Veeck signed as the first black player to play in the American League, and the great black pitcher Satchel Paige, whom, at 42, Veeck signed as the league's oldest rookie.

Veeck's other innovations include the first exploding scoreboard, the first "giveaways" and the first uniforms with players' names on them. He staged weddings at home plate and once presented his team's manager with a left-handed pitcher by having him pop out of a cake. Veeck also gave baseball, and the world, Harry Caray and his immortal version of "Take Me Out to The Ball Game."

But Veeck's most famous stunt occurred this week (Aug. 19) in 1951 when he sent a dwarf up to pinch-hit for his St. Louis Browns. Eddie Gaedel stood 3'7" tall and when he strode to the plate the crowd let out a collective gasp, as did the plate umpire, who immediately objected. Veeck, however, had shrewdly filed Gaedel's contract with the American League office late on Friday, knowing it would be perfunctorily approved. He never listed Gaedel's height.

Powerless to stop a player with a valid contract, the umpires let Gaedel bat and he promptly walked on four pitches. He was quickly replaced by a pinch runner, and although the Browns eventually lost that game, Gaedel and Veeck were the talk of the country. American League President Will Harridge was not amused, however, and barred dwarfs from ever playing baseball again.

Yet if that was Veeck's most famous stunt, his most outlandish occurred five days later when he held "Grandstand Manager's Day." Veeck had stadium officials give fans a placard that said "Yes" on one side and "No" on the other, and during the game Veeck's publicity director flashed cards asking the fans what managerial move the team should make — bunt, steal, bring in a reliever, hit-and-run? — with the team doing whatever the majority of fans voted.

The "grandstand managers" did an excellent job. The Browns won that game 5-3, stopping a four-game losing streak that had begun in the game featuring Eddie Gaedel's first and only big league appearance.

Bill Veeck died in 1986, having lived a colorful life. He is — are you surprised? — a first-ballot member of the Baseball Hall of Fame.

© Kauffmann 2008

Bruce's History Lesson:
LBJ: The Tall Tale Texan

Say what you will about Lyndon Baines Johnson — and people have said all kinds of things about him — the man who was born this week (Aug. 27) in 1908 had a razor sharp wit. Once, as vice-president, LBJ went on a "fact finding" tour to Africa, and at one stop an African leader said to him, "Mr. Vice President, is it true that you were born in a log cabin?"

"No, no, you are confusing me with Abraham Lincoln," Johnson replied, before pausing and adding, "I was born in a manger."

He was also a great storyteller, as are most denizens of the Lone Star State, but our 36th president — famous for landmark Civil Rights legislation as well as the debacle in Vietnam — truly had a Texan's knack both for telling a good story and using it as a political parable.

To illustrate American grit and flexibility in the face of hard times, for example, Johnson loved to tell the story of the Depression-era job applicant desperately seeking a teaching position. A member of the school board asked him if the world was round or flat.

"I can teach it round *or* flat," the applicant responded without hesitation. "You make the call."

But one of Johnson's (and my) favorite stories was the one he would tell to illustrate the fact that absolutely no act of self-promotion was too low or shameless for a politician.

The story goes like this: In the early 1930s in Louisiana, convicted murderers were sometimes executed by public hanging. Naturally, these hangings attracted large crowds of onlookers, many of whom, we can suppose, attended for motives not solely relegated to the need to see justice served.

169

In any case, the one legal addendum to this public hanging custom was that the condemned was allowed five minutes to say his (or her) "last words" in public — whatever they might be. So on the day in question the sheriff, having led the condemned man — let's call him Slim — up to the gallows, turned to him and said loud enough for the crowd to hear, "Slim, in accordance with the laws and customs of the great state of Louisiana, you have five minutes to say your piece before going on to your just reward."

All eyes turned to Slim, who squirmed, looked down at his feet, and finally turned to the sheriff and said, "You know me, sheriff. I ain't much for words. Let's jes' get on with it."

Suddenly a hand went up and a voice in the crowd shouted out, "Excuse me, but if he doesn't want his five minutes, can I have them?! I'm Bob Mason and I'm running for city council in next month's election!"

© Kauffmann 2008

Bruce's History Lessons:
Tragedy at the Olympic Games

Thirty years ago this week (Sept. 5) a tragic event first taught the rest of the world what everyone in the Middle East already knew — that the Palestinians and the Israelis were mortal enemies. It was a lesson made more stark by the venue in which this tragedy occurred — the Summer Olympic Games in Munich, Germany. After all, as everyone knows, during the Olympics all political, religious and ideological differences are to be put aside.

Even so, before dawn on September 5, eight armed Palestinian terrorists, calling themselves Black September, broke into the apartments occupied by Israeli athletes in Munich's Olympic Village, shot two Israeli wrestlers and took nine others hostage. Two Israelis managed to escape.

Immediately thereafter, Black September leaders announced their demands, which included freeing 236 Arabs then being held in Israeli jails and providing air transportation so that Black September and the hostages could fly to an undisclosed location. Otherwise, the terrorists warned, they would begin killing hostages one by one.

For the next several hours the world watched in horror as German police surrounded the Israeli compound and began negotiating with the terrorists. Six deadlines came and went, and several offers were made and rejected, including paying a ransom and replacing the Israeli hostages with German officials. But finally a special terrorist task force agreed to Black September's request for air transportation to Cairo, Egypt, where — it also was agreed — the 236 newly freed Arab prisoners would be waiting.

At the Munich airport, however, the situation turned violent when German police launched a surprise attack against the terrorists, hoping to overwhelm them and free the Israelis. But after a ninety-minute standoff, all nine hostages plus five terrorists and one German policeman were dead. The remaining terrorists were captured.

The next day, adding insult to serious injury, Olympic officials announced that despite the horrible tragedy, the Games would continue. Insisting that canceling the Games would mean a victory for the terrorists, Olympic officials held a memorial service on September 6, and the following day the athletic events resumed. Several pro-Israeli organizations immediately filed protests, while others demonstrated against the decision.

Which was nothing compared to the criticism the German government received for approving the botched rescue attempt. Claiming that the rescue was hastily conceived, badly planned and ineptly executed, critics accused the Germans of everything from incompetence, to insensitivity, to aiding and abetting in the murder of Jews — a charge that, given certain events that occurred in Germany some 30 years *prior to* 1972, was especially painful.

And sadly ironic. Germany had lobbied hard to host the 1972 Olympics to prove to the world that a new Germany had finally emerged out of the ashes of the old.

© *Kauffmann 2008*

Bruce's History Lessons: September 12th and the Invocation of NATO's Article 5

"The condition upon which God has given liberty to man is eternal vigilance."

– John Curran

Fifty-eight years ago the North Atlantic Treaty Organization (NATO) was created when 12 Western democracies joined together in a military alliance whose purpose was mostly defensive. World War II was a fresh memory, but the greatest threat to peace in 1949 was the Soviet Union, which had dropped an "Iron Curtain" — in Churchill's memorable phrase — around the nations of Eastern Europe, strangling their freedoms and rigidly controlling their economic, cultural and political institutions. The Western European democracies feared greatly that the Soviet army, the largest in the world, would someday invade their territories and do the same to them.

So did America, which joined NATO to help defend its members. U.S. troops were stationed in Europe both as a defensive force in case of a Soviet attack and as a "tripwire," meaning that should any American blood be shed it would ensure an American retaliation that might eventually involve nuclear weapons. The intent was to make crystal clear to the Soviets that, as Article 5 of the NATO charter stated, an attack on one NATO member was considered an attack on all, including America.

It worked. Not once in NATO's history did the Soviet army enter NATO territory, meaning that not once was Article 5 ever invoked, and with the dissolution of the U.S.S.R. in 1991 and the release of its Eastern European satellites from its grip, NATO was considered history's most successful military alliance.

And then on September 11, 2001, the world changed forever and so did NATO. On September 12, 2001, after five hours of deliberation among NATO members, NATO's secretary general, Lord George Robertson, not only invoked Article 5 of the NATO charter for the first time in history, but did so with an expanded definition of NATO's mission. No longer would NATO exist solely to protect members from threatening states, but also from threatening entities such as terrorist organizations. Upon proof that the September 11 attacks came from a foreign origin — and a month later it was definitively shown that al Qaeda and Osama bin Laden were behind them — then this attack on America would be considered an attack on all NATO members.

And so, for all of our disagreements, past and present, with our NATO allies over how best to meet the menace of terrorism, we should not forget on the anniversary of the terrible tragedy of September 11 that our allies stood with us when it counted. Indeed, the irony is that after 50-plus years of thinking America would one day have to come to the aid of its NATO allies, it was the NATO allies who came to the aid of America.

© Kauffmann 2008

Bruce's History Lessons:
"The Battle of the Sexes"

Of all the monuments to the madness that was the 1970s — disco, mood rings, leisure suits, beanbag chairs, Richard Nixon and even the Vietnam War — none quite matches the event that occurred this week (Sept. 20) in 1973. That's when a 55-year old former Wimbledon champ turned tennis hustler named Bobby Riggs met women's tennis star Billie Jean King in a tennis match to decide, for all practical purposes, which was superior — feminism or chauvinism. Winner take all.

The event itself — labeled "The Battle of the Sexes" and held (appropriately) in the Houston Astrodome — was a triumph of hucksterism. Riggs, who hatched the idea of playing the best women tennis players as a way to return to the spotlight, and make a buck in the process, had earlier defeated the world's top woman player, Margaret Court. "I want Billie Jean King!" Riggs declared immediately after his victory. "I want the women's libber!" This proved to be such good copy, Riggs enthusiastically assumed the mantle of "Men's Liberation" spokesman and number one "male chauvinist pig."

"Women belong in the kitchen and the bedroom," Riggs gleefully repeated to reporters in the months leading up to the match, predicting that he would demolish King and deflate the women's lib movement. Thanks to Riggs' promotional efforts, public interest in the match quickly grew, and on the night it was held 30,000 fans were in attendance and 40 million watched on TV.

They got their money's worth before the match even started. Riggs made his entrance in a chariot pulled by gorgeous young women, while King entered in a carriage carried by University of Houston football players clad in mini-togas. Prior to play Riggs presented King with a giant Sugar Daddy sucker. King gave Riggs a pig.

The match itself was anti-climactic. King destroyed Riggs in straight sets, 6-4, 6-3, 6-3, overpowering him with her serve-and-volley game, and even Riggs admitted after the match that King was too good for him. Riggs soon faded back into obscurity while King went on to have one of the great careers in all of tennis.

And, thanks to Bobby Riggs, one of the most lucrative, for the irony was that the "Battle of the Sexes" greatly contributed to the popularity of the women's game. "They owe me a piece of their paychecks," Riggs joked years later, and it was true, as even King — who had fought hard to achieve parity in the prize money paid to women — would admit. Or as Rosie Casals, another women's player who had once called Riggs "an idiot," would put it after Riggs died in 1995, "For a male chauvinist, he did a lot of good for us."

Game, set and match.

© *Kauffmann 2008*

Bruce's History Lessons:
The Man Who Put "Supreme" in the Supreme Court

John Marshall, born this week (Sept. 24) in 1755, was the greatest chief justice ever to serve on the U.S. Supreme Court. Before Marshall, the Supreme Court was "supreme" in name only. After him, it was the law of the land.

Marshall was a Virginian, but unlike peers such as Tom Jefferson and James Madison — Southerners to the core — Marshall joined the Northern-dominated Federalist Party of President John Adams, who, after losing to Jefferson in the presidential election of 1800, promptly appointed Marshall chief justice. Adams wanted to ensure a Federalist presence in the new government as a way of checking the Jeffersonian Republican majority. Since judicial appointments were for life, Jefferson would be stuck with Marshall.

Jefferson also would find, to his horror, that before leaving office Adams had "stuck" him with several more last-minute appointments, having named 42 new Federalist justices to the bench. Their appointments had been confirmed, but not all had been delivered when Jefferson was inaugurated, so he directed his secretary of state, James Madison, to void those tardy appointments. Jefferson reasoned that since these appointees did not physically possess their appointments, the president was not bound by them and could select his own justices. One of the denied appointees, William Marbury, promptly sued Secretary Madison, and the case, *Marbury vs. Madison*, produced the most important Supreme Court decision in history.

But first, Marshall, who would render that decision, found himself in a bind. If he ruled that Madison must allow Marbury's appointment, he knew Jefferson would ignore him, thus weakening the court's authority. If he sided with Jefferson, it would appear the court was cowering before presidential power, also weakening its authority. So Marshall took a masterful middle path. First, he ruled that Marbury was legally entitled to his appointment. But then Marshall ruled that since the Supreme Court is an appellate court it lacked the authority to enforce its ruling in *Marbury* because the case was not previously tried in a lower court. In effect, Marshall upheld the right of the court to tell the legislative and executive branch what was and wasn't legal, but avoided a confrontation it could not win.

By this decision Marshall established for posterity the "right of judicial review," meaning that the courts became the ultimate interpreters of the Constitution. This gave the judicial branch of our government, which had been considered the weakest branch, power equal to the executive and legislative branches.

With that power, the courts could defend the liberties of American citizens against encroachments by the other branches, which may be why — or so legend has it — when Marshall died in Philadelphia in 1835, the Liberty Bell was rung so hard in mourning, it acquired its famous crack.

© Kauffmann 2008

Bruce's History Lessons:
Of Machines and Men

What effect can a machine have on the affairs of a nation? Take the example of the cotton gin, invented by Eli Whitney in 1793, and the subsequent invention of the mechanical cotton picker, which was first demonstrated in Clarksdale, Mississippi, this week (Oct. 2) in 1944.

Before Whitney invented the "gin," only long-fiber cotton, the kind that easily separates from its black seeds, was commercially viable, and that was found only in the coastal areas of the Deep South. After the cotton gin, which made it easy to separate short- and medium-fiber cotton, cotton plantations spread throughout the South, and soon the South's entire economy was based on "King Cotton."

Of course, lots of cotton plantations necessitated lots of cotton pickers, and the American slave trade, which had been declining, suddenly grew dramatically from 1793 on. Slavery became a political and economic fact of life in the South, and protecting it from Northern attempts to end it, or prevent its spread, became a *casus belli* of the Civil War — the most tragic war in our history.

So it can be argued that a machine — the cotton gin — influenced American history from the turn of the 18th Century to the post-Civil War era.

Yet the former slaves who emerged from this post-war era found themselves in a new socio-economic order not much different from the old one. Because cotton plantations still needed cheap labor, and because blacks still needed to feed their families, slavery was replaced by sharecropping, a system that still exploited them, still segregated them, and still tied them to Southern cotton fields.

But another machine, the mechanical cotton picker, would change that, and in fact almost reverse it. Because each mechanical picker could do the work of 50 field hands, at one-seventh the cost, the need for black sharecroppers disappeared virtually overnight. Suddenly, the underpinning of the entire Southern economy — cheap black labor — was gone, leaving former sharecroppers with no reason to remain in the South and plenty of reasons to leave it.

The result has been called the greatest internal migration of a people in history, as some six million Southern blacks moved to large cities in the North and Midwest — Chicago, Detroit, Cleveland, New York and others — looking for work. This would forever change America's urban landscape, with all the attendant effects on northern economics, politics and culture.

But most of all this great migration forever changed the issue of race in America. What had been a Southern tragedy became a national tragedy, and solving the issue of race relations became a national priority — which it still is today.

What effect can a machine have on the affairs of a nation? A profound one.

© *Kauffmann 2008*

Bruce's History Lessons: Aleksandr Solzhenitsyn Wins the Nobel Prize

If, as now appears to be the case, the winner of the Nobel Prize for Literature must possess not only great literary skill but also great political courage, then there has been no worthier recipient than Aleksandr Solzhenitsyn, who was named the winner of that prize this week (Oct. 8) in 1970. A worthy heir to the great Russian writers of the past — Tolstoy, Dostoyevzky, Checkov — Solzhenitsyn's early novels, *One Day in the Life of Ivan Denisovich*, *The Cancer Ward* and *The First Circle* stand on their own as monumental literary achievements.

But it was his unabashed defiance and criticism of the oppression and violence practiced by leaders of the Soviet Union, from the Stalin era on, that makes Solzhenitsyn among the most admired writers in history. Sent to a forced-labor camp in 1945 for criticizing Stalin, Solzhenitsyn wrote *Ivan Denisovich* as a fictional account of his life as a "zak" — a political prisoner — deep in the bowels of the Soviet police state, and his follow-up novels further explored the universal theme of man pitting his courage and instinct to survive against the brutality of an unthinking, unfeeling dictatorial machine.

Although Solzhenitsyn was "rehabilitated" briefly during the de-Stalinization period of the early '60s, his constant criticism of the Soviet system soon caused his works, published widely in the West, to be banned at home. In 1974, after accusing him of treason, the Soviet government expelled him. Immigrating to America, he settled in Vermont.

The last straw for Soviet leaders was publication of Solzhenitsyn's greatest work, *The Gulag Archipelago*, a non-fictional account of the *other* great holocaust of the 20th Century, the imprisonment, torture and murder of countless millions of innocent Soviet citizens in an "island chain" (archipelago) of Soviet prison camps (gulags). Having survived the gulag himself, Solzhenitsyn had a "messianic" obligation to remember those who died and caution those yet born.

In the wake of the Cold War's end, and the "democratization" that has occurred in the Soviet Union, Solzhenitsyn was allowed to return to his country in 1994, where he continues to write and agitate the Soviet government to acknowledge and atone for its past. "I am confident that I will fulfill my tasks as a writer in all circumstances," he once wrote, "from my grave even more successfully and more irrefutably than in my lifetime. No one can bar the road to truth, and to advance its cause I am prepared to accept even death. But may it be that repeated lessons will finally teach us not to stop the writer's pen. At no time has this ennobled our history."

What has ennobled Russian history, and that of the world, is the life of Aleksandr Isaevich Solzhenitsyn.

© Kauffmann 2008

Bruce's History Lessons:
The Controversial Confirmation of
Clarence Thomas

Imagine the emotional roller coaster that retiring Supreme Court Justice Thurgood Marshall experienced after first hearing that the man nominated to replace him on the nation's highest court was a fellow African-American, and then discovering that this African-American was Clarence Thomas — a man as far to the right on the political spectrum as Marshall was to the left. In fact, Marshall's great claim to fame prior to serving on the Supreme Court was winning the landmark case, *Brown vs. The Board of Education*, which abolished the "separate but equal" doctrine that for so long had been used to discriminate against blacks. Yet Thomas would actually criticize *Brown*, calling it a misguided attempt to use social science to address constitutional issues!

Small wonder that when President George Bush nominated Thomas for the Supreme Court in 1991, his confirmation hearings were the talk of Washington — and that was *before* a University of Oklahoma law professor named Anita Hill, who once worked for Thomas at the Department of Education and later at the Equal Employment Opportunity Commission, came forward to accuse him of sexual harassment.

After that, the nationally televised confirmation hearings became a circus. The married Thomas vehemently denied Hill's charges, which included pressuring her to date him, boasting of his sexual prowess, and making pornographic references. Senators of both political parties quickly joined the fray, with conservatives calling Hill a liar (pointedly wondering why, if Thomas was harassing her, she kept following him from job to job) and liberals calling Thomas a liar. Outside special interest groups soon weighed in, especially women's groups, most of which found the male-dominated proceedings to be steeped in hypocrisy. Thomas himself called the confirmation hearings "a high-tech lynching."

Nationwide, the hearings also touched a nerve in the relationships between men and women, and the division was clear. In polls, men overwhelmingly believed Thomas was telling the truth, and in equal numbers women believed Hill. The debate raged in restaurants and classrooms, around the water cooler at work and around the dinner table at home. Rarely had America experienced an event that touched so many different emotions, or intertwined in such an intense and complex way so many disparate political, cultural and gender issues.

After all was said and done, of course, the Senate confirmed Thomas, this week (Oct. 15) in 1991 — although barely, 52-48 — and he has become, as expected, among the most conservative Supreme Court justices ever. As for Anita Hill, she has gone on to be a visiting professor, a guest speaker and an author. Her first book was the appropriately titled *Speaking Truth to Power*, although which of the two really was "speaking truth" will probably never be known.

© Kauffmann 2008

Bruce's History Lessons: Shootout At — Actually Near — the OK Corral

The words "History" and "Hollywood" have in common the letter "H" and three syllables, and practically nothing else. Take, for example, History's and Hollywood's versions of this week's events (Oct. 26) in 1881 in the aptly named town of Tombstone, Arizona.

According to Hollywood, the "Shootout at the OK Corral" — the most famous gunfight in the annals of the American West — occurred when the forces of law and order under Wyatt, Virgil and Morgan Earp, and that loveable John "Doc" Holliday, saved the town of Tombstone from those cattle rustling outlaws Frank and Tom McLaury, Ike and Billy Clanton and their friend Billy Clairborne, who had been waiting to ambush the poor Earps.

In reality, the shootout didn't even occur at the OK Corral, but in a vacant lot nearby, and while events surrounding the fight are disputed, some things are clear. First, the Earp brothers were nowhere near the sainted lawmen that Hollywood has made them. As for good ol' Doc Holliday of film and television, the real version was a drunkard, a gun-happy card cheat and possibly an armed robber.

As for those outlaws, the McLaurys and Clantons, they did engage in cattle thieving, but at — or more accurately *near* — the OK Corral that day they were as much sinned against as sinning. The shootout actually occurred because of an incident the night before in which Doc Holliday, with support from Morgan Earp and (versions differ here) the town's chief lawman, Marshall Virgil Earp, bullied and threatened the life of Ike Clanton. For Ike, a hothead and drinker himself, and his brother Billy, the code of the West virtually demanded revenge.

185

For his part, Marshall Earp had every right to enforce the law, and by bringing guns into town the Clantons and McLaurys undeniably broke it, but Earp's decision to deputize Holliday to help arrest the Clanton-McLaury gang was like pouring gasoline on a fire, and when the shootout began it was Holliday who fired first. When it was over, Bill Clanton and both McLaury brothers were dead, while Ike Clanton had fled the scene (Billy Clairborne's fate remains a mystery). Virgil, Morgan and Holliday were wounded, while Wyatt was untouched.

In Hollywood's version of this famous gunfight, justice prevailed, the bad guys got theirs and Holliday and the Earps, especially Wyatt, became legends. In History's version they barely escaped a murder conviction, partly because they were deputized lawmen and partly because there was no clear finding of fault on either side.

So in a sense, the "Shootout at the OK Corral" has become less of a shootout between the Earps and the Clanton-McLaurys and more of a shootout between Hollywood and History — a fight Hollywood clearly has won. Alas.

© Kauffmann 2008

Bruce's History Lessons:
Happy Birthday John Adams

Our second president, John Adams, who was born this week (Oct. 30) in 1735, would serve his country with a dedication that only one other Founding Father surpassed — the FF who preceded him to the presidency, George Washington. When Adams wasn't being asked to leave his home and family in Braintree, Massachusetts, to serve his country in Congress, he was asked to leave home, family and country to represent the latter in Europe — and he always went despite the toll it took on his family, his finances and his health.

In his day his importance to the nation was considered second only to Washington, and it was Adams himself, as leader of the Continental Congress, who convinced Congress to make Washington commander of the Revolutionary Army — thus making possible Washington's heroic destiny.

Adams also later convinced that Congress to assign another Virginian, Thomas Jefferson, the task of writing a document declaring America's independence from England. As historian David McCullough has noted, if Adams had done nothing other than those two deeds, his imprint on American history would be indelible.

But Adams did much more. His *Thoughts on Government*, written in 1775, was an early blueprint on how to arrange government institutions to ensure liberty among the people, and during the American Revolution it was Adams who secured a vital loan from the Netherlands that helped the Americans keep on fighting. Once that war was won, Adams also helped negotiate the peace treaty with England.

As America's first vice president (a job the loquacious Adams loathed as much because it rendered him as mute as it did powerless), he was the model of loyalty to Washington, while his own presidency, although controversial thanks to the infamous Alien and Sedition Acts, was a qualified success marked by terrible timing. Among other things, Adams sensibly kept an unprepared America out of a potentially disastrous war with France, even though the rest of the nation clamored for it. But news of the peace treaty eliminating all causes for that war arrived after the election of 1800, which he lost to Jefferson.

He also lost to Jefferson — or so he believed — his rightful place among the pantheon of American heroes. Adams was both jealous and astonished that Jefferson, whose only major contribution to the revolution was a document that Adams had assigned him to write, became the symbol of the revolutionary spirit. And even though the two men ended their lives as friends — forever linked by dying on the same historic day, July 4, 1826 — Adams was convinced he would never get his proper due.

He was almost right. It would take 175 years and David McCullough's wonderful book, *John Adams*, to give him that due at last.

© Kauffmann 2008

Bruce's History Lessons:
The Iranian Hostage Crisis

It was America's first first-hand experience with Middle Eastern terrorism, and although it now seems tame compared with the horrific events of September 11, the 444-day Iranian hostage crisis that began this week (Nov. 4) in 1979 was no less painful or frightening for the families involved, and no less frustrating for America.

The perpetrators of this crisis were Iranian "students" who stormed the U.S. Embassy in Iran's capital city, Teheran, and took 66 Americans hostage. They had the full support of Iran's spiritual and political leader, the Ayatollah Ruholla Khomeini, who had returned to Iran earlier in the year to take over the country from Iran's former leader, Shah Muhammad Reza Pahlevi. Pahlevi had fled the country after his people had turned against his dictatorial and often brutal rule, and Khomeini, whom the Shah had exiled from Iran 25 years earlier, never forgot that the Shah's reign had been engineered, and in many ways kept afloat, by U.S. power. Khomeini considered America a mortal enemy and denounced "The Great Satan," as he called America, at every opportunity. He was also virulently anti-Western, and upon taking power he outlawed all of the Western customs the Shah had adopted and instituted a strict Islamic Republic.

What triggered the hostage crisis was a decision by then-President Jimmy Carter to allow the deposed Shah, who had become terminally ill, to enter the U.S. for medical treatment, which so angered these "students" they attacked the U.S. Embassy. Although Khomeini had not ordered the attack, he quickly took advantage of it, demanding delivery of the hated Shah to Iran in return for release of the hostages. Carter rejected that demand and froze all Iranian assets in America, and thus began 14 months of mutual hatred and invective between both countries.

In this country, the hostages' plight became a national obsession. Nightly news coverage showed Iranians burning American flags and taunting the blindfolded hostages as they were dragged through the streets, and pressure on the Carter administration to act became so intense the normally dovish president finally approved a covert military rescue operation. It failed when two U.S. aircraft crashed into each other in the black of night. Eight American servicemen died.

In the last days of Carter's presidency a solution to the crisis was finally negotiated, and the hostages were actually freed on the day that Carter's successor, Ronald Reagan, was inaugurated. America rejoiced the return of her citizens, but the country was sobered by the knowledge that its great power had been countered by an enemy whose only real power came from a fanaticism fueled by unfathomable hatred and a martyr's indifference to death.

That kind of power, as we have learned, should not be underestimated.

© Kauffmann 2008

Bruce's History Lessons:
The Only Woman Medal of Honor Winner

From the Civil War to Somalia, America's military engagements have resulted in 3,459 Americans receiving the nation's highest military decoration, the Congressional Medal of Honor. Of those recipients, only one, Mary Walker, has been a woman. She received the Medal of Honor this week (Nov. 11) in 1865. Fittingly, that is Veterans Day.

Dr. Walker was a woman way ahead of her time. An avowed feminist 100 years before the term was coined, she was, among other things, a strong proponent of "dress reform," allowing women to dress in whatever made them comfortable, including trousers. In 1855, she also became the second American woman ever to graduate from medical school. After marrying a fellow doctor, Albert Miller (wearing a man's coat and trousers instead of a wedding gown), she and her husband began a practice in New York, but, alas, America was not ready for a female doctor, and both her career and her marriage foundered.

And then the Civil War began, and Dr. Walker traveled to Washington, D.C., to join the Union Army as a medical officer. Refused that position because of her gender, she volunteered, and was accepted, as an assistant surgeon, becoming the first female ever to have that job.

During her Civil War service, Dr. Walker tended to the wounded at the battles of Fredericksburg and Chickamauga, and while serving in the 52nd Ohio Infantry, where she allegedly spied for the Union, she courageously crossed into enemy territory to treat wounded soldiers and civilians alike. This eventually resulted in her capture by Confederate troops, and she spent four months in a Confederate prison before being released in a prisoner exchange of captured Union and Confederate doctors.

After the war, President Andrew Johnson authorized Dr. Mary Walker's Medal of Honor for Meritorious Service, but in 1917 Congress revised the medal's criteria to include only those in "actual combat," and Mary was asked to return her medal. She refused, and wore it openly until she died in 1919. In the years between the war and her death, Mary Walker became a social reformer, lecturer and writer, finally penning an autobiography, *Hit*, that was part life story and part commentary on society's treatment of women.

In 1977, President Jimmy Carter made official an Army board recommendation that Dr. Walker's Medal of Honor be officially reinstated. The board cited her "distinguished gallantry, self-sacrifice, patriotism, dedication and unflinching loyalty to her country, despite the apparent discrimination because of her sex." In 1997, Mary Walker deservedly joined the other distinguished names on the newly dedicated Women in Military Service for America Memorial.

© *Kauffmann 2008*

Bruce's History Lessons:
Madison's Federalist 10

The Federalist Papers, the most famous collection of newspaper columns ever published, helped persuade Americans to ratify the then-controversial U.S. Constitution, which had been finalized by Congress in 1787 but still needed the approval of the American people. Yet of the 85 papers written by the three authors, Alexander Hamilton, John Jay and (my hero, as regular readers know) James Madison, the most famous was Federalist 10, penned by Madison this week (Nov. 22) in 1787.

In it, Madison turned on its head the age's conventional wisdom, which was that a republican government could work only when a nation and its population were small in size. Larger territories were considered too unruly, too difficult to govern, and too ripe for "tyranny of the majority" (mob rule), in which majorities rode roughshod over the rights of minorities by virtue of their superior numbers.

Back then, the ideal republican model was Greece, a small nation with a tiny, homogeneous population of similar interests based on geographic proximity. This, it was believed, prevented serious conflicts among differing groups — there weren't any differing groups — thereby preserving political harmony.

In Federalist 10, Madison said, "Nonsense. The more the merrier." He thought one beauty of a large population was that people would inevitably split into factions — or coalitions — that would prevent such tyranny of the majority. Why would they do this? Simple self-interest.

Madison might agree, as his friend Jefferson wrote, that we are all *created* equal, but he knew that we *become* very different. We are raised with different values, we acquire different amounts of property (wealth) and we form different opinions. What's more, we constantly seek to promote our values, protect our property, and defend our opinions. And the best way to do these things is to ally ourselves with like-minded people. In numbers there is safety — and power.

This was the key to factions. You and I might join together in one faction to protest abortions because of similar religious beliefs, but we might split into different factions over taxes because of different incomes. Then we might re-join into a third faction over school vouchers because of similar experiences with public education.

Madison though that if the population kept shifting into, and out of, different factions, based on self-interest, there never would be one dominant majority in place long enough to cause any harm. But to ensure lots of factions, all counter balancing one another, the population needed to be large, which in turn requires lots of property.

The United States certainly had territory and soon acquired more. And sure enough, the population grew and factions were born. And they all behaved as Madison predicted, making America the longest-lasting republic in history.

© Kauffmann 2008

Bruce's History Lessons: Abe Lincoln's Thanksgiving

Because President Tom Jefferson thought observing a Thanksgiving holiday smacked of Royalism (he never explained why), he reversed George Washington's proclamation making the last Thursday of November an official day of thanks. There matters stood for 60 years until Sarah Hale, a Northern writer and editor, mounted a campaign that finally convinced President Abraham Lincoln to restore Thanksgiving. He did so in 1863, in the midst of the Civil War.

"The year that is drawing towards its close has been filled with the blessings of fruitful fields and healthful skies," his Thanksgiving proclamation began. "To these bounties, which are so constantly enjoyed that we are prone to forget the source from which they come, others have been added, which are of so extraordinary a nature that they cannot fail to penetrate and soften even the heart which is habitually insensible to the ever watchful providence of Almighty God."

To say that ol' Abe was putting an optimistic spin on matters would be a huge understatement. The year 1863 began with the Union army reeling from its disastrous defeat at Fredericksburg, and as the year progressed, and Union defeats piled up, Lincoln would fire one general after another — having already replaced McClellan with Burnside, he would replace Burnside with Hooker, Hooker with Meade — and still not find a commander equal to the Confederacy's Robert E. Lee. What's more, a troop shortage forced Lincoln to institute a military draft, which was so hated it sparked major riots in cities from Boston to New York.

Politically things were no better. Criticism grew over Lincoln's handling of the war, especially among Northern Democrats with whom Lincoln had always had a shaky relationship. One of their leaders had even urged Union troops to desert the army, forcing Lincoln to arrest him, and Lincoln's own chances of being re-elected in 1864 looked so slim, even a member of his own Cabinet considered running against him.

For all of that, Lincoln must have sensed that better days were ahead, something he helped ensure by making Ulysses S. Grant commander of the Union's western armies right after he issued the Thanksgiving Proclamation. And sure enough, by Thanksgiving of 1864, Grant — now commander of all Union armies — was driving Lee back to Richmond, General Sherman had captured Atlanta, and Lincoln had won re-election. The fortunes of war had turned, finally giving Lincoln a real reason to be thankful.

As for Sarah Hall, the woman who campaigned so hard to restore the Thanksgiving holiday, it turns out that she was also the author of the popular children's poem — now song — "Mary Had a Little Lamb." It is not known whether, at her first Thanksgiving dinner, Ms. Hall also had a little lamb.

© *Kauffmann 2008*

Bruce's History Lesson:
The "Infamous" Day <u>Before</u> Pearl Harbor

"For every action there is an equal and opposite reaction."

-Newton's 3rd Law of Motion

This week (Dec. 7) is Pearl Harbor Day, "a day that shall live in infamy" as President Franklin Roosevelt so memorably put it in the wake of Japan's devastating sneak attack on the Hawaiian harbor that served as the base for the U.S. Pacific fleet.

However, you might argue that another day this week in 1941, while not as infamous, produced an event of more lasting impact than Japan's surprise attack on Pearl Harbor. For it was on December 6, 1941, that several members of Roosevelt's administration met in Washington, D.C., to initiate an enterprise that would ultimately become the Manhattan Project. The Manhattan Project, you will recall, led to the development of the two atomic bombs that were dropped on the Japanese cities of Hiroshima and Nagasaki. To this day these bombs are still the only atomic weapons ever used in anger. The Atomic Age had dawned.

I bring this up because, as I have written repeatedly, "Mother History" (my version of Mother Nature) has an ironic sense of humor, to say nothing of a tendency to connect, sooner or later, a seemingly isolated series of events. This is one of those times. To wit:

On Saturday, December 6, 1941, the seeds of the atomic bomb are planted in the nation's capital, and the very next day, halfway across the world in Pearl Harbor, Hawaii, the event occurs that will set in motion the first use of that bomb.

But hold on — Mother History isn't finished. Although in hindsight Pearl Harbor was a disaster for the Japanese, when it occurred it was considered a great victory. In the immediate aftermath, both the Americans and the Japanese believed the attack had crippled America's Pacific fleet and rendered the United States helpless in preventing the Japanese from furthering their imperialistic designs in the Far East.

This would turn out to be untrue, mostly because America's aircraft carriers were safely out to sea at the time of Pearl Harbor, and aircraft carriers would prove to be much more vital to the naval conduct of World War II than battleships of the kind destroyed at Pearl. What's more, the Japanese had hoped the attack would intimidate Americans and shatter their morale, when in reality it aroused their anger. But at the time, the Japanese were unaware of this, and in Pearl's wake the tiny nation swelled with nationalist pride.

Certainly the Japanese people were in a festive mood on December 10, 1941, when parts of the daring naval fleet that had launched the attack at Pearl Harbor returned triumphantly — amid much fanfare — to the port city of...

Hiroshima.

© *Kauffmann 2008*

Bruce's History Lessons:
What If ...?

For years historians have speculated on how history might have changed if certain "near misses" and "What ifs..." had actually occurred. One that always makes me shudder is this: What if, when he was hit by a cab this week (Dec. 12) in New York City in 1931, Winston Churchill had died?

To set the stage, Churchill was in New York on a paid lecture tour, and having spent the day of December 12 writing, he was to dine that evening with American financier Bernard Baruch. But upon hailing a cab he realized he had forgotten Baruch's address. After he and the cabby had driven around 5th Avenue to no avail, Churchill decided to get out and walk. He thought he would recognize the house from the sidewalk.

From the Central Park side of 5th Avenue, Churchill decided to cross the street, but forgetting that Americans drive on the right — not the left like the British — he looked the wrong way to see if the street was clear. Satisfied, he entered the crosswalk, was promptly hit by another cab and was dragged several yards before landing hard on the pavement. Rushed to the hospital, Churchill was diagnosed with two cracked ribs, a head wound that had exposed bone, a mangled right foot and several cuts and bruises. He would also contract pleurisy.

But he would recover and later lead England to victory over Hitler and Nazi Germany. Had he not — had he died then and there — then whichever British leader was in power in June of 1940 would have gazed across the English Channel to find that Hitler controlled virtually the entire European mainland. Possessing neither Churchill's rhetorical gifts, nor his indomitable spirit, nor his intuitive understanding that compromise with Hitler was a fool's game, this leader would almost certainly have negotiated a peace with

Hitler that — in the (vain) hope of saving the British Isles — would have solidified Hitler's death grip on Europe and eventually doomed England.

Such a negotiated peace might even have involved some German say in England's internal affairs, but it most certainly would have forbidden any future alliance with the United States. Thus there would be no England to serve as the home base for the U.S. Army in 1944 (meaning no D-Day). With no nearby place to station troops, weapons or war material, America's ability to fight in Europe would have been so compromised that it would have had very little power to affect the outcome of the war.

In other words, a prostrate England and an impotent U.S. would have been no threat to Hitler, allowing him to fully concentrate on his bitter fight with the Soviet Union.

Germany would have won World War II.

© Kauffmann 2008

Bruce's History Lessons:
The Winter of Valley Forge

The words Valley Forge are synonymous with American suffering and hardship, and rightly so, for when George Washington led his beleaguered continental army into winter quarters in Valley Forge, Pennsylvania, this week (Dec. 19) in 1777, they would endure the harshest winter in memory and do so with little food, clothing or shelter. By contrast, just 18 miles away in Philadelphia, British General William Howe and his warm, well-fed troops were settling into snug quarters, happy to wait out a winter they were sure would be the last for the rebellious Americans.

They had good reason to think so. Of the 11,000 troops at Valley Forge, some 2,000 would die of disease and exposure before the winter was over. Frostbite was commonplace and many soldiers lost limbs to amputation. Those "bloody footprints in the snow" that history books describe actually occurred, and plaintive cries of "We want meat!" were heard nightly as starving soldiers, huddled in thin blankets, gulped bowls of equally thin gruel. They were, wrote the Marquis de Lafayette, the young French military officer who had joined Washington's staff, "An army of skeletons."

And it didn't have to be that way. The amazing subplot to the story of Valley Forge is that Washington made the conscious decision *not* to forcibly take the supplies his army so desperately needed from the inhabitants in the surrounding countryside, even though Congress had encouraged him to do so. Congress was willing to deprive the citizenry of their goods, to say nothing of their rights, to further the war effort, but Washington — farsighted as always — believed this would subvert the very liberties for which the revolution was being fought. In stark contrast to the British, who were earning the hatred of the people by stealing or forcibly taking their scarce supplies, Washington wanted to maintain the goodwill of the citizenry, whose ongoing support was crucial if the revolution was to succeed.

It was another testament to the character and genius of Washington, for not only did his army survive Valley Forge, becoming a tougher, more disciplined and more unified force in the process, but also Washington's selfless decision helped his army win a much more important battle — the battle of public opinion. As the war progressed, many thousands of former Loyalists switched their allegiance to the patriot cause, in great part because of the differences in how the two armies behaved in the field, and it was the British realization that they had lost the struggle for "the hearts and minds" of the people that, more than anything else, caused them to lay down their arms, surrender and go home.

Which made all of the suffering at Valley Forge worthwhile.

© Kauffmann 2008

Bruce's History Lessons:
The Visit From St. Nick

'Twas the night before Christmas and in many a home,
Our young will be listening to Clement Moore's poem.

This week (Dec. 24) in 1822, Clement Clarke Moore, a stodgy academic, whose most famous work at the time was the two-volume *Compendius Lexicon of the Hebrew Language,* was working in his home in New York City when his wife, who was roasting Christmas turkeys for the poor at their local parish, discovered she was short one turkey. Thus Professor Moore was sent into the snowy night to fetch another bird.

He made his journey in the common transportation of the time, a horse-drawn "sleigh," and legend has it that Moore had an inspiration while observing the cheerful, pot-bellied, white bearded sleigh driver who took him on his errand. With sleigh bells jingling as they glided over the snow-covered streets, Moore took out a pen and began composing a poem called "A Visit From St. Nicholas," which he read to his six children that night.

They were delighted and bragged of their father's poem to several family members, one of whom, upon learning that Moore refused to allow the poem to be published, secretly sent it to *The Troy Sentinel* in Troy, New York, which published it anonymously the following Christmas. It became an instant success.

That is the legend, and while many scholars believe its authenticity, others believe that Moore, a serious scholar himself, is more likely to have drawn from literary sources in composing his poem. One of them would have been Washington Irving's *Knickerbocker History,* which describes several Dutch customs, including that of a dark-robed character called *Sinter Klass,* who delivers presents, and lectures, to children each Christmas. Irving's book also describes rotund Dutch burghers, who dressed in red cloaks, wide leather belts and black boots. In addition, Moore might well have read another poem, "The Children's Friend," which was published a year earlier and describes "Old Santeclaus" on a sleigh driven by a single reindeer.

Whatever is the truth, and a combination of both is also possible, the irony was that Moore resented the celebrity his poem brought him when, reluctantly, he allowed it to be published under his own name in 1837. He thought the poem "undignified" and a "mere trifle" when compared to his serious scholarly works.

Of which not one is in print, or even remembered, today, while "A Visit from St. Nicholas," which later became "The Night Before Christmas," has been reprinted countless times. Indeed, for 170 years Moore's words have been the last heard by millions of children around the world before they drift happily off to sleep on Christmas Eve.

"Merry Christmas to all, and to all a good night."

© Kauffmann 2008

Bruce's History Lesson:
Guadeloupe and America's Birth

This week (Jan. 3) in 1760 Benjamin Franklin published his take on what would increasingly become an important debate in England: Canada or Guadeloupe? Its outcome would actually affect the birth of America.

The question was whether, in the wake of the French and Indian War (which by 1760 the British clearly were winning) Britain should toss the French out of Canada, making Canada part of the British Empire, or let the French stay and instead demand as the spoils of victory the annexation of the sugar-rich French island of Guadeloupe.

Certainly economics drove the argument for each position. On the pro-Guadeloupe side, gaining the island would double Britain's sugar production. This meant Britain could meet its own increasing demand for the stuff (someone discovered it greatly improved the taste of tea), as well as export it, which meant profits. On the pro-Canada side, the Canadian fur trade was also an economic boon to Britain, and, unlike Guadeloupe, Canada was huge, which meant potentially large population growth, which meant many customers for British goods.

But it was the political angle that had the most impact. Those wanting to keep Canada argued that to return it to France after years of warfare would outrage Britain's American colonists, who had fought the French alongside their British brethren. Certainly the colonists, including Ben Franklin, argued passionately that Britain should keep Canada, not only because it would expand commerce and wealth among the English-speaking peoples of America, Canada and Britain, but also because it would eliminate a sworn enemy — the French. The Americans feared that if the French were allowed to stay in Canada they would continue to use their allied Indian tribes to harass the American colonists.

Which was exactly right, and — to some forward-thinking Brits — exactly the point. If the British kicked the French out of Canada, they would also be eliminating the one threat to America so great that it kept the colonies dependent upon the Mother Country for assistance and protection. No French, no danger. No danger, no need for a British presence in America. No need for the British, no impediment to independence, which some British visionaries thought would then be a foregone conclusion given America's size and growing economic strength.

Sure enough, that is essentially what happened. The British opted to kick the French out of Canada, and the Americans quickly discovered that they had more grievances against their British cousins than things in common with them — including annoyance at Britain's attempts to tax them for the *cost* of the French and Indian War. Independence soon followed.

It isn't often that you can put the words "Guadeloupe" and "American independence" in the same sentence. But history is funny that way.

© Kauffmann 2008

Bruce's History Lessons:
Power Play: The Adoption of the
Designated Hitter Rule

Time magazine's "Fifth Worst Idea of the 20th Century" was approved this week (Jan. 11) in 1973 when the owners of the American League's baseball teams voted to adopt the designated hitter rule. To most baseball purists, only the Chicago "Black Sox" betting scandal of 1919 was a darker stain on the national pastime.

The rule was adopted to generate more offense in the American League, which, thanks to a lack of new talent — at least compared with the National League — was clearly the less interesting league to follow. Pitching so dominated the American League that in 1968, Boston Red Sox outfielder Carl Yastremski won the batting title with a .301 average, and the entire league hit only .230. American League owners faced declining attendance and revenues, and decided that increased scoring was the only way to increase interest. And so a rule was approved that stated, "A hitter may be designated to bat for the starting pitcher and all subsequent pitches in any game without otherwise affecting the status of the pitcher(s) in the game." As a result, for the last 30 years, weak-hitting AL pitchers have been replaced in the batting order by power hitters whose only job is to step to the plate four to five times a game. Most designated hitters are either bad fielders, or slowed by age, and therefore defensive liabilities.

But to baseball purists the rule itself is an egregious liability to the spirit of the game. Baseball's appeal, they contend, is more subtle than the brute force of football, the speed of hockey, or the athleticism of basketball — depending as it does on strategy, situational match-ups, statistical probabilities and, as often as not, just plain hunches. The fact that the DH takes away much of the managerial decision-making that baseball's purists find so entertaining, and relies instead on pure power, is sacrilegious.

And, given the scoring explosion prevalent in today's game, unnecessary. An influx of exciting young talent in the American League, plus bandbox new stadiums that turn routine fly balls into three-run homers, have radically increased the number of runs-per-game in both leagues, meaning there is no longer a need for an extra hitter to keep the runs coming and the game exciting.

To be fair, the DH does prolong the careers of many still-talented players, and the purist's cry that too many runs are being scored in today's game seems not to have resonated with the general public.

Which is why *Time's* fifth worst idea of the 20th Century may be around a while longer. Indeed, it already has lasted longer than *Time's* worst idea of that century — Prohibition — although it still lags behind the century's second worst idea — telemarketing.

© Kauffmann 2008

Bruce's History Lessons:
Elizabeth I

Interesting, isn't it, that throughout its long history England did its best to ensure that kings, not queens, ruled the country — elevating younger princes to the throne ahead of older female siblings, or even, on occasion, inviting foreign (male) royalty to assume the throne rather than be ruled by a native princess. Yet the two greatest monarchs in English history — at least the only two so consequential as to have entire "ages" named after them — are both women. Elizabeth and Victoria.

The former, Elizabeth I, was crowned this week (Jan. 15) in 1559, even though her chances of gaining the throne had been more remote than most English princesses. That is because before she finished childhood her father, Henry VIII, had her mother, Anne Boleyn, beheaded for adultery and treason, and then invalidated the marriage. That made Elizabeth illegitimate.

Even then, she was a distant third in line to the throne, after her *younger* brother Edward and her older sister Mary, although Edward's untimely death in 1553 did bring her one step closer. But she still had a ways to go given that ("Bloody") Mary's crowning put in power a fanatic Catholic who distrusted Elizabeth's Protestantism. What's more, Mary never forgot that Papa Henry had divorced *her* mom, Catherine of Aragon, to marry Elizabeth's mom, Anne Boleyn. Elizabeth continually faced imprisonment and even death at Mary's hands.

But somehow she survived and when Mary herself died childless, Elizabeth became queen, ruling England for 44 years before dying of old age. Yet it wasn't longevity that gave the word "Elizabethan" to the age. It was her courage, her diplomatic skills, her knack for picking good advisors and, most of all, her single-minded devotion to her country. "I will have but one mistress (England) and no master," she said upon turning down one of many marriage proposals. England was her mate for life.

It was during Elizabeth's reign that the English navy, commanded by Sir Francis Drake, defeated the mighty Spanish Armada (with considerable help from inclement weather), thus making England a world power and sowing the seeds for the coming British Empire. But perhaps Elizabeth's greatest contribution to both England and the world was the tone of moderation that she set. With great skill, Elizabeth was able to avoid plunging England into the religious strife and political turmoil that had dominated the reigns of her siblings. The resulting period of toleration not only allowed England to prosper economically, but also ensured a cultural and artistic flowering unlike any in history. Christopher Marlowe, Edmund Spenser, Ben Johnson and William Shakespeare are just some of the artists who prospered during the Elizabethan Age. Small wonder that many in England also call it their country's Golden Age.

Bruce's History Lesson:
The 24th Amendment

"All men are created equal," Jefferson wrote in our Declaration of Independence, yet a few years later in the Constitution his fellow Founding Fathers designated slaves as 3/5ths of a human being.

Which brings up a point. The genius of our Constitution, and the Founders who created it, is that they knew it was a far-from-perfect document, just as they were a far-from-perfect people. That is why they gave the Constitution the power to amend itself — to change for the better both the government and the country.

And as it happened, in the years since the Constitution was created, more amendments to it have dealt with "equality" than with any other issue. The 13th Amendment abolished slavery, the 14th guaranteed equal protection under the law, the 15th guaranteed the right to vote regardless of "race, color, or previous condition of servitude," and the 19th afforded the same right regardless of sex.

And then there is the 24th Amendment, which was ratified this week (Jan. 23) in 1964 as one answer to the attempts by many Southern states to preserve *inequality* by passing state laws that circumvented or defied both the spirit and intent of federal law. For example, even though the right to vote was guaranteed by the 15th Amendment, several Southern states passed laws that imposed a variety of conditions on black Americans to deny them that right. One such condition was a poll tax, which black voters had to pay before they could enter the voting booth. Many Southerners defended the tax by saying that a property qualification (i.e. having enough wealth to be worthy of voting) was as old as America itself, but Civil Rights advocates countered that because the tax fell disproportionally on blacks, it violated the 14th Amendment's equal protection clause.

And so Congress passed the 24th Amendment, which said that neither the states nor the federal government could deny a citizen the right to vote because of failure to pay a tax of any kind. It was one more step on that long road to equality under the law.

What's more, its passage emboldened the Civil Rights movement to press then-President Lyndon Johnson for a comprehensive Voting Rights Act that, among other things, ensured federal intervention and support for minority attempts to register to vote.

Congress passed that act in 1965, and in combination with the 24th Amendment, it resulted in a quarter of a million new black voters by the end of the year. A decade later that number had more than tripled, and blacks also began serving in Congress and state legislative bodies in record numbers. At least in the eyes of the law, all men, and women, finally were "created equal."

© Kauffmann 2008

Bruce's History Lessons:
Julia Ward Howe and the
Battle Hymn of the Republic

This week (Jan. 28) in 1908 Julia Ward Howe, a Civil War-era author, abolitionist and — as we shall see — songwriter, became the first woman ever elected to the American Academy of Arts and Letters. It was a fitting tribute to a life of unceasing dedication to human rights.

Born in 1819, Julia Howe, together with her husband, Sam Howe, founded and edited the *Abolitionist,* which was the premier abolitionist newspaper during the Civil War. In 1861, their work on behalf of the anti-slavery cause came to the attention of President Lincoln, who invited the Howes to Washington.

While there, she often passed by the soldiers stationed around the Capitol building, many of whom she overheard singing a popular marching song, "John Brown's Body," which had gained widespread fame as a memorial to the firebrand abolitionist who had led a doomed raid on Harper's Ferry, West Virginia, in the hopes of igniting a slave insurrection.

Listening to "John Brown's Body" during that visit, and having witnessed a skirmish between Union and Confederate troops in nearby Virginia, Howe decided she could write better lyrics to the tune than such lines as "John Brown's body lies a-moldering in the grave," so back at her hotel room one night she pulled out her copy of the Book of Isiah and began composing. The result was "The Battle Hymn of the Republic," whose opening line, "Mine eyes have seen the glory of the coming of the Lord," was certainly more poetic than anything in "John Brown's Body."

It was also more inspirational, and after "The Battle Hymn of the Republic" was published in *The Atlantic Monthly* (earning Howe a whopping five dollars), it quickly gained a loyal following, first among civilians in the North and then among the soldiers. According to legend, the hymn moved President Lincoln to tears and it became the unofficial anthem of the Union.

Today, "The Battle Hymn of the Republic" is considered one of America's three anthems, after "The Star Spangled Banner" and "America, the Beautiful." As for Julia Howe, after the Civil War she moved on from civil rights to women's rights, co-founding with Lucy Stone the New England Women's Club, which later became the American Woman Suffrage Association, which later merged with Susan B. Anthony's National Woman Suffrage Association to become the National American Woman Suffrage Association (NAWSA). Among the legacies of NAWSA is the 19th Amendment, giving women the right to vote.

Howe died in 1910 and in 1998 was inducted into the National Women's Hall of Fame. She was acclaimed as "an advocate … of great causes of human liberty; [and] sincere friend of all that makes for the elevation and enrichment of women."

Including a good patriotic song.

© *Kauffmann 2008*

Bruce's History Lessons:
Birth of a Nation

It is no small feat to direct a movie that makes the American Film Institute's list of the *One Hundred Greatest Movies* of all time and earns you the reputation as the father of cinema. It is also no small feat to direct a movie that makes the National Association for the Advancement of Colored People's (NAACP) list of the worst movies of all time, and earns you the reputation as the inspiration for the rejuvenation of the Ku Klux Klan. Director David Wark "D.W." Griffith did both, and *with the same movie*. Originally titled *The Clansman,* which was later changed to *Birth of a Nation*, the film premiered this week (Feb. 8) in 1915.

From the standpoint of advancing the cinematic craft, *Birth of a Nation* was an artistic triumph and a pioneering technological marvel. With his talented cinematographer Bill Bitzer, D.W. Griffith introduced a variety of unprecedented film techniques, including total-screen close-ups, night photography, fade-ins and outs, cross cutting between scenes to give the impression of simultaneous action, panoramic long shots, moving camera shots and even flashbacks. Griffith also insisted on thorough rehearsals of scenes before shooting, which significantly raised the acting quality.

That said, from a societal and historic standpoint, *Birth of a Nation* was an ugly, racist distortion of the post-Civil War Reconstruction period. Focusing on the plight of two families, one Northern, the other Southern, the film portrays blacks as lazy, morally degenerate and sexually promiscuous, while the Ku Klux Klan is portrayed as the principled defender of Southern life in general and the sanctity of Southern white women in particular. One graphic scene in which an accused black rapist is castrated was so offensive — all the more so because it was not unheard of in the real South of 1915 — Griffith agreed to edit it out of later versions of the film.

Even so, the NAACP and other protest groups managed to have the film banned in several states, while riots broke out in many places where it was shown. Never in American history had a film so polarized the public, especially since, despite its suppression, it set box office records and remains today among the most profitable films ever made.

It also remains among the most controversial. Many historians believe that the renewed popularity of the Ku Klux Klan, whose membership had faded before 1915, but from that year until 1925 swelled to more than 3 million, was in part a legacy of *Birth of a Nation's* heroic portrayal of this anti-black, anti-Catholic, anti-Semitic and anti-immigrant hate group.

In sum, D.W. Griffith raised cinema, and racial stereotyping, to an art form. That is no small feat — and one very mean feat.

© Kauffmann 2008

Bruce's History Lessons:
Tragedy in the Sky

That death is always looking over their shoulder is well understood by those brave men and women who have the honor to be called astronauts, and the crew of the Columbia was no exception. Which calls to mind our most historic space flight, the 1969 Apollo 11 mission to the moon. If space travel is still fraught with risk in 2003 — more than 30 years of technological advancements since Apollo 11 astronauts Neil Armstrong and Edwin Aldrin first stepped on our moon — imagine the sense of danger back in the late 1960s when America's space program was still in its infancy.

That is why, a few weeks before Apollo 11 was scheduled, astronaut Frank Borman suggested to presidential speechwriter (later *New York Times* columnist) William Safire that the Nixon administration be prepared for a possible Apollo 11 tragedy, especially if — as was very conceivable — the lunar module that put Armstrong and Aldrin on the moon was unable to bring them back to the Apollo 11 spacecraft. This meant they would be stranded for eternity and they would either die a slow, horrible death, or commit suicide to spare themselves and their families that gruesome ordeal.

Safire agreed and drafted the following remarks, which, thank goodness, President Nixon never had to deliver. But as you will read, Safire's words can still serve as a memorial and a testament to the courageous crew of the *Columbia*:

Fate has ordained that the men who went to the moon to explore in peace will stay on the moon to rest in peace. These brave men, Neil Armstrong and Edwin Aldrin, know that there is no hope of their recovery. But they also know that there is hope for mankind in their sacrifice.

These men are laying down their lives in mankind's most noble goal: the search for truth and understanding. They will be mourned by families and friends; they will be mourned by their nation and the people of the world; they will be mourned by a Mother Earth that dared send two of her sons into the unknown.

In their exploration, they stirred the people of the world to feel as one; in their sacrifice they bind more tightly the brotherhood of man.

In ancient days men looked at the stars and saw their heroes in the constellations. In modern times we do much the same, but our heroes are epic men of flesh and blood.

Others will follow, and surely find their way home. Man's search will not be denied. But those men were the first and they will remain foremost in our hearts.

For every human being who looks up at the moon in the nights to come will know that there is some corner of another world that is forever mankind.

Amen.

© *Kauffmann 2008*

Bruce's History Lessons:
The Accidental Planet

"Everything existing in the universe is the fruit of chance and necessity."
                                                                    -Democritus

In 1905, one of America's greatest astronomers, Percival Lowell, concluded that there were not — as was then believed — eight planets in our solar system, but nine, although he couldn't determine where the ninth one was.

Lowell came to this conclusion after discovering that the orbits of the seventh and eighth planets, Uranus and Neptune, were "perturbed" by a mysterious force — a force Lowell believed was the gravitational pull of this unseen "ninth" planet. Thus Lowell figured that if he could calculate "Plant X's" approximate location, he would eventually discover it with a telescope. He never did and Lowell died without proving his theory.

Fast-forward to this week (Feb. 18) in 1930, where an astronomer named Clyde Tombaugh is sitting in an observatory named after Percival Lowell himself. Tombaugh is looking through a telescope that shows photographs of identical fields of stars taken weeks apart, when suddenly he notices that a faint speck has jumped between the stars, which only a moving planet would do. Eureka! Planet X! Just as Lowell predicted!

Amid much fanfare, the existence of this ninth planet was announced and a quest for a proper name was conducted. While many of Lowell's followers wanted it named after him, traditionally planets were named after mythological gods, so eventually Pluto, the Roman god of the underworld, was chosen, both because — at about 360 degrees below Fahrenheit — the planet would make any underworld proud, and because the planet's initials would be PL, the same as Percival Lowell's.

It was a feel-good end to a story about dogged determination, justification and a connection between two generations of astronomers. And it was completely wrong. For one thing, it was later discovered that Pluto's size — it is smaller than our moon — could not create a gravitational pull strong enough to affect the orbits of Uranus or Neptune. For another, a later visit by the spacecraft Voyager 2 determined that there really was no real discrepancy in the orbits of either planet. In other words, there never was a Planet X.

This makes the discovery of Pluto one of those happy accidents that sometimes occur in science, even though, given its size and origins, there has been a move afoot to "downgrade" Pluto from planet to asteroid.* Which would be unfair. After all, Pluto orbits the sun and its gravity pulls it into a spherical shape — generally the two criteria for a planet.

Pluto's mysteries — it is the only planet never to have been visited by one of our spacecraft — may reveal themselves in 2006 if a planned mission to Pluto, "New Horizons," is funded. Given NASA's current problems, however, that is a very big "if."

© *Kauffmann 2008*

*In 2006, after the term "planet" was defined for the first time, Pluto was reclassified as a member of the new category of dwarf— or minor — planets. Boo.

Bruce's History Lessons:
The Birth of the Republican Party

According to polls, on many economic and social issues there is a deep chasm between the positions taken by today's Republican Party and those favored by America's black population. The Bush Administration's recent opposition to the University of Michigan's admissions practices, in which preferences are awarded to black and Hispanic applicants, is only the latest example. Small wonder the current ratio of black Democrats to black Republicans is about 9 to 1.

I bring this up because, coincidentally, this week (Feb 28) in 1854, in the town of Ripon, Wisconsin, the Republican Party was founded by former members of the Whig, Free Soil and No-Nothing parties. This new Republican Party's organizing principle was ... opposition to the expansion of slavery!

Their first presidential candidate, John C. Fremont, was such an abolitionist that he scared mainstream voters ("mainstream" then meant tolerance of slavery), and he and his fledgling Republican Party were trounced in the general election by the Democratic Party and their presidential candidate, James Buchanan.

By 1860, however, thousands of former Whigs had flocked to the Republican Party, angered at both the Kansas-Nebraska Act, which threatened to extend slavery into the Western territories, and the Supreme Court decision on the former slave Dred Scott, which not only returned Scott to slavery, but also said that owning slaves was Constitutionally permitted. Among those former Whigs aghast at these events was a young lawyer and sometime politician named Abe Lincoln, who, by winning the 1860 presidential election, became the first president of the modern Republican Party.

For their part, southern Democratic politicians, infuriated at Lincoln's election and terrified that slavery (upon which much of the southern economy depended) was threatened, led their respective states into secession, resulting in the Civil War.

It would last four bloody years, but when it was over, and the North had won, the then dominant Republican Congress promptly passed laws ensuring the freedom and legal equality of black Americans. The 13th Amendment, outlawing slavery, passed in 1865. The 14th Amendment, with its clause extending "equal protection" to all Americans, passed in 1866. The 15th Amendment, which extended voting rights "regardless of race, color, or previous condition of servitude," passed in 1869. In almost every instance, Republicans were opposed by southern Democrats and the bitter hatred that the South felt toward Republicans ensured that the Democratic Party would control southern politics for the next 100 years.

As we celebrate Black History Month this year, my how things have changed. A party born to free black Americans and extend to them the blessings of citizenship is now seen as insensitive to their aspirations. A party that fought a Civil War to keep them in servitude now considers them its most loyal followers.

© *Kauffmann 2008*

Bruce's History Lessons:
Reversal of the Republican and
Democratic Party–Part II

Last week in this space I wrote of the historic reversal that has occurred with respect to how African-Americans view the Republican and Democratic parties since the birth of the Republican Party just prior to the Civil War. As I noted, one organizing principle of the Republican Party in the 1860s was *opposition* to the expansion of slavery, while Southern Democrats viewed slavery's spread as the *sine qua non* of their continued existence. Thus, back then, blacks revered Republicans and distrusted Democrats. "My," I wrote last week, "how things have changed."

Actually, my how things have changed with respect to the entire philosophy of the two parties. Today, Democrats are considered the party of activist, nationalist government, while the Republicans are considered the party of minimalist national government, preferring to devolve governing power back to the states. Yet, as with African-American relations, this was an exact reversal of the 1860s when Republicans were the activists and Democrats were the state's rights minimalists.

Partly this was because the Republican Party rose out of the ashes of the old Whig Party and therefore inherited the Whig fixation with using government power to promote "internal improvements" — meaning improving roads, building canals, expanding railroads, encouraging industry, and any other means of enhancing America's ability to modernize by moving information, goods and people across the country.

What's more, Republicans controlled the federal government immediately after the Civil War, a war that added about 50,000 people to the federal bureaucracy. Any post-war national initiatives — Reconstruction being the most prominent — would by necessity be the federal government's job and it would need added resources and power to complete it.

Also, at least in the Republican North, the Civil War had spurred massive post-war industrial growth, whether it was those railroads that now began to stretch across the continent thanks to Republican land grants and bond issues, or the various types of machinery being installed in new factories, which — thanks to Republican protective tariffs and a Republican-controlled banking system that lent money to entrepreneurs seeking capital to start new businesses — were springing up all over the northern United States.

In contrast, the South, being more agrarian, traditional and insular, was both resistant to change and felt threatened by the growing role the federal government was playing in America's daily life. Southern Democrats clung to the old political arrangements in which state and local governments held sway.

Which makes it amusing to hear Republicans complain today about the evils of "big government," and equally amusing to hear Democrats long for the "good old days" of federal government activism. My how things have changed, which sometimes can be amusing, but should never be surprising. Change is history's one constant.

© Kauffmann 2008

Bruce's History Lessons:
FDR's Fireside Chats

Regular readers will learn, if they don't already know, of my admiration for the communication skills of British Prime Minister Winston Churchill, whose war speeches from 1940 until 1944 enthralled the world and helped ensure Allied victory in WWII. Some people listen to music on long road trips. I listen to BBC recordings of those speeches.

But (to borrow from Churchill) we should not give "short shrift" to the communication skills of our own leader during that period of our history. President Franklin Delano Roosevelt was also a man of uncommon rhetorical gifts, and he used them to great effect during both the war and the Great Depression that preceded it. And chief among his rhetorical "tools" was what the journalist Robert Trout dubbed FDR's "fireside chats." Roosevelt gave the first of those "chats" this week (March 12) in 1933.

They were actually radio broadcasts, but FDR's down-to-earth, almost avuncular delivery style made it seem as if the president and his listeners were all sitting around a warm fire, calmly discussing the great challenges that America faced. This was all the more so because, the medium being radio and the family fireplace being a common evening gathering spot for Americans in 1933, it was an image easily evoked.

The first "fireside chat" dealt with the banking crisis. Because millions of panicked Americans had attempted to withdraw their savings from the nation's banks, and because most banks were then on shaky financial ground due to their investments in businesses and industries that were failing by the thousands, the government had been forced to close the banks for more than a week — spreading even more panic and chaos. Thus, in his address on March 12, Roosevelt calmly — but without a hint of condescension — explained how the banking system worked and told his listeners that

225

the banks would re-open the next day. Roosevelt also announced that in the future the federal government would guarantee most bank deposits.

The "chat" was a resounding success both politically and in terms of stemming the financial crisis. When the banks opened the next day very few bank runs occurred, and all were handled to the satisfaction of the depositors. FDR had not ended the Depression, but he had taken the first steps toward changing America's mind-set.

Roosevelt would go on to give a total of 30 "fireside chats" — averaging in length about 25 minutes — on everything from the state of the economy to the progress of the war. His last "chat," given in June of 1944, urged Americans to "Swell the mighty chorus to bring us closer to victory!" How? By buying War Bonds.

Yes, back then Roosevelt (and Churchill) actually talked that way. And their people loved it.

© *Kauffmann 2008*

Bruce's History Lesson:
King James the First (non-smoker)

This week (March 24) in 1603, James I, the son of Mary Queen of Scots, became King of England, succeeding the great Elizabeth I, who had died hours earlier after the longest and most successful reign in England's glorious history.

Although a Protestant, James was married to a Catholic wife, Anne, which may explain why, prior to his ascension to the throne, he had hinted that he might allow more religious tolerance than had most of his predecessors, who — with the notable exception of "Bloody Mary" Tudor — had persecuted Catholics unmercifully. (Appalled at this, Bloody Mary had persecuted *Protestants* unmercifully, hence earning the sobriquet "Bloody.")

Unfortunately, foreshadowing modern politics, James went back on this promise to be more tolerant of Catholicism, which set in motion a plot by a group of angered Catholic fanatics who intended to blow him and Parliament to smithereens. Called the Gunpowder Plot, it was supposed to occur on November 5, 1605, but it was foiled when one of the plotters, Guy Fawkes, was discovered and arrested just before he could light several kegs of gunpowder that had been placed in the basement of a building next door to Parliament. Ever since, England has celebrated Guy Fawkes Day with bonfires and general revelry (and you thought the Brits had no sense of humor).

Yet if James I is known mainly for being the target of this plot (and for commissioning the King James Bible), he has one other claim to fame, which, I suppose, has not been better advertised due to the strenuous efforts of our still-powerful tobacco lobby.

It seems that during the trial of the Gunpowder Plot members, James — who secretly attended the trial — was angered that the condemned men were smoking tobacco so prodigiously, especially since he, James, had emphatically condemned the use of tobacco in a pamphlet he had recently written titled "Counterblast to Tobacco." In this pamphlet, James called tobacco "a custom loathsome to the eye, hateful to the nose, harmful to the brain, and dangerous to the lungs."

Let's see now ... more than 400 years ago, James I recognized that tobacco was un-cool (loathsome to the eye), gave you bad breath (hateful to the nose), was addictive (harmful to the brain) and caused cancer (dangerous to the lungs). It would be another 350 years before the American Medical Association got around to that conclusion and to this day the tobacco lobby still hasn't figured it out.

So three cheers for James I, the first English monarch to understand the harmful effects of smoking. Alas, his lecture was wasted on the accused in the Gunpowder Plot, who had more pressing health concerns. Trial or no trial, they were headed for the gallows and they knew it.

© *Kauffmann 2008*

Bruce's History Lesson:
The Equal Rights Amendment

This week (March 22) in 1972, Congress passed a Constitutional amendment that had been introduced in every new Congressional session since 1923. Finally, the Equal Rights Amendment (ERA) — which stated that "Equality of rights under the law shall not be denied or abridged by the United States or by any state on account of sex." — would go to the states for ratification.

By law, ratification by three-fourths of the states — a total of 38 — was needed, and by custom Congress placed a seven-year deadline on the ratification process, something that hardly looked like an obstacle after 22 of the required 38 states ratified the amendment in the first year. But soon opposition mounted, led by, ironically, a woman, Phyllis Schlafly, whose Eagle Forum claimed that the amendment would harm women more than help them. Schlafly and conservative allies argued that, among other things, the ERA would erode the workplace laws that protected women from having to perform physical tasks as demanding and dangerous as those performed by men — an argument that resonated among many members of labor unions. Anti-ERA forces also argued that the amendment would threaten alimony in contested divorces, overturn privacy rights, put women in combat and legally sanction homosexual marriages. They also opposed the ERA as yet another federal power grab.

As a result, as 1979 — the seven-year deadline — approached, only 13 more states had ratified the ERA, which was three short of the necessary 38. Feminist groups such as the National Organization for Women (NOW) then appealed to Congress for an extension of the deadline, which Congress approved, making the new deadline June 30, 1982.

And then along came Ronald Reagan and the rise of a conservative backlash against liberalism, feminism and what was perceived to be a decade-long period of left-wing social engineering run amok. The ERA was doomed. When the 1982 deadline passed, the amendment was still three states short of ratification and both Congress and the nation turned to other matters.

But there is a postscript. Since 1982, the amendment has again been re-introduced in every new Congress, and a movement is afoot to use — of all things — the "Madison Amendment" to remove any deadline to ratification and make legally binding the approval of the original 35 states that ratified it between 1972 and 1982.

And what is the "Madison Amendment" you ask? It is the amendment (my hero) James Madison originally proposed, and Congress passed, in 1789, dealing with Congressional pay raises. The states declined to ratify it in 1789, but did so in 1992. ERA proponents argue that if what is now our 27th Amendment can be ratified 203 years after Congress approved it, then there is hope yet for the ERA.

© Kauffmann 2008

Bruce's History Lessons:
The Pony Express

On this day (April 3) in 1860 a young man named Henry Wallace mounted his horse in St. Joseph, Missouri, and headed west toward Sacramento, California. At the same time in Sacramento, John Roff mounted his horse and headed for St. Joseph. Both men carried packages containing mail, newspapers and other material, which it was hoped would arrive at each destination within 10 days. The package that Wallace had started out with arrived in Sacramento in exactly that time — Roff's package just hours later. The Pony Express was born.

It would not live long. It was unprofitable and would soon give way to better "technology" — the telegraph and the railroad. But in America's imagination, it lasts to this day as a legendary symbol of America's pioneer and entrepreneurial spirit.

It was created because, for America's merchants and bankers on both coasts, travel by carriage was too slow — taking up to three weeks to cross the continent. As a result, three businessmen, William Russell, Alexander Majors and William Waddell, saw a market opportunity in a speedier delivery system in which relay teams of fresh riders and horses, strung out across the continent, could deliver goods and information in a much shorter time. The partners purchased 600 broncos, chosen for their fleetness and endurance, and hired 80 young men (none over 120 pounds) whose horsemanship, bravery and knowledge of the country and its various Indian tribes was unparalleled.

The Pony Express was an instant hit, and tales of the riders' bravery and endurance soon spread nationwide, helping to make several riders famous, including Wild Bill Hickok and Buffalo Bill Cody. Legend has it that Buffalo Bill, having ridden his allotted 85 miles to the next relay station, found that his relief had been killed, so he re-mounted and rode another 85 miles.

Finding no relief at the end of the line, he turned around and rode back two more legs of the return trip — at total of 340 miles in one day. Other riders faced similar endurance challenges, and many were attacked by Indians, yet during its entire existence the Pony Express lost only one delivery.

Alas, the company lost lots of money, and when — in October of 1861 — a trans-continental telegraph line was finally completed, information suddenly took minutes, not days, to deliver. The Pony Express was dead.

But, interestingly, it may have given the nation new life because for a brief but critical period the Pony Express was the fastest and most reliable means of communication between the East and West — especially California. Thus some historians credit the Pony Express with helping to ensure that the western states and territories remained pro-Union leading up to, and during, the Civil War.

© Kauffmann 2008

Bruce's History Lessons:
Old Soldiers Never Die.
They Just Get Sacked.

This week (April 11) in 1951, in the midst of the Korean War, President Harry Truman fired for insubordination the general in charge of U.S. forces in Korea, Douglas MacArthur.

At the time, Truman's job approval was at a record low, while MacArthur was the darling of the American public and a demigod to most members of Congress. As a result, after the firing, many in Congress called for Truman's impeachment, and mail to the White House overwhelmingly supported MacArthur. He was, after all, the man who had helped win World War II, and his brilliant generalship in Korea, including a daring invasion of the port city of Inchon, had turned the tide of that war, rallied our South Korean allies and driven the North Korean invaders back across their half of the Korean peninsula, from which they had launched the attack (in 1950) that began the war.

What the American public did not know, however, was that in MacArthur's frenzy to pursue the North Koreans as they retreated further North towards China, he ignored the president's and the Joint Chiefs of Staff's repeated orders not to encroach on the Yalu River, which bordered China, for fear of provoking the Chinese and causing them to enter the war on North Korea's side. And when the Chinese did just that in response to MacArthur's nearing the Yalu, the tide of the Korean War turned again. MacArthur's army was now badly outnumbered and faced annihilation. Having earlier predicted "certain victory," MacArthur now called for the use of atomic weapons to bail out his army. When Truman refused that demand, MacArthur began publicly questioning Truman's judgment. That was the last straw and Truman, supported by the Joint Chiefs, fired MacArthur.

Although Truman then gave a nationwide address explaining why he sacked the general, MacArthur, as he put it, "had the last word" by giving an emotional farewell speech to a joint session of Congress and a nationwide radio and television audience. Reminiscing on his entire career of military service, MacArthur ended his remarks with a now-famous line from an old army ballad — "Old soldiers, never die, they just fade away."

Which, to his complete astonishment, MacArthur actually did. Fully intending to run for president on the strength of his popularity, MacArthur's quest was derailed first by later press accounts that detailed his defiance of Truman's orders, and second by his own inability to articulate a political agenda that resonated with the American people. After 1952, MacArthur faded from the spotlight, and while Truman also quickly left public life, there is no question which of these two men has been treated better by History.

And History, as we know, always gets "the last word."

© *Kauffmann 2008*

Bruce's History Lessons:
The Death of Lincoln

"I think we are near the end at last," Abe Lincoln told William Seward, his secretary of state, in early April of 1865.

He was referring to the Civil War. Confederate General Robert E. Lee had just surrendered to Ulysses S. Grant, ensuring that America's bloodiest and costliest conflict would end in victory for the Union forces under Lincoln's command.

Alas, little did Lincoln know that his own end also was near. It came this week (April 15) in 1865 at the hand of assassin John Wilkes Booth during a show at Ford's Theatre in Washington, D.C.

But, amazingly, Lincoln did have a foreboding of how his life would end. In what would have made a riveting Shakespearean tragedy, a few weeks prior to his death Lincoln had a dream so haunting that he finally shared it with his wife Mary and members of the White House staff. In the dream, which was undoubtedly the result of Lincoln's recurring fitful sleep (itself the result of the terrible burdens of his office), Lincoln found himself wandering the corridors of the White House searching for the origin of a terrible sound, the sound of people wailing. "I went from room to room," he told Mary and the others, "No living person was in sight, but the same mournful sounds of distress met me as I passed along."

Finding himself "puzzled and distressed" at this mystery, Lincoln wandered into the East Room, where — as he told his listeners — "I was met with a sickening surprise." A corpse wrapped in funeral clothing was in the center of the room, with soldiers stationed around it. "Who is dead in the White House?" Lincoln had cried in the dream, only to be told, "The President. He was killed by an assassin!"

When Mary and the others expressed their horror at the dream, Lincoln, realizing how much he had scared his listeners, tried to make light of it, but his attempts at humor fell flat. Finally, he passed it off by telling the gathering, "Well, let it go. I think the Lord in His own good time and way will work this out all right."

If so, then Lincoln was right when he had said in his Second Inaugural Address of a month earlier, "The Almighty has His own purposes." Lincoln's untimely death made a Southern slave owner and sympathizer, Andrew Johnson, president, which changed forever the course of post-war Reconstruction and precipitated a Constitutional crisis so grave that it resulted in Johnson's impeachment, the first ever impeachment of an American president. In the ensuing Senate trial, Johnson escaped being found guilty by one vote.

Prophecy, perfidy, death and dissension. Shakespeare would have been impressed.

© *Kauffmann 2008*

Bruce's History Lessons:
Earth Day!

This week (April 22) in 1970 about 20 million people across the United States first celebrated Earth Day by holding rallies, parties, picnics, demonstrations and other gatherings that were, in various degrees, a mixture of politics, social consciousness, general revelry and — the original goal — grassroots environmentalism. Today Earth Day is celebrated in about 140 countries, making it an unqualified success, although success on behalf of what is still being debated.

If anyone deserves credit for creating Earth Day it is probably Gaylord Nelson, the environmentally conscious senator from Wisconsin who, in 1969, proposed a national educational awareness campaign on the growing crisis of the environment. Nelson hoped to merge the new proactive environmental movement — mostly populated by "back to nature" young adults — with his political goal of passing laws that would protect the nation's natural resources. From this idea Earth Day was born, although as Nelson conceded, no government or even civic entity ever took charge of coordinating Earth Day on a nationwide basis. "It took on a life of its own," he said.

As a result, the original message — the importance of protecting Mother Earth's natural resources or suffer the life-threatening ecological consequences — was diffused as different groups, with different agendas, in different parts of the country, celebrated Earth Day in their own way. In Hoboken, New Jersey, Earth Day participants threw a casket into the Hudson River with the names of the nation's polluted waterways "buried" inside. At Indiana University, Zero Population Growth advocates (and not a few feminists) threw birth control pills into the crowd as a reminder that unmanaged population growth could overwhelm Earth's resources. In Washington, D.C. (where I was on April 22), an "Earth Day" rally stretching from the Capitol to the Washington Monument was marred somewhat by the fact that the mountains of trash left behind took clean-up crews the better part of two days to collect and dispose of.

Which is not to say that Earth Day hasn't had a positive effect on the environment. It has contributed to the passage of laws such as the Clean Air Act, the Clean Water Act, and the Endangered Species Act. What's more, Earth Day is an annual reminder that being better stewards of our environment is in everyone's interest.

But to put things in perspective, I borrow from author Michael Crichton, who wrote in his novel *Jurassic Park* that the whole idea of "protecting Earth" is somewhat mislabeled. As one of his characters points out, Earth hardly needs protection since it will still be around even if, due to our own folly, human life becomes unsustainable. His point is clear: Earth Day isn't about protecting Earth from us. It's about protecting us from us.

© Kauffmann 2008

Bruce History Lesson: Washington's First Inaugural Address

George Washington gave his first Inaugural Address this week (April 30) in 1789, and it is a little known fact that (my hero) James Madison wrote the address.

But let me digress for a moment. Having worked as a speechwriter for 15 years, my interest in Madison was piqued by the fact that he had the best speechwriter's job in history. For one thing, as Washington's top speechwriter, Madison penned most of the president's speeches to Congress, including the first Inaugural Address. But Madison was also the leader of the House of Representatives (then more important than the Senate), so he wrote all of the congressional *replies* to the presidential addresses. As historian William Lee Miller has written, Madison was like E.B. White's two-headed lamb, "who could sing in two-part harmony and cross-question herself for hours."

This arrangement worked particularly well for Madison in April of 1789 because he wanted Washington to deliver a specific message in his first address to Congress and the country. He wanted the president to remind Congress that it had the power to further amend the Constitution if the people deemed it necessary. Having been in the thick of the battle to get the Constitution ratified in the first place, Madison knew that many of "the people" had only approved the Constitution on the promise that amendments spelling out a number of their specific rights would be added later.

What's more, Madison realized that, as times change, so must governments, something the amendment process would always make possible. But he also wanted the Constitution to have a durability that would allow it to weave itself into the fabric of America's life. So he and his fellow Founding

Fathers gave the Constitution an amendment process that struck the perfect balance between adaptability and permanence. It is *possible* to amend the Constitution, but it isn't — nor should it be — easy.

In any event, here is William Lee Miller's lovely description of Madison's role in Washington's inaugural message to Congress regarding amendments. It comes from Miller's wonderful book on Madison, *The Business of May Next.*

"And what did Madison say in this exalted indirect conversation with himself 200 years ago? President Washington's Madison-drafted address suggested that Congress might want to exercise the power delegated by the Fifth Article of the Constitution — the power to propose amendments to the Constitution. The House's Madison-drafted response to the Madison-drafted presidential address said, yes, we just might do that. President Washington's very short Madison-drafted response to the House's Madison-drafted response to the president's Madison-drafted address did not disagree."

All this "agreement" in part accounts for the 27 amendments (the first 10 being our Bill of Rights) added to our Constitution since 1789.

© *Kauffmann 2008*

Bruce's History Lessons:
The 2nd Continental Congress

Sometimes it's not where you stand, but where (and when) you sit.

Imagine that it is mid-April of 1775 and you have just been elected to the Second Continental Congress of America, representing your colony — not yet state — in what is not yet the United States but still a part of the British Empire. As you head for Philadelphia, where this Second Continental Congress is convening, you are keenly aware of the growing tensions between the 13 American colonies and the British government, which has attempted to usurp certain rights that you and your fellow colonists have always reserved for yourselves, including the right of self-taxation. But you also are aware that while there has been *talk* of revolution and independence, so far it has only been talk. Most of the more moderate colonial leaders, probably including you, believe that eventually things will smooth over.

And then, at some point during your journey to Philadelphia, you learn that there has been a skirmish between colonial "Minutemen" and a contingent of British troops at Lexington and Concord, Massachusetts, and that men on both sides have died.

So by the time you take your seat in this Second Continental Congress as it convenes this week (May 10) in 1775, you have no idea whether it will resemble the First Continental Congress — in which the delegates mostly made resolutions, discussed issues, gave speeches, took votes, passed proclamations, and then went home — or whether it will be something very different.

It will be something very different thanks to the shedding of American blood at Lexington and Concord. Indeed, by May 11, this Second Continental Congress has become, much to the surprise and chagrin of you and your fellow delegates, the *de facto* government of a nation-in-the-making that is about to go to war with the most powerful military force in the world.

Talk about your historic bait-and-switch. Believing you were going to Philadelphia to join a debating society, you find that you are now being called upon to actually govern a country! First, you must raise an army and appoint a military commander. Next, you must develop a position paper justifying to the world your decision to break with Great Britain. After that you must figure out how to finance the war. Then you must seek diplomatic recognition of your independence from the other European states. And finally you must pass binding resolutions — you have no authority to pass laws — unifying the 13 colonies and rallying them to win the war.

Miraculously, you are successful, but unlike today's politicians, the job done and your time in Congress served, you quit, go home and never once think about running for re-election.

Not surprising, all things considered.

© Kauffmann 2008

Bruce's History Lessons:
Blood, Sweat and Tears

When he became British prime minister — over the objections of many members of Parliament and the deep misgivings of his king — Winston Churchill knew that he had his work cut out for him, as evidenced by his first address to the House of Commons, which he gave this week (May 13) in 1940. At the time of his speech, the armies of France, Belgium and the Netherlands were being attacked by an unprecedented combination of German air power and highly mobile mechanized armored forces. A sense of panic and impending doom had begun to spread throughout those three nations, and Britain, whose British Expeditionary Force also was fighting in France, was itself in a state of high anxiety.

Understanding this, Churchill used the last section of his speech to outline a bold, if unspecific, plan for British resistance to the German military juggernaut that Adolf Hitler, Germany's ruthless leader, had so painstakingly (and illegally) built.

"You ask, 'What is our policy?'" Churchill began. "I will say: it is to wage war by sea, land and air with all our might and all the strength that God can give us. To wage war against a monstrous tyranny never surpassed in the dark and lamentable catalogue of human crime. That is our policy."

He continued. "You ask, 'What is our aim?' Sir, I can answer in one word. Victory! Victory at all costs! Victory in spite of all terror! Victory however long and hard the road may be!"

He reflected somberly on the stark alternative. "For without victory there is no survival." He paused — the only long pause in his speech. "Let … that … be … realized. No survival for the British Empire! No survival for all that

243

the British Empire has stood for! No survival for the urge and impulse of the ages, that mankind will move forward toward its goal."

Having let that sink in he engineered a calculated mood swing. "But I take up my task with buoyancy and hope!" he exclaimed. "I feel sure that our cause will not be suffered to fail among men. At this time I feel entitled to claim the aid of all and I say, 'Come! Then! Let us go forward together with our united strength!'"

Which the people of Britain then proceeded to do, and — as we all know — victory over the "monstrous tyranny" that was Nazi Germany eventually was achieved.

Interestingly, earlier in this same speech Churchill uttered what became perhaps his most famous line when he listed the following as his qualifications for the office of prime minister: "I have nothing to offer but blood, toil, tears and sweat!"

That was, of course, a bit disingenuous. He failed to mention courageous leadership and inspirational rhetoric.

© Kauffmann 2008

Bruce's History Lessons:
Bonnie and Clyde

When Bonnie Parker met Clyde Barrow in 1930 they were both dirt-poor Texans with no future. She was 19 years old and was tending bar because her then-husband was in jail. He was 20, with a hard face and harder eyes. He had been in trouble with the law since he was 15. They were, like so many others in the era of the Great Depression, aimless and angry at the cards they had been dealt.

So they decided to re-shuffle the deck. Beginning in 1932, after Bonnie helped spring Clyde from a Texas jail, they went on a crime spree that spanned five states and included robbing gas stations, restaurants, grocery stores and banks. It also included killing a dozen people, nine of them law enforcement officers.

But their crime spree captured the imagination of the public, especially the poor, who lived vicariously through the adventures of Bonnie and Clyde. The two always seemed to stay one step ahead of the law, sometimes escaping seconds before the police arrived. And on those occasions when the law did catch up to them, they escaped by shooting their way out, leaving dead and wounded in their wake.

As a result, much of America saw them as modern-day Robin Hoods, striking back at a capitalist system that had left the average Joe behind, and a heartless government that seemed to spend most of its time foreclosing on people's homes, farms and businesses. Pictures of Bonnie and Clyde posing in front of their famous V-8 Ford, guns in hand and puffing cigars, were splashed across newspapers nationwide.

As their fame grew, their capture became a government priority, and by 1933 even the Bureau of Investigation (later the FBI) was after them. But it was Texas Ranger Frank Hamer who, in May of 1934, received a tip that the Bonnie and Clyde gang was holed up near Gibsland, Louisiana. Hamer, accompanied by four other officers, set up an ambush on the main road near the hideout and waited. This week (May 23) at about 9 a.m. the officers saw an approaching car, and when they identified the passengers as Bonnie and Clyde, they began firing their weapons. Some two minutes and hundreds of rounds of ammo later, Hamer opened the car door where Bonnie and Clyde lay very, very dead. Fifty rounds had entered each of their bodies.

Bonnie and Clyde were buried in separate cemeteries in Texas. Frank Hamer became a celebrity in his own right and was honored on the floor of Congress. The bullet-riddled V-8 Ford made the rounds at state fairs where, for a quarter, anyone could have a look. It was both lucrative and — too late to do Bonnie and Clyde any good — perfectly legal.

© Kauffmann 2008

Bruce's History Lessons: Madison, Democracy, a Republic and Iraq

"The merit of our Constitution was, not that it promotes democracy, but checks it."

— Horatio Seymour

Begging the reader's forgiveness for again turning to (my hero) James Madison as the topic for a column, I nevertheless thought it would be an instructive lesson to apply Madison's thoughts on government to the situation now facing America and Iraq.

This is prompted by calls for a "Democratic Iraq" to rise from the ashes of Saddam Hussein's dictatorship. The truth is, as Madison recognized in 1787 when he presented his plan for our new government at the Constitutional Convention, a "democratic" government in which the majority rules would be almost as bad for Iraq as its past dictatorship in which a minority (of one) ruled.

Recall that in the 1780s, America was governed by the Articles of Confederation, which, being a pure "democracy," and giving most powers to the individual states, had no federal safeguards against majority rule. As a result, majorities could use their superior numbers to pass any laws they pleased, and true to the realities of human nature, most such laws tended to further their own interests, usually at the expense of the minority.

For example, in Rhode Island in the 1780s (as in most places) there were more debtors than creditors, so it was common practice for this debtor "majority" to pass laws that devalued the worth of their debts, or in some cases made those debts disappear. This was certainly in the interest of the debtors, but not the creditors and, in the long term, not the country. The

Founding Fathers called this "tyranny of the majority." A less genteel phrase would be "mob rule."

This is why Madison worked to create a republican government with enough power to check the excesses of pure democracy. For one thing, "the people" do not decide the issues in a republic, they decide *who* will decide the issues by voting for elected representatives of (it is hoped) sound judgment and experience. That is one check against the potential tyranny of "majority rule."

Another is the Bill of Rights, which spells out certain rights that can't be violated regardless of what a majority says in the voting booth. And a third is the independent judiciary, which can overturn a majority decision simply by finding it unconstitutional.

Food for thought in Iraq, where establishing a pure democracy would undoubtedly result in the overwhelming election of Shi'ite clerics. After all, Shi'ites compose the majority — about 60 percent — of the Iraqi population.

Now imagine "democratically" putting Shi'ite clerics in power before establishing the legal safeguards mentioned above. If you think the result will be a government that represents all of the Iraqi people, then you have not been watching the evening news lately — or reading the front page of this newspaper.

© *Kauffmann 2008*

Bruce's History Lessons:
The Israeli Osirak Attack

This week (June 7) in 1981, eight Israeli pilots flying U.S.-made F-15 and F-16 fighter jets, departed Israel's Etzion airfield and flew 650 miles to a location near Baghdad, Iraq, where Iraqi leader Saddam Hussein had built a French-designed, Osirak-type nuclear reactor that Israel feared would soon produce nuclear weapons. Facing no Iraqi resistance — the attack was a total surprise — the Israelis destroyed the Osirak reactor and returned safely to Israel.

And *then* the explosion occurred. In Europe, in the Soviet Union, and particularly in the Arab world, Israel was denounced as an international outlaw and warmonger, and even the United States joined the other members of the United Nations Security Council in a unanimous resolution that "strongly condemned" Israel's actions. Many critics also claimed Israel had violated the U.S. Arms Control Export Act, which prohibited foreign nations from using American-made military equipment "except in self defense."

But to Israel, bombing Osirak *was* an act of self-defense. Having spent years watching Saddam Hussein relentlessly build up his military arsenal, including medium-range missiles that could reach Israel, the tiny Jewish state felt it could not allow Saddam Hussein to "go nuclear," and it was clear to Israel that Osirak would have a nuclear weapons capability within two to five years. Prime Minister Menachem Begin made what he called his "most difficult decision" to destroy Osirak because he feared he might not be in office when Osirak finally went on-line, and he wasn't sure the more dovish Israeli Labor Party would have the fortitude to destroy Osirak once it had crossed the nuclear threshold. A survivor of the Holocaust, Begin had made a solemn vow that Israel would never be threatened by a holocaust again — nuclear or otherwise.

Fast-forward ten years to 1991. Saddam Hussein, who has previously used chemical weapons on Iran and his own people, invades Kuwait and threatens to use the same weapons on both Israel and on American forces rushing into the Middle East to defend Kuwait's neighbor, Saudi Arabia, and eventually force Hussein out of Kuwait. The simple fact that — thanks to Israel — Hussein did not have a nuclear weapons capability radically altered the military balance in that war and allowed the American-led coalition to defeat Iraq without precipitating a nuclear Armageddon.

Lo and behold, condemnation turns to commendation. In October of 1991, then-U.S. Defense Secretary Richard Cheney spoke before the Jewish Institute for National Security Affairs, saying. "Let me tonight, in front of this group, thank my good friend David Ivy (chief of the Israeli Air Force in 1981) for the action Israel took ... There were many times during the (Gulf War) that I gave thanks for the bold and dramatic action taken some ten years before."

© *Kauffmann 2008*

Bruce's History Lessons: Poetic Justice: The Miranda Decision

Shakespeare's admonition that some men have greatness — or at least fame — "thrust upon them" would certainly seem to apply to Ernesto Miranda, a career criminal who in 1963, while in Phoenix, Arizona, was arrested for armed robbery and the rape of an 18-year old retarded girl. After a lengthy police interrogation, Miranda signed a confession to both crimes, and was subsequently found guilty.

In repeated appeals, however, his lawyers argued that Miranda had not known when he confessed that he had a Constitutional right against self-incrimination, and three years later the case *Miranda vs. Arizona* was argued before the Supreme Court. This week (June 13) in 1966, the court's landmark, and controversial, 5-4 decision was handed down.

The court ruled that Miranda's confession was obtained illegally and therefore his conviction was overturned. Noting that the right to refrain from self-incrimination rests in the 5th Amendment, the court said that this "guarantees to the individual the right to remain silent unless he chooses to speak in the unfettered exercise of his own will." Such a choice, the court added, may be made only after he has been informed that it is not compulsory, *and* after he has been informed that he may first consult with an attorney, who may be present during any interrogation.

From all of this "legalese" came what is now famously known as the "Miranda Warning." If you are ever arrested, the arresting officer must first advise you that "You have the right to remain silent. Anything you say can and will be used against you in a court of law. You have the right to speak to an attorney, and to have an attorney present during any questioning." The only exceptions are questions related to establishing your identity, such as your name and date of birth.

Today, of course, the Miranda decision is among the most famous in our history and has probably sparked more debates about civil liberties than any other Supreme Court decision.

Which brings us to the story of Ernesto Miranda himself. Although his original confession was ruled inadmissible and his 1963 conviction was overturned, by 1966 new evidence conclusively linking Miranda to the robbery and rape was found, and he was again convicted in a new trial. Even more interesting, after spending 11 years in jail, Miranda was released on parole, whereupon he promptly got in a barroom brawl and was stabbed to death. A prime suspect was arrested, but after being informed of his Miranda rights, he chose to remain silent and was released. To this day, no one has been charged with Miranda's killing.

Meaning that, in the case of Ernesto Miranda, justice was finally served — as was poetic justice.

© *Kauffmann 2008*

Bruce's History Lessons:
The Greatest Treasure Hunt in U.S.
History

In early 1945, Nazi Germany was a defeated nation. Her borders were overrun by U.S. troops invading from the West and Soviet troops pouring in from the East. Berlin was rubble, as were many German cities. The German army was a pathetic mix of old men and teenagers. World War II was essentially over.

But the post-war world was already on the minds of the Allies, and somewhere in Germany lay the greatest post-war treasure of all — German scientists whose knowledge of rocketry was so advanced that they had developed the infamous "V-2" rockets that had rained terror and mayhem on London from their launch site at a place called Peenemunde on the German Baltic coast. American military leaders were well aware of these elite German scientists, as were the Soviets, and both armies wanted very badly to find them. The knowledge they would impart to whoever captured them would be invaluable.

And so the "treasure hunt" was on, with U.S. and Soviet troops scouring Peenemunde and nearby areas in search of these rocket scientists, who, for their part, were trying to decide what to do next. They knew Germany had lost the war, but they were convinced that their research had unlimited potential for intercontinental and even space travel, and they wanted to ally themselves with whichever nation would best support their work.

After some discussion, these scientists made their decision. "We despise the French, we are terrified of the Soviets, we don't believe the British can afford us, so that leaves the Americans," was one scientist's apt description of their choice. And so, while the Americans and Soviets searched for them, they began searching for Americans to surrender to. Eventually they succeeded, and soon Germany's most accomplished rocket scientists, including the great Wernher von Braun, were safely in America. Operation Paperclip, as the capture of these scientists was called, was finally concluded this week (June 20) in 1945.

Talk about the "spoils of war." Overnight, America, which had lagged far behind both Germany and the Soviet Union in rocket development, became the leader in this new scientific field — a field that everyone knew would shape both the military and civilian worlds of the future. Sure enough, put in charge of America's space program, von Braun and his colleagues would soon develop an intercontinental ballistic missile (ICBM) that could carry both warheads and astronauts into space.

Yet in hindsight, as important as it was that America captured this treasure, it was doubly important that the Soviet Union did not. If you doubt that, imagine these German scientists — in 1945 the greatest in the world — being put at the service of Josef Stalin at the dawn of the Cold War.

© Kauffmann 2008

Bruce's History Lessons:
Watergate's Smoking Gun

When Richard Nixon became the first U.S. president to resign from office rather than face certain impeachment and removal from the presidency, he may have looked back at this week, specifically June 23rd in 1972, as his political undoing.   For it was on June 23 that Nixon fired what came to be known as the "Smoking Gun." Willingly and knowingly, as caught by his own secret tape recordings of conversations in the Oval Office, Nixon discussed with his chief aide, Bob Haldeman, a plan to obstruct the FBI's investigation of the break-in and burglary of the Democratic National Committee Headquarters at the Watergate complex in Washington.

While Nixon previously had not been aware of the break-in, he quickly learned that it had been planned and executed by members of his own re-election campaign, meaning that if the FBI investigation was not sidetracked, the break-in would eventually be traced to the White House. As a result, Haldeman recommended, and Nixon agreed, that they should order Vernon Walters, the deputy director of the CIA, to call Patrick Gray, the acting director of the FBI, and tell Gray that he should back off of his Watergate investigation because it might uncover covert CIA activities that were not related to Watergate, but had sensitive national security implications that should never come to light. Since some of the Watergate burglars had connections to the CIA-directed Bay of Pigs invasion of Cuba a decade earlier, Nixon and Haldeman believed that their scenario, which they knew was a red herring, sounded plausible.

As a result, later that day, Vernon Walters told Pat Gray that for national security reasons, the FBI should limit its investigation to the five men under arrest for the Watergate break-in.

Of course, as history records, the Watergate investigation expanded way beyond the Watergate burglars, thanks in large part to two indefatigable reporters from *The Washington Post* named Bob Woodward and Carl Bernstein. Soon Senate hearings on Watergate were under way, which resulted in the discovery of a number of shady and illegal campaign activities by the Nixon campaign, including political espionage, illegal wiretapping, money laundering and campaign contribution violations. And in July of 1973, a Nixon aide startled the nation by revealing that Nixon taped his White House conversations.

From then on Watergate became a battle between attempts by the Watergate special prosecutors to obtain those tapes, and Nixon's attempts to keep them out of reach. And when Nixon lost that battle after the U.S. Supreme Court ruled he must release the tapes, his end was inevitable.

"Words are loaded pistols," Jean Paul Sartre once wrote. By openly discussing obstructing justice, Nixon fired the "smoking gun" that, politically, proved to be a mortal wound.

© Kauffmann 2008

Bruce's History Lesson:
Jefferson and Adams Live

It is arguably America's greatest historical coincidence. Exactly 50 years to the day after the Declaration of Independence announced America's birth as a nation on July 4th, 1776, the Declaration's author, Thomas Jefferson, and the man who recommended him for the job, John Adams, both died. The date was July 4th in 1826.

For both men it had been a remarkable half century, one in which they had begun as allies, but had spent much of as political enemies. Fortunately, in the last few years of their lives they became friends again through a remarkable correspondence in which, among many other subjects, they shared their recollections of the nation they had helped create and their hopes for its future.

It was John Adams, after all, who had first noted Jefferson's "felicity of expression" in recommending that the young Virginian take first crack at a written declaration explaining to the world why "…these United Colonies are, and of Right ought to be Free and Independent States," which Jefferson penned in prose unmatched in American history. Their budding friendship then blossomed in the 1780s as both men served together on several diplomatic missions to Europe. It continued in George Washington's administration, where Adams served as vice president and Jefferson as secretary of state.

But friendship turned to friction when their evolving political philosophies began to put them at odds. In the 1790s Adams had become *de facto* head of the Federalist Party, whose belief in a stronger central government had always been an anathema to Jefferson. Their differences came to a head in the presidential election of 1800, in which Jefferson succeeded Adams and promptly reversed many of Adams's most important presidential acts (including repeal of the hated Alien and Sedition Acts — the latter essentially made it a criminal offense to criticize the government). Adams, who was notoriously thin skinned and always convinced that his contribution to America's founding would never be fully appreciated, was especially bitter at Jefferson's undoing of his presidential handiwork, and the two subsequently became estranged. It was only through a mutual friend, Dr. Benjamin Rush, that their affection for each other was finally rekindled and lasted until that fateful fiftieth Fourth.

Of course, neither man knew of the other's demise. Jefferson died first, sometime around two in the afternoon at his Virginia home near Charlottesville, and his last words were "Is today the 4th?" Adams died some three hours later in his Massachusetts home near Quincy, and his last words were "Jefferson lives."

Obviously, Adams was mistaken in the short term, but as it would turn out, he was prophetic in the long term. One hundred and seventy-seven years later, Jefferson still lives. And so does Adams.

© Kauffmann 2008

Bruce's History Lessons:
The Lady is a Veep (Candidate)

This week (July 12) in 1984, Geraldine Ann Ferraro, a three-term member of the U.S. House of Representatives from Queens, New York, made history when Democratic presidential candidate Walter Mondale announced that she would be his running mate. That made her America's first woman vice-presidential candidate on a national party ticket.

If Mondale, an unapologetic liberal, wanted to give the American voter a clear ideological choice between the Democratic ticket and the Reagan-Bush Republican ticket that the Democrats would face in the November election, he did well by picking Ferraro, whose time in Congress had been marked by a strong liberal voting record, especially with respect to women's rights, and in particular support for the Equal Rights Amendment.

Ferraro came by those issues honestly. She was just eight years old when her father, an Italian immigrant, died, and her mother went to work as a seamstress. After getting her high-school diploma as a 16-year-old, she went to college on a full scholarship. Upon graduation she taught in the New York City public school system while attending law school at night. After marrying John Zaccaro, a realtor, she spent the next 13 years raising her three children before joining the Queens County District Attorney's office. There her work in the area of sex crimes, child abuse and domestic violence against women caught the attention of local Democratic Party leaders, who recruited her to run for Congress in New York's 9th district.

While Ferraro was in Congress, her most notable legislative achievement was her sponsorship of the Women's Economic Equity Act, which ended pension discrimination against women, provided employment opportunities for displaced homemakers and enabled homemakers to open their own

Individual Retirement Accounts. But it was her job as head of the 1984 Democratic Platform Committee that brought her to Mondale's attention, and after debating whether to choose her or San Francisco Mayor Dianne Feinstein (now a U.S. Senator), Mondale finally chose Ferraro just prior to the Democratic National Convention.

In her acceptance speech at that convention she said, "Tonight, the daughter of an immigrant from Italy has been chosen to run for vice-president in the new land my father came to love," and later she told the convention that her selection, "sent a powerful signal to all Americans ... If we can do this, we can do anything."

The November election was, alas for the Democrats, anti-climactic. The Reagan-Bush ticket beat Mondale-Ferraro in a landslide, winning every state but Mondale's home state of Minnesota and Washington, D.C.

But if Ferraro did not achieve her ultimate goal, she earned a place in history as a trailblazer, as Elizabeth Dole, Hillary Clinton and many other women who have sought, or will seek, the nation's highest political office are well aware.

© Kauffmann 2008

Bruce's History Lessons:
Hitler's Struggle

Perhaps the most famous quote from Adolf Hitler's autobiography *Mein Kampf* (My Struggle), which was first published this week (July 18) in 1925 in Germany, is this:

"The great masses of people ... will more easily fall victim to a big lie than to a small one." Certainly, in Nazi Germany from 1930 until 1945, the great mass of people fell for one after another of Hitler's big lies, thereby plunging Europe and much of the globe into a horrible world war.

But ironically, Hitler's *Mein Kampf* was itself the big truth. The book was both a mirror to Hitler's soul and an accurate, step-by-step blueprint of his master plan for Germany's and Europe's future. And no one outside of Germany believed a word of it.

After all, it was too demented, what with its plan for "higher breeding" in which Aryan Germans must follow "natural law" by mating only with their own kind, and so avoid producing "inferior offspring" that would weaken the Fatherland and leave Germany prostrate before its many enemies.

It was too perverse, what with its call — in page after page — for a state policy to eradicate the vile Jewish race, including subjecting them to "poison gas," in order to ensure a racially pure German nation.

It was too fantastic, what with its clearly stated intention to rid Germany of all vestiges of democracy and instead give total power to one strong leader (guess who?) who, unfettered by the drag of political parties, a free press or established state institutions, would dictate to the *volk*, the people, what must be done.

And it was certainly too bizarre, what with its statement that "might alone makes right," and its clarion call for Germany to become the greatest military power in the world so that it could first annex Austria (Hitler's place of birth), next invade and conquer Czechoslovakia, Poland and the rest of Eastern Europe, and finally overrun the Soviet Union — all to gain *lebensraum* (living room) for a master race of Aryan Germans.

Every one of these goals, policies, practices and pronouncements was spelled out in *Mein Kampf,* which was such a best seller in Europe, its royalties made Hitler wealthy. Thus had one European statesman from 1930 to 1939 — when World War II started — bothered to read or take seriously *Mein Kampf,* he would have known exactly what Hitler was planning and might then have been able to coordinate a multi-national response that would have stopped Hitler before it was too late.

Actually, one European statesman did read it, and he tried to tell the world what it said. But no one believed him either until it was almost too late. His name was Winston Churchill.

© Kauffmann 2008

Bruce's History Lessons:
A Ford in Our Past

This week (July 23) 1903 Henry Ford sold his first car. Before the year ended he and the Ford Motor Company that he founded would sell another 650 of them.

Then in 1908 he introduced the famous "Model T," and five years later he installed a moving assembly line in which stationary workers assembled cars using standard, interchangeable parts. As a result of this groundbreaking business practice, by 1916 the Ford Motor Company had sold nearly a million cars and earned profits of $60 million. Before the Model T was discontinued in 1927, sales reached 15 million cars and the automobile was no longer the plaything of the rich. The middle class had joined the party.

Meaning that Henry Ford revolutionized the way America both worked and lived. The assembly line, in which each worker repeatedly performed the same function, was a quantum leap in operational efficiency and greatly reduced production time. As a result, Ford's output increased dramatically, while costs actually decreased even though Ford paid his workers twice the standard wage of the times. Ford saw this as a way to retain good workers, thus saving the retraining costs common with high turnover. He also thought a higher paid workforce would better be able to afford his cars.

As for changing the way America lived, by putting the automobile within the economic reach of millions of Americans -- he was also among the first to offer an installment payment plan -- Ford made the nation more mobile. In addition to enjoying freedom of speech, the press and religion, America suddenly enjoyed the freedom to move (which, to most Americans, is practically its own religion). The legacy of this new-found freedom includes the suburb, the further economic development of the rural South and far West, the modernization of much of America, and — through the interstate highway system — an interconnectedness that greatly contributed to America's sense of being one nation.

Ford had his faults. He was authoritarian and anti-Semitic, and for someone so open to new ideas, he stubbornly clung to his Model T design long after rival automobile manufacturers were introducing new models annually. Partly as a result, by the 1930s General Motors was outselling Ford.

But he was a visionary. Before he died in 1947, he bequeathed most of his considerable personal fortune to the Ford Foundation, a nonprofit organization he founded to "Strengthen democratic values, reduce poverty and injustice, promote international cooperation and advance human achievement." Since its inception it has given out more than $80 billion in grants worldwide.

Small wonder the name "Ford" — be it the foundation, the company, the car or the man himself — is synonymous with the word "driven."

© Kauffmann 2008

Bruce's History Lessons: The Top Secret Mission of the USS Indianapolis

This week (July 30) in 1945, with the war in the Pacific winding down, the *USS Indianapolis* was halfway between Guam and the Philippines when a torpedo from a Japanese submarine slammed into its hull. Moments later a second torpedo hit the fuel tanks and powder magazines, causing an explosive chain reaction. Three hundred men died instantly or went down with the sinking ship, leaving to their fate the 900 remaining crewmen who had jumped overboard into the sea. Fortunately, distress signals had been sent before the ship went down, so the survivors had a reasonable expectation of a routine rescue.

Unfortunately, unbeknownst to these men, the *USS Indianapolis* had not been on a routine mission. Rather, its mission was so secretive, and attended by so many security precautions, that the fate of the *Indianapolis* would not be known for several days. As a result, the 900 men floating on rafts, life jackets and ship debris had to endure for four days and nights, unprotected from the elements, with little food or water, and with many wounded and bleeding from the ship's explosion.

And then the sharks came. Smelling the blood and sensing the commotion on the ocean surface, shark attacks began early on the morning of the 30th and continued for the entire ordeal. Men already paralyzed with fear watched in horror as the dorsal fins began their encirclement, and one-by-one the men were attacked, many pulled under to become the victims of a shark feeding frenzy. When they were finally rescued, only 317 of the ship's 1200 man crew had survived.

A number that would later dwindle by one. The ship's captain, Charles McVay, subsequently became the only U.S. naval commander ever court-martialed for a ship's sinking. During court-martial proceedings it was noted that he had ceased using the "zigzagging" avoidance course used by allied ships to avoid enemy subs in the shipping lanes, and although such a decision is a captain's prerogative, depending on the weather, and although McVay's surviving crewmen defended him, the charge stuck. Overcome with guilt, McVay committed suicide.

So why was the mission of the *USS Indianapolis* so guarded? It was the cargo. Days earlier, the ship had docked at the Pacific island of Tinian, where it had unloaded the atomic bomb that, a week later, would destroy the Japanese city of Hiroshima and change the nature of war.

Speaking of sharks, for my money, the most gripping scene in the movie *Jaws* is not the shark itself, but the scene in which the boat captain, played by Robert Shaw, describes being a crewman on the *Indianapolis* and watching the sharks take so many of his comrades. That scene alone is worth renting the movie.

© *Kauffmann 2008*

Bruce's History Lessons:
Damn the Torpedoes!

While the Civil War produced a number of famous army officers — Grant, Sherman, Lee, Longstreet — it produced only one famous naval officer, the Union's Rear Admiral David Farragut, and today his fame stems as much from a curse he uttered in a moment of exasperation as from anything he actually did. For it was this week (August 5) in 1864, during an attack on a Southern stronghold in Mobile, Alabama, along the Gulf Coast, that Farragut uttered the immortal words, "Damn the torpedoes, full speed ahead!"

Actually, what he is believed to have said was, "Damn the torpedoes! Four bells! Captain Drayton, go ahead!"

By way of background, for most of the Civil War, the South had controlled the ports along the Gulf of Mexico, including the port at Mobile Bay, enabling Confederate officials to maintain a critical supply line in which food, ammunition and other necessities could be imported from overseas, and then sent to armies in the field. But by 1864, the North had shut down, captured or quarantined most of these coastal ports, leaving only a few ports open to Southern blockade-runners. One of the most important of these ports was in Mobile, and Farragut was determined to shut it down as well. Therefore, on August 5, he launched an attack against Mobile Bay with four ironclads and seven sloops-of-war, including his own flagship the *Hartford*.

But Mobile Bay was well defended. In addition to being protected by two forts, a number of gun ships and its own ironclad, the *Tennessee*, the waters in the bay were strewn with mines, or as they were called at the time, torpedoes.

Sure enough, during the initial attack, Farragut's lead ironclad, the *Tecumseh*, struck a "torpedo" and began sinking, which — because of the attack plan, the narrowness of the bay and the plethora of "torpedoes" — threatened to cause a major aquatic traffic jam as the Union ships behind the *Tecumseh* came to a halt, not knowing how, or whether, to proceed.

Admiral Farragut, who had climbed to the highest rigging of his own ship to get a panoramic view of the battle, was too high up to understand what was happening directly below, so he shouted, "What is the trouble?!" When told, "Torpedoes," he uttered his famous curse and order to resume the attack. As a result, his own ship surged past the others and led the way to a complete Union victory that shut down Mobile and helped cut the South off from its overseas supply routes.

It was probably the most important naval victory of the Civil War, yet today our nation's first rear admiral, David Farragut, is known more for his curse than his courage. Which proves that sometimes words speak louder than actions.

© *Kauffmann 2008*

Bruce's History Lessons:
The Babe

George Herman "Babe" Ruth, the greatest baseball player who ever lived, died this week (Aug. 16) in 1948 of throat cancer. For the next two days his body lay "in state" at the main entrance to Yankee Stadium, also known as "The House that Ruth Built." More than 20,000 fans showed up to pay their respects.

To most sports fans Ruth's story is familiar. Born the son of a saloonkeeper in Baltimore, Maryland, his early years were troubled and his parents placed him in a Catholic-run orphanage to instill in him some discipline. There Ruth learned to play baseball and by his 18th birthday his baseball prowess had caught the attention of the entire city, including Jack Dunn, the owner of the minor league Baltimore Orioles franchise. Dunn quickly signed Ruth to a professional contract, but because Ruth was still a teenager, Dunn had to become his legal guardian. As a result, Baltimore sportswriters dubbed Ruth "Dunn's baby," which, combined with his cherubic face and youth, soon was shortened to "Babe."

Financial difficulties later forced Dunn to sell Ruth's contract to the Boston Red Sox, where he broke in as a pitcher and led the Sox to World Series titles in 1915, 1916 and 1918. By 1919, however, Ruth's abilities as a hitter exceeded even his pitching skills and he moved to the outfield so that he could play every day. That year, Ruth captured the major league home run title with 29 round trippers — this at a time when a dozen home runs was considered Herculean.

And then, as every baseball fan knows, Red Sox owner Harry Frazee sold Ruth to the New York Yankees to help cover some debts and the fortunes of both clubs changed forever. Ruth would lead the Yankees to seven World

Series, winning four of them, while the Red Sox have not won the World Series since. "The curse of the Bambino" (one of Ruth's many nicknames) has haunted Red Sox Nation for 83 years.

As with his baseball life, Ruth lived his personal life to the fullest. He partied with the best of them, drinking and carousing until all hours, chasing women and gorging himself at the dinner table. But he never forgot where he came from, and his charitable work and visits to hospitals, schools and orphanages touched the lives of thousands of children. Also, he never said no to an autograph request.

Today, Babe Ruth is buried in the Gates of Heaven Cemetery in Hawthorn, New York. Assuming God is both merciful and a baseball fan, it's a safe bet that, his many transgressions notwithstanding, "The Babe" made it to — and through — the actual gates of Heaven.

© Kauffmann 2008

Bruce's History lesson:
The 19th Amendment

When John Adams and his fellow Founding Fathers were in the Continental Congress in 1776, working on whether or not to declare independence, his wife Abigail wrote him a letter advising him to "remember the ladies." She meant that the Framers should not forget the rights of the fair sex in any set of new laws that they devised.

History does not record Abigail's initial reaction to John's resulting handiwork, but it's possible that, for a while anyway, the Adams family was about as cheerful as "The Addams Family." Later laws, including those in the Constitution, not only forgot the ladies, they ignored them.

Undaunted by this oversight, Abigail's descendants soon began to band together to gain equal political rights and power. In 1848, for example, they held the first women's rights convention — the Seneca Falls Conference — in upstate New York. There, Elizabeth Stanton wrote a declaration of independence purposely modeled after Tom Jefferson's.

"All men and all women are created equal," she wrote, adding, "The history of mankind is the history of repeated injuries and usurpation on the part of man toward woman." And just as Tom had included in his Declaration a long list of grievances against King George III, so did Ms. Stanton sprinkle hers with a list of grievances against (every) Tom — and Dick and Harry.

The Seneca Falls Conference jump-started the women's movement, eventually resulting in the formation of the National American Woman Suffrage Association (NAWSA). Led by Stanton, Susan B. Anthony and Lucy Stone, NAWSA worked tirelessly to gain support for an amendment granting women's suffrage, only to be repeatedly rebuffed by Congress. After the Civil

War, for example, the 14th and 15th Amendments to the Constitution granted citizenship and suffrage to blacks but ignored women.

Then along came America's entry into World War I, which NAWSA publicly supported in the hopes of reaping political reward when it ended. Yet it wasn't politics but instead the practical contribution women made to the war effort that would be crucial to their cause. Millions of females, including large numbers of suffragettes, worked in hospitals, office buildings, relief agencies, businesses and even factories — both military and civilian. Wherever there was a void left by men sent to fight in Flanders and France, women filled it.

And filled it so well that when the war ended, their desire for equality could no longer be denied. Having proved that they could shoulder the responsibilities of citizenship, they deserved to share in the rights of citizenship. As a result, Congress finally passed, and sent to the states for ratification, the 19th Amendment, which gave women the right to vote. It was ratified this week (Aug. 18) in 1920 when Tennessee became the 36th state to give its approval.

At long last "the ladies" had achieved equality under the law.

© Kauffmann 2008

Bruce's History Lessons:
Not a Man of His Time

There is a phrase that we use to defend historic figures whose conduct, centuries later, looks questionable in light of our present day mores. We say, "He was a man of his time."

For example, when Abe Lincoln is called racist because, although he despised slavery, he spoke out against the races mixing, we say, "He was a man of his time." Or when President Andrew Jackson, while ushering in a new democratic era, ruthlessly and cruelly re-settled the American Indians against their will, we say, "He was a man of his time."

But one man was never "a man of his time" — our first president, George Washington, and my two examples above serve to reinforce his singular greatness. On both the issue of slavery and the Indians, Washington was a man ahead of his time.

Yes, Washington owned slaves, but unlike his countrymen, he believed that slavery itself, not genetic inferiority, prevented the advancement of African-Americans, which is why his will not only instructed that all of his slaves be freed upon his death, but also that, piece-by-piece, his Mount Vernon home was to be sold and the proceeds used to care for his freed slaves for generations to come.

This was both generous and visionary, because Washington — *again, unlike his countrymen* — did not believe that, once freed, blacks should be shipped back to Africa. Washington understood that their future was in America. Providing his former slaves with long-term financial support was his way of helping them prepare for that future.

The same was true of his view of American Indians. Washington was not alone in understanding that the western migration of white settlers was inevitable, and that the implications of this migration were ominous for the Indian tribes who roamed those western lands. But Washington was alone in his solution. He did not call for the Indians to leave or be destroyed. He called for them to change their way of life and be saved.

In an "Address to the Cherokee Nation," which he gave this week (Aug 25) in 1796, Washington asked the Indians to abandon their "hunter-gatherer" way of life because it took up too much land — land white settlers would eventually seize. Instead, Washington suggested that Indians should become farmers, which would make them the neighbors of white farmers instead of the enemies. By living side-by-side in similar socio-economic circumstances, Washington envisioned whites and Indians gradually and peacefully assimilating.

Interestingly, in this address, Washington provided added incentive by reminding the Indians that he too was about to resume farming, having recently announced that he would soon voluntarily relinquish power and return to private life.

In the 18th century, a man who did that was *way* ahead of his time.

© *Kauffmann 2008*

Bruce's History Lessons:
Searching for Bobby Fischer

Imagine a Russian football team, at the height of the Cold War, winning the Super Bowl by destroying the New England Patriots and you have some idea of the magnitude of chess grandmaster Bobby Fischer's defeat of the Soviet world champion, Boris Spassky, at Reykjavik, Iceland, this week (Sept 1) in 1972. It made Fischer America's first world champion in a sport long dominated by Soviet players. Thereafter, many would consider Bobby Fischer the greatest chess player ever.

He was certainly the greatest American player ever, having become the youngest U.S. master at age 14, and at 15 the youngest international grandmaster. He also won eight U.S. chess championship titles, which has never been duplicated.

He also was considered the most exciting and creative chess player ever. Unlike most grandmasters, who at that level are so familiar with one another's game that they often play for draws, Fischer liked to attack and demoralize his opponent into fatal mistakes. As a result, Fischer actually won a high percentage of his games. "I like the moment when I break a man's ego," he once explained.

All of this, plus a brashness akin to rudeness — he would regularly insult Soviet players and accuse them of fixing matches — made Fischer a media favorite, and when he went to Reykjavik to play Spassky it was dubbed "the chess match of the century." PBS coverage of the match, which was essentially a shot of a large chessboard with pieces moving around, became the highest-rated PBS broadcast to that point. In addition to Fischer's youth— he was just 29 — and colorful personality, the chess match was seen as a clear metaphor for the Cold War.

In the first game, Fischer, who had complained about everything from the prize money, to the cameras, to the chessboard's surface, played poorly and lost, which prompted more complaints and threats. Fed up, the match promoters told Fischer he had forfeited game two, awarding it to Spassky.

Now down 2-0, Fischer finally got serious, easily winning game three, and as the days went by his game got ever stronger, while Spassky's became weaker. Finally, on September 1, Spassky resigned and Fischer was champion.

The chess world was stunned, not only because Fischer had won, but also because he had won virtually alone. It was Fischer, his chess books, practice boards and genius, against Spassky and several dozen Soviet grandmaster assistants, plus all the resources of the chess-obsessed Soviet state.

A legend was born, and although in the 30 years since, Fischer's career has gone nowhere, and his personality has degenerated into paranoia, schizophrenia, rabid anti-Semitism and anti-Americanism bordering on treason, there is no taking away his place in the history of chess — or of sport.

© Kauffmann 2008

Bruce's History Lessons: The 28th Amendment

In the past 212 years, only 27 amendments have been added to the Constitution, including the original 10, the Bill of Rights, but for those of you wondering what might make an appropriate 28th, let me suggest that you first recall (as if you could forget) the events of this week (Sept. 11) in 2001.

First the World Trade Center and the Pentagon were hit by three hijacked airplanes piloted by al Qaeda terrorists, and in the skies over Pennsylvania a fourth hijacked plane was headed for Washington, D.C. However, because that fourth plane was 40 minutes late taking off, allowing its passengers to learn via cell phone calls from loved ones that they too were being hijacked, they fought the terrorists for control of the plane. As a result, that plane crashed in Pennsylvania instead of what is now believed was its intended target, the U.S. Capitol building where Congress sits.

Which begs the question: Had the terrorists in the last plane successfully crashed into Congress, how many of our nation's lawmakers would have died? And more to the point, had a considerable number of them perished, how would the government run?

It is not a theoretical question. When U.S. senators die or are incapacitated, the governor of their home state can replace them by special appointment, but the Constitution only allows members of the House of Representatives to be replaced through special elections, something that would take many months to organize in the chaotic wake of a successful terrorist attack on Congress. In the meantime, the House could well lack a quorum, which the Constitution states is a prerequisite before it can conduct official business.

As things stand today, 218 of the 435 members of the House are needed for a quorum, and whether a direct hit on the Capitol building would have killed that many is anybody's guess. But had it happened, from a Constitutional standpoint Congress would be unable to make laws, including declaring war or passing spending bills designed to fund war-making or counter-terrorist activities.

Granted, either the Senate, or more probably the White House, would assume some "emergency powers" to deal with such a crisis, but in addition to being unconstitutional it might well smack of being dictatorial, and invite some kind of inter-governmental branch power struggle.

Which brings us to the idea of a 28th Constitutional amendment, something many legal experts, most prominently Norman Ornstein of the American Enterprise Institute, are advocating. Ornstein favors a simple amendment that grants Congress, regardless of quorum, the authority to establish guidelines for selecting temporary members in an emergency.

Something to think about given that, if at first they don't succeed, al Qaeda has been known to try, try again.

© Kauffmann 2008

Bruce's History Lesson: James Garfield and the Disappointed Office-Seeker

Quick, what do you know about James A. Garfield other than the fact that he was a U.S. president (our 20th) and that he met an untimely death this week (Sept. 19) in 1881 at the hands of what historians invariably describe as a "disappointed office seeker"?

Probably nothing, and you aren't alone. Granted, Garfield was no great shakes as a president (how could he have been, he was shot shortly after taking office), but it still seems unfair that a former president's only claim on the nation's historical memory is inextricably connected with the assassin who gunned him down.

"It always says the same thing," the comedian Robert Klein once noted about Garfield. "It says 'Shot by a disappointed office seeker.' You look in a grade school history book and what do you find? You find, 'George Washington ... Father of our Country. Thomas Jefferson ... Declaration of Independence. Abe Lincoln ... Emancipation Proclamation. James A. Garfield ... Shot by a disappointed officer seeker.'

"Even if you look him up in the dictionary," Klein joked, "it reads, *'Garfield, James A.; see Office Seeker, Disappointed.'*"

And the sad part is, Garfield had potential. He was one of the most dedicated and experienced politicians ever to hail from Ohio, where he served in the state senate. And his ability to lead men in battle earned him the distinction of being the youngest brigadier general in the Civil War. Battlefield courage even earned him a second general's star, but in 1863 Garfield resigned his military commission at the direct request of President

Lincoln, who wanted him to run for Congress (Lincoln had plenty of military generals but not enough effective Republican politicians). Ohioans got the message and promptly elected him to the U.S. House of Representatives, where he remained for 17 years until running for the Senate in the election of 1880. Although he won that race, he never served because he also became the Republican's compromise candidate for president in the 1880 election — an election he also won.

Interestingly, as president, one of Garfield's pet projects was civil service reform; he thought job seekers should pass a written examination before getting a government job. Alas — adding insult to irony — Garfield had no chance to address this issue before being gunned down by the aforementioned office seeker, a lawyer named Charles Guiteau, who had wanted to be Garfield's ambassador to France but was turned down.

That, of course, begs the question: Would this job seeker have fared better, and therefore been less "disappointed," if Garfield had been able to introduce a written-examination requirement for most government positions? Probably not — Guiteau was mentally unstable — but as is so often the case in history, we'll never know.

© Kauffmann 2008

Bruce's History Lessons:
Her (Sandra) Day in Court

In a sense, two cases of legal discrimination 120 years apart led to the event that occurred this week (Sept. 25) in 1981 when Sandra Day O'Connor was sworn in as the first woman justice in the history of the Supreme Court. For it was in the 1830s, while working in her father's law firm, that Elizabeth Cady Stanton saw first-hand the gender discrimination that would convert her into a feminist and inspire her to lead the woman's movement toward equal rights.

And it was in the 1950s, after graduating near the top of her class at Stanford law school, that one of the beneficiaries of Elizabeth Stanton's equal rights crusade — the young Sandra Day from El Paso, Texas — experienced such pervasive gender discrimination that no law firm would hire her for a job commensurate with her talent and school ranking, forcing her to turn to the public sector as a deputy county attorney in San Mateo, California. From that humble beginning, Sandra Day O'Connor — she married John Jay O'Connor shortly after graduation — would serve as a civilian lawyer for the army, an assistant attorney general for the state of Arizona, and an Arizona state senator, where she became the first woman ever to serve as majority leader of a state senate. She left the Arizona senate when then-Governor Bruce Babbitt appointed her to the Arizona Court of Appeals, where she served for two years before President Ronald Reagan nominated her for the Supreme Court.

The appointment was both good politics and the honoring of a pledge Reagan had made during his presidential campaign — that he would nominate a woman to the Supreme Court "at the earliest opportunity." O'Connor replaced the retiring Potter Stewart, a conservative judge appointed by President Eisenhower in the 1950s, and although O'Connor was considered a moderate on the abortion issue, her supporters believed that she was sufficiently conservative to uphold the doctrine of judicial restraint.

In hindsight it hasn't quite worked out that way. Although she sided with the court's conservative faction early on, in recent years Justice O'Connor has emerged as a more pragmatic conservative with an activist streak. Often voting with the liberal wing, she has become, in the court's parlance, a "swing vote" who could go either way on an issue, but tends to chart a moderate course that — her supporters contend — helps ameliorate the often sharply divided court.

In that sense, O'Connor is like many of the Supreme Court justices who have preceded her, defying both the expectations and the political and social agendas of the presidents who appointed them. The one difference is that O'Connor does it from the perspective of a woman. Elizabeth Cady Stanton would be proud.

© Kauffmann 2008

Bruce's History Lessons: Big Red

In ESPN's list of the top 50 athletes of the 20th century, 49 of them relied on two legs to help them achieve their athletic glory. Only one — ranked 35th of the 50 — relied on four legs, which is usually the case with horses.

But this was not your usual horse. This was Secretariat, "Big Red" as he was called, arguably the greatest racehorse of all time. In 1973, when this son of Bold Ruler and Somethingroyal won the Triple Crown, he was the first horse to do so in 25 years, and he set a world record in two of those three races (a malfunctioning clock in the other race, the Preakness, prevented him from setting a record there as well). In the Kentucky Derby, which he won by 2 and 1/2 lengths, Secretariat crossed the finish line in 1:59.25, becoming the only horse ever to break two minutes.

But it was in the Triple Crown's final leg, the Belmont Stakes, that Secretariat became a legend by winning in a world-record time of 2:24 and finishing an astonishing 31 lengths ahead of his nearest rival. The gap between Secretariat and the second-place horse, Twice A Prince, was so wide that CBS Television, which broadcast the race, had to use its widest-angle lens and even then it barely was able to fit the two horses in the same shot.

And history was made. The following week "Big Red" was on the cover of *Time, Newsweek,* and *Sports Illustrated.* That year he earned "Horse of the Year" for the second year in a row. "Big Red" fever became so widespread, the William Morris Agency was hired to oversee his personal appearances. Not since Seabiscuit in the 1930s had a horse so captured the imagination of America, and the speculation over which of those two magnificent animals would prevail in a head-to-head duel is debated in bars and race tracks even today. Most give the nod to "Big Red."

After the Belmont Stakes, Secretariat raced six more times, winning four and finishing second twice. In November of '73 he was retired and put to stud at the Clairborne Farm in Kentucky, and although he sired more than 600 foals in a stud career spanning 16 years, including the 1988 Preakness and Belmont Stakes winner, Risen Star, none of his offspring could ever match the standard he set.

Suffering from the terrible pain of laminitis, a hoof disease, Secretariat was given a lethal injection and died this week (Oct. 4) in 1989. An autopsy revealed that his heart was more than twice as large as that of the average horse, which only confirmed medically what Secretariat's legions of fans instinctively had known all along.

© *Kauffmann 2008*

Bruce's History Lesson:
Lincoln's Editor

William Seward, whose fame rests mostly on his decision to purchase Alaska from the Russians in 1867 — a purchase that was ridiculed then, but is viewed somewhat differently today — died this week (Oct. 10) in 1872. In homage I focus on a lesser known, but critical task that he performed as Abe Lincoln's secretary of state.

It is late in February of 1861 and Lincoln, the president-elect, is drafting his first Inaugural Address. Earlier in the month, seven southern states had established a new nation, the Confederate States of America. In Lincoln's mind, this new nation is illegal and its perpetrators are in a state of rebellion that could destroy the Union.

Lincoln is not exactly angry, but he is perturbed, and it shows in the first draft of his address. He calls the new Confederate government, "legally nothing." He calls its creators "treasonable." He says these rebels must "submit" or else. And, finally, he ends his address as follows: "*In your hands, my dissatisfied fellow-countrymen, and not in mine, is the momentous issue of civil war. The Government will not assail you unless you first assail it. You can have no conflict without being yourselves the aggressors. You have no oath registered in heaven to destroy the Government, while I shall have the most solemn one to 'preserve, protect, and defend it' ... With you, and not with me, is the solemn question of, 'Shall it be peace, or a sword?'*"

And then Seward is asked to review it. Seward suggests that the new government be called "void" rather than "nothing," so as not to seem dismissive. He softens "treasonable" to the less inflammatory "revolutionary." He asks the rebels to "acquiesce" rather than "submit," the former being more dignified. He is, in a sense, advising Lincoln to be more accommodating, so as not to insult his wayward countrymen and harden their position.

285

Finally, realizing that Lincoln's ending implies that any war would be the South's fault alone, Seward advises adding a softer final paragraph that reminds both the South and North of their shared heritage. Lincoln accepts this advice and re-works Seward's suggested language. The result is among the most eloquent passages in the history of American speechmaking:

"We are not enemies, but friends. We must not be enemies. Though passion may have strained it must not break our bonds of affection. The mystic chords of memory, stretching from every battlefield and patriot grave to every living heart and hearthstone all over this broad land, will yet swell the chorus of the Union, when again touched, as surely they will be, by the better angels of our nature."

Buying Alaska is one thing. Serving as Abe Lincoln's editor is something else entirely.

© *Kauffmann 2008*

Bruce's History Lessons:
The OPEC Oil Embargo

Of the many "weapons of mass destruction" that have come out of the Middle East in modern times, the one that had the greatest effect on the United States — at least the U.S. economy — was unleashed 30 years ago this week (Oct. 17). That is when leaders of the Organization of Petroleum Exporting Countries (OPEC) met in Algiers and cut oil exports to all nations that had assisted Israel in the 1973 war against invading Arab armies led by Egypt and Syria.

That war, which was launched during the Jewish holiday, Yom Kippur, initially caught Israel by surprise, but after early battlefield losses, Israel regained the initiative, thanks to U.S. airlift of weapons and supplies, plus additional military assistance from Denmark and the Netherlands. By mid-October the war had turned so sharply against the Arab armies, OPEC decided to act. It declared that oil exports would be reduced by five percent every month until Israel evacuated not only its gains from the Yom Kippur War, but also its territorial gains from the Six-Day War of 1967.

Israel refused to withdraw from any of the occupied territories and the price of OPEC oil soon increased by 70 percent. And then, that December at an OPEC conference in Iran, OPEC hiked oil prices another 130 percent, while imposing a total oil embargo on the U.S., the Netherlands and Denmark.

The result in America was a major energy crisis and severe economic dislocation. In the decades leading up to the '70s, American dependence on foreign oil had risen sharply as domestic production declined, and even though OPEC was not a major U.S. supplier, in the wake of its embargo, panic spread throughout the country. Price gouging and long lines at the pump were the norm, and given oil's effect on all aspects of American economic life, inflation soon reared its ugly head.

By the following year, however, tensions had cooled and a negotiated agreement between Israel and Syria led to a lifting of the embargo. While oil prices remained high, most Western nations responded by developing, or relying on, alternative energy sources, including nuclear power and the increased use of coal. And by the 1980s, the combination of these alternative energy sources, increased energy conservation, and the need for many OPEC nations to increase exports to pay for expensive public works and construction projects, led to an oil glut and lower prices.

But the years passed, memories grew short and the SUV was born. In 1973, when the embargo began, oil imports to America were 36 percent of our total. Thirty years later, while we search for other kinds of "weapons of mass destruction" in the Middle East, imports have risen to 58 percent.

© Kauffmann 2008

Bruce's History Lesson:
Reach Out and Touch Someone

Forty-three years on the planet and the only black man John F. Kennedy had ever spent any time with was his valet. Yet the two-minute phone call he made this week (Oct. 20) in 1960 to Coretta King, the wife of America's most important black leader, Martin Luther King, probably made Kennedy, and not Richard Nixon, president.

It all started when, in the middle of the 1960 presidential campaign, King was put in a hard-time Georgia prison on a trumped up charge related to an old traffic violation. Worried about King's safety, members of his entourage implored both the Kennedy and Nixon presidential campaigns to intervene with Georgia political leaders on King's behalf.

For both candidates, such intervention posed a political risk, not only because it could cost them the South, which was still segregated and significantly racist, but also because — and this is not usually remembered — in those days blacks traditionally voted Republican. Thus Nixon's camp declined to help, seeing little to gain (the black vote was already theirs) but plenty to lose by aiding the controversial civil rights leader. Ditto Kennedy's camp. Why jeopardize Southern votes to help a member of an ethnic group that habitually supported the other party?

Fortunately for Kennedy, a young aide named Harris Wofford had the idea that if there was nothing specific the democratic candidate could do for King, perhaps it wouldn't hurt to at least call Mrs. King to offer his sympathy and moral support. When the idea of phoning Mrs. King was proposed to Kennedy by his brother-in-law, Sergeant Shriver, Kennedy replied "What the hell. It's the decent thing to do." Kennedy made the call, talked for about two minutes, and forgot about it soon after.

But King's family and friends did not forget. King's father, "Daddy King," who was one of the most powerful leaders in the black church community, promptly announced that he was switching his vote from Nixon to JFK, and other black leaders, especially black church leaders, followed suit. In addition, sensing a unique opportunity in this black church support, Kennedy's campaign secretly distributed through a nationwide network of black churches a pamphlet that quoted black leaders praising Kennedy's courage in phoning Coretta King. The goal was to influence the black vote — especially in the North — without alerting, and thereby jeopardizing, the mainstream white vote — especially in the South.

Did it work? In 1956 Eisenhower and Nixon got 60 percent of the black vote. In 1960 Kennedy, without losing significant Southern support, got 70 percent of the black vote, a switch that more than accounted for his victory margins in Illinois, Pennsylvania, Michigan and New Jersey. Those states totaled 95 electoral votes. Kennedy beat Nixon by 84 electoral votes.

© Kauffmann 2008

Bruce's History Lesson:
The Federalist Papers

Perhaps the most important newspaper columns in American history began publication in New York newspapers this week (Oct. 27) in 1787. Called *The Federalist Papers*, they were published under the pen name "Publius," but were actually penned by a trio of Founding Fathers — (my hero) James Madison, Alexander Hamilton and John Jay. These papers were an attempt by the "Federalists" to defend their decision, made in Philadelphia the previous summer, to junk the weak Articles of Confederation that had been governing America and replace them with a new Constitution that, among other things, called for a strong "federal" (central) government.

Given the reverence in which the Constitution is held today, we forget how controversial it was during the beginnings of our republic. But in truth this new Constitution was vehemently opposed by the "Anti-federalists," who feared giving new powers to a central government. Having recently been governed by a strong "central power" — King George III — they much preferred that the *states* posses most power, and at least initially they had the public's support.

But through this series of columns, Madison, Hamilton and Jay argued that without a strong central government America could not regulate commerce among the states, or make treaties on behalf of the states, or issue a uniform currency, or ensure sound fiscal policy, or defend the nation's shores, or promote its interests abroad. The result, according to the authors, would be monetary chaos, high tariffs and other impediments to trade; a weak, fractious confederation that would be easy prey to the large states of Europe; and eventually the dissolution of the union.

Further, the columns met the anti-federalists' fears about a strong central government head on, explaining that the powers given this new government were *shared* among three different branches, which would all check one another. And finally, the authors explained why the framers had created a "republican" as opposed to purely "democratic" government. Madison in particular used his columns to point out the need to temper public opinion with sound judgment, and the wisdom of providing many checks against unbridled majority rule — both of which the Articles of Confederation had lacked. "In all cases where the majority are united by common interest or passion," Madison wrote, "the rights of the minority are in danger."

Brilliantly written and argued, *The Federalist Papers* were instrumental in turning the tide of popular opinion in support of this new Constitution. Fittingly, its future was assured when the two most important states in the union, Hamilton's and Jay's native state of New York, and Madison's native state of Virginia, finally voted their approval.

© Kauffmann 2008

Bruce's History Lessons: The Power to Make War

With the debate over the legitimacy of war in Iraq foremost in the public's mind, and with the Democratic presidential contenders simultaneously debating who did, or did not, or (John Kerry) did not *intend* to vote to authorize that war, it might be useful to review just what our Founding Fathers were thinking when it came to who had the power to authorize and fight America's wars. The timing is also appropriate because this week (Nov. 7) in 1973, Congress passed the War Powers Act, which sought to remind presidents that the Constitution vested Congress, not the president, with the power to declare war.

But not the power to "make war," which is an important distinction. When the Framers were debating the Constitution in 1787, they originally proposed that Congress be given the war-making power. As (my hero) James Madison noted, since history has shown that "the executive is the branch of power most interested in war, and most prone to it," prudence dictated putting that power somewhere else — notably the legislative branch.

That said, the Framers worried that granting Congress the power to "make war" would be too cumbersome. In the event of a surprise attack, for example, a Congress comprising two branches and hundreds of elected officials would be too slow to respond. Only a single decision maker — namely the president — could effectively respond in time. As a result, the original words "make war" were replaced by "declare war" with respect to Congress's Constitutional war powers. In effect, Congress would decide *when* America would wage wars, but the president would decide *how* those wars would be waged.

For most of history this compromise worked well, but in 1950, when North Korea invaded South Korea, President Harry Truman committed

U.S. forces to the conflict without congressional authorization. Truman argued that Korea was a "police action," which did not require congressional approval. Opposition Republicans in Congress vehemently disagreed.

That "police action" logic took a quantum leap in Vietnam, and by 1973, Congress was fed up with what it saw as the Nixon Administration's secret war making and illegal usurpation of its authority to declare and fund America's conflicts. In response, it passed the War Powers Act, which allows presidents only 90 days to keep troops in combat without a specific congressional authorization.

I note in closing that, with respect to our war against Iraq, President Bush did request and receive a congressional resolution. What's more, since many of the Democrats now seeking his job voted to approve that resolution, their criticism has shifted to whether he leveled with them about the seriousness of the Iraqi threat.

That's a problem the Constitution's Framers could never have anticipated. After all, George Washington was their president.

© *Kauffmann 2008*

Bruce's History Lessons:
The U.N. Declares
Zionism is Racism

"A great evil has been loosed upon the world."

- Daniel Moynihan, U.S. Ambassador to the United Nations,
describing U.N. Resolution 3379, which equated Zionism with racism

When, this week (Nov. 10) in 1975, the United Nations General Assembly passed Resolution 3379, which condemned Zionism as both "racism" and "a threat to world peace," it did so by more than a two-to-one margin. Naturally, every Arab state in existence voted for 3379, as did the Soviet Union and its satellite countries. Then again, also voting for 3379 were Brazil, Turkey and many African nations with ties to neither the Soviets nor the Arab world.

Equally disturbing were the nations that abstained, thereby signaling a moral indifference to a state, Israel, that was the only democracy in the Middle East, that had never engaged in colonialism, and that had never fought a war except in self-defense. Abstaining nations included Japan, Greece, Venezuela, Kenya and Zaire.

U.N. Resolution 3379 was, quite simply, an organized campaign of anti-Semitism meant to de-legitimatize Israel, make it a pariah in the community of nations, and —at least in much of the Arab world — eventually dismember and destroy it. Giving such intentions the imprimatur of United Nations support remains one of the U.N.'s most dishonorable actions.

And it was both bad law and bad history. Prior to 1975, the legitimacy of Zionism and an Israeli state had been internationally recognized both by the League of Nations and by the United Nations itself, in 1947, when Israel's statehood was approved. At that time, the U.N. wanted to partition the western part of Palestine into an Arab and a Jewish state. The Jews accepted the U.N.'s plan. The Arabs rejected it and in 1948 started a war to overturn it — a war they lost.

But that was then and this is now. Although the U.N. finally rescinded 3379 in December of 1991, today Israel is the only member of the United Nations not permitted to sit on the U.N. Security Council. Today Israel is the only country whose membership in U.N. commissions is severely restricted.

Today, the U.N. has a "Day of International Solidarity with the Palestinian People" — November 29. No such day exists for Israel or the Jewish people.

Last year, the U.N. Commission on Human Rights passed 7 resolutions condemning various Israeli actions. That was six more than Cuba, Iran, Iraq, Afghanistan and Russia each received.

Speaking of bad history, November 10, 1975, was the 37th anniversary of the culmination of Kristallnacht — the "night of shattered glass" — in which Nazi Germany first began its campaign of genocide against the Jews. That anniversary was no doubt lost on the supporters of U.N. 3379. Not so the citizens of Israel.

© *Kauffmann 2008*

Bruce's History Lessons:
The Stealth Bomber

The B-2 "Stealth" Bomber, which was first revealed publicly this week (Nov. 22) in 1988, has been called the most survivable aircraft ever built — and that was by its detractors! At more than $40 billion for development, and a cost of $1 billion per plane, the B-2 is among the most expensive pieces of military equipment in history, and many members of Congress from both parties thought the price was far too steep. But the B-2 meant jobs — lots of them — in politically powerful California and elsewhere, so it managed to deflect all attempts to kill it. It even survived the disappearance of its original reason for existence, the Soviet Union, which collapsed in 1991. In the wake of that collapse, however, the original order of 132 B-2 Bombers was reduced to 21, thereby increasing the per-plane cost to the aforementioned billion dollars.

It is called the "Stealth" bomber because of its ability to escape detection. Although its wingspan equals half a football field, it has special coatings and materials, plus a revolutionary "flying wing" design (resembling a boomerang), that make it extremely difficult to locate visually, acoustically, electromagnetically, with infrared or by radar. With one refueling the B-2 can go anywhere in the world, and its payload is 40 thousand pounds of weapons, both conventional and/or nuclear. And unlike conventional aircraft, its "invisibility" allows it to penetrate heavily defended areas virtually at will, making it one of the most feared weapons in America's military arsenal.

In fact, as its supporters point out, the beauty of the B-2 is that it can be as dangerous to an enemy as a nuclear-tipped intercontinental ballistic missile, yet it is safer, more versatile and — a critical advantage — less destabilizing because it can be more easily recalled.

Which is not to say that the B-2 hasn't had problems. The "stealth" materials that make it invisible are vulnerable to varying weather conditions and therefore require more repair and maintenance than was originally estimated. And in terms of whether to build more B-2s, or instead build (many) more conventional aircraft, the plane's price tag remains an issue, especially since its detractors believe cruise missiles and "stealth" fighter planes can neutralize enemy air defenses just as easily as the B-2 can penetrate them — at much less cost. Thus when the B-2's supporters claim, as they often do, that it does the job of 75 conventional aircraft, its detractors counter that its cost *equals* that of 75 conventional aircraft.

A major advance in U.S. bomber modernization, or flying white elephant? One thing is for certain, as America grapples with its air defense posture for the 21st century, the debate over the B-2 Bomber won't end anytime soon.

© *Kauffmann 2008*

Bruce's History Lessons:
Mr. Hitsville U.S.A

When you think of the assembly line in the car business, you think of the Ford Motor Company. When you think of the assembly line in the music business you think of Motown Records. There's a reason for that. Motown's founder, Berry Gordy, who was born this week (Nov. 28) in 1929, built the Motown Record Company based on the business principles he learned while working at a Ford assembly plant in Detroit in the early 1950s.

Ford's chief business principle was, of course, the moving assembly line in which identical parts traveled down a conveyor belt, passing by workstations where additional parts were added, until the finished product emerged at the end of the line. Gordy believed this concept could be adapted to the music business, so when he started Motown Records in 1959, he quickly established a team of "musical assembly workers." They included a "house band" with a distinct musical sound, a standardized song-writing team, an in-house marketing group, and even staff choreographers who could take raw talent off the streets of Detroit and — in an assembly-like succession of training sessions — teach it to sing, talk, dress and dance in a way that could be acceptable to crossover white audiences as well as African-Americans.

It was mass-produced music, much of it based on songs Gordy himself composed while working at Ford. The tedium of the job, combined with the rhythmic pounding of the machinery, allowed Gordy to compose songs in his head, which he then frantically wrote down during coffee breaks.

Those musical musings, plus Gordy's Ford-based business model, produced such hit makers as Stevie Wonder, Smokey Robinson, Marvin Gaye, Martha and the Vandellas, The Temptations, The Four Tops and the biggest hit maker of them all — the musical equivalent of the Ford Mustang — The Supremes.

By the mid-1960s Gordy's Motown empire, labeled "Hitsville U.S.A.", included eight record labels, a publishing company, a managing service and a record for musical chart busting unrivaled at the time. In 1966, 75 percent of Motown's releases made the musical charts.

But from 1970 on, Motown went into decline. Many artists left for other record labels, convinced that Gordy was cheating them out of royalties, or ignoring them to focus on a favored few such as The Supremes' lead singer, Diana Ross. As a result, Motown was never the same, and in 1988 Gordy sold it to a business conglomerate.

Still, any man ultimately responsible for "Dancing in the Streets" (Martha and the Vandellas), "My Girl" (The Temptations), "I'll Be Doggone" (Marvin Gaye), and "Tracks of My Tears" (*the great* Smokey Robinson) deserves immortality, which Gordy received in 1990 when he was inducted into the Rock and Roll Hall of Fame.

© Kauffmann 2008

Bruce's History Lessons:
The Election of 1824

What almost happened in the Bush-Gore election of 2000, namely a deadlocked national presidential election being decided by the House of Representatives, actually did happen this week (Dec. 1) in the presidential election of 1824. And that isn't the only similarity between the two elections.

The candidates running in the 1824 election were John Quincy Adams, who had been secretary of state in the previous administration of James Monroe; Henry Clay, America's most famous United States senator; Andrew Jackson, national icon and war hero; and William Crawford, Monroe's secretary of the treasury. Yet when the votes were tallied, no candidate had received an electoral majority, meaning that, in compliance with the 12th Amendment to the Constitution, the House would have to choose among the top three vote getters.

The top three were Jackson, Adams and Crawford, which left Clay the odd man out. But it also made Clay a potential kingmaker. Whoever he supported would probably become president, meaning that the winning candidate would be very grateful, and beholden, to Clay.

As history records, Clay threw his support behind Adams, and when Adams subsequently won the House election and became president, he appointed Clay his secretary of state. Thus did Jackson and his followers accuse the two men of making "a corrupt bargain."

On the surface the charge had merit. Clay had long sought the presidency, and in those days the surest political steppingstone to that office was the position of secretary of state. Thomas Jefferson, James Madison, James Monroe and now Adams himself had gained the presidency from that office, so Clay's appointment put him on the fast track. What's more, it was known that Clay and Adams had met privately prior to Clay's decision to support Adams.

On the other hand, Clay's support of Adams was completely defensible. Both were "National Republicans" who supported an activist national government that would build highways, canals and railroads, plus create a national bank to encourage the growth of industrialism. This was an anathema to Jackson and his Democratic party of populists and farmers.

Whatever the truth, and most historians believe any Clay-Adams "bargain" was more implicit than complicit, Adam's victory so enraged Jackson and his followers that they vowed revenge against Adams in the election of 1828 — a vow they made good on by defeating Adams and denying him re-election.

Which is interesting because in 2000, Al Gore's Democratic supporters, just like Andrew Jackson's, felt that their man was robbed, and they vowed revenge on Bush in the following election. Whether they succeed or not remains to be seen, but one other similarity should give Bush's supporters pause. George W. and John Quincy are the only two men whose fathers also were president. Both dads were denied re-election.

© Kauffmann 2008

Bruce's History Lessons:
A Good Walk Spoiled

"A good walk spoiled."

-Humorist Samuel Clemens describing a round of golf.

The golf tee was patented this week (Dec. 12) in 1899, which allowed golfers to achieve more distance on their drives and created God knows how many jobs in the tee manufacturing industry. Other than that, it was just another small change in a sport that has seen many since the Scots first invented it early in the 15th century.

The sport was a good match for the stoic, unflappable Scottish temperament, although — alas for the rest of us — while the game turned out to be easily exportable, stoicism was not, which helps explain the number of broken clubs rusting at the bottom of so many golf course water hazards around the world. But in any case, golf became so popular in Scotland the Scottish Parliament had to pass laws prohibiting its play because Scottish warriors were neglecting their military training in pursuit of the little brown ball (the first golf balls were made of leather and feathers, presumably in the hopes of increasing their "flight").

These laws were mostly ignored, and became somewhat problematic when Scotland's own King James IV became an avid golfer — a passion he passed down to his granddaughter, Mary Queen of Scots, who, while living in France, frequently played. And since it was customary for royalty to be accompanied by attendants, she was followed around the course by young men called *cadets*, a name that was later translated in Scottish to "caddy," or "caddie," which is what we now call the young men who tote golf bags for the mostly rich, white, out-of-shape country club golfers who play the game on weekends.

In turn, Mary's passion for golf was shared by her son, who became England's King James I. When James was not dodging assassination attempts by Catholic fanatics such as Guy Fawkes, he was often on the links, and soon much of England was playing the game. From the British Isles, it was exported to the European continent, and then to places like America, where today nearly 30 million people play — a figure that, thanks to golf superstar Tiger Woods, is expected to increase dramatically.

And speaking of fanatics, golf has had its share, which has inspired many a joke poking fun at the devotion it inspires. My favorite involves the foursome that was playing a local course one Sunday afternoon when a funeral procession passed nearby. This prompted one player to back away from his putt, turn toward the line of cars, and silently bow his head until it passed.

"That was thoughtful of you," said his playing partner.

"It was the least I could do for my wife," the man replied.

© Kauffmann 2008

Bruce's History Lessons:
The Wright Stuff

In my favorite museum in the world, the Air & Space Museum located in Washington, D.C., star status is accorded the tiny biplane that forever changed history 100 years ago this week. On December 17, 1903, in Kill Devil Hills, North Carolina, two brothers named Wilbur and Orville Wright successfully completed the first-ever flight of a self-propelled, pilot-controlled, heaver-than-air aircraft.

Orville was the first to go airborne in their propeller-driven biplane — aptly named the Flyer — lasting a total of 12 seconds. Wilbur took the most successful flight of that historic day, remaining airborne for 59 seconds and traveling 852 feet. The five witnesses gathered at Kill Devil Hills, near Kitty Hawk, registered complete astonishment, as did the world when news of the historic flight quickly spread.

The two brothers, who grew up in Dayton, Ohio, were both gifted engineers and wizards at mechanical design. In 1892 they opened a bicycle shop that was soon thriving, and profits from their business, plus the experience in mechanical problem-solving that the business gave them, allowed them to indulge in their long-held dream of building the world's first airplane.

First, however, they researched every previous attempt at manned flight, using that information to design an experimental glider. Next, the brothers wrote the U.S. Weather Bureau asking about a suitable spot to conduct glider tests. They were told that Kitty Hawk, a village on North Carolina's Outer Banks, had suitable winds and sand dunes on which a glider could land softly. In 1901 they conducted their first successful tests of a glider at Kitty Hawk, and the experience helped them construct a wind tunnel where they then tested wings and airframes of every size and shape.

The next year when they returned to Kitty Hawk, their glider flights were uniformly successful. It was time to add an engine.

Back in Dayton they designed a small internal combustion engine and built a new aircraft around it. They then returned to Kitty Hawk, re-assembled their plane, and on December 14 first attempted manned flight. Unfortunately, the engine stalled on take-off and the plane crashed. But after spending three days repairing the plane, they tried again and when Orville finally guided the Flyer into the air on that December morning, the modern aviation age also took wing.

And what a flight it has been, sending us across countries and continents, around the world, into space, to the moon, to Mars, to distant galaxies and beyond. Indeed, while the Flyer rests on its laurels in the Air & Space Museum, one of its progeny, the Pioneer 10 spacecraft, having long ago left our solar system, is heading toward the constellation Taurus, which it should reach in 2 million years.

© Kauffmann 2008

Bruce's History Lessons:
A Christmas Present from George

In December of 1776, the prospects for the American Revolution seemed bleak indeed. The nation's tiny, demoralized army and its humiliated commander, George Washington, had retreated across the Delaware River to Pennsylvania, having been routed by the British army in New York and New Jersey. Even Washington's own officers had lost confidence in him, and some were plotting his removal.

For their part the British were so pleased with the war's direction, they had gone into winter quarters, but not before the British commander, General Howe, established several military outposts throughout New York and New Jersey, from which he would launch new offensives once the weather improved in the spring.

One of those outposts was in Trenton, New Jersey, and as General Washington gazed in that direction from his makeshift headquarters across the Delaware River, he decided that desperate times called for desperate measures. He would attack that outpost on Christmas Day, sending an invasion force across the river in order to catch the British by surprise.

And so, in the early morning of December 25, 1776, three columns of American troops set out across the Delaware, and although progress was good initially, a driving rain soon turned to snow, and high winds and strong currents hampered their progress. As a result, only one of Washington's columns made it across the river, and he and his men still had a 10-mile hike to Trenton.

That hike ranks among the most desperate and important military marches in American history. Just as it began, the weather turned ferocious — howling winds and a mixture of sleet, snow and ice drenched the men, froze their extremities and made the footing so treacherous that many soldiers fell, never to get up again.

Yet on balance, the weather was a Godsend because the British stationed in Trenton — actually, most were German mercenaries — were so confident that no attack was possible in the terrible storm, they were caught by surprise and completely overwhelmed when Washington and his men suddenly appeared.

Militarily, the victory at Trenton was not significant, but as a morale booster it was a critical turning point in the war. That is because on January 1, most of Washington's men were eligible to go home, their terms of enlistment having expired. Prior to Trenton, most of them surely would have done so, leaving Washington — and America — without a real army. But their morale and spirits now restored, many decided to stay on, and as word of the victory at Trenton spread, new enlistees joined up.

There would be many dark days ahead, but George Washington's heroic "crossing of the Delaware" and victory at Trenton was a timely, and welcome, Christmas present to the new nation.

© Kauffmann 2008

Bruce's History Lessons:
The Lord of Middle Earth

With the third installment of John Ronald Reuel (J.R.R.) Tolkien's magnificent trilogy *The Lord of the Rings* now in movie theaters nationwide, it seems appropriate to visit with the man himself, especially since he was born this week (Jan 3) in 1892.

His literary career began in his early twenties when his talent for linguistics helped earn him a scholarship to Oxford University, where he studied Old and Middle English. For fun, Tolkien also began inventing his own languages.

Graduating from Oxford in 1915, Tolkien joined the army and fought in the trenches during World War I, but after developing trench fever he was sent home to recuperate. It was during his recovery that Tolkien first began writing stories about "Middle Earth," creating characters, magical creatures, entirely new languages and histories that would lay the groundwork for his two most famous works, *The Hobbit* and *The Lord of the Rings*.

In 1918 Tolkien returned to Oxford, where, except for a brief professorship at Leeds University, he would spend the rest of his academic life. At Oxford, Tolkien published several acclaimed studies and translations of Old and Middle English stories, including the legend of the Knights of the Roundtable.

This interest in legends would manifest itself in his own writings, and was reinforced by his friendship with England's other literary giant, C.S. Lewis (*The Lion, the Witch and the Wardrobe*), who also taught at Oxford. Tolkien and Lewis both loved a tall tale, especially one with mythological origins, and so the two scholars started an informal study group called "The Inklings," which met weekly in Lewis's quarters at Oxford to discuss mythology, literature, religion and many other topics. It was during these weekly meetings that Tolkien first read aloud excerpts from *The Hobbit* and the first book of his great "Ring" trilogy, *The Fellowship of the Ring.*

Both Lewis and Tolkien also were firm adherents of Christianity, and its influence on their work is undeniable. In Tolkien's case, the themes of good versus evil — think Gandalf and Aragon struggling against the Dark Lord Sauron — the call to sacrifice and heroism, and the prevalence of magic and miracles in the "Rings" trilogy are manifestations of his religious convictions and his passion for mythology. Indeed, Tolkien believed that mythology shared religion's power to enrich the spirit and explain universal truths.

When J.R.R. Tolkien died in 1973 he had gained a following rare among writers — he was as revered on college campuses as he was in literary circles. And rightfully so. *The Lord of the Rings* trilogy is as fine, and fun, a piece of writing as ever there was.

And speaking of miracles, the movie versions of the trilogy actually do it justice.

© *Kauffmann 2008*

Bruce's History Lessons:
The Lesson of Der Alte

This is the story of a man, Konrad Adenauer, who became the leader of West Germany in 1949, shortly after Germany's defeat in World War II had divided the nation into East and West, had destroyed the country's economy, had eradicated its infrastructure, killed millions of its people, sent its leadership packing and branded it a pariah among nations.

In other words, Germany in 1949 resembled Iraq today. How Adenauer turned West Germany into a respected member of the world community, while restoring its economic vibrancy and national pride, may provide some lessons for both the alliance now occupying Iraq and its critics.

Adenauer was born this week (Jan.5) in 1876, meaning he was already 73 when he became West Germany's new leader. "Der Alte" — "the old man" — as his countrymen called him, had been a wily enough politician to stay out of the clutches of the Nazis during the war, while still exhibiting an utter contempt for them. But contempt was an emotion no effective post-war politician could afford, and one of Adenauer's earliest and most controversial decisions was to adopt amnesty laws that absolved many of the most ardent Nazis of their war crimes, while also passing laws that restored hundreds of thousands of Nazi party members and sympathizers to their old jobs — including government jobs.

Although this directly defied Allied wishes, Adenauer reasoned that to build a new state, he needed the skills and experience of these former Nazis. Further, he thought that prosecuting them, or refusing to allow them back into German society, would breed massive discontent, while offering them a fresh start would ensure their allegiance to the new state. Adenauer knew that his policies papered over the monstrous crimes perpetrated by the Nazis,

311

but his first priority was to create stability and then a sense of normalcy in Germany. Once the country was strong enough, Adenauer reasoned, those difficult questions about guilt and responsibility could be debated without the fear of tearing the country apart.

Adenauer's second controversial decision was to bind the country to the West as a bulwark against Soviet expansionism. "We belong to the West, not the East," Adenauer insisted, and to those Germans who preferred remaining neutral in Europe in order to play the East and West off each other, Adenauer replied, "The moment that happens, Germany will become a (Soviet) satellite."

That Adenauer's policies were successful is confirmed by the unprecedented prosperity and worldwide acceptance that Germany has achieved since 1949. It is also confirmed by the fact that Adenauer was elected to four terms as German chancellor.

Food for thought for both President Bush, and those seeking his job, with respect to our approach to post-war Iraq today.

© Kauffmann 2008

Bruce's History Lessons:
Madison Weighs In

Memo to: Supreme Court Justice Sandra Day O'Connor, principal author of the majority decision upholding the McCain-Feingold Campaign Finance Reform Act

From: James Madison (deceased), principal author of the Constitution and Bill of Rights

Re: Your Constitutional reasoning

Dear Mrs. (sorry, Ms.) O'Connor: I am spinning in my grave here. What part about the First Amendment's language "Congress shall make no law abridging the freedom of speech" do you not understand? McCain-Feingold, which Congress made into law, severely restricts political speech. Therefore, your ruling that it passes Constitutional muster is incorrect. And I know of what I speak. I wrote the First Amendment!

McCain-Feingold states that no radio or TV political advertisements paid for by independent organizations can say the name of a candidate for federal office within 30 days of a primary or 60 days of a general election. In other words, neither the National Rifle Association, nor the Sierra Club, can criticize a specific candidate whose voting record they find abhorrent. *That*, my black-robed friend, is abridgment of free speech!

It also undermines one of my core principles — namely, that republican government works best when *all* Americans, not just the rich, have an equal opportunity to join with other like-minded Americans to protect their political interests. Alone, John Doe does not have the political influence of, say, Bill Gates (boy, do I wish I'd owned a computer in 1785), but if John wants to leverage his influence by forming a political organization with Tom, Dick and Harry to promote a cause that they all believe in — whether it's

313

gun ownership or environmentalism — they should have the right to freely express that cause in any way, and at any time, they see fit. That includes running so-called "issue ads" critical of opposing candidates right before a primary or election. That's when political expression is the most important because that's when voters are the most attentive!

Now I will admit that one man's — sorry, person's — "issue ad" is another person's "attack ad," but so what? Passionate speech, including speech that attacks opponents, is a part of politics, and no court should decide what speech is too "passionate" to be allowed. Granted, as senators McCain and Feingold both know, most "attack" ads attack incumbents because incumbents have public records that can be criticized. No wonder they want to abridge such speech — it hurts their chances of re-election. But is it the Supreme Court's job to protect incumbents?

In the America I envisioned in 1789, every citizen has an equal right to engage in political expression and association. McCain-Feingold makes some citizens more equal than others. That makes it unconstitutional. That means you should re-consider.

Thanks for listening. Dolley says hi and adds, "You go, girl."

© Kauffmann 2008

Bruce's History Lessons:
The Birth of Robert E. Lee

Robert E. Lee was born this week (Jan. 19) in 1807, and as is well known, he became one of the greatest military generals in American history, repeatedly managing to outwit, outmaneuver and defeat Union armies that were superior in numbers, and that were better equipped, supplied and reinforced. Had Lee not fought for the Confederacy, the Civil War would have been over in months, not years, which would have changed forever Abe Lincoln's place in history, to say nothing of the history of slavery, Reconstruction, the Republican and Democratic parties, and North-South relations.

And the irony was that no man in the U.S. Army in 1860 was more pro-union than Lee, whose pedigree was as American as they came. His father, "Light Horse" Harry Lee, was among George Washington's most trusted military commanders during the Revolutionary War, and — irony of ironies — Harry Lee was the man President Washington chose to stamp out the new nation's first secessionist threat, the Whiskey Rebellion of 1794.

His son, Robert E. Lee, even married into Washington's family; Lee's wife, Mary Custis, was the great granddaughter of Martha Washington and, through adoption, George Washington himself. Lee's military career was also pure Americana — he graduated from the U.S. Military Academy at West Point, and later became its superintendent. Finally, Lee led the force that put down John Brown's attempt to foment a slave rebellion at Harper's Ferry, West Virginia, a rebellion meant to start a civil war.

Small wonder that as the Civil War loomed, President Abe Lincoln offered Lee the one job that Lee had always wanted, command of the U.S. Army. Not only would it have allowed Lee to follow in the footsteps of his own father, but also in those of his relative by marriage, the "Father of Our Country."

Yet Lee not only refused Lincoln's offer, he resigned his commission in the army.

He did so because the only tie stronger than his tie to America was his tie to his home state of Virginia. Lee knew that in the event of war, Virginia would secede from the Union, and he could never, as he put it, "raise my hand against my birthplace, my home." Five days after refusing Lincoln's offer, Lee became commander of Virginia's forces, and later a brigadier general in the Confederate Army. From there his rise to commander of all Confederate forces was inevitable.

Of course, despite Lee's brilliant generalship, the Confederacy lost the war, but it never tainted Lee's reputation, at least not in the South where he is more revered today than any man before him or since.

A Confederate soldier put it well. "I've heard of God," he said, "but I've *seen* General Lee."

© *Kauffmann 2008*

Bruce's History Lessons:
The King Who Lost America

George William Frederick of the House of Hanover died, mercifully, this week (Jan. 29) in 1820. In America his passing caused a minor stir among the people, due mostly to the fact that he was the last British monarch to rule over them. King George III, as he was more commonly known, died totally blind, nearly deaf and completely insane, having suffered for years from a blood disease that affected the brain. It also was said that he died of a broken heart, having never gotten over the loss of his American colonies.

Not that George doesn't deserve his share of the blame for that loss. Although Parliament gets most of the responsibility for the ill-advised and ultimately counter-productive decision to impose direct taxation on America, George deserves most of the blame for refusing to compromise with America's bid for some measure of economic and political sovereignty. After seeing his grandfather, George II, and great grandfather, George I, fritter away both power and privilege to a resurgent Whig Party in Parliament, George III was determined to regain the upper hand, and his dealings with the colonies reflected his dealings with all who tried to erode his power and influence. To George, it was "My way or the (Royal) highway."

Which was unfortunate because, right up until the Declaration of Independence itself, the colonists had mostly blamed Parliament for their quarrel with the mother country, believing that their good King George was being misled and ill informed about Parliament's hard-line stance. As a result, although the colonists insisted on the power to control their internal affairs, such as direct taxation, they were perfectly willing to let their king hold sway over external affairs, such as regulating trade, which was 10 times more profitable for England than any tax revenue it could ever have collected from the colonists.

317

This classic "penny wise and pound foolish" approach to America cost George his most profitable trading relationship and may well have heightened his dementia. By 1811 he was so delusional that he once began conversing with a tree, thinking it was the King of Prussia (Prussian kings were wooden, but not *that* wooden). Shortly thereafter he was stripped of his powers in favor of his son, the Prince of Wales, who was appointed Regent until George III finally died. At that point, the son, whom George detested, became King George IV.

An excellent movie of this historic period is *The Madness of King George*, starring the fine English actor, Nigel Hawthorne. The title refers to George's mental state, but it could just as easily refer to his decision to pursue a policy that ultimately left America no choice but to go its own away.

© Kauffmann 2008

Bruce's History Lessons:
The Hedgehog

"The fox knows many things. The hedgehog knows one big thing."

– Isaiah Berlin

Ronald Reagan, born this week (Feb. 6) in 1911, was a hedgehog from his tail to his snout. And the one big thing he knew was that Communism was an ideology devoid of a single redeeming factor, and that its chief practitioner, the Soviet Union, was the greatest threat to human freedom, and world peace, in all of recorded history.

And so, from his days as president of the Screen Actors Guild, where he battled a significant Communist presence, to his days as president of the United States, Ronald Reagan made it his highest priority to end what he called the "evil empire" of Communist-driven totalitarianism that the Soviet Union had created in Eastern Europe, and had inspired — and supported — in many parts of Asia, Africa and Latin America.

His plan to do this began with reversing a policy that a previous president from his own party had created — *détente*. Whereas Richard Nixon had resigned himself to "co-existing" with the Soviets, even to the point of propping up their tenuous economy with investment, loans, credits and improved trade relations, Reagan took a diametrically opposite approach. His goal was to force the Soviets into an ever-spiraling level of military spending that would eventually bankrupt them and force them to choose between imploding and changing.

Thus did Reagan embark on a military spending spree that resulted in a 600-ship Navy, a vastly expanded air bomber force, legions of new missiles and weapons systems, and his pride and joy, the Strategic Defense Initiative

(SDI). Dubbed "Star Wars" by its critics, it was meant to be a space-based missile defense system that could shoot down Soviet intercontinental ballistic missiles.

To be sure, Reagan's military spending contributed to trillion dollar budget deficits in the United States, but when all was said and done, the U.S. managed to survive deficit spending. The U.S.S.R. did not. The *coup de grace* was SDI, which may have been a pipe dream (and as envisioned certainly would have been staggeringly expensive), but it convinced then-Soviet Premier Mikhail Gorbachev that radical changes were needed in the Soviet system, or the country would fall further behind the West. The "evil empire" soon fell, much to Reagan's credit.

As a postscript, in 1994 a special on PBS television (not exactly a conservative mouthpiece) detailing the Soviet Union's demise included an interview with Victor Kulikov, the former head of the Soviet Warsaw Pact military forces. During the interview, Kulikov said of SDI, "It was a piece of adventurism, an attempt to mow us down economically, to force us to spend all of our resources on counter-measures."

He adds glumly, "Unfortunately, it worked."

© *Kauffmann 2008*

Bruce's History Lessons:
The St. Valentine's Day Massacre

The dominant color at the warehouse on Clark Street on Chicago's North Side was red that day (Feb.14) in 1929, which should have been fitting since it was Valentine's Day. But it wasn't red roses or red hearts that were all over the place — it was red blood. Seven men, six of them members of gangster George "Bugs" Moran's mob, had been brutally gunned down in the most spectacular, and famous, gangland hit in American history, the "St. Valentine's Day Massacre."

Police immediately suspected that Moran's chief rival, Al "Scarface" Capone, was behind the murders, and most historians agree. Yet to this day Capone's guilt has never been proven. For one thing, Capone was in Florida during the hit, and, for another, the killers were never caught, thanks to the fact that the massacre was an extremely clever and meticulously planned operation.

Indeed, Chicago police at first were puzzled that Moran's gang members — all well-armed, hardened criminals — were so easily disarmed and killed, not even putting up a fight. Police also were puzzled by the fact that, immediately after the shooting, eyewitnesses saw two police officers escorting two men, both with their hands up, out of the warehouse. According to police records no officers should have been anywhere near the area at that time.

But eventually, the puzzle became clearer. Two of the four killers who entered the warehouse that day were dressed as policemen, making it relatively easy to fool Moran's gang members into thinking it was a routine bust. That explains why they allowed themselves to be disarmed. What's more, by leaving the crime scene with the two "policemen" escorting two men they had "captured," it made the eyewitnesses think the police had the situation under control. That explains why no one called the police until hours after the killers had escaped — everyone thought the police were already there.

In the end, the St; Valentine's Day massacre spelled the end of Bugs Moran's operations in Chicago — he never recovered from the ignominy — but the massacre also probably contributed to Capone's own demise. Although Chicago's denizens had for years endured mob hits, robberies, beatings and shootouts among rival gangs, the St. Valentine's Day Massacre was such an outrage, they finally had had enough. Public pressure and a crusading media — not to mention a police force angered at being impersonated — resulted in a law enforcement crackdown on organized crime. Moran was even forced to leave Chicago and eventually went to prison for robbery.

As for Capone, he too eventually went to prison, although in an amusing irony, he was not convicted for spilling red blood, but for spilling red ink. In 1931, Capone was found guilty of income tax evasion.

© Kauffmann 2008

Bruce's History Lessons:
The Indispensable Baron

Historically, one of the more amusing foibles among many European "royalty" — a foible that continues to some extent even today — is that the length and grandiosity of their official names and titles are almost always in inverse proportion to the likelihood that they have any more noble lineage than do you or I.

So it was with Lieutenant General Friedrich Wilhelm Ludolf Gerhard Augustin Baron von Steuben, whose claim to be a wealthy German baron was as bogus as his insistence that he had once held high rank under Frederick the Great. Yet unlike the hundreds of other foreigners who came to America during the Revolutionary War hoping to wangle out of Congress a high military commission and commensurate salary, Baron von Steuben's arrival at Valley Forge this week (Feb. 23) in 1778 was an answered prayer. Militarily, few Americans, let alone foreigners, were more important to the success of America's Continental army than was von Steuben, whose genius at military training and discipline was the one thing America's revolutionary forces sorely needed.

It was von Steuben who quickly grasped the unique character of the American citizen-soldier and organized his training and drilling regimen to accommodate it. "You say to your (European) soldier, 'Do this,' and he does it," von Steuben explained in a letter written from Valley Forge to a friend. "But here I am obliged to say to a soldier, 'This is the reason you ought to do that,' and then he does it."

Partly as a result, von Steuben was able to turn a disorganized and badly demoralized collection of individuals into a disciplined, cohesive fighting unit. He taught Washington's army how to use bayonets in close combat.

He showed them how to maneuver in ranks, curing them of the tendency to fight in single file. He taught them to concentrate their musket fire for more deadly results.

What's more, von Steuben turned many of the drills into competitions, which made them more fun. It also didn't hurt that von Steuben's mercurial personality — he could be ecstatic one moment and apoplectic the next — and his tendency to curse in his native German (his English was so bad, he usually needed a translator) became an ongoing source of amusement to the troops, who soon grew fond of their ebullient drillmaster. Both von Steuben and his training methods became a sport at Valley Forge, which was a very welcome change of pace.

As was the performance of the army that emerged from Valley Forge in the spring of 1778. Thanks in great part to Baron von Steuben — an imposter as a nobleman, but the real deal as a military man — America was on its way to winning the Revolutionary War.

© Kauffmann 2008

Bruce's History Lessons:
Uncle Walter Turns Against the War

Given the general disfavor in which "the media" is now held, it may be hard to believe that in the 1960s the most trusted person in America was the anchorman for the CBS Evening News, Walter Cronkite. In survey after survey Americans cited "Uncle Walter," as he was affectionately known, as the man they most trusted for honesty and objectivity. When he signed off his evening broadcast by saying, "And that's the way it is, [on such-and-such date]," millions of Americans took it as gospel.

Which is why his broadcast this week (Feb.27) in 1968 was such a crucial turning point in the fortunes of both the Vietnam War and the man leading America's effort to wage that war — President Lyndon Johnson. On his February 27th broadcast, Walter Cronkite denounced America's presence in Vietnam.

He had just returned from his own fact-finding tour of Vietnam, and what he found convinced him that victory was impossible in this "burned, blasted and weary land." Cronkite told his millions of viewers that the war was "a stalemate," and that the only "rational policy" was "to negotiate" an end to it.

Among the millions watching that broadcast was President Johnson himself, a man with unsurpassed political antennae. "If I've lost Walter Cronkite," he reportedly said to one of his aides, "I've lost Middle America."

He was right. Prior to Cronkite's broadcast, both the Gallup and Harris polls showed that 61 percent of the American people strongly supported the war — up five percent from the previous month — and even favored stronger military measures if they were deemed necessary. Among those stronger measures was continued bombing of North Vietnam, which was supported by 70 percent of the country. Yes, there was resistance to the war, but it came mostly from the nation's college students, who were seen by Middle America as a bunch of drug-taking, promiscuous fruitcakes.

After February 27th things changed dramatically. In early March, Americans who thought the war was a mistake outnumbered supporters 49 – 41 percent, and Johnson's job approval ratings plummeted. Adding injury to insult, on March 12 in the New Hampshire presidential primary, challenger Eugene McCarthy stunned Johnson by gathering 42 percent of the vote, which prompted Johnson's chief political rival, Robert Kennedy, to jump into the presidential race. Three weeks later Johnson announced he would not run for re-election.

It is an oversimplification to say that Walter Cronkite brought Johnson down. There had long been an undercurrent of bewilderment about the war, exacerbated by conflicting government pronouncements, troop escalation and rising body counts. On the other hand, Cronkite's seminal broadcast marked a clear denouement. Imagine Dan Rather, Tom Brokaw or Peter Jennings having that kind of influence today.

© Kauffmann 2008

Bruce's History Lessons: Lincoln's Second Inaugural

Walk up the steps of the Lincoln Memorial in our nation's capital, enter the hallowed room where the statue of Abraham Lincoln resides, and look to your left. There, inscribed on the wall, you will see *not* the greatest speech ever written by an American, but the most important speech. The Gettysburg Address literally changed the country. It confirmed for posterity that this nation was "conceived in liberty" and founded on the proposition that "all men are created equal." In this speech, Lincoln brilliantly reminded his countrymen that the intellectual foundation on which America stood was not the Constitution, a document that at the time allowed slavery, but the Declaration of Independence. The Gettysburg Address purified the nation, gave it a nobler creed, and made it more worthy of preserving.

Now — still standing before Lincoln's statue — look to your right to the wall across from the Gettysburg Address. There you will see inscribed Lincoln's Second Inaugural Address. This *is* the greatest speech ever written by an American, and it was delivered this week (March 4) in 1865 on the occasion of the ceremony that for the second time made Lincoln president of the United States.

The Second Inaugural also conveyed an important message: that although both sides had sought to avoid the Civil War they had been waging for four years, and although both sides prayed to the same God for assistance in that war, the prayers of neither side could be answered fully because "God has his own purposes." Lincoln was subtly suggesting that the causes of the war could be laid at the feet of both sides, which is one reason why the Union side, at that point clearly winning the war (Lee would surrender to Grant a month later), must be charitable in its treatment of the defeated South.

But enough — let's let Lincoln's words do the talking, for they are greater than any I could conjure to describe them. Herewith my favorite passage from one of my favorite speeches:

"Fondly do we hope, fervently do we pray, that this mighty scourge of war shall speedily pass away. Yet, if God wills that it continue, until all the wealth piled by the bond-man's (slave's) two hundred and fifty years of unrequited toil shall be sunk, and until every drop of blood drawn with the lash shall be paid by another, drawn with the sword, then as was said three thousand years ago, so still it must be said, 'the judgments of the Lord are true and righteous altogether.'"

With all due respect to Thomas Jefferson, Lincoln is the greatest writer ever to serve as president. And for my money, the greatest president ever to serve the nation.

© Kauffmann 2008

Bruce's History Lessons:
New York Times Co. v. Sullivan

Your humble columnist and the newspaper that publishes this column both owe a great debt to the Supreme Court for the landmark case, *New York Times Co. v. Sullivan,* which, as much as any legal decision ever rendered, protects a newspaper's ability to seek out the truth.

Our story begins in 1960, when the *Times* published an advertisement placed by a civil rights group that criticized certain "Southern violators of the Constitution." At the time, members of the nascent civil rights movement were being harassed, incarcerated and beaten by avowed segregationists, especially in Montgomery, Alabama, where L.B. Sullivan served as police commissioner. Sullivan took offense at the ad's generic description of actions by "the police," even though the ad never mentioned him by name. He sued the *Times* for libel, seeking $500,000 in damages.

In the subsequent trial, which occurred in Montgomery, an all-white jury awarded Sullivan the full amount, and when lawyers for the *Times* appealed to the Alabama Supreme Court on First Amendment grounds — that restricting freedom of the press was unconstitutional — the court ruled against them, arguing that the First Amendment did not protect slanderous statements, which the lower court ruled had occurred in this case because several statements in the advertisement, although trivial, were incorrect. Worse, Alabama's Supreme Court took the lower court's ruling a step further, stating that when *any* government department is criticized, then *any member of that department* can sue for libel. That ruling, had it stood, would have given blanket immunity from criticism to all branches of government.

It also would have returned us to the year 1800, when President John Adams instituted the infamous Alien and Sedition Acts, the latter of which made it a crime to criticize members of his government. However, when Tom Jefferson replaced Adams, the Sedition Acts were immediately repealed and every editor arrested under them released.

Which was exactly the historic precedent that the *Times* lawyers used in arguing before the U.S. Supreme Court that First Amendment protections did apply in this case, and that criticizing public officials is a long-standing right. The Supreme Court agreed, and this week (March 9) in 1964, it handed down its decision, stipulating that as long as there was "absence of malice" — meaning that any incorrect statements were not made on purpose — then criticism of government officials is protected speech.

To gauge how important *NYT v. Sullivan* was to the free press we enjoy today, consider this. Exactly a decade after it was handed down, the Nixon administration and the national media were fighting an all-out war over press coverage of the Watergate break-in. Ask yourself whether that battle might have ended differently had *NYT v. Sullivan* not been in effect.

© *Kauffmann 2008*

Bruce's History Lessons: Jemmy Madison: Underrated and Mostly Ignored

We come again to the birthday of (my hero) James Madison, this week (March 16) in 1751, a birthday I periodically remind readers of for one reason. No one else does.

Regular readers know my complaint. Madison is responsible for two of the three documents on which America is founded. Jefferson wrote the Declaration of Independence, but Madison created the Constitution and the Bill of Rights, earning him the title "Father of ..." the former document and "Chief Architect of ..." the latter. Yet there is no national monument to him, no holiday commemorates his birth, and now — a brand new complaint — *there is no best selling biography of his life!*

Think about it. Biographies of Jefferson are everywhere — many of them, such as *American Sphinx* by Joseph Ellis, quite good. Ditto Washington, who not only is the subject of several popular biographies, but also is the centerpiece of every history of the American Revolution.

Same with Ben Franklin who was recently the subject of two outstanding and popular biographies, *The First American* by H.W. Brands, and *Benjamin Franklin* by Walter Isaacson. And Alexander Hamilton was the subject of the best biography I have read in many years, Ron Chernow's very popular, highly acclaimed *Alexander Hamilton.*_

Even John Adams, the one Founder who was convinced history would ignore him and future generations would forget him, scored with a best-selling biography by "America's Historian," David McCullough. (While alive, Adams complained bitterly of his supposed future anonymity. Does

331

McCullough's book prove that even in history, "the squeaky wheel gets the grease"?)

But no such biography has been written for Madison. The question is, why?

The answer seems to be as follows: Unlike Washington, Madison did not earn glory on the battlefield, nor become America's first and only unanimously elected president. Unlike Jefferson, Madison did not pen immortal prose, nor make a huge land purchase, nor get accused of sleeping with his slaves.

Unlike Franklin, Madison was not a scientist whose experiments were studied worldwide, or an inventor whose inventions are still in use today. Unlike Hamilton, Madison did not create our monetary system, nor die gloriously in a duel. And unlike Adams, Madison was not lucky enough to die on the same day as Jefferson — and on July 4th, 1826, the 50th anniversary of independence.

And then there is the fact that, of them all, Madison was the least concerned about his place in history. Indeed, as I have written, in June 1836 when Madison himself was dying, his many admirers wanted him to take stimulants in the hope he could last until that July 4th, the 60th anniversary of independence, thereby ensuring his immortality. Madison politely declined and died a week early.

© Kauffmann 2008

Bruce's History Lessons: Liberty, Death and Immortality

This week (March 23) in 1775, a young Virginian named Patrick Henry uttered seven words that would ensure his fame forever.

He uttered them in support of the people of Boston, who for almost a year had suffered under a series of British regulations that had shut down the city and put its people under house arrest. The "Intolerable Acts," as these regulations were called, had closed Boston's port to trade, had modified Boston's charter and taken away its right of self-government, had legalized the quartering of British troops in the homes of Boston's citizens, and had denied Boston the right to bring to trial British officials charged with crimes.

In response, civilian leaders of colonial America met at the First Continental Congress in Philadelphia in late 1774, where they passed measures calling for an economic boycott of Britain, as well as resistance to the British Parliament's ongoing attempts to regulate America's internal affairs. This Continental Congress then issued a proclamation asking America's 13 colonies to unite in support of these measures.

Thus did Patrick Henry and other prominent Virginians gather on March 23 in St. John's Church in Richmond to consider this proclamation. Weighing on their minds was not only the fact that supporting it could lead to war with the mother country, but also the fact that Virginia was America's largest, most influential colony, and historically its most pro-British. Whatever Virginia decided would profoundly affect the other colonies.

In this atmosphere, Henry rose to speak. From notes taken at the meeting, he began his speech slowly and with a moderate voice. "The question before the House is one of awful moment to this country," he said. "For my own part I consider it to be nothing less than a question of freedom or slavery."

His voice rising and his cadence sharpening, Henry then reviewed the patient attempts of the colonies to stand up for their rights and Parliament's mean-spirited attempts to thwart them. "Our petitions have been slighted. Our remonstrances have produced additional violence and insult ... we have been spurned!" he said.

And finally, he crossed the Rubicon, demanding defiance to Britain. "There is no retreat but in submission and slavery!" he exclaimed. "Our chains are forged! Their clanking may be heard on the plains of Boston! The war is inevitable — and let it come!

"Is life so dear, or peace so sweet, as to be purchased at the price of chains and slavery?" he asked, and then added in conclusion, "I know not what course others may take; but as for me, *give me liberty or give me death!*"

Patrick Henry would get liberty and, eventually, death. But thanks to those final words, he would also get immortality.

© Kauffmann 2008

Bruce's History Lessons:
The 15ᵗʰ Amendment to the Constitution

The 15th Amendment to the U.S. Constitution, which was adopted this week (March 30) in 1870, has two sections. The first states that "the right of citizens of the United States to vote shall not be denied or abridged by the United States or by any State on account of race, color, or previous condition of servitude." The second section states that "Congress shall have power to enforce this article by appropriate legislation."

This post-Civil War amendment, like its predecessor, the 14th, was designed to prevent the pervasive discrimination against African-Americans, both former slaves and free blacks, that historically had consigned people of color in America to second-class citizenship.

And for a brief period during Reconstruction it worked. In every southern state, the 15th Amendment empowered African-Americans to join with white allies and sympathizers to elect pro-equality candidates — including African-American candidates — to Congress and to state and local governments. The result was an increase in political power, social acceptance and material worth for African-Americans from all walks of life.

However, in the post-Reconstruction period there was a political, economic and even physical backlash against both the "carpetbagger" northerners — those who had come south to help administer Reconstruction — and their African-American allies, as a resurgent southern Democratic Party used both legal and illegal methods to take back power. Under the "states' rights" banner, for example, racist organizations such as the Ku Klux Klan began assaulting blacks, while other, more moderate southerners — motivated partly by cultural racism, but also angered by northern meddling in their political affairs — supported "Jim Crow" laws that emasculated the 14th and 15th Amendments and oppressed African-Americans.

For example, while the 15th Amendment stated that no person can be denied voting rights because of "race, color, or previous condition of servitude," it said nothing about denying them the vote because of a literacy requirement, or the means to pay a poll tax, or any of the other "conditions" that politicians began using to deny African-Americans their voting rights. Additionally, while the 15th Amendment's second section gives Congress the power to enforce the first section, it doesn't say Congress *has* to use it. And from the 1880s on, a southern-dominated U.S. Congress ignored the 15th Amendment, making it toothless.

And there matters stood for nearly 100 years until the Civil Rights movement of the 1960s forced Congress to pass, among other laws, the 24th Amendment, which declared the poll tax illegal, and the Voting Rights Act, which protected all citizens seeking to register to vote.

Politically enfranchised once again, after 1965 the percentage of African-Americans who voted went from 23 percent to 61 percent, thereby restoring both the spirit, and the letter, of the law that was the 15th Amendment.

© Kauffmann 2008

Bruce's History Lessons:
Saving Mount Vernon

In 1854, the place where the Father of Our Country played father to his family was a run-down, dilapidated shambles. Washington's home, Mount Vernon, which was so beloved to him that he kept giving up power to return to it, had a collapsed roof and rotted front portico. Most of the windows were broken, the inside staircases were destroyed, the furniture was in disrepair, and it needed a coat of paint. Someone wrote that a strong wind would likely blow the entire edifice down.

It was, in short, a national disgrace, as Louisa Cunningham discovered when she viewed Mount Vernon from the deck of a boat that passed by it on the Potomac River. Shocked by its ruinous state, she wrote her daughter Ann that something must be done. Ann Cunningham decided to do something.

She created the Mount Vernon Ladies Association with the aim of publicizing Mount Vernon's tragic condition in order to raise enough money to buy it from its current owner, John Washington (a great grandnephew of Washington), and restore it. To this end, she and the other association members wrote letters to newspapers, held fundraisers, gave speeches and even lobbied politicians both in Congress and in the Virginia legislature

At first progress was slow, both in terms of raising funds and negotiating with John Washington, who refused to even consider selling the home to a group of ladies. Fortunately, Cunningham's cause came to the attention of the age's most famous orator, Edward Everett (whose much admired address would precede Lincoln's at the Gettysburg battlefield in 1863), who volunteered not only to make Washington's home the subject of future orations and newspaper articles but also to donate his fees to the association's fundraising efforts.

With their financial picture brighter, the ladies turned to negotiating with John Washington, whose refusal to sell the famous, but endangered home had generated widespread condemnation from the many newspapers that increasingly were taking up the ladies' cause. This only hardened Washington's position, but at a meeting between Cunningham and Washington, Cunningham — rather than condemning him as well — expressed condolences for the criticism he was receiving. That set in motion a change of heart and finally Washington agreed to sell Mount Vernon to the Mount Vernon Ladies Association for $200,000. The sale was consummated this week (April 6) in 1858, and by 1860 Mount Vernon was on its way to becoming what it is today — a majestic, much visited memorial to America's greatest leader.

As for Ann Cunningham and the Mount Vernon Ladies Association, they are honored today as the pioneers of America's historic preservation movement, whose national association, the National Trust for Historic Preservation, once employed me — albeit briefly — as a writer.

© *Kauffmann 2008*

Bruce's History Lessons:
Under God

A while back I wrote what I thought was an inoffensive column on Patrick Henry's most famous speech, but from the deluge of e-mails I received, apparently I was mistaken. Readers took offense at this paragraph in the column: "Is life so dear, or peace so sweet, as to be purchased at the price of chains and slavery?" he (Henry) asked and then added in conclusion, "I know not what course others may take; but as for me, *give me liberty or give me death!*"

As readers pointed out, in between those two sentences Henry invoked "Almighty God." By leaving that out I was, as one reader put it, engaging in historic revisionism and joining the movement to "remove God from the public arena and thought."

That was not my intent, but as the Supreme Court considers the issue of whether the words "under God" in the Pledge of Allegiance violate the "separation of church and state," it might be useful to re-visit the religious proclivities of the Founding Fathers. It might even give us insight into the Pledge controversy.

The Founders were, let's be clear, a religious bunch, with a firm belief in a Creator who, as Jefferson put it, endowed them "with certain unalienable rights." They did believe in a "wall of separation" between church and state, but only in the sense that they did not want the state to sanction any particular religion. They had seen how a state-sponsored religion, namely the Anglican faith, had led to religious strife in England, and they wanted no part of that. To them freedom of religion meant all Americans were free to observe any faith they wanted to, without state interference, which is why the First Amendment not only reads, "Congress shall make no law respecting an establishment of religion," but also reads, "or prohibiting the free exercise thereof."

What's more, the main political quarrel the Founders had with the mother country was rooted firmly in religion. If, as the Founders insisted, their unalienable rights come from God, and not from the "state" — in this case Britain's Parliament — then it follows that they answered only to God, and therefore had every right to resist Parliament's attempts to impose its will on them.

That is what the Knights of Columbus were getting at when they petitioned Congress to insert the words "under God," into the Pledge in 1954. To them, that would make the Pledge a daily reminder to all Americans that they had God-given rights no government authority can ever take away.

In that sense, a Pledge that includes the words "under God" is true to the beliefs of the Founders, which is why I believe the Supreme Court will leave the words in.

© Kauffmann 2008

Author's note: The Supreme Court did indeed rule that the words "under God" were permissible in the Pledge of Allegiance.

Bruce's History Lessons: The Mystery of William Shakespeare

This week (April 23) in 1616, William of Stratford-on-Avon, better known as William Shakespeare, passed away. The greatest writer in the history of the English language was buried in an unmarked grave without ceremony or public notice. Astonishingly, his will, which meticulously detailed his household goods, made no mention of anything related to literature.

And then there is his life. Born the son of a tradesman, he could not have received much education, and there is no record that he ever owned any books. Research does show that he was a sometime actor, that he helped manage a theatre company, and occasionally dabbled in real estate. The chances are slim that he would have ever been to court, traveled abroad, spoke a foreign language or had any knowledge of the law.

Which is puzzling because half of Shakespeare's plays are set in foreign countries, most of them exhibit a profound understanding of the royal court, whole passages of them are in foreign languages, and many demonstrate a knowledge of the legal system. What's more — talk about genius — William of Stratford, actor, theatre manager, property manager, husband and father of three (before he was 21), somehow found the time to produce 36 plays in 26 years!

Or did he? Given these discrepancies, was William of Stratford really Shakespeare? A growing number of scholars say no. These scholars disagree about who really was Shakespeare. Some say Christopher Marlowe, others Francis Bacon. But the man most believe was the real William Shakespeare is Edward de Vere, the 17th Earl of Oxford.

The circumstantial evidence is compelling. De Vere, who was a regular at Queen Elizabeth's court, was a talented poet and playwright, traveled extensively, spoke several languages, and studied the law. Also, many events in Shakespeare's plays mirror events in de Vere's life. *Hamlet* is practically autobiographical. His father-in-law, Lord Burghley, bore an uncanny resemblance to the character Polonius, and some of Hamlet's lines in the play reveal an insider's knowledge of Burghley's life. What's more, de Vere's private correspondence contains phrases and passages that also are found in Shakespeare's plays.

So why would de Vere write under a pen name? Because as a court insider, whose plays often criticized the monarchy, he may have feared that acknowledging his authorship would cause him political problems. As to why he chose "Shakespeare," his nickname was "Spear-shaker" — given to him because of his jousting skill and because his family crest was a lion brandishing a spear.

Finally, as a matter of record — and contrast — among the many who paid their respects when de Vere died, was Elizabeth's successor, King James I, who had several "Shakespeare" plays produced in tribute.

What was it "Shakespeare" said? "A rose by any other name …"

© *Kauffmann 2008*

Bruce's History Lessons:
Barbie's Dollmaker

One day when Ruth Handler was watching her daughter Barbara play with her paper dolls, the young mother had an epiphany. Girls don't play with dolls because they like pretending to be mommies, Handler thought. They play with dolls because they like pretending to be bigger girls.

And so Handler, who together with her husband Elliott had founded the Mattel toy company, decided to develop a revolutionary new doll, one that actually had the figure of a "bigger girl." She named the doll "Barbie," her daughter's nickname, and when the doll was introduced at the 1959 American Toy Fair, a cultural and marketing phenomenon was born. A year later an astonishing 350,000 Barbie dolls had been sold.

Handler actually based Barbie on the more woman-like figure of a German-made doll called "Lilli," which, like Barbie, came with different costumes. But while Lilli buyers had to purchase new dolls to get new outfits, Handler decided to follow the "Sell-the-razor-cheap-and-make-money-on-the-blades," business model. She marketed Barbie's costumes separately and wound up making a fortune on both the doll and the clothes.

That decision proved wise in more ways than one because, through her costumes, Barbie was able to remain relevant to the ever evolving mores, and buying habits, of young girls. While early Barbies were brides, cheerleaders and ballerinas, for example, Barbie later became an astronaut, a surgeon and a businesswoman. Of course, Malibu Barbie, in a bathing suit, and Totally Hair Barbie, with hair from head to toe, remain two of the best-selling ever, confirming Handler's belief that little girls want to be big girls and have big girl fun.

Big girls also have boyfriends, and in 1961 Mattel introduced Ken (named after Handler's son), plus friends Midge and Grown-up Skipper for Barbie to

343

hang with. But it is Barbie who remains the cultural and sales phenomenon. Since 1959, 1 billion Barbies have been sold and today, worldwide, two are sold every second.

Of course, with every product that successful, controversy is sure to follow, and several women's groups have objected to Barbie's measurements, which are the equivalent of 38-21-33 on a real person. Handler defended Barbie's figure by saying that on such a small scale, it was the only way her clothes would look good on her, but critical comments have ranged from "obscene" to giving young girls "unrealistic expectations."

Whatever the case, Handler, who died this week (April 27) in 2002, remained unapologetic and proud of her creation — both the doll and her company. And Barbie continues to remain relevant, as evidenced by the fact that, this past Valentines Day, she finally found the nerve to dump that dull, wimpy Ken.

Totally Available Barbie — available at a store near you.

© *Kauffmann 2008*

Bruce's History Lessons: The Miracle Mile

This week (May 6) in 1954, Roger Bannister, a 25-year-old medical student from Oxford, England, achieved one of the most famous milestones in the history of sports when he became the first human to run a mile in less than four minutes. When he crossed the finish line at Oxford's Iffy Road track his time was a breathtaking 3:59.4, although most in the crowd never learned the exact time until later. That is because when the track announcer began by saying Bannister's official time was "three minutes and ..." the crowd erupted in a chorus of cheers, drowning out the rest.

Their joy was understandable, especially since it had been nine years since Gundar Hagg of Sweden had set the world record of 4:01.3 seconds. Even back then, nine years was an eternity for a world record to stand, but more importantly, because so many had tried, and failed, to break the four-minute barrier, it had become conventional wisdom that running a sub-four-minute mile was a physical impossibility

Bannister disagreed, thinking the four-minute barrier was more psychological than physical, and so, relying on his medical training, he began exploring new ways to prepare both physically and mentally for a mile in under four minutes. Bannister studied the scientific principles behind running, including the mechanics of motion, but he also mapped out a way to gain a psychological edge during his race. Bannister recruited two other milers, Chris Basher and Chris Chataway, as pacemakers, hoping that they could push him into running a faster pace than he normally would on his own.

On the day of the historic race, conditions were hardly conducive to record breaking. Rain had soaked the track and a strong crosswind was blowing as the race began. But Bannister raced as planned, with Basher serving as pacemaker for the first half of the race, and when he tired Bannister signaled Chataway to take the lead. Bannister stayed close until, with just 350 yards left, he gave his final kick, virtually sprinting to the finish line, which he crossed at 3:59.4. His race subsequently was dubbed "The Miracle Mile."

After Bannister, breaking the four-minute barrier became commonplace (proving that it was mostly a psychological hurdle), and Bannister himself ran several more sub-four-minute miles before retiring from racing at the end of 1954. In 1955 he wrote a book about his experiences, *The Four Minute Mile*, and then became a doctor.

In 1975 Bannister was knighted by Queen Elizabeth and today, at the age of 75, he remains active in the fields of medicine and sports.

It might be said that Roger Bannister was the first to achieve his "15 minutes of fame" in less than four minutes.

© Kauffmann 2008

Bruce's History Lessons:
What Churchill Faced

It is 1940. You are Winston Churchill and you have become British prime minister this week (May 10) in part because your repeated warnings of the mortal danger that Nazi Germany posed to Europe, although long ignored by most European governments — including the one you just replaced — have been proven correct.

Your reward for this uncanny prescience? You now head up a nation that is virtually alone in facing Hitler and the Nazis. As you assume your duties, France and the Low Countries are being conquered by Germany in a stunning display of mobility and power. This means the German army will soon have troops stationed in those nations and the German navy will have French and Belgian ports just a short hop across the English Channel, which they can use to launch naval operations against you. Also, the German *Luftwaffe* (air force) will have close-by French airfields from which to launch bombing raids on your territory.

Meanwhile your army, the British Expeditionary Force, which had been fighting in France, is trapped at Dunkirk on the French coast. It will miraculously escape the Germans, but must leave most of its military equipment behind. So you face massive rearmament problems. Actually, you face them anyway, because the government in power before you did little or nothing to rearm against the Germans, fearing that such actions would anger them.

Wait, things get worse. In June, Italy, which you hoped would remain neutral, enters the war on Germany's side, meaning your entire base of operations in the Mediterranean, to say nothing of the Middle East, is now threatened. This will spread your beleaguered navy even thinner. And of course, most of central and eastern Europe is already under Nazi control, and the Soviet Union has signed a pact with Germany that made them allies and allowed them to carve up Poland.

And don't look now, but isn't that the heavily armed, imperialistic nation of Japan that is threatening your commercial interests and colonial possessions in the Far East? Its hunger for the mineral riches, rubber and oil produced in that region is undisguised and growing. In September it will sign a Tripartite Pact with Germany and Italy.

Finally, don't be too hopeful about an alliance with the only other free and democratic world power. America is enjoying its isolationism and wants no part of another European scrap.

That is the situation Churchill faced when, against the wishes of his own king, George VI, and much of Parliament, he became prime minister. That he was still able to unite his nation and lead it to victory in World War II is why I have made him my "Man of the 20th Century."

Any arguments?

© Kauffmann 2008

Bruce's History Lesson:
Brown vs. the Board of Education

Fifty years ago this week (May 17, 1954) America recovered some of her promise when the Supreme Court handed down its unanimous opinion in *Brown vs. the Board of Education*. In its wake, the legally sanctioned principle of "separate but equal" treatment of whites and blacks in the nation's public schools became a thing of the past.

The ruling that had sanctioned "separate but equal" treatment was *Plessy vs. Ferguson*, which held that segregating the races was not discriminatory provided each race had access to "equal" facilities. Legally, the ruling was specious. Practically, it was a joke, especially in the South where white schools were equipped with modern teaching tools, while "equal" black schools were lucky to have blackboards and chalk.

In Topeka, Kansas, this disparity was not lost on Oliver Brown, whose daughter Linda was forced to pass by a spiffy whites-only school to attend a run-down black school farther away. Nor was it lost on Thurgood Marshall, the black head lawyer for the National Association for the Advancement of Colored People. Marshall had been looking for a test case to overturn *Plessy*, in particular a case in a border state where racism was less ingrained than in the Deep South. Smartly, Marshall attacked segregation at its edges and then used those victories as stepping-stones toward his ultimate goal of abolishing it nationwide. Thus when Brown sued the Kansas school system, Marshall took his case, intending to bring it to the Supreme Court.

When it got there, recently appointed Chief Justice Earl Warren quickly saw *Brown* as a way to end this "separate but equal" segregation charade, but he felt that on an issue this divisive only a unanimous decision by the

Supreme Court would have the legal and moral force to compel acquiescence, if not total acceptance.

That would be no small feat because his fellow justices included several monumental egotists, one skeptical Southerner, a "go-it-alone" maverick and a die-hard segregationist. It took Warren's considerable negotiating skills to do it, but he finally got everyone to agree that Linda Brown's 14th Amendment rights to equal treatment were being violated.

Warren read the court's unanimous decision from the bench, with this ending: "We conclude that ... the doctrine of 'separate but equal' has no place. Separate educational facilities are inherently unequal."

The decision stunned the nation, and although it was only the beginning of the journey toward a new integrated America, it definitely marked the end of the old era in which segregation based on race, creed or color was sanctioned by law.

In that sense, although it wasn't a "trial" *per se*, one could argue that for African-Americans, *Brown vs. the Board of Education* was the "Trial of the Century."

© Kauffmann 2008

Bruce's History Lessons: A Treasonous Gathering

This week (May 25) in 1787, enough delegates having arrived in Philadelphia to reach a quorum, the conference that later became known as the Constitutional Convention officially began. Today the Constitutional Convention is considered the preeminent meeting of America's greatest leaders — a gathering of demi-gods who somehow found the fortitude and enlightenment to create a blueprint for the longest lasting democratic republic in history.

Back then, however, the convention could more plausibly have been considered an act of treason, and had the vast majority of the delegates who arrived in Philadelphia known in advance what was the convention's true purpose, they would have immediately headed back home. They *thought* they were there to amend the Articles of Confederation, which had governed America for the past six years. Instead, unbeknownst to them, they were there to junk the Articles completely and create a brand new document — a constitution — that radically shifted power from their home states to a central, "federal" government. Call the Constitutional Convention the greatest "bait-and-switch" in history.

And call (my hero) James Madison and Alexander Hamilton, the two men who perpetrated this fraud, the greatest hucksters of their time. Both men were convinced that the weak Articles were leading the country to ruin and needed to be replaced with something entirely new, but because the 13 states had all sworn an oath of allegiance to the Articles, any open attempt to break with them was tantamount to committing treason. Not that many of the states would be all that eager to break with a government — the Articles — that gave *them* most powers, in favor of one that gave many of their powers to a "federal government" of indeterminate size, shape and location.

No wonder Madison and Hamilton kept the convention's true purpose a secret.

But Madison in particular knew that eventually he would have to reveal his true intentions to the other delegates, at which point it was highly likely that they would quit the convention in disgust. So Madison, always thinking ahead, did the one thing necessary to prevent such an outcome. He persuaded George Washington to lead Virginia's delegation to the convention. Washington's presence — and to a slightly lesser extent Ben Franklin's — gave the convention an imprimatur of respectability that inoculated it against charges of treason and also convinced the other delegates of the seriousness of the undertaking they were being asked to join.

That "undertaking," as we all know, produced a government that in only slightly altered form still governs us today and is the model for the world.

It is a government based on the rule of law, which is ironic given that the convention that created it was, for all intents and purposes, illegal.

© Kauffmann 2008

Bruce's History Lessons: Spring Cleaning

It being springtime I thought I would do some spring cleaning. Specifically there are reader issues to address and some "Frequently Asked Questions" (FAQ) to answer.

Issue number one: I appreciate greatly the ever-increasing volume of mail that I get and I pride myself on answering every single reader e-mail, good or bad, agree or disagree, in awe of my range of knowledge or in disbelief at the depths of my ignorance.

But my mail volume has grown to the point that I can only answer each reader once. I cannot, as some readers seem to wish, get into a back-and-forth debate on every column. If I did that I wouldn't have time to actually write the column. So if you e-mail me with a comment, I will e-mail you back, even if it's only to thank you for writing. If you e-mail me a week later with a comment on that week's column, I will e-mail you back again. But if you then e-mail me again with a comment on my response to your first comment, please do not expect a reply. On the bright side, it means you get in the last word.

Issue number two: I am not a professor, nor do I have a doctorate, so there is no need to address me as either "Professor Kauffmann," or "Doctor Kauffmann" (although both have a nice ring). I prefer Bruce.

FAQ number one: My columns are not published in book form. I hope to do so eventually and I promise I will notify you when publication occurs. Indeed, my plan is to shamelessly devote an entire column to hawking the book's publication. My suggested column headline will be "Bruce's History Lessons Now in Book Form! Readers Flocking to Bookstores!" Alas, my editors always change my suggested headlines.

FAQ number two: My favorite book on James Madison is *The Business of May Next* by William Lee Miller. Miller also wrote an excellent book on Abe Lincoln titled *Lincoln's Virtues."* William Manchester's two books on Churchill — his *The Last Lion* series — are still the two best books I have read on that great man. On George Washington, James Thomas Flexner's book *Washington: The Indispensable Man* is excellent.

General interest books I recommend include *Founding Brothers* by Joseph Ellis, a look at our Founders; *April 1865* by Jay Winik, a dissection of the most important month of the Civil War; *Dreadnought* by Robert K. Massie, a brilliant review of the run up to WW I, and *The Fifties* by David Halberstram, which demolishes the notion that the 1950s were a sleepy, uneventful decade between World War II and the swinging '60s.

There, the place looks cleaner! I'll do it again next year.

© *Kauffmann 2008*

Bruce's History Lessons:
You've Lost That Loving Ruling

Arguably the most ironically named case in the history of the U.S. Supreme Court was decided this week (June 12) in 1967 when, in *Loving v. Virginia*, the Court struck down the state of Virginia's law against interracial marriage, ruling that it violated the rights of Mildred and Richard Loving as guaranteed to them under the 14th Amendment's Equal Protection Clause.

In 1958, Richard Loving, who was white, and his wife, Mildred, who was black, had married in Washington, D.C., because their home state of Virginia upheld anti-miscegenation laws forbidding whites from marrying people of different races. But after their wedding the Lovings immediately returned to Virginia where they lived together for a year before being convicted of violating Virginia's anti-miscegenation law. The presiding judge, pointedly noting that God's decision to place the different races on different continents proved that God "did not intend for the races to mix," sentenced Richard Loving to a year in jail, but then suspended the sentence in return for a promise that the Lovings would leave the state and not return for 25 years. Forced to move back to Washington, D.C., the Lovings decided to initiate a lawsuit challenging the constitutionality of Virginia's law forbidding their marriage.

That lawsuit was first heard in the Virginia Supreme Court of Appeals, which upheld the constitutionality of Virginia's law, ruling — among other things — that Virginia had a right to "preserve the racial integrity of its citizens" and prevent "a mongrel breed of citizens." More astonishingly, the court based its judicial reasoning on the rather novel principle that, since laws forbidding inter-racial marriage applied "equally to the white and the Negro participants," such laws "do not constitute invidious discrimination based on race."

Not surprisingly, the Lovings appealed, and their appeal reached the Supreme Court a year later. In its unanimous decision regarding the constitutionality of anti-miscegenation laws, the Court held that legal distinctions based on race were not only "odious to a free people" but also were subject to "the most rigid scrutiny" under the 14th Amendment's Equal Protection Clause. When held to such scrutiny it was clear that Virginia's anti-miscegenation law had no legitimate purpose other than "invidious racial discrimination." Anti-miscegenation laws were therefore unconstitutional, the Court said, meaning that Virginia's, and similar laws in 15 other states, were subsequently null and void.

Of course, today the hot-button issue is not laws forbidding marriage between those of a different race, but marriage between those of the same sex. Given the striking similarities — and differences — between these two issues, it will be interesting to see if the Supreme Court gets involved and if so what, if anything, it decides and what legal reasoning it uses to render that decision.

© *Kauffmann 2008*

Bruce's History Lessons:
Auschwitz: The Scene of the Crime
(of the Century)

Even today, if you scoop up a handful of dirt from the ground at Auschwitz, the Nazis' most famous World War II concentration camp, you can find fragments of human bone, the remains of some 2 million Jews, gypsies and other "subhumans" who died at Auschwitz and its sister camp Birkenau (Auschwitz II) between 1940 and 1945. That number, 2 million, is *one third* of the total number of dead commonly referred to when discussing the Holocaust.

From all over Nazi-occupied Europe, Jews were shipped by train to Auschwitz, located near Krakow, Poland, where they were separated into three groups: those who would die immediately (the old, the infirm), those who would die eventually (the young, the fit for work), and those who would die gruesomely (twins, dwarfs and the deformed — the subjects of experiments by doctors such as the "Angel of Death," Nazi physician Josef Mengele).

Death also came in several forms, the most humane being to line up the victims and shoot them. Others were sent to the gas chambers where they were literally strangled by the suffocating effects of a cyanide gas called Zyklon-B. The rest were starved, beaten, tortured or worked to death, or were killed by any number of camp diseases — typhus and dysentery the most common — which spread easily among the unsanitary living conditions. Inmates slept three to a bunk, shared one toilet (a hole in a wooden bench), and except when working were locked in their barracks even in the most oppressive heat.

As a result, as many as 20,000 people a day perished, making disposal of the bodies a daunting challenge — one that was met at first by mass graves and later by crematoriums that operated around the clock. A joke among the camp's guards was that the only way a prisoner could escape Auschwitz was "up the chimney."

Auschwitz officially opened this week (June 14) in 1940, and although it was just one of many camps working to fulfill Adolf Hitler's order that Europe's Jews be destroyed, Auschwitz today has become *the* symbol of the Nazis' — and by extension all of mankind's — capacity for evil.

Ensuring that no one ever forgets about that capacity is one reason the Polish government, in cooperation with several Jewish organizations, made Auschwitz a museum in 1946, and since then approximately 35 million people have visited it. For many, their visit was a life-altering experience.

To enter this "museum," which is surrounded by the same barbed wire fence the prisoners faced, you pass through a small gate with a cruelly mocking sign above it that reads, *"Arbeit macht frei"* — "Work makes you free."

At Auschwitz, it wasn't work that made you free. It was death.

© *Kauffmann 2008*

Bruce's History Lessons:
Ronald Reagan, R.I.P.

"Even God realized He couldn't change the past. That's why He created historians."

- Anon

Michael Beschloss is a serious historian. He says that no accurate assessment of Ronald Reagan's presidency can be made for another 30 years. Beschloss' point is well taken. There will be a decade or so of hagiography — we are already seeing it — in which Reagan is depicted as the winner of the Cold War, the force behind 18 years of economic prosperity, and the champion of human freedom.

This will be followed by the "counter-revolution" in which revisionist historians completely debunk the earlier assessments, painting Reagan as a bumbler, an intellectual lightweight, a warmonger, the instigator of class warfare, a racist, sexist and worse.

This will be followed by an amalgam, in which everything blends together, resulting in an above average president who had some notable accomplishments and made some serious mistakes. Put him in the second row of "near great" presidents.

Bruce Kauffmann is not a serious historian. He says that Ronald Reagan was the most important president of the second half of the 20th century and arguably the most important person. Kauffmann doesn't care whether his point is well taken or not. He sides with those who believe Reagan's economic policies — but much more important his ability to communicate to an America mired in "malaise" that "America's best days are ahead of her" — helped spur the sense of optimism that is always the foundation of risk-taking, entrepreneurialism and job creation. Kauffmann points to the fact that from 1982, when Reagan supported Federal Reserve Chairman Paul Volker's successful attempt to squeeze inflation out of the economy, to 1988 when Reagan left office, economic growth was an astonishing 4.7 percent a year, while unemployment went from nearly 11 percent to 5.3 percent.

Kauffmann sides with those who credit Reagan with bringing down the "Evil Empire," resulting in a bloodless revolution in Eastern Europe — and within the Soviet Union — that freed a half-dozen countries and hundreds of millions of people from that empire's grip. For proof, Kauffmann cites the admission of high-ranking Soviet officers that this was so.

Kauffmann sides with those who think Reagan believed America was the most important thing to happen in modern history, and that what America had become — a nation based on the rule of law, on the superiority of market-based economics, and on individual freedom grounded in a respect for the rights of others — is what the world wants to become. And Kauffmann thinks that, thanks to Ronald Reagan, the world is much closer to that goal.

Kauffmann puts Reagan at the end of the first row of "great" presidents. And Kauffmann believes Reagan will still be there 30 years from now.

© *Kauffmann 2008*

Bruce's History Lesson:
Madison's Pen

My hero, James Madison, died this week (June 28) in 1836. As a president, our fourth, he was no great shakes, but as a "Founding Father" he was second only to Washington, for he was the creative genius behind two of the three pillars of our nation's founding. Jefferson wrote the Declaration of Independence, but Madison is responsible for the Constitution and Bill of Rights.

Imagine almost single handedly drafting the blueprint that would be the basis for the world's longest-lasting representative government. For all intents and purposes that is what Madison did in 1786, in his private study, in his beloved home Montpelier, where — in the greatest one man "skull session" in history — he pored over hundreds of books on governments of the past in an effort to discover what had worked, what hadn't, and why.

There are bookworms and then there are *bookworms*, and it isn't every student who can plow through the strengths and weaknesses of the Amphyctionic Confederacy of 16th century Greece, the Helvitic Confederacy of 14th century Switzerland or the Belgic Confederacy of the 1600s. Madison did, and he made lists of the defining features of those governments, both good and bad. From those lists Madison began to form his ideas of how human nature affected government, and vice versa. He concluded that a successful government must not ignore or work against human nature, especially our very human tendency to act in our own self-interest. Rather, government should minimize its damaging effects and, when possible, turn self-interest "to the support of liberty and republican government."

That is why Madison formulated a government with shared powers, all of which "would check each other." That is why he constructed a "Republican," or representative government, instead of a pure democracy. Madison wanted the wishes of the masses — based naturally on *self* interest — to be filtered through the judgment and wisdom of elected representatives, who would more likely act in the *national* interest. And that is why he assembled a Bill of Rights, so that the God-given rights of the minority could never be violated by the numerical power of the majority.

As I have written before, it is dismaying how little respect is paid to Madison's importance. No national monument stands in his honor, no holiday is set aside for his birth, and even his live-wire wife, Dolley, gets more press. But as George F. Will once wrote, *"If we really believed the pen is mightier than the sword, the nation's capital would be named not for the soldier who wielded the revolutionary sword, but for the thinker who was ablest with a pen. It would be Madison, D.C."*

I, for one, would live in that city.

© *Kauffmann 2008*

Bruce's History Lessons:
For Whom the Bell Tolls

This week (July 8) in 1776, the now-famous Liberty Bell rang out from the steeple of the Pennsylvania State House — known today as Independence Hall — to alert the public that the first ever reading of the recently completed Declaration of Independence was about to occur. The Continental Congress had adopted the Constitution on July 4, but it took another four days to have it printed in a form suitable to for a public reading.

Speaking of constitutions, the Liberty Bell itself had been commissioned in London in 1751 to mark the 50th anniversary of Pennsylvania's original constitution. Made of copper and weighing 2 thousand pounds, the bell — it would not gain its famous nickname "Liberty Bell" until 1839 when that phrase was coined in a poem — arrived in Philadelphia in 1752, but cracked when first rung, necessitating that it be melted down and recast. When the second bell also proved defective, it was recast again and the third time proved the charm. In 1753 it was hung from the steeple of the Pennsylvania State House where it would be rung to announce special events such as sessions of the Pennsylvania Assembly.

Over the years it also would ring to commemorate special occasions, such as — in perfectly ironic order — the ascension of King George III to the British throne in 1761; a meeting to plan defiance to King George's controversial Stamp Act tax in 1765; the revolutionary battles of Lexington and Concord that were fought against King George and his government in 1775, and — annually — the day, July 4, in which they first proclaimed their intentions to defy King George and go their own way as a separate nation.

Finally, closing the historic circle, after that revolution was victorious, the Liberty Bell would toll every February 22, commemorating the birthday of the man, George Washington, who led America to victory and nationhood.

Of course, what has added to the Liberty Bell's luster is the now famous crack that it suffered in 1835, when — or so legend has it — it was rung so hard in commemoration of the death of America's greatest Supreme Court Justice, John Marshall, that it developed a slight crack. That crack expanded to its present size in 1846 while again tolling to mark Washington's birthday, and experts subsequently decided the Liberty Bell was no longer suitable for ringing. However, it continued to be "tapped" to commemorate events of historic importance, such as on June 6, 1944, when the Liberty Bell's ring was recorded and broadcast across the United States to commemorate D-Day.

Today, for its own protection, the Liberty Bell is encased in a special pavilion in front of Independence Hall. A visit to see both is a trip well spent.

© Kauffmann 2008

Bruce's History Lesson:
Elbridge Gerry-manders

"Fame is a bee. It has a song. It has a sting. So, too, it has a wing."

-Emily Dickinson

Were he alive today, Elbridge Gerry, born this week (July 17) in 1744, would likely think he felt the sting of fame far longer than the song, for it is his terrible fate to be famous — or more appropriately, *infamous* — for an act of legislative skullduggery that, at the time, seemed to Gerry and his compatriots to be a relatively harmless partisan political maneuver.

This is a man, after all, who justly earns the title "Founding Father." A graduate of Harvard College, Gerry was a leader of the colonial resistance to Britain prior to the American Revolution; he signed the Declaration of Independence; he twice served in the Continental Congress; he helped draft America's Constitution (he would not sign it, despairing the lack of a Bill of Rights and the amount of power granted the federal government); he served in the first U.S. Congress as a representative from Massachusetts; he was twice elected governor of that great state and ultimately gained the second highest office in the land when he served as vice-president during (my hero) James Madison's second term as president.

So what *is* Gerry famous for? He is famous for dividing Massachusetts into a series of strangely shaped congressional districts in order to ensure that his political party, the Democratic-Republicans, maintained its majority over the Federalists in the Massachusetts General Assembly. One of these newly created districts struck an observer as resembling a salamander, which — when combined with the name "Gerry" — resulted in the now-famous political term, *gerrymandering*.

The legacy of this political act is, of course, still with us today. At one time or another, in every state in the Union, the political party in power has attempted to re-draw congressional districts to ensure that it *stays* in power, and in modern times the issue has become so controversial — and has taken on so many new dimensions — that gerrymandering cases have even reached the Supreme Court. To give one example, several years ago the Supreme Court ruled unconstitutional a state's attempt to gerrymander districts to ensure the election of minority candidates.

It has been said that it is better to be damned than forgotten — to feel fame's "sting" rather than have it take "wing" — and perhaps Gerry would agree with that. While gerrymandering was an accepted practice in the early 1800s, today it connotes back-room dealing, deception and political intrigue. Yet if it weren't for the term "gerrymandering," nobody would remember Gerry at all, just as nobody remembers the other very important and powerful Founding Father who served as James Madison's first vice-president.

Go ahead, then, name him.

© *Kauffmann 2008*

Bruce's History Lessons:
The Plot to Kill Adolf Hitler

Of the myriad attempts to kill Adolf Hitler and end World War II before further disaster struck Germany, the most famous occurred this week (July 20) in 1944 when a group of army officers led by General Ludwig Beck and Colonel Claus von Stauffenberg tried to assassinate Hitler during a meeting at his Wolf's Lair headquarters in East Prussia.

As luck would have it, von Stauffenberg, a long-time anti-Hitler conspirator, was invited to attend the July 20 meeting, whose agenda was Germany's worsening situation on the Eastern front. Von Stauffenberg joined the meeting holding a briefcase, which he placed on the floor near the table where Hitler sat. In the briefcase was a bomb timed to blow up in minutes. Moments later, Von Stauffenberg mumbled that he had to step out for a moment, but when he left the room he also left the building. The bomb went off minutes later.

But Hitler was spared. One of the assembled officers inadvertently pushed von Stauffenberg's briefcase further under the table, so when it went off, the table's thick supports cushioned the blow, and Hitler, although badly burned and suffering ruptured eardrums, was otherwise unharmed.

Von Stauffenberg, convinced that Hitler was dead, flew back to Berlin to begin a coup, but reports soon surfaced that Hitler was alive and after general confusion and a number of arrests, the conspirators were routed. Beck shot himself to avoid capture, and von Stauffenberg was executed. The last, best hope to end the war by ending Hitler's life had failed.

Interestingly, there was one man on the Allied side who was not at all upset that this assassination plot failed — the American president, Franklin Roosevelt. In fact, Roosevelt was almost relieved because he believed that only by defeating a Germany with Hitler as its leader could the Allies demand unconditional surrender and wipe the slate clean of Germany's wartime leadership. Roosevelt feared that if Hitler was killed by German bigwigs in either the army or the Nazi party, they might then insist on a negotiated settlement in which some of them were allowed to stay in leadership positions in post-war Germany. Certainly such a settlement would be tempting to many Americans and British weary of four years of war.

Roosevelt knew better. He also knew that if Hitler was killed prematurely, a Hitler cult would arise in Germany, which might have sparked underground resistance after the war ended.

And finally, Roosevelt was glad the plot failed because he shared the view of a savvy British colonel who later expressed amazement that anyone would think killing Hitler prematurely was a good idea. After all, this colonel marveled, "Hitler was doing such a wonderful job of losing the war!"

© Kauffmann 2008

Bruce's History Lessons: The Riddle of Jimmy Hoffa

Teamsters President Jimmy Hoffa was one of the giants of the modern labor movement, so perhaps it is fitting that — according to rumor — he is buried under Section 217 of Giants Stadium at the Meadowlands in New Jersey. This rumor is based on the fact that this week (July 30) in 1975 Hoffa disappeared without a trace from a restaurant in Detroit, Michigan, allegedly the victim of kidnapping and murder by members of organized crime.

Whatever motive mobsters might have had for wanting Hoffa dead probably stemmed from his attempts to make a comeback as undisputed leader of the Teamsters Union, which he previously had built into one of the most powerful unions in the country. Becoming Teamsters president in 1957, Hoffa quickly established a reputation as a tough boss and ruthless bargainer. In 1964 he negotiated the union's first contract with the nation's trucking companies and at the height of his leadership the Teamsters had some 2 million members, making it a mighty political force.

However, he also gained a reputation for shady dealings and for having close ties with organized crime, and in 1967, after a prolonged trial, Hoffa was sentenced to 13 years in federal prison for jury tampering, conspiracy and pension fraud. Defiant as ever, he refused to give up his position as Teamsters president, and in that he had the support of the majority of Teamsters members.

But by 1971, Hoffa, nearing 60 years old, wanted out of prison and was ready to make a deal. Then-President Richard Nixon, undoubtedly seeing a political benefit in gaining the goodwill of the Teamsters leader, agreed to commute Hoffa's sentence on the condition that he resign as head of the union and refrain from union activities. Sure enough, Hoffa supported

Nixon for re-election in 1972, but he soon reneged on his promise to stay away from Teamsters activity. By 1973 it was an open secret that Hoffa was working to replace his successor, Frank Fitzsimmons, as Teamsters boss.

Which is where the theory that the mob caused his death comes in. Organized labor and organized crime have long been cozy, and in the case of the Teamsters, Hoffa's attempts to alter the status quo — and the attention those attempts were getting from both the media and federal law enforcement — might have been seen as a threat to the interests of both union and mob leaders.

That said, the only thing certain about the disappearance of James Riddle Hoffa, who was officially declared "presumed dead" in 1982, is that his middle name is an appropriate one. That and the fact that if he *is* buried in Giants Stadium, it has had no appreciable affect on the team's football fortunes.

© Kauffmann 2008

Bruce's History Lesson:
Hiroshima

"Now I am become death, the shatterer of worlds."

- Vishnu, Bhagavad-Gita

This week (Aug. 6) in 1945 the world's first atomic bomb hit its primary target, the Aioi Bridge in Hiroshima, Japan. At the time, no one knew that the political and moral fallout of the resulting explosion would be more widespread, and last much longer, than the radiation fallout. In fact, the political and moral fallout spread around the world, and lasts to this day.

Was the bomb the only way to force Japan's surrender, short of a costly and deadly invasion, or — as many still claim — would more patience, combined with a less extreme use of force, have done the trick?

My answer is: Only the bomb could have forced Japan's surrender.

Of the suggested "less extreme" alternatives, the first, a naval blockade, would have been costly, time consuming, and — given that by 1945 Americans were sick of sacrificing for the war effort — hard to sustain. Also, the Japanese saw surrender as a political problem, not a resource problem, so success would have been uncertain.

A second alternative was continued firebombing of Japanese cities, which already had killed more than 100,000 Japanese. But in terms of casualties there was little difference between saturation firebombing and the atomic bomb, and the latter — needing a single plane and crew — was safer and more efficient.

Finally there was the option of invading Japan, which had to be considered from the following perspective: 1. The recent battle against the Japanese at

Okinawa had cost 50,000 American lives. 2. In the three months since Harry Truman became president, U.S. battle casualties against the Japanese were half of what they had been in the previous *three years*. 3. Some estimates of casualties in a mainland invasion approached 1 million. Japanese military leaders, having lost touch with reality, were prepared to commit national suicide in one glorious final battle, and to that extent the entire Japanese citizenry was preparing to die defending their sacred homeland. Indeed, even after Hiroshima, a second bomb dropped on Nagasaki, and two orders from Japan's Emperor to surrender, many hard-liners still refused. Some plotted to capture the Emperor and wage guerrilla warfare in Japan's mountains.

In sum, the atomic bomb was the only way to force Japan's surrender and Truman was right to use it. Or as George Elsey, an aide to Truman put it, "He (Truman) could no more have stopped it (the bomb) than a train moving down a track. It's all well and good to come along later and say the bomb was a horrible thing. The whole goddam war was a horrible thing."

A war, we should recall, that the Japanese started.

© *Kauffmann 2008*

Bruce's History Lesson:
The Wall

Construction of the Berlin Wall separating Soviet-controlled East Berlin from Allied-controlled West Berlin began this week (August 13) in 1961, and although "The Wall" was one of the most hated symbols of the Cold War, it may well have prevented a hot war.

To discover why, recall the tense situation that existed between the U.S. and the Soviet Union in the summer of '61, in which Berlin was the most important but not the only flashpoint. Months earlier, the Bay of Pigs disaster, in which American-backed Cuban exiles failed to overthrow Cuban leader Fidel Castro — a Soviet ally — had made the new U.S. president, John Kennedy, look foolish and weak in the eyes of Soviet Premier Nikita Khrushchev. Khrushchev's impression of Kennedy's weakness was only reinforced in a subsequent summit meeting at which Khrushchev bullied Kennedy unmercifully and threatened to cut off all Allied access to West Berlin (although West Berlin was controlled by the Allies, the city itself was located in the heart of East Germany, which the Soviets controlled).

As the Soviets saw it, Kennedy's only choice in that event was to acquiesce to the Soviet takeover of West Berlin, or start a war that would probably go nuclear. The Soviets did not believe Kennedy would "sacrifice New York to save Berlin," as the saying went, meaning he would not risk a nuclear retaliatory attack on U.S. territory by defending Berlin with nukes.

But there was another, more important, factor driving Soviet behavior over Berlin — the mass exodus of citizens from East Berlin into West Berlin. If some way to stop this exodus wasn't found, the Soviets faced a propaganda nightmare — Germans "voting with their feet" to live in the West — and an

East Germany bereft of the skilled human resources it would take to rebuild the country after the devastation of WW II.

For his part, Kennedy was determined to protect West Berlin at all costs, even nuclear war. Humiliated in Cuba and challenged by Soviet proxies in Southeast Asia, he saw Berlin as the ultimate test of Western resolve. If the U.S. backed down there, then no country would ever again put its faith in American promises.

Therefore, determined to prove his mettle, Kennedy gave a major speech calling for an arms build-up and for nationwide civil defense measures, and again reiterating that West Berlin was sacrosanct. The speech impressed Khrushchev, who then solved his own problem, the mass exodus of East Berliners, by building a wall — *the* "Wall" — separating the two Berlins.

That hated "Wall," of course, came tumbling down on November 9, 1989, ending — thank God — the Cold War. But there is no getting around the fact that its construction may well have averted a world war.

© Kauffmann 2008

Bruce's History Lessons:
Wendell Willkie: At the Water's Edge

For those who remember him at all, Wendell Willkie was the guy with the funny name who ran against President Franklin Roosevelt in the presidential election of 1940. Since Willkie lost that election he has faded into obscurity, but part of the reason he lost was a courageous decision he made this week (August 17) in 1940 when he gave his speech accepting the Republican nomination for president.

Certainly Willkie was the surprise Republican nominee that year, having beaten the heavily favored candidate, Thomas Dewey. Because Willkie's career had been in business, not politics — indeed, he had never held political office — it was assumed that he had no chance against Roosevelt. He wasn't even a real Republican, having spent most of his life as a Democrat, only changing parties because he thought Roosevelt's government was becoming too heavy-handed in how it treated business.

But in 1940 there was one political issue that made Roosevelt vulnerable to defeat — instituting a military draft. After dodging the topic for months, Roosevelt finally publicly endorsed mandatory selective service legislation, both because he knew how pitiful was the battle readiness of the American military and because he knew how dangerous was the situation in Europe where Adolf Hitler's Nazi Germany now ruled the continent.

The American public, however, happy in its isolationism, did not share Roosevelt's concerns about Europe, and when he supported a draft a powerful combination of liberals, pacifists and concerned parents, particularly mother's groups, erupted in protest. Their opposition was so passionate, and their numbers so large, that Roosevelt believed they might "easily defeat the Democratic ticket — (Henry) Wallace and myself."

Yet no one knew where Willkie stood on the issue, although all knew it was tailor-made for his political exploitation. If he came out against the draft, not only might he defeat Roosevelt in November, but also his opposition would probably defeat passage of the selective service legislation that had come before Congress.

Willkie's answer to the mystery was delivered in his August 17 acceptance speech to a crowd of 200,000 supporters in Elwood, Indiana. Noting that America could not remain isolated from the unhappy events in Europe, Willkie stated unequivocally that "some form of selective service is the only democratic way in which to assure the trained and competent manpower we need in our national defense."

In essence Willkie put the good of the country ahead of his political career. When Roosevelt learned what Willkie had said, he remarked, "Willkie has lost." FDR was right, but the selective service legislation passed, enhancing America's national security.

Wendell Willkie is one of my un-sung heroes of history. He proved that there really was a time when politics stopped at the water's edge.

© Kauffmann 2008

Bruce's History Lessons:
Chicago, the Summer of '68

"So your brother's bound and gagged/And they've chained him to a chair/Won't you please come to Chicago/Just to sing."

– Graham Nash, "Chicago"

This week (August 26) in 1968 the city of Chicago descended into madness. It was the opening of the Democratic National Convention in which Vice President Hubert Humphrey would best the anti-Vietnam War candidate, Eugene McCarthy, for the presidential nomination. But that was a sideshow to the main event, the violent clash between Chicago Mayor Richard Daley and his police force, and the thousands of war protestors who had come to Chicago to support McCarthy's candidacy and force the convention to accept a "peace plank" that would quickly end America's presence in Vietnam.

The influx of anti-war demonstrators actually had been anticipated by leaders of the Democratic Party, many of whom had suggested moving the convention to another city. But Mayor Daley assured his fellow Democrats that no hippie protesters were going to disrupt his city — he would maintain order whatever the cost.

He certainly tried, and the result was non-stop television coverage of Middle America's sons and daughters being beaten senseless by Chicago's finest and shoved into police wagons night after night outside of the convention center. The scene so disgusted most of America that Daley's reputation never recovered and Chicago's barely did.

The worst of the violence occurred on August 28th as 15,000 protesters gathered at Chicago's Grant Park for a rally. There they first learned that the peace plank had been defeated and in anger they decided to march on

377

the convention center. At Michigan Avenue they were met by police, who had been ordered to clear the streets, and in the ensuing melee not just demonstrators, but many bystanders, were punched, clubbed, maced, tear gassed and arrested. Some were later hospitalized and the "Battle of Michigan Avenue," as it was dubbed, was caught on film and broadcast nationwide.

Later that evening, in what was decidedly an anti-climactic moment, Hubert Humphrey won the democratic nomination and pledged to continue President Lyndon Johnson's Vietnam policy, which was to keep fighting until concessions were won at the bargaining table. That position, together with the infamy the Democrats earned in Chicago that year, helped ensure Humphrey's defeat in the general election.

In Chicago's aftermath, some 600 demonstrators had been arrested and more than 1,000 were treated for injuries. A study later commissioned to determine the cause of the violence put most of the blame on the Chicago police. In response, Mayor Daley gave his police force a pay raise.

"In a land that's known as freedom/How can such a thing be fair/Won't you please come to Chicago/For the help that we can bring. We can c-h-a-n-g-e the world!"

© *Kauffmann 2008*

Bruce's History Lessons: The American Scholar

This week (Aug. 31) in 1837 the writer and teacher Ralph Waldo Emerson gave a speech at the Harvard Chapter of the Phi Beta Kappa Society that, from a cultural perspective, would change forever the way American writers and philosophers thought. The speech, which Oliver Wendell Holmes called "our intellectual Declaration of Independence," was titled "The American Scholar." Many still consider it the most important speech ever delivered by an American that did not have a political purpose.

Rather, Emerson's address sought to explain how Americans could achieve a higher consciousness that would allow them to live meaningful lives. To that end Emerson made two central points.

First, he noted that book learning was the beginning, not the end of intellectual discovery and wisdom. Books can inspire original thinking, but they should not be a substitute for it. "I had better never see a book than be warped by its attraction clean out of my own orbit and made a satellite," Emerson declared. Books look backward, while true genius looks forward. One can only develop one's "Over-Soul," Emerson insisted, by also studying nature, by thinking for oneself, by developing intellectual self-confidence, by reveling in one's individuality and by taking creative action. That was true of religious books as well, Emerson believed. The Bible, the Koran, the Torah — all are foundations of religious thought and awareness, but men should still seek their own truths so that they can "read God directly" and not be mired in "other men's transcripts."

The other central point of Emerson's speech was that the American scholar must create his own intellectual and artistic identity separate from the Old World — Europe. Although by 1837 America was Europe's equal, and even its superior, in terms of politics and economics, culturally it still considered itself Europe's handmaid. Emerson called on America's writers, artists and scholars to declare their cultural independence from Europe, just as the Founders had declared America's political independence. America was a land of new frontiers, Emerson insisted, intellectual as well as geographical, and unlike Europe, which was mired in old traditions and fettered by limitations on freedom of expression, America was a country founded on freedom. America's thinkers should embrace that freedom and lead a new intellectual renaissance.

Emerson's speech was a revelation to America's budding intellectual movement and in its wake some of the great writers and thinkers of the day found their voice. Henry David Thoreau, Walt Whitman, Nathanial Hawthorne and many more all began writing the books that not only would define their careers but also shape America's distinct literary and intellectual identity.

Small wonder "The American Scholar" speech, although little known today, ranks as one of the most important events in American history.

© Kauffmann 2008

Bruce's History Lessons:
Telecommunications:
One Legacy of 9/11

If this week wasn't the anniversary of such a tragic event — Al Qaeda's terrorist attack on America — it would be a delicious irony. On September 11, 2001, America's burgeoning telecommunications industry, which the federal government regulates, probably saved the federal government.

Recall that after three hijacked planes hit the World Trade Center and the Pentagon early on September 11, there was still a fourth plane missing — United Flight 93 — which had left New Jersey bound for California but had changed course without authorization and also was presumed to be under the control of terrorists. However, unlike the other planes, which met their horrific ends before anyone knew what was happening, Flight 93 was delayed taking off, so by the time it was airborne the fact that young Arab men were hijacking passenger planes had been broadcast nationwide, not only by established news organizations but also by individuals with cell phones and computers.

Among those with cell phones, and in-flight Airphones, were the passengers on Flight 93, who soon were talking to loved ones on the ground about what had happened in New York and Washington. Thus the Flight 93 passengers quickly surmised that the terrorists who had control of their plane intended to crash it into a target of some financial, cultural, military or political importance. As a result, as the world knows, those passengers wrestled the terrorists for control of the plane, causing Flight 93 to crash into a field in Pennsylvania.

Everyone on board died, but the intended target — now thought to be the U.S. Capitol — was spared and, as a result, the federal government was likely saved. For as I wrote in this column last year, had the Capitol been hit it is possible that enough members of the House of Representatives would have died to prevent Congress from being able to reach a quorum. From a Constitutional standpoint, without a quorum Congress can't function, and because the Constitution provides no means for holding timely emergency elections for new members of the House, legally speaking the federal government could have been in limbo for months. In effect, there would have been no government.

The point being that, thanks to telecommunications products that not only are state of the art but also are affordable, accessible and pervasive, an informed citizenry was able to fight back against the terrorists in ways that — as the 9/11 Commission's recent report makes crystal clear — the U.S. air defense system failed spectacularly to do.

The further point being that the federal government, which regulates the telecommunications industry, should ensure that this industry is allowed to continue to grow and advance. In hindsight, it is producing not just tools of communication, but weapons of defense.

© Kauffmann 2008

Bruce's History Lessons:
The Star Mangled Banner

This week (Sept. 14) in 1814, in the thick of the War of 1812 between Great Britain and America, a young lawyer from Baltimore, Maryland, named Francis Scott Key approached British authorities in the hopes of learning the whereabouts of a physician friend thought to have been incarcerated by the British for "unfriendly acts." For his troubles, Key himself was detained on one of the British warships that had sailed into Baltimore Harbor to attack Fort McHenry, the city's last defense against British occupation.

The attack, which Key witnessed from the ship's deck, began in the evening hours of September 13th with a massive naval bombardment of Ft. McHenry, and ended the next morning. Thousands of salvos "bursting in air" were fired against the fort, but to Key's astonishment, the "dawn's early light" revealed that the American flag — Old Glory — "was still there," tattered and full of holes, but in one piece, flying above the battered, but also in one piece, American fort. Inspired, Key jotted down the words (including the above quotes) that would become the lyrics to the "Star Spangled Banner." Not incidentally, Ft. McHenry's survival was a turning point in the War of 1812. Unable to breach the fort's defenses, the British ended their siege of Baltimore and four months later the war ended with the Treaty of Ghent, which ultimately was more pro-American than pro-British.

As for Key's immortal words, they were immediately published in a Baltimore newspaper, and not long after that his patriotic sentiments were set to the music of a popular English drinking tune, "To Anacreon in Heaven." In due time, "The Star Spangled Banner" was adopted as the country's unofficial theme song by a number of patriotic organizations, including the U.S. armed services, and in 1931 it was made the official American national anthem through a resolution passed by Congress.

Today, of course, "The Star Spangled Banner" is mostly performed at grade school ceremonies and organized sporting events, and it is a toss-up as to which group mangles the lyrics and the tune worse — the school kids or the singers, often paid professionals, who assault our eardrums with their renditions at major league football, basketball and baseball games. Granted, Key's lyrics are difficult to remember, and the aforementioned English drinking tune may have been the worst possible choice to set the lyrics to. It fights the words, forcing the singer to stretch out and distort many lyrics, often making them unrecognizable.

Call it "The Star Mangled Banner," which (unfortunately, given its author's last name) is usually sung "off-Key," and which, as every Little Leaguer knows, only has one memorable line: "…AND THE LAND OF THE FREE, PLAY BALL!"

© *Kauffmann 2008*

Bruce's History Lessons:
The Constitutional Amendment Process

This week (Sept. 25) in 1789 America's first Congress under our new Constitution approved 12 amendments to that Constitution and, in compliance with that same Constitution's instructions, sent them to the states for ratification (they ratified 10; our Bill of Rights). Given recent movements to once again amend the Constitution with both a ban on burning the American flag and a ban on same-sex marriage, it seems appropriate to review what the Founders were thinking when they decided to create an amendment process.

They were thinking that it should be *possible* to amend the Constitution, but not *easy*. They clearly understood that as times change, so must governments, but they wanted the Constitution to have a durability — a permanence — that would allow it to weave itself into the fabric of American life. Put more plainly, if the Constitution was to be obeyed — to be "the law of the land" — it needed to gain the public's respect and reverence. That would not happen if the document was so pliable, one generation's Constitution would be radically different from the next generation's.

That is why it takes two-thirds of Congress to approve a Constitutional Amendment and three-fourths of the states to ratify it — an uphill climb if ever there was one — and *that* is why, in the 215 years since our original 10 amendments, we have only added 17 more.

What's more, as the Founders intended, the majority of our approved amendments deal with protecting individual rights, leaving public policy — for the most part — to be determined by the executive and legislative branches. Voting rights in particular have dominated the amendment process: the 15th Amendment extended voting rights to African-American males; the 19th Amendment extended them to women; the 23rd Amendment gave voting rights to residents of Washington, D.C.; the 24th Amendment abolished poll taxes, which had prevented African-Americans from voting; and the 26th Amendment lowered the voting age to 18.

Indeed, the wisdom of narrowing the types of amendments proposed to those dealing with individual rights was proven when the one amendment clearly dealing with a national public policy issue, the 18th Amendment establishing Prohibition, proved such a disaster it was repealed by the 21st Amendment — the only time an amendment has met that fate.

Food for thought as we ponder the implications of banning flag burning or same-sex marriage by Constitutional amendment. In my mind, the first, flag burning, however heinous, *is* political speech (what other possible motivation could there be for burning an American flag?) and therefore is a protected right, and the second, the sanctity of traditional marriage, is a national issue that should be decided in the legislative arena, not the courts.

The Founders, from my readings, would agree.

© *Kauffmann 2008*

Bruce's History Lesson:
The Dan Rather I Knew

I guess it was inevitable that I would get e-mails from readers asking me what I think of the whole Dan Rather scandal, in which Dan and CBS News were found to have engaged in shoddy journalism for relying on forged documents in their "60 Minutes II" story that claims President Bush disobeyed orders and failed to take a physical while in the Texas Air National Guard. As it turns out, at the end of my column several newspapers that publish it note that I used to write for Dan, a plug I was unaware of until I began getting e-mails from readers saying, "You used to write for Rather? No wonder he sounds like such a moron." (Thank you for sharing.)

Well, yes, I did write for Dan. From 1989 to 1991 I wrote his radio broadcast, "Dan Rather Reporting, News, Analysis and Commentary," which ran afternoons on CBS News Radio, and it was a great job. While Dan and I would occasionally discuss the stories he thought were important, mostly he let me choose what stories I thought should be covered. If he didn't agree, I would start over or he would write himself that day, and he was always free to edit — which he often did.

In any event, working for the man for several years — I also wrote speeches for him — I got to know him fairly well and let me say this about Dan personally. I liked him. He was thoughtful, considerate, self effacing almost to a fault, a voracious reader, big on self improvement, like me a fan of history and — this may sound strange — a real gentleman. He was a true Texan in that sense that Texans may let their hair down around other men, but they are always gentlemen to ladies.

I also want to go on record as saying the Dan I knew was nowhere near the left-wing media crazy he is so often labeled. In some ways he was very conservative and it should be noted that the person who wrote for Dan before me was Peggy Noonan, who went on to pen speeches for Ronald Reagan and George Bush (I) and now writes for *The Wall Street Journal.* Not exactly a bleeding-heart liberal, our Peggy, nor am I, and it is to Dan's credit that he hired us both.

As for Dan's present difficulties, obviously he has gotten himself into some Texas-sized trouble and the repercussions will last a while. The great irony, of course, is that Dan made his reputation covering the Nixon White House during the Watergate scandal. He of all people should know that it isn't the original mistake that brings you down. It's the attempt to obstruct, delay and cover-up.

© Kauffmann 2008

Bruce's History Lessons: Eugene McCarthy Runs for President

In July 1967, U.S. forces fighting in Vietnam reached an astonishing 500,000 soldiers and, unsurprisingly, the drumbeat of political protest was getting louder.

But fortunately for then-President Lyndon Johnson, this political dissent was mostly confined to college campuses, where the hair on both the young men and women students had grown noticeably longer, the clothes they wore increasingly stranger, the music they listened to progressively more inscrutable and the mind-altering stimulants they imbibed decidedly more illegal.

As a result, these "hippie" protestors taking to the streets or taking over college buildings antagonized Middle Americans a lot more than they worried the political status quo, and the more thoughtful of the protest leaders knew it. They realized that if they ever were going to effect change, they had to work within the system. They had to convert the anti-war movement from an amorphous "protest" to a targeted political challenge, which meant they needed a political candidate to rally behind.

The obvious choice was Bobby Kennedy, the former attorney general and younger brother of slain president John Kennedy. Bobby's antipathy for Johnson was well known and his relative youth and emerging liberalism made him the perfect candidate. But Bobby declined, thinking it political suicide to challenge a sitting president of his own party.

So they turned to another idealistic candidate, the maverick senator from Minnesota, Eugene McCarthy, who this week (Oct. 7) in 1967 declared his candidacy for president with the goal of ending the Vietnam War as quickly as possible.

Like moths to a flame, the anti-war movement rallied to McCarthy's cause. Students from around the country signed up as volunteers, many — under the banner "Clean for Gene" — even shaving their beards and cutting their hair so they would be more presentable to the "average Joe" Americans whose doors they would be knocking on to pass out McCarthy leaflets.

What they lacked in experience they made up for in enthusiasm, and although the Johnson administration dismissed these "kids for McCarthy" as amateurs, they got America's attention. And as the fighting in Vietnam got progressively worse, and television coverage of it got progressively better, public opinion shifted. Middle Americans started to turn against the war, and as a result McCarthy won 42 percent of the vote in that year's New Hampshire primary, which so shocked Lyndon Johnson that he withdrew from the presidential race.

Interestingly, Bobby Kennedy also was shocked, but in a different way. Sensing a political opportunity, and considering himself, not McCarthy, the true leader of America's youth, Bobby jumped into the race, meaning that the anti-war protest movement, which once had no candidate to support, suddenly had two. Politically, 1968 was to be a year of surprises — some good, some very bad.

© Kauffmann 2008

Bruce's History Lessons: Teddy Roosevelt's Life-Saving Speech

Having worked as a professional speechwriter I have long believed that in the 20th century perhaps only Winston Churchill could give a speech longer than 25 minutes and still hold the audience's attention, which is why I maintain that the shorter the speech, the better. But Theodore "Teddy" Roosevelt, our 26th president, would probably disagree with me. This week (Oct. 14) in 1912, a long speech saved his life.

It was around 5:00 p.m. on that October day that Roosevelt, who had been president from 1901 to 1908 and was again running as a third-party candidate, emerged from a Milwaukee hotel on his way to a campaign rally downtown. Suddenly, a voice rang out, "Any man looking for a third term as president ought to be shot!" and a deranged anarchist named John Schrank fired a revolver point blank into TR's chest. Fortunately, because TR had stuffed the very thick manuscript of that evening's campaign speech into his chest pocket, the bullet was slowed by the paper and only wounded him. The bullet missed his heart by centimeters.

Bleeding from the wound, TR nevertheless insisted on attending the rally and delivering his speech, although he would not give the speech as written, but an edited version of it that included the fact that he had been shot. "I don't know whether you fully understand that I have just been shot," TR announced to the stunned audience, "but it takes more than that to kill a Bull Moose." The "Bull Moose Party" was Teddy's name for the political party he had formed in order to run again for president. "The bullet is in me now," he added, "so I cannot make a very long speech."

He then proceeded to defend himself against the "foul mendacity and abuse" that had been "heaped upon me" by his two opponents, President William Taft, who had been TR's handpicked successor for president, and the democratic challenger, Woodrow Wilson. TR also briefly outlined his accomplishments as the former president and his political vision of a nation in which, through honest compromise, capital interests and labor interests could achieve harmony.

For someone unable to "make a very long speech," TR managed to talk for 45 minutes before being rushed to a nearby hospital to have the bullet removed. Fearless as always, he continued to campaign in public for the rest of the race. He would even make his physical toughness a campaign theme.

Alas, to no avail. Roosevelt and Taft essentially split the Republican vote, handing the election to Woodrow Wilson. As a result, this episode may be the only time in history that a speech saved a politician's real life, but had no effect on his political life.

© Kauffmann 2008

Bruce's History Lessons:
Flunking College

This week's lesson is prompted by the upcoming presidential election and the clamor to change, or even eliminate, the Electoral College in the wake of the fiasco of the last presidential election. Why did the Founding Fathers set up an Electoral College and what is it supposed to do? Call this column another in my series, "What *Were* the Founders Thinking?"

First of all, they were thinking compromise. Like most issues that came before the Constitutional Convention in 1787, the election of our president got caught up in the "Big State vs. Small State" debate. The small states, fearing their presidential choices would never garner enough popular votes, wanted each state to have an equal number of votes in choosing a president (like their equal representation in the Senate), while the big states, for similarly obvious reasons, wanted a nationwide popular election. The Electoral College split the difference, giving each state electoral votes equal to its number of representatives *and* senators.

The Founders also were thinking regionally. While population size determined how many representatives states could send to Congress, the original Constitution allowed Southern slave states to count slaves as 3/5th of a person in determining their population — thereby increasing their congressional representation and power. But slaves obviously would not be allowed to vote in presidential elections, meaning such elections would greatly diminish the South's ability to choose presidents. So Southerners supported the Electoral College, which (as noted) awarded states electoral votes based on congressional representation.

The Founders also were thinking "big picture." They feared popular elections because they didn't think the "people" — that mass of humanity scattered along the Eastern Seaboard — would ever learn enough about the different candidates to choose wisely. There was no national media, so how were the voters, mostly yeoman farmers, to familiarize themselves with national candidates, let alone their positions on issues? Thus the Electors originally were intended to filter out unfit candidates by choosing a few truly worthy ones.

And who would then make the presidential selection? Believe it or not, the Founders expected that at this point the election would go to the House of Representatives where a majority vote would choose the president. What we fear today — elections being "thrown into the House" — was an outcome that the Founders considered entirely plausible. In effect, the Electoral College would serve as the nominating process with the House the final arbiter.

If this system sounds confusing, it is, which perhaps is why there have been so many attempts to change it, especially since about half of the reasons the Electoral College was originally created are no longer valid.

Then again, there are some good reasons to retain the College, which is another column for another time.

© Kauffmann 2008

Bruce's History Lessons:
The Charge of the Light Brigade

Forward, the Light Brigade!/"Charge for the guns!" he said/Into the valley of Death/Rode the six hundred.

— Alfred Lord Tennyson

As every school child knows, the cavalry charge that occurred this week (Oct. 25) in 1854, during the Battle of Balaclava between Britain and Russia in the Crimea, was the most courageous cavalry charge in history.

And as every scholar knows, it was also the most idiotic. Like the "whispering game" that children play, in which a message is whispered to one child after another, resulting in a final message that bears no resemblance to the original, the Charge of the Light Cavalry Brigade against well-defended Russian artillery resulted from a vague military order given by the army commander, Lord Raglan, to a confused subordinate, Captain Nolan, who got it further wrong when delivering it to the cavalry commander, Lord Lucan, who further garbled it in orders to the Light Brigade's commander, Lord Cardigan. Thus did Cardigan charge the wrong position.

This combination of courage and idiocy is one reason the Charge of the Light Brigade is considered such a quintessential example of Britain's Victorian Age. After all, the cavalry commander, Lord Lucan, and the brigade commander, Lord Cardigan, were brothers-in-law, yet they were feuding over a matter of honor and therefore neither was speaking to each other nor permitting their staffs to communicate. This virtually ensured confusion over military position.

What is more, befitting the times, the military rank that both men had achieved was due more to political connections and social standing than any martial skills. Thus when Lord Cardigan, against all common sense, led his "six hundred" (actually 673) into the "valley of death," where Russian artillery were well fortified, it was a certainty that many men would be killed. The final tally was 272 deaths, a casualty rate of about 40 percent.

Which leads us to the final proof of how "veddy British" the charge was. It became the stuff of legend. A monstrously wrong-headed suicide mission, arising from repeated blunders, struck a unique chord in Victorian England. Lord Cardigan, who somehow managed to survive the charge, became a national hero. Poems were written about the charge, including one of the most famous in English literature (quoted above). Parliament passed resolutions of praise, and British school children study it to this day. Meanwhile, the earlier charge of the British Heavy Brigade, *which was a total military success*, is completely forgotten.

But, oh, the charge was "a feat of chivalry," as a member of Parliament put it, although French General Pierre Bosquet, who watched the charge, and whose troops eventually rescued what was left of the Light Brigade, probably put it better when he commented, "It's magnificent. But it isn't war."

© Kauffmann 2008

Bruce's History Lessons:
The Electoral College: Part 2

"The best argument against democracy is a five-minute conversation with the average voter."

-Winston Churchill

In my previous column on the Electoral College, in which I explained the reasons the Founders established it, but also some of its flaws, I promised to follow-up with a column outlining its advantages. From the reader response I got, including several readers who sent me articles on the topic, the Electoral College seems to be a subject of interest. So call this column "Electoral College Part 2: The Defense."

For starters, recall that the Founders did not create a democratic government in Philadelphia in 1789. They created a republican government because they wanted some checks against pure, unalloyed democracy in which the majority ruled. The Electoral College is one of those checks.

Now imagine that we do away with it and choose our presidents by the very democratic method of a nationwide popular vote. The first result will be the undermining of the two-party system. Every Tom, Dick and Harry who looks in the mirror and sees a president will run for the job and the eventual winner might garner less than 30 percent of the vote. Talk about a president lacking a mandate!

So, you say, let's have a run-off first. Leave aside the fact that we have now lengthened the campaign season by having at least two elections — first the run-off and second the general election (at double or triple the expense, *meaning more fundraising!*) — the main problem is that a run-off could well eliminate some of the centrist candidates in favor of extremists on either the left or right. If you don't believe me, check out France where that happens on a regular basis.

What's more, popular elections with myriad candidates practically demand backroom deal making. As some of the dozen or so candidates inevitably lose steam, many will propose bargains with the current frontrunners, backing them in return for political favors or jobs. That's something the Electoral College and the two-party system have made less likely.

Speaking of lengthy campaigns, without an Electoral College, which forces candidates to focus on electoral-rich states, presidential campaigns will truly be national as the last candidates standing fight over every piece of geography with a large population center. That may sound like a good thing, but think back to the ferocious disputes, legal and otherwise, over the legitimacy of the vote totals in Palm Beach, Florida, in 2000. In a close popular election you might have to multiply that by the hundreds, maybe thousands.

The Founders had a deep skepticism about giving power to the *demos* — the people — and they established the Electoral College as one way to temper that power. In my mind, wisely.

© Kauffmann 2008

Bruce's History Lessons:
And the Wall Came Tumbling Down

My vote for the most significant historic event in the second half of the 20th Century occurred this week (Nov. 9) in 1989 when the Berlin Wall that had separated East and West Germany — but in a larger sense had separated the Eastern bloc countries of Europe and the Soviet Union from the Western bloc countries of Europe and the U.S. — came tumbling down. The "Wall" was the ultimate symbol of the Cold War, and as such its removal heralded the Cold War's end.

For the West — for America and its West European allies — the fall of the Wall and subsequent relaxation of Cold War tensions evoked many emotions, from euphoria over the end of a 50-year threat of nuclear annihilation; to the smug satisfaction that history had endorsed its belief in the superiority of market-based economic systems and pluralistic political systems; to the giddy anticipation that reduced defense budgets would mean sounder economies and more just societies.

And yet that paled in comparison with the emotions experienced by the East — by the ordinary citizens of those countries located behind an "Iron Curtain" controlled by a ruthless dictatorship in Moscow. For them, and that included the ordinary citizens of the Soviet Union itself, the fall of the Wall meant the end of much more than the threat of nuclear war or of the illusion that command economies and socialist political systems were, as Karl Marx once said, the "wave of the future."

It meant the end of the only way of life that most of them had ever known. It meant the end of government control of all economic output, all property, all movement, all information and all opinion. It meant the end of the imprisonment, torture, death or disappearance of tens of millions of

399

people for the simple crime of having displeased the state. It meant the end of the suppression of religious observance; it meant the end of the deadening uniformity of their drab lives and the end of the slow coarsening of the human spirit that is the inevitable result of unrelieved hopelessness.

True, it also meant the end of a cradle-to-grave dependence on the state for a job, housing, medical coverage, old-age security, and the many other economic and social benefits that were the so-called hallmarks of socialist systems. So in that sense, the removal of the chains of totalitarianism has been replaced by the "chains" of individual responsibility and initiative.

For the East *and* the West, that is both the challenge and the promise of the fall of the Wall, which is why this event is memorable not only because of its effect on our past century, but also because of its portent for our present one.

© Kauffmann 2008

Bruce's History Lessons:
The Heidi Game

Unbeknownst to most Americans, a major battle in our nation's *Kulturkampf* (culture war) occurred this week in 1968. It was a rout.

The battlefield was, fittingly, that square little box that millions of Americans spend their evenings and weekends watching. On Sunday, November 17, professional football's Oakland Raiders were playing the New York Jets and NBC was broadcasting the game nationwide.

But it was not just any game. The Raiders and Jets not only were two of the best teams in football — each had a 7-2 record — and not only did they feature many of the game's marquee players, including Jet's quarterback "Broadway Joe" Namath, but also they had developed a rivalry that approached pure hatred. Winning this game meant ultimate bragging rights, both for the players and their rabid fans.

What's more, the game was a classic. There were five lead changes, several amazing plays — both Namath and Oakland's quarterback, Daryle Lamonica, threw for more than 300 yards — and a slew of penalties that resulted from several vicious hits, cheap shots and fights. In other words, a fan's delight, and with just over a minute left in the game, the Jets kicked a field goal to give them a 32-29 lead. As NBC went to commercial break millions of fans watching sat back in anticipation of a thrilling finish.

Which they never got to see. In part because of the many penalties, the game had run over its three-hour time limit and at 7 p.m. NBC was contractually obligated to broadcast the made-for-TV movie "Heidi." To the horror of millions of football crazies, coming out of the commercials they were greeted not with the sounds of behemoth ballplayers grunting on a football field, but the sounds of a pig-tailed goat herder yodeling on a mountain.

The fans went berserk, especially when they learned of the game's miracle finish in which the Raiders scored two quick touchdowns to win 43-32. The switchboard at NBC headquarters lit up with so many fan complaints that the phone system crashed. The next day NBC's president apologized publicly and in the wake of the "Heidi Game" the NFL wrote contracts that bound the networks to broadcast games in their entirety — a television first.

Today, of course, sports — but especially football — dominates the American cultural scene. In the years since 1968, college football has become more popular than ever, while pro football has given us Monday Night Football, Thursday Night Football, Saturday playoff football and the granddaddy of them all, the Super Bowl, which boasts the 10 most watched television events in history.

As for "Heidi," a movie designed for wholesome family viewing, it is still shown occasionally, a quaint artifact from America's cultural days of yore.

© *Kauffmann 2008*

Bruce's History Lessons:
D.B. Cooper's Perfect Crime?

There was a time — how innocent those days seem — when hijacking an airplane could earn the perpetrator cult status, and a good example of that was the hijacking that occurred this week (Nov. 24) in 1971 when, on a Northwest Orient flight from Portland to Seattle, a man named "D.B." Cooper handed a note to a flight attendant that indicated he possessed a bomb. After allowing the attendant a quick glance into a briefcase, where she saw something resembling a bomb, Cooper demanded $200,000 in cash and four parachutes.

On his orders the plane then landed in Seattle, where authorities met his demands. In return, Cooper allowed the other passengers to exit the plane, and then ordered the plane back into the air, instructing the pilot to head to Mexico and fly at a low altitude. Next, Cooper ordered all crew members into the cockpit and moments later — somewhere over the Lewis River in southwest Washington — he jumped out of the plane and into a violent thunderstorm. Given the plane's 10,000-foot altitude, the outside temperatures were estimated at below zero, with winds swirling at approximately 150 miles-per-hour. Cooper was wearing a suit, a raincoat and sunglasses.

He was never seen again. Although most people believe the weather conditions killed him, the terrible storm actually delayed a search for him, and when an extensive manhunt was finally conducted, it turned up nothing.

And a legend was born. The story of D.B. Cooper, an average Joe who got away with one of the most daring crimes in history, was front-page news in every newspaper in America. A movie was even made of his deed, and to this day his is the only unsolved hijacking ever committed in the United

States.   Some called his robbery and escape "the perfect crime" because he left investigators with absolutely nothing to go on — no suspects, no leads, no accomplices, no evidence. Although in 1980, while playing near the Columbia River, a young boy discovered $6,000 of the ransom money (serial numbers matched FBI records), no one knows today whether D.B. Cooper died that November day in a remote Washington forest or whether he has been living the good life ever since.

Actually, no one even knows who D.B. Cooper was. Despite thousands of tips called in and tens of thousands of dollars spent investigating him, all that is known is that Cooper smoked Raleigh cigarettes, knew a bit about aerodynamics and liked whiskey.

Which is fitting because every November 24th for the past 33 years residents of the nearby town of Ariel, Washington, gather at a local bar to hoist a whiskey — or two — in homage to the average Joe who, seemingly, committed the perfect crime.

© Kauffmann 2008

Bruce's History Lesson:
Rosa Parks

"Thank you Miss Rosa, you are the spark, that started our freedom movement. Thank you Sister Rosa Parks."

The Neville Brothers

Leaving work on December 1 in 1955, Rosa Parks, a part-time seamstress and full-time employee of a department store in Montgomery, Alabama, boarded a city bus for home after a very hard day. Her feet were sore, her shoulders ached and her whole body was exhausted. And as it would turn out, so was her patience.

She took a seat in "no man's land" — a section in the middle of the bus that was neither specifically reserved for whites, as the front section was, nor for blacks, as the rear was (unless whites needed it). In Alabama, as in many Southern states in 1955, segregation was a reality, Federal laws notwithstanding. And on Montgomery city buses, drivers even had the power to expand the white section of the bus as they saw fit. So when a white man boarded her bus Rosa Parks and three other passengers were told that "no man's land" was now "Whites Only" and they had to move. The others complied. Parks refused.

It was not exactly a spur of the moment decision. As an NAACP member who had attended desegregation workshops in which blacks and whites had treated each other with mutual respect, Parks had foreseen the day when she might no longer meekly tolerate the humiliating sense of powerlessness and second-class status that Alabama's segregation forced on its black citizens.

Which is why her subsequent arrest for violating local segregation laws presented the city's black leadership with a long-sought opportunity to legally challenge Montgomery's segregated public transportation system. And as an added benefit, the arrest of this respected, church-going woman had stirred the black community into initiating a boycott of the Montgomery bus system

Her arrest also brought to prominence a young Baptist preacher named Martin Luther King, Jr., who was chosen to lead the boycott mostly because — as a relative newcomer to Montgomery — he had made no enemies among the city's black leadership. It would prove an inspired choice, not only because of his courage, determination and insistence on non-violent protest, but also because, challenged to rally the black community, King began to find his voice as a public speaker. Thanks in great part to his rhetoric, blacks boycotted the bus system for almost a year despite the economic and physical hardships it caused them.

And in the end they prevailed when, in November of 1956, the United States Supreme Court, without even listening to argument, ruled that Alabama laws requiring segregation of its public transportation system were unconstitutional. A "spark" had become a fire that would not soon be extinguished.

© Kauffmann 2008

Bruce's History Lessons:
Pearl Harbor and
Cultural Ignorance

As is well known, America's tragic involvement in Vietnam was due in part to its ignorance of the history and culture of the Vietnamese people — yet another example, or so conventional wisdom says, of the white man's ignorance of the Oriental mind.

But sometimes it's Oriental ignorance of our ways that leads to tragedy. The Japanese attack on Pearl Harbor, which occurred this week (Dec. 7) in 1941, is the quintessential example of that. Simply put, if the Japanese had better understood how the American people thought, and how the American political system worked, there would have been no war.

To review, in the late 1930s Japan was bent on creating an empire that included much of East Asia. Japan had already conquered Manchuria and parts of China and, with most of Europe trying to fend off Nazi Germany, it was beginning to move against European colonial possessions in the East Indies.

But there was one major obstacle to the imperialist designs of Japan's war leaders — the United States. America's president, Franklin Roosevelt, refused to acquiesce to Japan's expansionist plans, and knowing that those plans depended on Japan's ability to import critical raw materials such as iron, oil and aviation fuel, Roosevelt ordered an embargo of the sale of those materials to Japan.

Of course, Japan could make up for those embargoed goods by continuing to conquer countries in the Indies and using their raw materials, but the Japanese were convinced that doing so eventually would cause America to declare war on them. Their only course of action, they believed, was to launch a devastating blow against America that would cripple its war-making capability and demoralize its citizens. Pearl Harbor was the result.

In making this decision Japan made two critical mistakes. The first — the most well known — is that, rather than demoralize Americans, Pearl Harbor aroused and angered them. The "sleeping giant" awoke and exacted its revenge.

But the more important mistake Japan made was assuming that its actions in East Asia would provoke America into a war. Had Japanese leaders better understood how isolationist America was — how unconcerned Americans were about a region halfway around the world that most of them couldn't locate on a map — Japan would have known that a direct attack on American soil was the *only thing* that would arouse the country's martial spirit. Japan's leaders also mistook Roosevelt's animosity toward their expansionism for his ability to do anything about it. Because *they* could bring Japan into a war regardless of public opinion, they assumed Roosevelt could, too.

Those mistakes — the result of cultural, political and historical ignorance — are why Pearl Harbor is not only a "day of infamy" for America, but for Japan as well.

© *Kauffmann 2008*

Bruce's History Lessons:
Ludwig Beethoven — Superstar

Ludwig van Beethoven, born this week (Dec. 16) in 1770, is generally considered the most important musical composer in history. Granted, Mozart may be more popular, and among critics Bach has his disciples, but the argument over who was "number one" aside, there should be no argument over who was the most influential. Beethoven, hands down.

He began as a pianist *extraordinaire*, moving from Germany, his birthplace, to the pinnacle of the musical world, Vienna, where he became a successful performer and teacher. By his twenties he also was composing, specializing in piano sonatas that were both popular and critically admired. Before he turned 30 he had added three piano concertos and two symphonies to his playlist, and his future seemed as bright as his talent.

And then he began going deaf. In an irony that only God could explain, the world's greatest musician eventually lost his hearing, which so depressed him that he withdrew from society and even contemplated suicide.

Yet, in another irony that God probably couldn't explain, Beethoven's deafness may have made him the great composer he became. His inability to hear seemed to liberate him musically, and his social withdrawal made him indifferent to the accepted standards of the time. He began to create compositions that, as he said to one critic, "are not for you but for a later age."

Those works, which he never heard, are among his greatest ever, and include his famous Choral Symphony, no.9 in d minor, and his Piano Sonata No. 29 in B flat major. What's more, the volume of Beethoven's work never slacked. Except for that short period when his depression was most intense, Beethoven continued to create a quantity of music that was matched only by its quality. When he died he had written (by my count) 32 piano sonatas, 10 sonatas for the piano and violin, five piano concertos, nine symphonies and a number of string quartets.

But perhaps his most important contributions to classical music were his innovations. He showed how versatile the piano could be, transforming it into the focus of most classical compositions. He often discarded the traditional four-movement scheme in favor of six or even seven movements. He expanded the size of the orchestra and increased the length of symphonies, thereby widening their scope. Most important, he brought passion to his music, transforming it from merely "classical" into a romantic style that deeply influenced both his contemporaries and those who followed. They include Brahms, Schubert, Strauss, Mahler and even Tchaikovsky.

When Beethoven died in 1827 more than 10,000 people attended his funeral, and his works were being played from London to St. Petersburg and beyond.

He was, beyond doubt, music's very first superstar.

© Kauffmann 2008

Bruce's History Lessons:
America's Tiny Ally

The next time a tiny mosquito lands on your arm looking for lunch, slap her (only female mosquitoes "bite") dead, but then remember her contribution to the country we live in. For without the mosquito, the Louisiana Purchase, which was finalized this week (Dec. 20) in 1803, might never have occurred. Which means that gaining the middle third of America (including the states of Louisiana, Arkansas, Missouri, Iowa, Minnesota, North and South Dakota, Nebraska, Oklahoma and parts of Montana, Wyoming and Colorado) would have been a lot more difficult, and might well have involved going to war.

To set the scene, in 1800 the territory that would become the Louisiana Purchase was part of France's colonial empire, as were several islands off the Florida coast, including Haiti, where French plantation owners depended on the slave labor of native Haitians to keep their plantations profitable. But in 1801, a Haitian general named Toussaint L'Ouverture led an uprising of Haitians against the French. After fierce fighting his forces captured Haiti's largest city, Santo Domingo, giving Toussaint control of the entire island.

Heeding the pleas of the French planters, France's emperor, Napoleon, sent a large and well-equipped French army to Haiti to quell the uprising, but Toussaint's brilliant generalship, combined with the staggering losses the French suffered at the hands of the malaria-carrying mosquito, turned the tide and forced Napoleon to agree to a peace treaty that gave Haiti its independence. A few months later, with the bitter taste of that Haiti adventure still in his mouth, Napoleon concluded that his holdings in the New World — including his territory on the North American continent — were more trouble than they were worth. He decided instead to focus on expanding his European empire, and needing cash to finance that expansion, he offered to sell the Louisiana territory to the United States for the bargain price of $15 million dollars. President Thomas Jefferson quickly agreed to the deal, engineering the greatest act of his presidency.

And it was made possible in part by one of the tiniest, yet deadliest and most resilient creatures in nature. No living thing in history has killed more humans than has the mosquito, yet after years of being subjected to eradication measures such as widespread chemical spraying — including the use of DDT — mosquitoes are more numerous than ever, as are global cases of malaria, dengue fever and West Nile virus.

All of which are reasons to fear and loathe that whiny sound the mosquito makes just before she lands on you, which she will undoubtedly do often this coming summer. But after you squash her, salute her. In 1801 she helped win a war that helped double the size of your country.

© Kauffmann 2008

Bruce's History Lessons:
The Wall of Separation

Perhaps the most unintentional Constitutional argument in history was initiated this week (Jan. 1) in 1802 when President Thomas Jefferson wrote a letter to the Danbury Baptists in Connecticut proclaiming that there was "a wall of separation between Church and State." Ever since, those who argue that, Constitutionally, religion and politics must never mix have used Jefferson's "wall" to support their argument.

Yet Jefferson's letter to the Baptists was less a discourse on the First Amendment's religious establishment clause ("Congress shall make no law respecting an establishment of religion") and more a campaign letter meant to boost the Republican Jefferson's political standing in an area dominated by the rival Federalist party. Jefferson had hoped his letter would score political points with the Baptists, who thought there was too much state support of the rival Congregationalists in New England, but he wound up angering Baptist leaders by seeming to advocate total separation of religion from public life, something the Baptists — who had asked Jefferson to declare a national day of "fasting" — would not support.

What's more, Jefferson's hallowed reputation notwithstanding, connecting his "wall" to the First Amendment is a stretch given that Jefferson had nothing to do with the writing, passage or ratification of that amendment, or any of the other nine that comprise our Bill of Rights. This accomplishment belongs to (my hero) James Madison, and during the time Madison was writing the Bill of Rights and shepherding it through a recalcitrant Congress, Jefferson wasn't even in the country. He was serving as America's minister to France.

For that reason, Jefferson always deferred to his great friend Madison on Constitutional questions, and Madison's attitude toward religion in public life might best be put, "The more the merrier." As early as 1785, while observing a dispute between Episcopalians and Presbyterians in his home state of Virginia, Madison made the point that he preferred them in conflict rather than in coalition because religious freedom was furthered when differing religious groups were all competing for adherents — what today we might call "competing in the marketplace of ideas."

What Madison, Jefferson and the other Founding Fathers feared was *not* a mix of religion and politics — indeed, while in the midst of their most important politicking they held daily prayer services. Rather, they feared the "establishment" of one government-sponsored religion that would inevitably inhibit the practice of all others, which is exactly what had happened with the state-sponsored Anglican Church in England, a nation from which many of their forebears had emigrated for exactly that reason.

Perhaps that is why the First Amendment, in addition to preventing Congress from making laws with respect to the "establishment" of a religion, also prevents Congress from "prohibiting the free exercise thereof."

© Kauffmann 2008

Bruce's History Lessons:
E-Mails, We Get E-Mails:
The Year in Review

One of the joys of writing this column (trust me, it ain't the money) is the feedback I get from readers. To borrow from Ana in *The King and I*, while I am teaching you, you are teaching me in your e-mails agreeing, arguing, praising, excoriating, expanding, putting into context, and — yes — correcting.

This past year was no different, so I decided to devote this column to the reader feedback I liked, or learned from, the most in 2004. I will do it every year from now on.

Not surprisingly, my column on dropping the atomic bomb on Hiroshima generated lots of mail, including one from Ted Kircher, a reader of *The Reading Eagle* (PA), who wrote that we should have demonstrated the bomb's power *before* killing Japanese with it. "The U.S. should have dropped one atomic bomb off the east coast of Japan — preferably due west of Tokyo harbor — so that prevailing winds would carry most radiation out to sea. In addition to taking pictures, we could have had the highest ranking Japanese (war) prisoners observe the explosion and then release them back into Japan so their explanations would not be tainted by U.S. influence. If after a few weeks Japan had not yet surrendered, then we should have continued bombing."

A thoughtful point.

But my favorite e-mail of 2004 came from Sheila Demmel, who reads *The Dubuque Telegraph-Herald* in Iowa. In response to my column on "The Heidi Game," in which NBC enraged millions of football fans by pulling the plug on a nail-biting Jets-Raiders football game to show the movie "Heidi," she wrote, "I thought you might enjoy a story from the other perspective. Our girls were four and six at the time. They had asked every day for a week if this was the night "Heidi" was on TV. Each day we told them no, until the magic day arrived. They had been good all day because that was part of the deal. If they were good, they could stay up and watch the whole movie. Supper was over and baths had been taken. I can see them yet dressed in their pajamas anxiously waiting for the start of 'Heidi.' They were so excited when the awaited time, 7:00 o'clock, finally came. They would have been devastated had the movie been delayed. Just as sports fans were upset, had it been the other way around, many children would have been very disappointed. It isn't hard to figure out the importance of this event in our lives, since I still remember it vividly 36 years later...From a sentimental Mom."

I wrote Mrs. Demmel back that she was absolutely right.

Keep 'em coming in 2005 and have a terrific new year!

© *Kauffmann 2008*

Bruce's History Lessons:
Thomas Nast

This week (January 15) in 1870, an American tradition was born when America's first great political cartoonist, Thomas Nast, first drew a cartoon donkey to symbolize the Democratic Party. In this historic cartoon, which was drawn for *Harper's Weekly*, the donkey (Nast actually drew a "jackass") represented the Democratic-controlled newspapers of the post-civil war South, but later came to symbolize the entire Democratic Party, thereby giving those cartoonists who followed in Nast's footsteps a way to represent that political party — and ideology — in their work. And four years later, in another cartoon for *Harper's Weekly*, Nast introduced the elephant as the symbol for the Republican Party. In this cartoon, the elephant bore the words "Republican vote," and Nast chose such a large animal as a way to convey the widespread support for the Republican president, Ulysses S. Grant, with whom Nast had a longstanding friendship.

Born in Germany in 1840, Nast immigrated with his family to America, where he discovered his talent for illustration. And even though his first job at *Harper's Weekly* was as a Civil-war correspondent, his dispatches from the battlefield often included on-the-scene sketches, which quickly became more popular than his writings. After the war his job description changed to "cartoonist," a position he would hold for another 25 years, during which time his cartoons commented on every political issue of the day. In fact, Nast's influence was such that no presidential candidate he supported ever lost an election.

But his real interest was exposing political greed, corruption and cronyism, and by 1870 he found a perfect target in New York's legendary William "Boss" Tweed and the corrupt Tammany Hall political machine Tweed led. Nast's cartoons on the misdeeds of Tweed and Tammany were so effective that Tweed once offered Nast a half-a-million dollar bribe to back off. "I don't care what the papers write about me because my constituents can't read," Tweed supposedly said. "But them damn pictures they can see!"

Outraged at the bribe attempt, Nast went after Tweed with renewed fervor and helped put him behind bars. And even after Tweed escaped jail and fled to Spain, it was another Nast cartoon on Tweed that actually led to his recapture. A local Spanish official recognized Tweed from a Nast drawing re-printed in a Spanish paper, and turned him over to the authorities, who shipped him back to America.

Nast died in 1902, but not before making one other significant contribution to American culture. He drew the first illustrations of Santa Claus based on the "St. Nick" described in Clement Moore's poem "The Night Before Christmas."

The symbols for our two major political parties and Santa himself. Not a bad legacy for any artist.

© Kauffmann 2008

Bruce's History Lessons:
A Royal Wedding

This week (Jan.25) in 1858 a royal wedding took place that was designed to align the fortunes of Europe's two most important powers, Great Britain and Germany's chief principality, Prussia.

The bride was Victoria, or "Vicky," the oldest child of England's longest serving queen, Queen Victoria, and her husband, Prince Albert. The groom was Frederick, or "Fritz," the son of King William of Prussia.

The marriage was primarily the brainchild of Prince Albert, who dreamed that Great Britain and an eventually united Germany, under Prussian leadership, together would guide Europe into a future of liberalism, progress and prosperity. Albert recognized that the conservative King William was adverse to change, but he hoped that William's son and heir, Frederick, would embrace new ideas, especially if they came from his beautiful and intelligent bride-to-be, Vicky. With Vicky counseling her husband once he became Germany's ruler, the future of a Europe influenced by Victoria and Albert on one throne, and their oldest child on the other, seemed — to Albert — bright indeed.

It would not, alas, turn out that way. Frederick died shortly after becoming king so his and Vicky's oldest son, William II, became ruler in his stead. Kaiser (German for "Caesar") William II, as he called himself, would later plunge Germany and Europe into history's first world war.

But that was in the future. In the present there was a wedding to plan, which promised to be a grand affair except for one not-so-minor hitch. Queen Victoria wanted the wedding to be held in England, while King William wanted it in Prussia.

The Prussians fired the first volley of this diplomatic *contretemps* by announcing that, adhering to tradition, Prussian princes must marry in Berlin. But Queen Victoria fired the final volley, using language that makes it clear why she is considered among England's greatest rulers — indeed, why an entire "age," the Victorian Age, carries her name.

"[The Prussians] are not to entertain the possibility of such a question," she wrote dismissively of a Berlin wedding. "The Queen could never consent to it, both for public and private reasons, and the assumption of it being too much for a Prince Royal of Prussia to come over and marry the Princess Royal of Great Britain in England is too absurd to say the least. Whatever may be the usual practice of Prussian princes, it is not every day that one marries the eldest daughter of the Queen of England. The question must therefore be considered as settled and closed."

And settled and closed it was.

As a postscript, as the newlyweds left St. James Chapel in London (not Berlin), they were serenaded by Mendelssohn's "Wedding March," the first time it ever was played at a wedding.

© *Kauffmann 2008*

Bruce's History Lessons:
Betsy Ross: Did She or Didn't She?

This week (Jan. 30) in 1836 Elizabeth Ross, a three-time widow, died in the city she had lived in most of her life, Philadelphia, which happens to be the city that birthed not only the Declaration of Independence and the Constitution, but also the flag that symbolized the nation formed by those two documents. And Elizabeth "Betsy" Ross, according to legend, also happens to be the maker of that flag.

But legend and fact are two different things, and the controversy over whether Betsy actually did sew our first "Old Glory" continues to this day. Since most historians require documented proof before they subscribe to a theory, and since there is no irrefutable documentation that Betsy designed the flag, there can be no definitive ending to this story. But it's an interesting story all the same, and if I had to come down on one side, I would say she did design our first flag.

As the story goes, in June of 1776, George Washington, Robert Morris and George Ross, the uncle of Betsy's first husband, visited Betsy, a professional upholsterer and seamstress, at her Philadelphia shop and asked her to design a national flag. These three men, who served on the Flag Committee established by the Continental Congress, showed Betsy a rough sketch of an American flag, to which Betsy made several alterations, including changing the proposed six-pointed star to the five-pointed star we have today. Betsy then retired to her sewing room where she made the famous flag.

And where did this story originate? From Betsy Ross's grandson, William Canby, who told a meeting of the Historical Society of Pennsylvania that as an 11-year-old boy he was told this story by Grandma Betsy herself, just before she died. What's more, sworn testimony by Betsy's daughter and other family members supported Canby's claim, meaning that if the story is false, Betsy Ross herself was lying. Given that this God-fearing Quaker woman had absolutely no reason to lie, the story seems credible.

Also, choosing her to sew the flag was entirely plausible. She was a known seamstress who had previously sewed flags for the Pennsylvania State Navy, and not only had she prayed in the same church as George Washington — her pew was right next to his — but also she had previously sewn buttons for him. And of course her late husband's uncle, George Ross, being an admirer of Betsy's talents, a friend of Washington's *and* a member of the Flag Committee, likely would have recommended her.

True story or not, Betsy's tale was believed by enough people in 1887 — when the evidence was much fresher than it is today — that her home was designated a national historical landmark. Which it remains today.

© Kauffmann 2008

Bruce's History Lessons: Washington Elected President

This week (Feb 4) in 1789, George Washington was unanimously chosen by the electors of the recently established Electoral College to assume the duties of the first president of the also recently established United States of America. In Washington's mind, such an honor, great as it was, paled in comparison with the sense of burden and responsibility — and even foreboding — that he felt at the thought of the task before him.

For one thing, Washington doubted his ability to do the job. He was a military man, not a politician. He had little formal education and no experience in law or government. Winning wars, even wars against the world's greatest military power, seemed easy compared to creating a government.

For another, the task really was daunting. At the Constitutional Convention in Philadelphia two summers earlier several of the more intractable issues were papered over with the understanding that they would be resolved once the government was in action. As a result, much of the Constitution's language was vague, or in many cases said nothing at all about what powers would be needed to meet what responsibilities, and who would exercise those powers. As one historian put it, the government created by the Constitution was "George Washington and a blank piece of paper." It would take a lot of work to fill that piece of paper up.

But third, and most important, the stakes were so high. What the people of America were trying to prove — against all odds and certainly against all precedent — was that representative government could last, and that a people could govern themselves without needing a monarchy or dictatorship to do it for them. In Europe, in Latin America, in the Far East and most everywhere else around the globe, power was vested in a single king or dictator, or among a minority of hereditary elite — all of whom expected, or were fervently hoping, that the American experiment would fail.

If it did fail, Washington knew that it would undoubtedly be a long time before such an experiment was tried again. He also knew that much of the responsibility for that failure would be his, which is why when he set out on his journey from Mt. Vernon to New York to take the presidential oath of office he was filled with "more anxious and painful sensations than I have words to express."

So all hail to Washington and the other Founders he chose to help him make the American experiment work. Given the odds, given the size of the challenge and given the historic importance of meeting it, they have rightly earned their place in the American pantheon. "The Father of Our Country" most of all.

© Kauffmann 2008

Bruce's History Lessons:
Happy Birthday, Honest Abe

My choice for America's greatest president, Abe Lincoln, who *just* edges out Washington, was born this week (Feb. 12) in 1809. It is fitting that Lincoln's birthday and Washington's (Feb. 22) are the two presidential birthdays celebrated as a national holiday, albeit as the clichéd "President's Day," and albeit annually on a Monday, whether or not that day actually coincides with either of their births.

No matter. Washington, more than any other, created the country, and Lincoln, more than any other, saved it. A combined holiday beats no holiday.

Lincoln was born in Kentucky but raised in Indiana, where his parents moved in 1817, in part because Kentucky allowed slavery while Indiana did not. Being Baptists, the Lincolns disapproved of slavery, and young Abe's lifelong antipathy to that execrable institution can be traced to his early upbringing.

And yet what stands out so clearly about Lincoln's early life is how unique an individual he was and how immune he was to the standard mores and accepted practices of the time.

Consider that time and place: the early 1800s on America's frontier. In Kentucky, Indiana and later in Illinois, where Abe would live as a young man, it was a rough-and-tumble world where hunting and farming were a way of life, where survival was for the fittest, and where the men were hard as nails. They all drank, smoked, fought and cursed.

Except Lincoln, who was tall and strong, yet never once was in a fight that he instigated. Lincoln never drank alcohol, smoked tobacco or used profanity. Nor did he hunt, and although he farmed out of necessity, he hated it and vowed to leave it.

And then there were his politics. Illinois, where Lincoln came of age, overwhelmingly supported the Democratic Party and its great leader, Andrew Jackson. Yet Lincoln's political hero was the Whig leader, Henry Clay, and so Lincoln became a Whig.

So why would this most political of animals join a party that had no political future in his own state? Because Whigs supported government initiatives to build better roads, to improve river navigation, to build railroads so that goods and services could move more reliably from place to place. Whigs also supported high tariffs to keep out foreign competition while the nation's fledgling manufacturers got started, and Whigs supported a national bank because it would provide needed capital to begin new businesses. In short, the Whig Party was the party of national self-improvement, which mirrored Lincoln's own, lifelong goal of personal self-improvement.

Later in life, of course, the Whig Party gave way to the Republican Party, which Lincoln first led. And national self-improvement gave way to national self-preservation — which Lincoln had something to do with as well.

© Kauffmann 2008

Bruce's History Lesson:
The Japanese Internment

This week (Feb. 19) in 1942, President Franklin Roosevelt signed Executive Order #9066, which forced all people of Japanese descent living within 300 miles of the Pacific Coast to leave their homes and businesses for relocation camps further inland. It was arguably his most controversial presidential decision.

The order sprang from the Japanese attack on Pearl Harbor a year earlier — an attack that the U.S. military had proof was aided by unidentified Japanese-Americans still loyal to their ancestral homeland (one intercepted Japanese cable described "connections with our second generations working in airplane plants for intelligence purposes.") That, plus the general hysteria resulting from Pearl, and the numerous defense plants in California, led FDR to conclude that Japanese residing along the West Coast were a security threat.

In hindsight, forcing all Japanese-Americans into camps because of the actions of an unknown few clearly violated their Constitutional rights, and clearly was FDR pilloried for it (his wife Eleanor his harshest critic). Yet from a historic perspective, there actually is some "grey" to this seemingly black-and-white issue.

For one thing, FDR was not the first president to use "military necessity" to justify assuming broad war powers. Abe Lincoln did the same thing in the Civil War, suspending several Constitutional protections, including writs of *habeas corpus*, because he believed that his more pressing Constitutional duty to save the nation gave him the power to temporarily suspend certain rights. Indeed, throughout history when there is a grave threat to national security, American presidents tend to think more like military officers than ACLU lawyers, putting what they believe to be the defense of the nation ahead of civil liberties.

Secondly, it should be noted that there were actually two "classes" of Japanese affected by FDR's order — the *Issei*, who were legal immigrants but not citizens, and the *Nisei*, who were born on American soil and therefore legally citizens. Relocating the *Nisei* did run afoul of the Constitution, but the *Issei* were another matter. In 1942, they were subject to the Alien Act, which gave FDR the power to "apprehend, restrain, secure and remove alien enemies."

All this said, acting against an entire racial class because of the actions of a few violated the letter and spirit of American law, something the Supreme Court finally confirmed when it ruled that FDR's order was unconstitutional. Of course, by that time America was winning the war and the "threat" posed by these Japanese-Americans was so minimal that FDR was happy to rescind Executive Order #9066.

Contributing to this war-winning effort, by the way, were many thousands of brave and loyal Japanese-Americans from other parts of the country, who had enlisted and fought heroically for their homeland, America.

© Kauffmann 2008

Bruce's History Lessons:
The Sandinista Defeat

We have seen it before. The recent elections in Iraq—which in terms of participation exceeded even the most optimistic forecasts—are not the first example of the elemental law of nature that says all people, regardless of race, creed, religion or origin, prefer freedom and empowerment over enslavement and tyranny.

For it was this week (Feb. 25) in 1990—just 15 years ago—that the people of Nicaragua stunned the world by going to the polls and voting to end the decade-long rule of Nicaragua's leftist military dictatorship, the Sandinistas. Swept out of office in that historic election was the avowed Marxist and leader of the Sandinistas, Daniel Ortega. Swept into office with a plurality of 55 percent of the vote was Violeta Barrios de Chamarro, a tiny, frail-looking widow of a former newspaper editor. Chamarro's party also took control of the National Assembly.

That the Sandinistas even agreed to hold elections, given their grip on power, was something of a surprise, but can indirectly be traced to then-President Ronald Reagan's support for the Contras, a group of anti-Sandinista rebels that engaged in guerilla attacks against the Sandinistas from bases in Honduras and Costa Rica. Granted, Reagan's support for these "freedom fighters," as he called them, was controversial, and eventually Congress cut off funds for the Contras, citing their own human rights abuses. But through private funding and—as the American public later learned—illegal, clandestine support for the Contras from members of the Reagan administration, the Contras managed to stay in the field, fighting the Sandinistas at every opportunity.

Looking to end the Contra threat, Ortega then made a deal with the leaders of those countries the Contras were using as bases to stage their raids.

If these leaders would shut down the Contra bases within their borders, the Sandinistas would agree to hold free elections. Ortega and the other Sandinista leaders undoubtedly thought that the result of those elections would be a foregone conclusion, given their overwhelming military power and political control.

They were wrong, in part because they overlooked how miserable the economic conditions in Nicaragua were, and in part because they ignored the general drift away from Marxist dictatorships that was occurring worldwide at that time, especially in Eastern Europe. But in the end, as was true in Iraq, the Sandinistas underestimated the courage of their own people and the universal allure of freedom.

As a postscript—and to their credit—the Sandinista army and security forces allowed the peaceful transfer of power to Chamarro and her party, and in the intervening years many Sandinistas have participated in the democratic process, even occasionally winning office.

Hopefully, that is a harbinger of Iraq's future as well.

© *Kauffmann 2008*

Bruce's History Lesson:
The Articles of Confederation

The American journey from being subjects of the King of England to a self-governing republic under the United States Constitution was a trip with many detours. One of the most significant of those detours, the ratification of the Articles of Confederation and Perpetual Union, occurred this week (March 1) in 1781. It gave America its first national government, and like most first stabs at something, there was room for improvement — as members of Congress quickly recognized. Indeed, when they sent the Articles to the states for ratification back in 1777, they wrote an accompanying letter that said, in effect, "We know this isn't perfect, but it was really hard to create a government that accommodated your 13 different sets of interests and priorities."

The larger problem with the Articles, however, was that they were toothless. Since the colonists had fought their revolution in great part because they wanted to rid themselves of a powerful "central government," namely King George III and Parliament, they weren't about to replace one such central power with another. As a result, the Articles gave most powers to the state governments, including the power to tax, regulate trade, issue currency and raise standing armies. What's more, the Articles made no provision for a strong executive — indeed, there was no executive at all, just a unicameral legislature that could *ask* the states for money and troops, but had no enforcement powers should the states refuse to comply (which they usually did).

The inadequacies of the Articles were clearly recognized during the war, which America managed to win in spite of them, but in the war's wake, serious Americans began re-evaluating the effectiveness of the Articles. Perhaps some were motivated by the fact that, adding insult to injury, the Treaty of Paris ending the war with England languished for months because the states never bothered to send enough representatives to Congress to approve it, and under the Articles Congress had no power to command their attendance!

In any case, several motions to revise the Articles were subsequently proposed, but because unanimous approval was necessary, all failed until Alexander Hamilton and (my hero) James Madison convinced enough state representatives to assemble in Philadelphia in 1787 to discuss "improvements" to the Articles. That gathering became known as the Constitutional Convention, and it produced, after junking the Articles entirely, the Constitution that still governs us today.

To give the Articles their due, they did manage to hold America together until the fear of a strong central authority subsided and more balance between state and federal power could safely be established. Think of the Articles as a dress rehearsal. In hindsight, their achievement was to make the actors more comfortable with the real thing.

© *Kauffmann 2008*

Bruce's History Lessons:
Old Hickory and the Volunteer State

Early in the year 1812, as the history books note, the fledgling United States and the world's greatest military power, Great Britain, were once again moving inexorably toward war. The underlying cause of the coming conflict was "impressment," in which armed British naval officers boarded American ships at sea and forcibly "impressed" American seamen into service on British war ships. Britain claimed these Americans were really British seamen who had deserted, and while that was sometimes true, mostly it was not. In reality, Britain was at war against France, and the British navy needed sailors, so they took them where they found them, regardless of their actual citizenship or the national flag under which their ship sailed.

Another less contentious but equally problematic issue was the fact that, 30 years after the American Revolution, there was still a British presence on the American continent, including British forts left over from the Revolution. This rankled many Americans.

Certainly it rankled Major General Andrew Jackson of Tennessee, who this week (March 7) in 1812 issued a call for Tennessee "volunteers" to follow him in a campaign to conquer "all the British dominions upon the continent of North America!"

His call struck a nerve, and so many sons of Tennessee answered him it earned the state the nickname it carries today — "The Volunteer State." Legend has it that every able-bodied man in Tennessee joined Jackson's cause, and while the real number is closer to 3,000, such an army of Tennessee sharpshooters was a potent force and Jackson was thrilled to offer then-President James Madison the services of his troops against the British usurpers.

Madison, however, declined Jackson's offer, not only because war hadn't yet been declared, but also because Jackson himself was considered a dangerous loose cannon who had made many powerful enemies.

When Jackson realized his services were not wanted, he became so angry he decided on his own to train, equip and march his men down to New Orleans, but when he got there he was told to dismiss his men and give their weapons over to the ranking army officer in the area. Jackson refused and promptly marched his men back to Tennessee. During the hazardous journey back, Jackson so inspired his men with his willingness to endure hardship and his indomitable spirit that they called him "as tough as Tennessee hickory." The nickname "Hickory" stuck, and as he aged it became "Old Hickory," the nickname Jackson also carries today.

One march, two famous nicknames. And two years later, in 1814, Jackson would return to New Orleans where his resounding defeat of the British at the "Battle of New Orleans" would ensure his legend and one day make him president.

© Kauffmann 2008

Bruce's History Lessons: The Man Who Made Abe Lincoln President

Roger Taney, the fifth man to achieve the highest position in American jurisprudence, chief justice of the United States Supreme Court, was born this week (March 17) in 1777, one year into America's war for independence. Before his life ended he would become famous for authoring the most controversial Supreme Court decision in history, the Dred Scott decision.

But he would also, as we shall see, be the man who made Abe Lincoln president — both literally and figuratively.

Our story begins with Taney's decision in the infamous Dred Scott case. Dred Scott, a former slave, had sued in federal court for his freedom, claiming that when he had traveled with his former owner into a U.S. free territory, it was tantamount to making him a free man upon the death of his owner, which subsequently occurred. Taney thought otherwise. In his final ruling, Taney stated that not only were slaves *not* citizens — and therefore could not sue in federal court — but also he ruled that Congress could not forbid slavery in any of the U.S. territories.

To many Americans, including Abe Lincoln and fellow members of the newly formed Republican Party, Taney's ruling was political dynamite because it sought to put a Constitutional imprimatur on attempts by Southerners to expand slavery into the new territories in the West — something most Republicans, whose ranks included former Whigs and Free Soil Party members, adamantly opposed. They acquiesced to the fact that slavery was legal in the South — at that time the Constitution specifically permitted it — but they believed that if slavery was prevented from spreading it would eventually die out. They saw Taney's ruling as a way to give slavery new life.

Taney's Dred Scott decision not only caused a split in the Democratic Party, it also angered many thousands of anti-slavery Americans who subsequently joined the ranks of the Republican Party, thereby giving it enough political power to help make Abe Lincoln its first president in 1861. In effect, it was Taney's decision that indirectly — "figuratively," if you will — put Lincoln in the White House.

Yet if that is how Taney figuratively made Lincoln president, how did he literally make him president? In one of those ironic twists of historic fate, Taney was still chief justice of the Supreme Court on Inauguration Day in 1861, and therefore it was he who administered the oath of office that made Abe Lincoln America's 16th president.

When Roger Taney died in 1864, the outcome of the Civil War he helped start was still in doubt, but there is no doubt that, by his ruling in Dred Scott, Taney also helped ensure that the one man who could win that war was in a position to do so.

© Kauffmann 2008

Bruce's History Lessons:
Truman's Loyalty Oath

President Franklin Roosevelt's World War II executive order interning Japanese-Americans in relocation camps because of their suspected disloyalty to the United States was, by most accounts, the most controversial executive order ever issued. If so, number two was probably President Harry Truman's Executive Order #9835, which was signed this week (March 21) in 1947. Its purpose was to perform "loyalty checks" on all members of the federal government to determine whether they were patriotic Americans, or whether they were members of — or even sympathetic to — groups with "totalitarian, fascist, communist or subversive" tendencies.

In the order's wake, Loyalty Boards were established in every department of the federal government and employees were subject to loyalty investigations based on information supplied by the FBI. In most cases those being investigated had no opportunity to examine or rebut this FBI-supplied information, which often came from paid informers or people with secret identities.

The main goal was to uncover cases of domestic espionage, but even "reasonable doubt" about someone's personal loyalty could result in dismissal from one's job. There were no judges or juries, nor was there anything approaching due process, although there were Loyalty Review Boards to handle appeals.

As he would later admit, this order was not Truman's finest hour, nor was it his smartest decision because the end result was the exact opposite of what he intended. With the Cold War heating up and anti-communist hysteria increasing, Truman had been attacked repeatedly by Republicans for being "soft on communism," so he hoped his executive order would toughen his image and dampen criticism. Instead, the broad scope of the investigation

— reaching as it did into every branch of the government — only reinforced the impression that both the government and the Truman administration were riddled with spies, subversives and "commies." This resulted in even greater hysteria — to say nothing of absurdity. At one point the Cervantes Fraternal Society, the Committee for the Negro in the Arts, the League of American Writers and the Chopin Cultural Center were suspected of "disloyal" activity.

Small wonder that over the next three years some 2 million people were investigated under the order, although not one case of espionage was proved. True, about 140 people were dismissed from their jobs for "questionable loyalty," but few, if any, of these dismissals would have stood up in a real court of law.

And Truman's executive order had one other unexpected and unfortunate repercussion. It laid the groundwork for a junior senator from Wisconsin to give a speech in 1952 claiming that "205 known communists" worked in the State Department. That speech sent anti-communist hysteria to even greater heights and earned its author, Joe McCarthy, everlasting fame as the progenitor of "McCarthyism."

© Kauffmann 2008

Bruce's History Lessons:
Adolf Hitler-Political Prisoner

April Fool's Day is traditionally the day for practical jokes, but in 1924 in Germany this week (April 1) the joke was on the German people. That was the day Adolf Hitler was sentenced to five years in Germany's Landsberg Prison for leading the Beer Hall "Putsch" (coup) of 1923, in which he and a cluster of followers had tried to overthrow the German government. Yet the joke was that instead of destroying his political career, the trial and his subsequent conviction for treason gave his political aspirations a tremendous boost.

For one thing, the trial attracted nationwide press coverage, which made the little known Hitler a household name in Germany. For another, Nazi sympathizers in the government made sure the trial's appointed judges were sympathetic to Hitler's politics. As a result, the judges allowed Hitler to use the trial — and the media coverage it generated — as a soapbox to espouse his political, racial and social beliefs.

Hitler took full advantage of the opportunity. Rather than deny the charges against him, he reveled in them, boasting that he purposely tried to overthrow the government in 1923, but he explained that his motivation was to take back Germany from the "traitors" who had "betrayed" the country by prematurely suing for peace at the end of World War I. Hitler's long-held contention that Germany had not lost World War I, but had been "stabbed in the back" by Jews, Communists and spineless bureaucrats, resonated with many Germans, and his trial afforded him the perfect opportunity to communicate that message on a national scale.

By the time the trial ended Hitler had morphed from defendant into political superstar, and he used his closing statement to send a clear message of his future intentions. "The man who is born to be dictator is not compelled," Hitler exclaimed. "He wills it! He is not driven forward but drives himself!"

Hitler concluded by telling the judges that, "It is not you, gentlemen, who pass judgment on us. That judgment is spoken by the eternal court of history ... (and) she acquits us."

The judges agreed, and only found him guilty on the assurance that he would be treated well in prison and granted early parole.

They got their wish. Hitler got a private cell with a view of the grounds and was allowed gifts and visitors. His longtime assistant and fellow Landsberg inmate, Rudolph Hess, even became his private secretary, and in the scant nine months that Hitler was incarcerated he dictated to Hess his autobiography, *Mein Kampf,* which was a blueprint of how he planned to take power in Germany and what he intended to do with that power.

World War II and the Holocaust were the ultimate results.

© Kauffmann 2008

Bruce's History Lesson: Dixie!

Among the most popular, unpopular and just plain controversial songs ever composed and sung was first heard in Mechanics Hall in New York City this week (April 4) in 1859.

Its composer, Daniel Emmett, was a veteran of the minstrel shows that had toured America and Europe in the pre-Civil War years when minstrel shows and churches were practically the only two outlets for new songs. Emmett had earlier composed a song called "Old Dan Tucker," which gained some popularity (and can even be heard around Boy Scout campfires today), but he never had a hit big enough to support himself solely as a songwriter, which was his ultimate goal.

Then one late Saturday evening in 1859, after the last show of the Bryant Minstrels, which he had joined two years earlier, Emmett was approached by the show's music director and asked if he could compose a quick "walk-around" (knock-off) song. "I need it by Monday, Dan," the director said.

That weekend, stuck in his house due to torrential rains, Emmett had a bad case of writer's block, and the blues to boot. "I wish I was in Dixie," he complained to his wife, and suddenly the light bulb went on. Emmett sat down and in an hour had composed the first verse and chorus. The rest of the song soon followed and his wife suggested he title it, "I Wish I was in Dixie's Land," a title that was later shortened to "Dixie."

The song was an instant hit, especially in the South, which by 1861 badly needed an anthem because it had just seceded from the former United States, whose unofficial anthem "The Star Spangled Banner," had no meaning for the secessionist South, not to mention very little connection with the newly created Confederate flag. And as it happened, when Confederate President

Jefferson Davis was inaugurated, he asked the band to play "Dixie," making it the *de facto* anthem of the Confederacy. From that time until the end of the Civil War, whenever Union marching bands played "The Star Spangled Banner" or its other anthem, "The Battle Hymn of the Republic," Confederate bands would always counter with "Dixie," including at Gettysburg where General George Pickett ordered his band to play "Dixie" right before his famous last charge.

The song's fame got an even bigger boost at the end of the war when President Lincoln, who called it "one of the best tunes I have ever heard," jokingly tried to claim it for the North as a "fairly captured" war prize, but the South stubbornly refused to give it up. To this day it remains — for better or worse — a musical symbol, and reminder, of the South's Civil War past.

© *Kauffmann 2008*

Bruce's History Lessons:
Coining The Cold War

If the Cold War ended on November 9, 1989, with the fall of the Berlin Wall, when did it officially begin?

A case could be made that it began this week (April 16) in 1947 when multi-millionaire financier Bernard Baruch coined the phrase "Cold War" in a speech he made in Columbia, South Carolina, at the unveiling of his portrait in the South Carolina House of Representatives. Born in South Carolina, Baruch was among the state's most famous native sons, having earned millions on Wall Street and having become influential in national politics and international affairs. An advisor to President Woodrow Wilson at the end of World War I, Baruch helped hammer out the economic provisions of the Treaty of Versailles that ended that war, and Wilson also appointed him to the Advisory Commission to the Council of National Defense.

Baruch also served as a critical advisor to President Roosevelt during World War II. A member of FDR's famous "Brain Trust," Baruch recognized early on that America would be dragged into the European conflict and he urged his country to begin building up its armed forces and stockpiling the raw materials — such as rubber and tin — that would be needed to wage the war.

Upon Roosevelt's death, Baruch became a trusted advisor to President Truman and served as a middleman between Truman and former President Herbert Hoovers, whose experience in international relief efforts would be invaluable in dealing with the problems of famine and social breakdown that were occurring in post-war Europe.

So Baruch knew of what he spoke when, instead of mouthing a few platitudes of gratitude at his portrait unveiling in South Carolina, he surprised everyone by launching into an impassioned speech lamenting the industrial labor problems that were then occurring in America — problems that Baruch believed made America weaker in an increasingly dangerous world. Baruch called for a new "unity" between labor and management that included no-strike pledges from unions and no-layoff pledges from management. Only by growing stronger economically, Baruch argued, could America — then emerging as a superpower — counteract the increasingly evil designs of the Soviet Union.

"Let us not be deceived," Baruch said in his speech, "We are today in the midst of a cold war. Our enemies are to be found abroad and home ... our unrest is the heart of their success."

Baruch's "Cold War" speech, while not as famous as the "Iron Curtain" speech given a year earlier by Winston Churchill, helped focus the attention of America's policy makers on the growing deterioration of U.S. - Soviet relations. And not incidentally, his famous phrase was manna from heaven for newspaper editors around the country looking for a short, pithy way to describe those relations.

© *Kauffmann 2008*

Bruce's History Lessons:
Paul Revere's Ride

"Listen my children and you shall hear ... of the man behind the ride of Paul Revere. To most his name may sound foreign. Few have heard of Joseph Warren."

My apologies to Henry Longfellow, but the famous ride of Paul Revere, which occurred this week (April 18) in 1775, might never have happened the way it did were it not for a little known figure in our history, Joseph Warren. The American Revolution might have been different as well.

Some facts we know. In 1775, in response to the Boston Tea Party, Britain closed the city of Boston, angering all of America's colonists, who were openly talking of breaking with England. The man in charge of British troops in Boston, General Thomas Gage, realized that he lacked the troops to put down an uprising, so he hoped to avoid a fight by arresting rebel leaders. Gage ordered a small British force to march secretly to Lexington and arrest prominent rebels John Hancock and Sam Adams, who were hiding there. Gage also ordered this force to march to Concord and confiscate a cache of rebel weapons.

Alas for Gage, colonial leaders learned of his plan to arrest Adams and Hancock, and one of the most radical of those leaders, Joseph Warren, instructed Paul Revere and William Dawes to warn the two men of the danger to their safety. Had both men confined their mission to that, Adams and Hancock would have slipped away, frustrating Gage, although his soldiers might have succeeded in confiscating the weapons at Concord.

Instead, Warren — who badly wanted war with England — specifically instructed Revere to spread the word that "the Regulars are coming," which he knew would alarm the entire countryside and result in local militia quickly organizing against the British. Thus when Gage's troops arrived at Lexington they were greeted by armed militiamen. A shot rang out — "the shot heard 'round the world" — and the rest is history.

Thus the case can be made that Warren took it upon himself to start the American Revolution, in April, at Lexington and Concord. Certainly General Gage had no desire to fight at that time — as was noted, he lacked sufficient force to do so. And even members of the Massachusetts Congress had not planned on taking their stand then. A resolution they recently passed advocated colonial resistance only under specific conditions, including that any British force on the march had to exceed 500 in number and possess artillery. Gage made sure that his force that April day was under 500 and had no artillery.

Fame is fickle. Paul Revere, the messenger, is known to us all. Joseph Warren, who ordered the message in the belief that war would result, is not.

© *Kauffmann 2008*

Bruce's History Lessons:
The Birdman of America

John James Audubon, who was born this week (April 26) in 1785, was a rare bird, and in the 18th century his chosen profession, painting birds, was even rarer. Yet in many ways Audubon was the quintessential early American.

He came to America from Europe, having fled France to avoid conscription in Napoleon's army. Although he was penniless and spoke no English, he possessed that typically American mixture of optimism, self-confidence and energy, and he soon re-invented himself as man about town (Philadelphia) who wooed and won a wealthy farmer's daughter, Lucy Bakewell. In 1811, he and Lucy set off for frontier Kentucky with plans to become a mill owner and firearms merchant.

It was on that journey down the Ohio River to Kentucky that Audubon began sketching and recording observations about the varied species of birds he found along the way — sketches and notes that might have remained a hobby had Audubon's business ventures succeeded. But over the next few years the nation's banks began calling in their loans to pay off the Louisiana Purchase, which caused a financial panic and bankrupted millions of businesses, including Audubon's. So Audubon changed careers, dedicating his life to producing a book depicting all of the known birds in North America.

Today that book, *The Birds of America*, is considered the most influential nature book ever produced. Not only did Audubon's drawings reflect his lifelong observation of his subjects, but also, unlike other artists who painted from a distance, Audubon killed, mounted and *then* drew his subjects, giving his work a blend of authenticity and "interpretation" that was unique to Audubon. As has been noted by critics, Audubon's birds range from menacing apparitions to violent predators, their talons usually sunk into bloody prey,

447

their eyes wild and defiant. Audubon depicted the harsh reality that was nature.

As has also been noted by critics, Audubon's proficiency with a rifle and willingness to kill hardly squares with his reputation as a nature lover. But Audubon *was* both an environmentalist and conservationist who tried to educate his countrymen about a number of nature-related issues, including how birds helped control insect populations, and the growing environmental destruction of the Ohio River wildlife. Audubon even correctly predicted the extinction of several animal species.

The Birds of America made Audubon wealthy, which proved to be a double-edged sword. With the realization that his life's work was completed, Audubon began experiencing bouts of depression, mixed with excessive drinking and dementia. He died in 1851, but he would later rise — like another legendary bird, the Phoenix — to become the inspiration for the oldest and best-known conservation organization in America. The Audubon Society, founded in 1905, celebrates its centennial this year.

© *Kauffmann 2008*

Bruce's History Lessons:
The Original G-Man

Upon hearing of FBI Director J. Edgar Hoover's death, which occurred this week (May 2) in 1972, both criminals and civil libertarians probably breathed a sigh of relief. For despite his detractors' claims, Hoover was a trailblazer who compiled an extraordinary record of innovation and modernization in the field of law enforcement. And despite his supporters' claims, Hoover was a megalomaniac, a racist, a publicity hound and a control freak who skirted or broke the law whenever it suited his purposes.

Hoover's career in law enforcement began in 1917 when he joined the Justice Department right out of law school. He would be there for the next 55 years, going from identifying "radicals and subversives" (it taught him to cultivate informants), to working at the department's General Intelligence Division, then the Bureau of Investigation, and, finally — when he was 29 years old — the new Federal Bureau of Investigation, which he was asked to lead.

Hoover quickly put his personal stamp on this new bureau. He fired agents he thought were undisciplined and replaced them with college graduates willing to conform. He set up an Identification Division with a centralized fingerprint file. He established a crime laboratory, thereby introducing science to police work, and he set up a National Police Academy that trained an elite force of crime fighters.

And he got results. In the 1930s the FBI arrested thousands of holdover gangsters from the Prohibition period, and under Hoover's leadership the bureau virtually eliminated kidnapping, which had been that decade's crime of choice. The FBI went after Depression-era bank robbers with a vengeance, and communists during the Cold War. And with a genius for self-promotion, Hoover kept the public abreast of the FBI's successes.

But success bred megalomania and sycophancy. Flattery replaced ability as the way to advance in Hoover's FBI, and his sense of omnipotence led to his own law breaking. Hoover's vendetta against the Civil Rights movement and Rev. Martin Luther King Jr., for example, led to illegal wiretapping and attempted blackmail, and in later years reports of Hoover's somewhat bizarre lifestyle and the FBI's rogue enterprises badly tarnished Hoover's and the bureau's reputations.

But no president dared fire him and few dared cross him — a testament to his power and the fear he inspired — both of which are captured in this *probably* apocryphal story:

Hoover loved writing comments in the margins of the memorandums agents sent him, but one day an agent's memo was so lengthy, and had margins so narrow, Hoover was unable to comment. So he scribbled on the only blank space left on the memo, "Watch the borders!"

Immediately, FBI agents were dispatched to Canada and Mexico, where they patrolled the borders for a week.

© Kauffmann 2008

Bruce's History Lessons:
WWII and The Leadership Gap

As most history buffs know, when Adolf Hitler's German armies invaded France and the Low Countries at the onset of WWII, which they did this week (May 10) in 1940, Germany won a decisive victory, overrunning France and sending the British Expeditionary Force that was fighting in France scurrying back to England, lucky to have survived.

What most people don't know is that at the exact moment this German *blitzkrieg* (lightning strike) began, strictly speaking *neither France nor Britain had a fully functioning government.*

In Britain, there actually was a government in place, but no one was sure who headed it. Prime Minister Neville Chamberlain, whose policy of appeasing Hitler had collapsed in tatters, no longer had the confidence of the Labor Party, which refused to serve under him. So Chamberlain met to discuss his resignation with his two likeliest successors, Lord Halifax and Winston Churchill, and when Halifax declined to serve Chamberlain instructed Churchill to ask King George VI for permission to form a new government.

But before Churchill could meet with the king, Germany attacked, which put England in crisis mode. Chamberlain now was reluctant to resign, thinking changing leadership then would be counterproductive, and his followers agreed. Churchill's followers, however, insisted that a new government was critical, and when both Churchill and Chamberlain began issuing statements, political confusion resulted. There matters stood as the German Army poured through France.

In France, the situation was even worse. On May 9, French Premier Paul Reynaud told his cabinet that he would resign if they did not support his wish to fire General Maurice Gamelin, who then commanded France's armies. Reynaud believed Gamelin was both defeatist and incompetent, and that should a war with Germany come — as almost everyone expected it would — France could not win under Gamelin's command. Unfortunately for Reynaud, Gamelin had powerful supporters who objected to his sacking, so Reynaud abruptly resigned. He then dissolved his cabinet, meaning the French government was *fini.*

And later that day, when Gamelin learned what had transpired at the cabinet meeting, he resigned in indignation, meaning France had no government and no military commander.

Of course, realizing they were at war, both France and England quickly addressed the confused political situation. Britain's Labor Party again informed Chamberlain that it would only serve under Churchill, so Chamberlain resigned and Churchill formed a coalition government the next day. And in France, Reynaud rescinded his resignation and asked Gamelin to resume command of all French forces.

Still, lacking a functioning government, even briefly, is usually a mistake when a nation is trying to defend itself from attack, let alone defending itself from a *blitzkrieg* attack by what was then the most powerful army in the world.

© *Kauffmann 2008*

Bruce's History Lesson:
Hello Dolley!

America's second most famous First Lady (after Eleanor Roosevelt), Dolley Madison was born this week (May 20) in 1768, in North Carolina. She grew up in Virginia before moving with her Quaker parents to Philadelphia, where she married a Quaker lawyer named John Todd. They had two children, but in 1793 a yellow-fever epidemic took the life of her oldest child and her husband.

And then, in 1794, the widow Dolley Todd met and married (my hero) James Madison, whose political handiwork includes our Constitution and Bill of Rights. It was a classic case of opposites attracting. Madison was shy, serious and uncomfortable in large gatherings. Dolley, who soon traded her somber Quaker clothing for the latest colorful fashions, was warm, quick to laugh, an attentive listener and a born hostess. Together they made a formidable team.

Practically speaking, Dolley Madison is the only woman ever to serve as First Lady for two different presidents. Because her husband's great friend and political ally, Thomas Jefferson, was a widow when he became America's third president, he asked Dolley to serve as his hostess for official functions during his 8 years in office. Thus Dolley had plenty of experience with the social side of diplomacy and political fence-mending by the time her husband followed Jefferson with two presidential terms of his own.

It paid off handsomely. Dolley was the mistress of ceremonies at all White House social gatherings, which allowed "the great little Madison," as she called her diminutive husband, to slink off to a corner and talk politics with trusted aides and friends. Always the center of attention, Dolley could hold her own with European dignitaries, Middle East envoys, congressmen from both her husband's Republican Party and rival Federalists, and even the occasional Indian chief. One observer of Washington's social scene wrote of her, "It would be impossible to behave with more perfect propriety than she did."

And she was fearless, as perhaps the most famous episode in her life, the burning of the White House during the War of 1812, would prove. With the British literally at the door of the presidential mansion, she refused to flee until the famous Gilbert Stuart painting of George Washington was safely removed.

Perhaps that is why, even after a truly mediocre presidency, James Madison still enjoyed tremendous popularity when he and Dolley finally quit Washington for Montpelier, their home in Virginia. It may also explain why, after Madison had died and her finances forced her to sell Montpelier, she was welcomed back to Washington with open arms.

Indeed, until she herself died, an honorary seat was allotted her on the floor of the U.S. House of Representatives — the only woman ever so honored.

© Kauffmann 2008

Bruce's History Lessons:
A Man on the Moon:
JFK's Memorable Challenge

It was at a press conference on April 12, 1961, that President John Kennedy was asked a pointed, and loaded, question. Earlier that day America was stunned by the news that a Soviet cosmonaut, Yuri Gagarin, had just become the first human to travel into space, having orbited the earth three times in his spacecraft *Vostock I* before returning safely to earth. "Mr. President," a reporter asked Kennedy, "the Communists seem to be putting us on the defensive on a number of fronts — now again in space ... do you think there is a danger that their system is going to prove more durable than ours?"

It was the central question of that phase of the Cold War, and Kennedy had given it a lot of thought, especially since he had recently been burned by his disastrous decision to allow a CIA-planned invasion of Cuba by Cuban exiles bent on overthrowing Cuba's communist dictator — and Soviet client — Fidel Castro. The "Bay of Pigs" fiasco not only hurt Kennedy politically, it also diminished American prestige, while enhancing that of the Soviet Union. Thus to the question of which system, capitalism or communism, was the wave of the future, the answer seemed to be communism, based not only on recent geopolitical events, but also on each side's technological achievements.

Which is why, that morning, Kennedy had grilled his vice president and point man on the American space program, Lyndon Johnson, on what was being done to catch up to the Soviets.

"Can we put a man on the moon before them?" Kennedy asked. "Can we leapfrog them? If somebody can just tell me how to catch up!"

That somebody turned out to be Kennedy himself who, this week (May 25) in 1961, went before a special joint session of Congress and threw down one of the most famous national challenges in U.S. history.

"I believe," Kennedy intoned, "that this nation should commit itself to achieving the goal, before this decade is out, of landing a man on the moon and returning him safely to earth."

Kennedy's speech struck a nerve with the public and gave new life, and funding, to the space program. Project Mercury, which produced America's first manned sub-orbital flight, soon gave way to the more ambitious Project Gemini, which put men in space, and finally Project Apollo, which put Neil Armstrong, Buzz Aldrin and Michael Collins on the moon on July 20, 1969 — before the decade was out, just as Kennedy had promised.

Alas, Kennedy did not live to see it, at least not from an earthly vantage point. As the world knows he was assassinated in November of 1963, so perhaps — a merciful God willing — he got to witness it from higher platform.

© Kauffmann 2008

Bruce's History Lessons:
The Marshall Plan

This week (June 5) in 1947, in his address to the graduating class at Harvard University, Secretary of State George C. Marshall gave the most famous speech in American history that no one can quote one sentence from.

Marshall's speech proposed an American-initiated economic recovery program for a European continent devastated by World War II. The program's centerpiece was substantial American financial assistance to post-war Europe in order to alleviate the pervasive destruction, poverty and disease suffered by Europe's war-ravaged citizenry. Partly as a result of Marshall's speech, Congress passed a European Recovery Program — better known as "The Marshall Plan" — that over the next three years poured $13.3 billion into the economies of 16 European countries (more than $100 billion in current dollars).

Today, the Marshall Plan is remembered as a humanitarian gesture by a generous American people, but it might better be called an act of "enlightened self-interest." For one thing, the rampant poverty in post-war Western Europe was contributing to a breakdown of the social and political order, which the Soviet Union — having declined to participate in the Marshall Plan, while also forbidding its Eastern European satellite countries to participate — was exploiting by supporting increasingly assertive Communist parties in France, West Germany, Italy and other Western European nations. Preventing those nations from being dominated by Soviet-controlled Communist governments was a paramount American foreign policy objective, which the Marshall Plan helped achieve by stabilizing Western European economies and giving hope to the European people, thereby helping to prop up democratic governments in Western Europe.

In addition to political objectives, there was an economic incentive for the United States to help revive Western Europe. Simply put, the U.S. needed new markets for the products it was beginning to manufacture on a large scale as its massive wartime industrial infrastructure made the transition to the peacetime production of consumer goods. As Secretary Marshall and Congress both understood, an economically strong Western Europe could potentially be such a market, and as it turned out, the Marshall Plan's $13 billion investment was paid back a thousand-fold by the increased trade between America and Western Europe — trade that, at least initially, mostly consisted of Europeans buying American goods.

Winston Churchill called the Marshall Plan "the most unsordid act in history," which is not entirely correct given that American self-interest was one of its driving forces. But it certainly was one of the most consequential acts in history because it helped keep Western Europe democratic, capitalist and allied with America. Given the fact that America had to fight a Cold War with the Soviet Union and its Eastern European allies over the next 45 years, having Western Europe on our side was a very good thing.

© Kauffmann 2008

Bruce's History Lessons:
A Dickens of a Tale—and Life

"It was the best of times, it was the worst of times," not only in London and Paris during the French Revolution, but also in high school English classrooms across the country where Charles Dickens' famous novel A Tale of Two Cities is assigned. It was the worst of times because Dickens could be long-winded and murky, with ornate sentences, twisting plotlines and a lengthy list of complex characters. It was the best of times because when read carefully, and often, Dickens emerges as one of the funniest, most passionate, moral and important writers ever. A satirist and caricaturist as well as social reformer, Dickens wrote novels that brilliantly exposed the many injustices of the 19th Century, especially the brutal treatment and neglect of society's underclass.

Dickens came by his viewpoint honestly, and many of his books mirror his life. At the age of 12 he had to quit school and work in a shoe-polish factory, and his father eventually went to debtor's prison. After teaching himself to write, and discovering that he had a talent for describing everyday life, Dickens began submitting his observations on city life to magazines under the pen name Boz. When a collection of those observations, *Sketches by Boz*, proved popular, Dickens was asked by a publishing company to write a story in monthly installments, a story that became *The Pickwick Papers*. The book, which made the comic Samuel Pickwick into a national icon, also made Dickens an overnight success.

Financially solvent, Dickens turned to darker themes, including the attempts of society's poor to survive in the face of an unfeeling government, a hostile legal system, and the ravages of the fledgling industrial age, which produced a new upper class that was both malicious and corrupt. Yet running through the somber plots of his novels are a fascinating cast of secondary characters with a litany of idiosyncratic, often hilarious mannerisms. Dickens could be wickedly funny, while wickedly angry, brilliantly contrasting "the best and worst" of the human spirit, as books such as *Oliver Twist, Bleak House, Great Expectations,* and his most famous work, *A Christmas Carol,* still prove.

In his later years Dickens also wrote plays and musical dramas, and he traveled extensively, doing readings of his stories both in England and America. He died this week (June 9) in 1870.

Among English writers, only Shakespeare has been more analyzed, quoted and dissected, but the best description of Dickens' work I ever heard came from a high school student who was asked to describe the main message Dickens was trying to convey.

"That the world would be a better place," this student replied, "if we were all just a little nicer to each other."

© Kauffmann 2008

Bruce's History Lessons: West Point's First African-American Graduate

It is said that the army is the most color-blind institution in America. If so, it has come a long way since 1877 when — this week (June 14) — Henry Ossian Flipper became the first African-American to graduate from the U.S. Military Academy at West Point.

Talk about endurance. During his entire four years at West Point he was not spoken to once by a white cadet, let alone invited to attend a social function, a sporting event, a study group or even a meal. But perhaps in his case, silence was golden. Not only was he the first African-American to graduate — four had tried before him — but also he graduated 50th out of a class of 76 cadets, a not inconsiderable achievement given the many disadvantages he faced and the unequal treatment he suffered.

Commissioned a second lieutenant, Flipper was subsequently assigned to the 10th Cavalry, serving in Texas and Oklahoma, where his skills as an engineer and surveyor came in handy.

At Fort Davis in Texas Flipper was even promoted to acting assistant quartermaster and acting commissary of subsistence, which put him in charge of the fort's supplies and physical space. It was an honor, but one fraught with danger because it left him open to charges of misusing funds — charges that subsequently were leveled when it was discovered that army supply funds were missing. In the subsequent court martial Flipper was found innocent of embezzlement but guilty of conduct unbecoming an officer because he did not report the missing funds right away. Flipper maintained that the funds had disappeared specifically to bring charges against him and that he tried to find and replace the funds before reporting them.

Dismissed from the army Flipper became a surveyor and engineer in the Southwest, working for private companies. In 1893 his testimony in a suit over a land grant dispute between Mexico and Arizona helped save Arizona's landowners hundreds of thousands of dollars, which led to his appointment as special agent for the U.S. Court of Private Land Claims. Steadily Flipper distinguished himself in several land-related government positions, finally serving as assistant to the secretary of the Interior, then one of the highest government positions ever held by an African-American.

Flipper died in 1940 before he could clear his name and restore his army rank, but his descendants took up the cause and in 1976 the army — admitting that his court martial had been "unduly harsh and unjust" — gave him an honorable discharge, dated June 30,1882, the day he was court-martialed.

Fittingly, in Flipper's honor West Point now presents an annual award to the graduate who best exemplifies "the highest qualities of leadership, self-discipline and perseverance in the face of unusual difficulties."

© Kauffmann 2008

Bruce's History Lessons:
Five Who Made a Difference

After finishing a book on our greatest Supreme Court justice, John Marshall, it occurred to me that only Alexander Hamilton ranks above Marshall on the list of Americans who had a profound effect on our country but were never president. And then I thought, "Who else would make that list?"

Below are my top five choices and briefly why I chose them. I invite you, dear reader, to agree or argue with my choices, and even add to the list so that we have a "Top 10." Explain your choices in three sentences or less, and e-mail me at bruce@historylessons.net. In a subsequent column I will publish the choices I thought were best argued.

Alexander Hamilton. Not only was Hamilton the chief author of *The Federalist* Papers, which helped ensure ratification of the Constitution, but also, as our first treasury secretary, he created the financial system that enabled America to evolve from an agrarian-based economy to a country of industry, technology, trade and opportunity. America today is the country Hamilton envisioned and worked to build.

John Marshall. In his masterful decision in *Marbury vs. Madison*, Marshall single-handedly made the Supreme Court a co-equal branch of the federal government. His decision in that case established forever the right of "judicial review," meaning the courts became the final interpreter of the Constitution, thereby giving them the power to defend American citizens from encroachments by the other two branches.

Rev. Martin Luther King, Jr. Yes, America eventually would have addressed its most glaring injustice, the disenfranchisement and segregation of millions of Americans because of their skin color. But only through King's inspired leadership, and his courageously chosen non-violent path, were we able to address this injustice with a minimum of rancor and bloodshed. And he gave his life to that cause.

Eleanor Roosevelt. Franklin Roosevelt's presidency, considered the greatest of the 20th century, would not have been as great without her. Because FDR's polio prevented him from traveling the country, she went instead, visiting impoverished coal miners in West Virginia, destitute farmers in Oklahoma and poor blacks in the South, and her reports on these travels helped him shape social policies that are with us still. Her legacy also includes such causes as civil rights, child labor protection laws and women's equality — and such organizations as the U.N., the Red Cross and the NAACP.

Thomas Edison. In his lifetime Edison patented 1,093 inventions, including his most famous, a workable incandescent light bulb. He also invented the phonograph and the "kinetoscope" — today's movie projector — and he improved the design of both the telegraph and telephone. Edison put electricity to work, transforming it from a fad to the energy that runs America and the world.

© Kauffmann 2008

Bruce's History Lessons: U-Boote!

"Ich U-boote bauen!"

– Adolf Hitler

Had Hitler made good on his boast — "I will build U-boats!" — I believe Germany would have won World War II.

It is said that military leaders always fight the last war, but one who did not was the German Admiral Karl Doenitz. In the early 1930s, as Hitler began to build the military juggernaut he would use to launch World War II, Doenitz schemed to build a new generation of German submarines — U-boats — that he believed could destroy enough shipping in the Atlantic Ocean to starve Great Britain out of any war Hitler started.

But first Doenitz had to build a worthy boat. Having been sunk in a U-boat during WWI, he knew its limitations, so he spent the post-war years designing a boat that would be more elusive and more lethal, and could stay submerged longer. Called the *U-1*, it boasted a new battery that allowed it to stay submerged twice as long as previous U-boats, but its most important improvement was its torpedo, which was electrically powered — meaning no visual wake — and had a magnetic firing mechanism designed to explode under a surface ship's most vulnerable part, its keel.

This week (June 28) in 1935, Doenitz launched his first *U-1*, and its performance so impressed him that he went to Hitler with his plan. Let me build a fleet of 300 *U-1s*, he told the Fuhrer, and when war comes I will destroy of 700,000 tons of merchant shipping every month. At that rate England, an island that depended on imports for survival, literally would starve before the year was out and would have to sue for peace.

Hitler was ecstatic and re-affirmed his boast to build U-boats. Doenitz left the meeting convinced the coming war was won.

But as was often the case with the vacillating Hitler, his passion for U-boats cooled, in part because other German naval officers — with their own turf to protect — downplayed the importance of U-boats, and in part because of a character flaw that would repeatedly undermine Hitler's war planning. In a word, to Hitler the U-boat was not showy. U-boats went underwater, for goodness sake, while surface ships were majestic and intimidating, and with their Nazi swastikas flapping in the wind could steam into any European port in a mighty display of Nazi superiority and strength. U-boats may be lethal, but battleships were impressive.

And so Doenitz never got the U-boat fleet he envisioned and England survived long enough to keep Germany at bay until America entered the war. Ironically, by surviving, the British Islands became, in effect, the "battleship" on which America's military manpower and equipment were stationed. Without that "battleship" Germany would have won the war.

© *Kauffmann 2008*

Bruce's History Lessons:
July 4th:
What the Revolution Wrought

This week (July 4) in 1776, our Founding Fathers formally approved a written declaration that transformed 13 former English colonies into free and independent states. Briefly, let us look at why, and what was the result.

The Founders sought independence from England because they perceived a threat to their natural rights — to life, liberty, the pursuit of happiness — and to their legal rights as Englishmen — to representation in government, trial by jury, security in their homes, and control over their internal affairs (including taxation).

Yet when the revolution was won and independence established, the Founders looked at the resulting nation and saw problems. Under the Articles of Confederation that governed the country, most power was vested in each state, which was hardly conducive to a unified nation. What's more, within each state, the Articles gave power to popular majorities, which meant there were no safeguards for minority rights.

So the Founders junked the Articles and created a government that was both national, thus unifying the 13 states under one central authority, and Republican, which they considered an important check on majority rule. In essence, the majority of "the people" don't get to decide the issues. They get to decide who decides the issues by voting for candidates for office. This gave those elected officials a certain amount of freedom to vote for the larger good, rather than narrow self-interest.

But not too much freedom. The Founders also established frequent elections so the people could remove from office any officials who pursued policies consistently at odds with their constituents' wishes.

The Founders also created a constitution in which they enshrined "constitutive" rights that are above — and therefore cannot be abolished or altered by — any laws passed by their elected officials. Among these rights are the right to life, liberty and property, and if elected officials ever attempt to tamper with these rights, the people have the constitutive right to alter or abolish the government itself.

And then, to make sure everybody was clear on the concept, the Founders created a Bill of Rights that spelled out additional rights the people possessed. And they included in this document two amendments that said: (1) Just because a certain right is *not* mentioned in this Bill of Rights doesn't mean the people don't possess that right (9th Amendment); and (2) Unless a right (a power) is specifically given to the federal government in this Constitution, or specifically denied to the states, that right (that power) belongs to the states and their residents (10th Amendment).

In sum, our Founders created a system that unified the 13 states, promoted individual freedom, protected natural rights, made possible human progress, and became a model for the world. And then they rested. Happy 4th of July.

© Kauffmann 2008

Bruce's History Lessons: Madison Weighs In (Again)

Memo to: Supreme Court Justice John Paul Stevens, principal author of the majority decision in *Kelo v. New London.*

From: James Madison (deceased), principal author of the Constitution and Bill of Rights

Re: Your Constitutional reasoning

Dear Justice Stevens: I'm spinning in my grave again. In *Kelo v. New London* you stretch the definition of "public use" beyond anything I intended when I created the Bill of Rights.

To review: In New London's Fort Trumbull neighborhood, Suzette Kelo and the other families who live there own modest, but well-kept, unblighted homes — many having owned those homes for generations — and now they are to be evicted because you ruled that the 5th Amendment's "takings" clause, which says, "… nor shall private property be taken for public use without just compensation," allows New London to "take" those homes. And to what "public use" are these homes to be sacrificed? So that developers can build a riverfront hotel, private offices, a conference center, a health spa, and luxury townhouses and condominiums.

And *how* is that a public use? Because the rich fat cats who buy the luxury residences and use the upscale facilities will pay more in taxes than Suzette Kelo and her neighbors, thereby putting more money in the coffers of New London's municipal government.

Um, read my lips. "[It] is a just government, which impartially secures to every man, whatever is his own."

469

It's one thing to take property for real "public use" — *things the public actually uses* — such as highways, parks and even courthouses. That has been the purpose of the "takings" clause of the 5th Amendment — *my* 5th Amendment — since its establishment. We Founders recognized that sometimes the public good takes precedence over private interests, but when that happens those private interests must be fairly compensated. But "taking" from the less affluent and giving to the more affluent — which in light of your ruling will be the case 99.99 percent of the time — violates every principle we held dear in 1791.

Indeed, have you read my Bill of Rights lately? If so, you may have noticed two other amendments besides the 5th. The 3rd Amendment says no outsiders can be quartered in people's homes without their consent. The 4th says the people have a right to be secure in their homes against unreasonable searches and seizures. We were really big on protecting property in my day because we had so much experience with governments trying to take it away.

Which brings up one final question. If Suzette Kelo can lose her property simply because someone else can put it to more productive economic use, what is to prevent some rich Washington, D.C.-based developer from doing the same thing to yours?

© *Kauffmann 2008*

Bruce's History Lessons:
George McGovern: War Hero

Born this week (July 19) in 1922, former Senator George McGovern's historic claim to fame is that he was the Democratic candidate for president in the now-infamous Nixon-McGovern campaign of 1972. In that contest, which was mostly waged over Nixon's handling of, and McGovern's opposition to, the Vietnam War, the Nixon camp successfully portrayed McGovern as an ultra-liberal, "Blame America First" peacenik who would cede Southeast Asia to the Communists regardless of the cost to American prestige and security.

Certainly McGovern was a liberal. Among his campaign promises that year was a guaranteed annual income for every American, which to the typical middle-class wage earner sounded suspiciously like a government subsidy for the unemployed. What's more, McGovern's frequently uttered clarion call to "Come Home America!" from Vietnam and other foreign commitments left him vulnerable to charges of isolationism and defeatism. And skillfully did Nixon's team exploit that vulnerability (not always legally, as Watergate showed), which resulted in a Republican landslide in the November election. McGovern lost every state but Massachusetts, and in the election's wake, "McGovernism" became symbolic of a government-knows-best domestic policy and a knee-jerk pacifistic foreign policy. In some ways, the Democratic Party is still suffering from its brush with "McGovernism."

Which is surprising, at least in this sense. George McGovern was among the toughest, coolest, most skillful and courageous warriors ever to strap himself into the pilot's seat of a military airplane during World War II.

And it wasn't just any airplane. It was the B-24 long-range bomber, the hardest and most dangerous bomber to fly in that war. The plane was cramped, prone to malfunctions, deafeningly noisy and it vibrated almost uncontrollably. What's more, at the altitudes the plane flew, it was bitterly cold and oxygen was scarce, and that was *before* it entered the target areas, where enemy planes and anti-aircraft fire were constant.

What's more, it wasn't just a few dangerous missions that McGovern and his crew flew. They flew 35, the maximum the military allowed. On one of those missions two of McGovern's engines went out when one malfunctioned and the other was hit by enemy fire. McGovern coolly landed the plane on an emergency airstrip that was half the length of the runway required for B-24s. That earned him the Distinguished Flying Cross.

Speaking of surprising, during his presidential campaign, McGovern made what some thought was a courageous decision not to exploit his war record, which was literally unheard of in the annals of presidential campaign politics. Granted, Richard Nixon also played down his war record in the '72 campaign, but Nixon — that die-hard devotee of a muscular, *realpolitik* foreign policy — spent WWII serving as a Naval supply officer in the South Pacific.

© *Kauffmann 2008*

Bruce's History Lessons: A Top 10 Great Americans List

A month ago my column asked for suggestions for the most important Americans who were never president. I picked five — Alexander Hamilton, John Marshall, Martin Luther King, Jr., Eleanor Roosevelt and Thomas Edison, and asked for five more to make a "Top 10" list. Here is the response:

Ben Franklin was number one. As James Fidler of Canton, OH, wrote, "Franklin personified the ideal of rugged individualism and civic duty. He participated in the creation of every major document in our history, including the Declaration of Independence, the peace treaty with England, and the U.S. Constitution. Further, his idea of citizens forming organizations to provide for public safety and intellectual development helped create America." Others noted the importance of his diplomacy. "Without Franklin, no alliance with France; without that alliance, independence problematic," wrote Cole Dawson of Vancouver, WA.

Henry Ford was number two. Ross Gates of Muskegon, MI, wrote, "Henry Ford's vision of manufacturing defined the 20th Century. We wouldn't have been the arsenal of democracy during two world wars without the efficiency of his methods, and for proof compare the quality and quantity of manufactured goods before and after him." Mary MacKenzie of Portland, OR, noted Ford's business acumen, writing, "Ford paid his workers a wage that allowed them to purchase his cars."

Number three was, as dozens wrote, "The greatest inventor no one has heard of." (Including me). Nikola Tesla argued for alternating current (Edison favored direct current) and — fortunately — prevailed. Michael Germino of Los Banos, CA, wrote, "Edison's light bulb didn't power the

473

industrial revolution. The electric power and motors based on Tesla's patents are the force behind the world we have today."

Number four was George C. Marshall, President Roosevelt's top military advisor and President Truman's secretary of state. "As chief of staff during WW II, Marshall brilliantly directed strategic planning on a global scale," wrote R.L. Jenkins of Tipp City, OH, adding, "He also contributed to stabilizing our relations with China." John Morgan also of, Muskegon, MI, noted, "He oversaw the European Recovery Program, now called The Marshall Plan, an economic policy that helped Western Europe recover from the devastation of World War II."

Just one reader submitted number five, but I liked it so much I included it (hey, it's *my* column). "I vote for the common man," wrote Frank Lucrezi of Stroudsburg, PA. "The men and women who settled and built this nation, who crossed the mountains and rivers with only a dream and carved out farms and homes in the process. Their graves dotted the way west. Their independence and sense of freedom make us what we are today."

Well said, and my thanks to the more than 300 of you who participated. I learned a lot!

© *Kauffmann 2008*

Bruce's History Lessons: Richard Nixon's Last Night on the Presidential Yacht

This week (August 1) in 1974, President Richard Nixon was alone on the presidential yacht, The Sequoia, when he did something he had never done before.

But first some background. *The Sequoia*, which is now a national historic landmark, once carried presidents up and down the Potomac River, allowing them to unwind from the pressures of their job. At only 104 feet, *The Sequoia* is small compared with most yachts, but it is steeped in history. Built during Herbert Hoover's administration, *The Sequoia* hosted Franklin Roosevelt and Dwight Eisenhower when they planned the D-Day invasion. Harry Truman decided to use the first atomic bomb while on *The Sequoia* and later hosted the world's first nuclear arms control conference on the ship. John Kennedy celebrated his 46th birthday, which was also his last birthday, on it, while Lyndon Johnson used it to lobby for the 1964 Civil Rights Act.

But no president used *The Sequoia* more than Richard Nixon, who was on it 88 times, sometimes entertaining congressman and foreign diplomats, sometimes relaxing with friends and family, and sometimes just cruising alone. On August 1, 1974, he was alone.

Earlier that evening his friend Bebe Rebozo had joined him on board and as the two men talked Nixon finally decided that he would resign from the presidency for his role in the Watergate scandal. In the wake of the revelation that Nixon had obstructed justice, his political support had imploded and articles of impeachment against him had been introduced. All hope was gone and Nixon finally knew it.

After Rebozo left, Nixon retired to the main salon where he asked that he be left alone, with the lights off. Finally, as it grew dark, Nixon sat down at the piano (added during Truman's administration) and asked one of the ship's crew to bring him a glass of his favorite drink, 20-year-old Ballantine Scotch. Nixon's rule whenever he was on *The Sequoia* was two Scotches, and no more, but after the crewman had poured him his drink Nixon said — for the first and only time — "Leave the bottle."

Which the crewman did, although he later asked the ship's captain if he had done the right thing. "If the president says, 'Leave the bottle,' you leave the bottle," the captain replied.

And so that night, alone in the dark, with a bottle of Scotch and the realization that he would be the first president ever to resign in disgrace, Richard Nixon played the piano for himself. The tune he kept playing was "God Bless America."

Four days later, while on *The Sequoia* for the last time, Nixon informed his family of his decision to resign. Four days after that, on August 9, he did just that.

© *Kauffmann 2008*

Bruce's History Lessons: David Atchison's *Very* Short Presidency

David Atchison, the 12th president of the United States of America, was born this week (Aug. 11) in 1807 in Frogtown, Kentucky.

Now, I know what you're thinking. Frogtown, Kentucky?

No, no, actually, what you're thinking is, who the heck is David Atchison and when was he president? It's quite a story.

Atchison was a United States Senator from Missouri who had advanced to become president pro tem of the Senate in 1849, just when James K. Polk was set to step down as U.S. president and Zachary Taylor, who had won the presidential election of 1848, was set to replace him. In those days presidents were inaugurated on March 4 - not until Franklin Roosevelt's time were presidents inaugurated in January - and as it happened, March 4, 1849, fell on a Sunday.

Which was a big problem for the deeply religious Zach Taylor, who refused to be sworn in on the Sabbath, meaning that there was some question as to who would serve as president of the United States between Sunday, when Polk stepped down, and Monday when Taylor could be sworn in.

The question was answered on March 4th. Since, back then, the president pro tem became president of the United States in the event the elected president and vice president were unable to serve - and since Atchison, having retained his senate seat and his job as president pro tem, was the first person to be sworn in on Inauguration Day - he was, technically speaking, the president of the United States.

Several minutes later, the vice president-elect, Millard Fillmore, was sworn in, at which point he became acting president of the United States under Article 2, Section 1, Clause 6 of the Constitution. Atchison happily went back to being president pro tem, and the next day, Zachary Taylor was sworn in as president, restoring the political order.

Interestingly, President Taylor would die just sixteen months later from a gastro-intestinal disorder that was probably caused by eating a bowl of cherries too quickly and gulping down a glass of milk after a hot 4th of July celebration. That made Fillmore president once again, and his decision to support the Compromise of 1850 - Zachary Taylor had adamantly opposed it - helped avert a civil war at a time when the North was much less ready to fight such a war than it would be in 1860. Such is the fickleness of fate.

As for Frogtown's most famous native son, and president-for-three-minutes, David Atchison, he seems not to have been unduly affected by his (admittedly brief) stint as the most powerful man in the country. After technically assuming, and then relinquishing, presidential power, he spent the rest of the day in bed sleeping.

© *Kauffmann 2008*

Bruce's History Lessons: Napoleon Bonaparte: Not Another Washington

Look up the word "overachiever" in the dictionary and you might find next to it a picture of Napoleon Bonaparte, who was born this week (Aug. 15) in 1769. In 1804, when he was crowned France's emperor in a ceremony unrivaled for its pomp and splendor (Napoleon choreographed it himself), he became one of the most powerful and wealthy rulers in French history, which was quite an accomplishment considering that he began his life neither powerful nor wealthy.

Nor even French. Napoleon was Corsican, one of 13 children born to a middle-class family from the Corsican city of Ajaccio. (By the way, what *is* the deal with famous dictators and their homelands? Adolf Hitler was born in Austria, not Germany; Josef Stalin was born in Georgia, not Russia.)

Napoleon's rise to the top was meteoric. Having joined the French army as a First Lieutenant with a genius for artillery, he became a Brigadier General when he was 24, leapfrogging several more senior candidates in the process. He won his first major battle at 28, and at 30 he helped initiate a *coup d'etat* that established a ruling consulate with himself as First Consul. A year later he named himself commander of the French army, and in 1802 became Consul for Life and finally emperor.

Napoleon's legacy is well known, both the good and bad. His Napoleonic Code, a series of sweeping legal and social reforms, was much admired in its time, and parts of it are still in use today. Yet he was an absolute despot who despised his countrymen and treated his women, his advisors and even his soldiers with indifference and disdain.

As for his military career, if the rise was meteoric, so was the fall. In the wake of his disastrous decision to invade Russia in 1812, which ended in ignominious defeat and the loss of one-third of his army, his many enemies smelled blood, and a coalition of Russian, English and Austrian troops soon defeated him, freeing Europe from his control. (Napoleon was undoubtedly disappointed by Austria's involvement since his second wife, Marie Louise, was the daughter of Austria's emperor!).

Napoleon subsequently was exiled to the French island of Elba, but he escaped to attempt a military comeback. At Waterloo, however, as all know, he was again defeated by a combination of British and Prussian forces, and his military and political career was finally over.

"They wanted me to be another Washington," Napoleon complained late in his life, referring to George Washington's historic decision to relinquish power voluntarily. Napoleon clung to power like a lifeline, which may explain why Washington died peacefully in his Mt. Vernon home, while Napoleon died alone, depressed and imprisoned on the British island of St. Helena.

© Kauffmann 2008

Bruce's History Lessons:
The Misunderstood Guillotine

"The mechanism falls like thunder; the head flies off, blood spurts,
the man is no more."

–Dr. Joseph Guillotin, describing his guillotine to the
French National Assembly

The supreme irony of the guillotine — an irony that caused the good doctor who invented it to brood the rest of his days — is that it was designed for humanitarian purposes. In 1789, as the French Revolution was flowering and words such as "equality" and "brotherhood" filled the air, the normal barbaric punishments that the common folk suffered for serious crimes suddenly were seen as not in keeping with the equal status granted to all French citizens — peasantry as well as nobility — by the "Declaration of the Rights of Man" that the French Assembly had just adopted.

Those normal punishments, which included hangings, breakings on the wheel, and being drawn and quartered, were in stark contrast to the punishments enjoyed by the nobility, who, when they were sentenced to death, were quickly and mercifully beheaded, usually by sword.

Thus Dr. Guillotin's "machine" was seen as a post-Enlightenment technological wonder that quickly, painlessly and equally dispatched all who deserved to die, giving common criminals the same dignity and status previously enjoyed by the more privileged members of French society. In essence, the guillotine was death made democratic.

Alas, its combination of egalitarianism and efficiency — little skill was needed to operate it and maintenance was a breeze — made it the perfect vehicle for those in authority seeking to bend the French Revolution to their

481

own purposes. And given that a great many political factions would gain and lose power during the various stages of the Revolution, with state punishment one day followed by retribution the next, there was no shortage of heads for the guillotine to sever. By the time of "The Terror," the number of "criminals" in France had reached such epidemic proportions that the guillotine became both the instrument and the symbol of the Revolution's bloodiest period. Because it was never able to shake this reputation, it is seen today as one of the most heinous of death machines, and the good Dr. Guillotin is viewed as a heartless, even macabre executioner.

The ball (actually a head) first got rolling this week (August 21) in 1792 when Louis Collot d'Angremont, a secretary in the National Guard, became the first political victim of the guillotine in punishment for participating in a "conspiracy" against the government. Before the French Revolution was over some 10,000 people would join him, including France's King Louis XVI and his wife, Marie Antoinette.

Interestingly, France's last execution by guillotine occurred in 1977. In 1981, France outlawed capital punishment altogether, laying the misunderstood guillotine — like its many victims — finally to rest.

© *Kauffmann 2008*

Bruce's History Lessons:
Strom Thurmond's Record Breaking Filibuster

filibuster, n. an attempt by a member of a legislative body, especially of the Senate, to obstruct the passage of a bill by making long speeches, introducing irrelevant issues, etc.

As has been noted often in the debate over whether Democrats have a right to filibuster President Bush's judicial appointees, the longest individual filibuster in Senate history occurred when South Carolina's senior senator, Strom Thurmond, filibustered a proposed civil rights bill. That one-man filibuster, which lasted for an astonishing 24 hours and 18 minutes, finally ended this week (Aug. 29) in 1957. As part of his filibuster "speech" Thurmond read the entire text of the state of South Carolina's election laws. It was not exactly reminiscent of Winston Churchill at the height of his rhetorical powers.

The civil rights legislation Thurmond was filibustering against included the usual laundry list of provisions ending segregation in housing, in public transportation, and in public places such as restaurants, but the bill's most important provisions were in the area of voting rights, and what gave the legislation teeth — and therefore was an anathema to Southern politicians such as Thurmond — was language that said federal judges, not local juries, would determine if these voting rights were being infringed. In the 1950s most Southern politicians couldn't have cared less about what a civil rights "law" actually said because they knew that all-white juries in their states would decide the outcome as they saw fit. Putting that decision-making power in the hands of federal judges was another matter entirely.

And so virtually the entire southern contingent of the Senate began a filibuster, and when the filibuster stretched into its third week, pro-civil rights senators finally agreed to remove the language that gave federal judges total judicial review over civil rights violations. Satisfied, the Senate's southern bloc ended its filibuster.

But not Thurmond. The man who, in 1948, left the Democratic Party to start a new states rights "Dixiecrat" Party in protest of President Harry Truman's liberal civil rights policies, continued his own personal filibuster in defiant dissent against awarding any kind of franchise to African-Americans. Only after he was threatened with physical harm did Thurmond finally relent, end his "speech" and sit down.

Still, you have to wonder at his faithfulness to his convictions because in fighting to deny African-Americans equal rights as citizens, he was — as he secretly knew — denying those rights to his own daughter. Not long after Thurmond died in 2003, a woman named Essie Mae Washington-Williams claimed that she was Thurmond's illegitimate child, having been born to Thurmond and an African-American maid in the Thurmond household when Thurmond was just 22 years old.

Shortly thereafter the Thurmond family publicly acknowledged that her claim was true.

© Kauffmann 2008

Bruce's History Lessons:
Elvis Meets Mr. Ed

This week (Sept. 9) in 1956 America's cultural paradigm shifted. Elvis Presley made his first appearance on *The Ed Sullivan Show*. It was a clash of customs and a war between the forces of good and evil. Presley, representing evil, won handily.

To begin at the beginning, in 1956 the Elvis phenomenon was starting to spread nationally. Records such as "Don't Be Cruel," "Hound Dog," and "Heartbreak Hotel" were climbing not only the popular charts but the country-music and rhythm-and-blues charts as well, which had never happened before. Elvis was hot, but he was also controversial. With his perpetual sneer, his guitar slung low and suggestively, and hips that swiveled and gyrated when he performed live, he was as feared and loathed by parents as he was worshipped by their children. "Elvis the Pelvis," who in reality was a mild-mannered momma's boy, became the symbol of teenage rebellion and sexuality.

Ed Sullivan, a stone-faced former gossip columnist, had somehow come to host the most popular variety show on television, *The Ed Sullivan Show*. Utterly humorless, but with a voice and onstage manner that were grist for countless stand-up comics, Sullivan ran his show like a tyrant, and as a self-proclaimed guardian of public morality, he would only book entertainers whose wholesomeness was beyond question. Which is why he publicly proclaimed that Elvis would never appear on his show.

He would eat those words. Immediately, Sullivan's main competitor, which in 1956 was a variety show hosted by the comic Steve Allen, booked Presley for an appearance. Although Allen had no qualms about having Presley on his show, he did try to tone the singer down, dressing him in a tuxedo and casting him in the show's comedy sketches. As an attempt to "split the difference" it was an abject failure — Elvis fans hated the show — but as a ratings getter it was a huge success. For the first time ever, Allen's show drew more viewers than Sullivan's.

Sullivan was not amused. Fighting for decency was one thing. Losing viewers, advertisers and your number one rating was another. Sullivan's agents quickly booked Elvis for a three-show gig at an unheard of $50,000. This small but significant battle in the *Kulturkampf* had come to an end. Elvis had won.

But Sullivan still had one shot to fire. He ordered his cameramen to only shoot Elvis from the waist up, meaning the television audience never saw the singer's gyrating hips and pelvis thrusts. It was Sullivan's way of "splitting the difference," and although it was cleverer than Steve Allen's, in the end it was little more than a parting shot. The "King" as Elvis was soon known, became more popular than ever.

© Kauffmann 2008

Bruce's History Lessons: George Wallace — An American Original

Four-time Alabama governor and three-time presidential candidate George Wallace died this week (Sept. 13) in 1998. Perhaps only Richard Daley, Chicago's ubiquitous mayor, or Huey Long, Louisiana's colorful governor, had political careers as memorable as his.

As the "moderate" candidate in his first run for Alabama governor in 1958 Wallace was thrashed by an avowed segregationist, and he learned his lesson. Wallace promised he would never again get "out segged," and in his successful second try for the statehouse in 1962 his campaign theme was "Segregation now! Segregation tomorrow! Segregation forever!" It was a vow that was tested just six months later when black students attempted to enter the all-white University of Alabama, and three months after that when black children attempted to integrate several public schools.

Wallace lost those fights when President Kennedy sent federal troops to enforce integration, but his unyielding demeanor and populist rhetoric quickly made him a symbol of Southern resistance to "pointy headed bureaucrats" in Washington. His was the politics of resentment and anger — at the rise in crime, at forced busing, at draft-dodging hippies, at higher taxes and more government regulations — and he appealed not only to Southerners, but increasingly to blue-collar Northerners who shared many of those concerns. In fact, after a surprising showing in the 1964 presidential campaign, Wallace ran a third-party campaign in 1968 that earned him 10 million votes — or 13 percent of the total turnout — and made him a political force to be reckoned with.

He was back at it in 1972, running against both President Nixon and his Democratic challenger George McGovern, noting that "There isn't a dime's worth of difference between the two parties," but his campaign was cut short when a deranged gunman shot him during a rally in Maryland. Crippled and confined to a wheelchair, Wallace returned to Alabama to finish his term as governor, but from then on both his politics and his life would gradually, yet profoundly change. He eventually renounced the race mongering of his early years, moved to the political center, and courted and received substantial numbers of black votes as he won two more terms as governor.

In his last years Wallace went on something of an "apology tour" for his racist past, frequently meeting with black political and church leaders, granting interviews to liberal writers and editors, and fervently, if not altogether convincingly, explaining his early politics as simply a stand for Constitutionally protected states' rights against an overly intrusive federal government.

Fittingly, before Wallace died he would see just how far the politics of reconciliation and hope, rather than division and fear, could take a Southern governor when his Georgia neighbor, Jimmy Carter, became president in 1976.

© Kauffmann 2008

Bruce's History Lessons: Washington's Farewell

This week (Sept. 19) in 1796 George Washington delivered his Farewell Address. Simply put, its message to an American public that had never known life without him was, "You're on your own."

Actually, Washington never "delivered" the address. He sent it to a Philadelphia newspaper, *The American Daily Advertiser*, which published it on September 19th. Newspapers nationwide quickly re-printed it, alerting a stunned populace that this time Washington really was relinquishing the presidency (he had wanted to, and threatened to, at the end of his first term, but his advisors convinced him the country was not yet able to do without him).

His reasons for stepping down — thereby establishing a two-term precedent for presidents that was honored until Franklin Roosevelt — were myriad. First, he was getting old and his health was an issue. He wanted to live out his last years in the bosom of his family and his Mt. Vernon home. Second, he was tired of the job. Internecine struggles among his advisors had wearied him and constant sniping by opposition newspapers had angered him. In fact, the original draft of his farewell message was so maudlin and self-pitying that he sent it to his top advisor, Alexander Hamilton, for help with a re-write. This Hamilton did, which ever since has sparked a historic debate over whether the Farewell Address is Washington's or Hamilton's. (It's mostly Hamilton's language but unquestionably Washington's thoughts and ideas).

But the main reason Washington said farewell was his unshaken belief in republican principles. As many historians have noted, Washington was not only America's first president, but in many ways its first and only monarch. His god-like status among the people, combined with the fact that so much of his presidency involved setting precedents that would be honored by all who followed, gave him executive power far beyond what the Framers had envisioned, and Washington knew it. He could think of no gesture that would better affirm his allegiance to republicanism than the voluntary surrender of that power.

As for the message itself, it contained two major themes. First, Washington warned against the danger of faction, especially faction generated by political parties. Partisan politics was a "fire not to be quenched," he admitted, but "it demands a uniform vigilance lest, instead of warming, it should consume." In other words, unity was paramount for the nation to prosper.

Second, Washington cautioned against America involving itself in foreign causes. Foreign policy, he insisted, should be based on America's interests and none other.

The address was a critical triumph and contributed mightily to Washington's legend. America would soon be without Washington, but thanks in part to his Farewell Address, it would not be without a guidepost to the future.

© Kauffmann 2008

Bruce's History Lessons:
The Townsend Letter

The old adage that when you are in big trouble you'll try anything would certainly seem to apply to America's reaction to a letter written this week (Sept. 30) in 1933 by Dr. Francis Townsend, a semi-retired physician living in Long Beach, California. The good doctor, who like most Americans was suffering from the ravages of the Great Depression, had an interesting idea about how to solve the nation's economic doldrums, and he shared it in a letter to the editor of the local paper, The Long Beach Press-Telegram.

The main problem, Townsend wrote, is that the country has a surplus of workers, which was a widely shared opinion given the massive unemployment that the Great Depression had caused. But Townsend's rather novel solution was to summarily remove all workers over sixty from the workforce by offering them $200 a month to retire. The only requirement was that they spend the entire $200 in the month they received it. Townsend planned to pay for this monthly stipend through a 2 percent value added tax on every business transaction Americans made.

And how would his plan affect the nation's economic stagnation, deflation and unemployment? As Townsend saw it, the elderly could retire with dignity and a guaranteed income, which would then shrink the labor pool and raise wages for those still working. Further, by requiring that its recipients spend the entire stipend in the month they receive it, it would stimulate the economy — much like today's consumer-driven economy — resulting in a general economic recovery. Finally, the value-added tax would retire the national debt and replace all other forms of taxation.

To say the least, Townsend struck a nerve, and within a year of his letter's publication 5,000 "Townsend Clubs" had sprung up nationwide with

2 million members. Another 25 million Americans soon signed petitions demanding that the government institute Townsend's plan, and in the congressional elections of 1934 most of those elected from California owed their seats to Townsend support. Townsend himself became a celebrity, even testifying before Congress about his plan.

So, were Townsend's economic theories as practical as they were popular? Hardly. The monthly stipend would have doubled the national tax burden, and transferring purchasing power to the old at the expense of the working young would have decreased aggregate consumption. Finally, a value-added transaction tax would have been easy to avoid through monopolistic practices that reduced the number of taxable business transactions.

And so, fortunately, the Townsend plan was never tried, and the "Townsend phenomenon" finally faded away. But to be fair, President Franklin Roosevelt later proposed a government plan that had a number of provisions similar to Townsend's, especially with respect to the elderly. It was called Social Security.

© *Kauffmann 2008*

Bruce's History Lessons:
No Jack Kennedy

Call it the most famous political put-down of the last quarter-century, maybe longer.

It occurred this week (Oct. 5) in 1988, in Omaha, Nebraska, where the Republican candidate for vice president, Dan Quayle, was engaged in a vice presidential debate with the Democratic candidate for that office, Lloyd Bentsen. Quayle, a two-term senator from Indiana, had been presidential candidate George Bush's surprise pick to round out the Republican ticket, and from the moment he was chosen doubts about his experience and competency surfaced. Compared with the venerable Bentsen, a four-term senator from Texas with a face that looked chiseled in stone (who, ironically, became a senator by defeating the senior Bush in the Texas senate race in 1972), the 41-year-old Quayle seemed boyish and inept.

And he only reinforced that impression during their debate. Quayle was hesitant and seemed out of his depth, and when he was asked what he would do if he had to succeed President Bush, he struggled for an answer. Finally, in desperation, he said, "I have as much experience as Jack Kennedy did when he sought the presidency."

Bentsen pounced. Drawing himself up, his face the picture of disapproval, Bentsen said in his best stentorian voice, "Senator, I served with Jack Kennedy. I knew Jack Kennedy. Jack Kennedy was a friend of mine. Senator, you're no Jack Kennedy."

It was the highlight of the entire campaign. A *Washington Post* headline shouted "Bentsen Bags A Quayle," and footage of the audience applause and Quayle's stricken look was replayed on news programs for days. As a result, even though the Bush-Quayle ticket would later decisively defeat the

Democratic ticket of Michael Dukakis and Bentsen in the election, Quayle's reputation as a lightweight never recovered (his later misspelling of the word "potato" in a school classroom — he spelled it "potatoe" — didn't help).

Which was unfortunate because in many ways Quayle was a thoughtful, articulate and especially engaged vice president. Most Washington insiders thought he had a better staff than President Bush, and on social issues he could be particularly effective. His criticism of the TV sitcom "Murphy Brown," for example, whose title character bore a child out of wedlock, sparked a much-needed national debate about unwed motherhood as a "lifestyle choice."

Yet, as Quayle discovered, sometimes a single moment can define you forever, and for him that debate debacle was it. Then again, as a friend of mine noted, if Quayle had been thinking on his feet — something good politicians are supposed to do — he could have easily turned the tables on Bentsen.

"The moment Bentsen said to Quayle, 'You're no Jack Kennedy,'" my friend explained, "Quayle should have replied, 'You're right. For starters, I've been faithful to my wife.'"

© Kauffmann 2008

Bruce's History Lessons: General Lee Goes to College

The Confederacy's greatest general, Robert E. Lee, died this week (Oct. 12) in 1870, and since his exploits in the Civil War are well known, I thought I'd share the story of his post-war life, specifically his acceptance of an offer, in 1865, to become president of a run-down, war-ravaged, southern university in Lexington, Virginia.

In 1865, Washington College, like the rest of the South, was a once-proud institution — George Washington himself had supported it financially — that had fallen on hard times. It had suffered extensive damage during the Civil War, including frequent pillaging by Union troops, and when Lee accepted the job only four teachers and about 40 students remained at the school.

In other words, Lee once again faced formidable odds. And interestingly — as was the case during the Civil War when he turned down President Lincoln's offer to command the Union armies and instead accepted an offer to command Confederate troops — when Lee accepted the Washington College job, he turned down several other job offers that were more lucrative than the $1,500 annual salary the financially strapped southern college was paying. But as he said, "I have led the young men of the South in battle. I must now teach their sons to discharge their duty in life."

To that end, Lee immediately went to work. He revised the curriculum, adding to the traditional (classical) studies several more practical scientific and engineering courses. During the Civil War Lee had seen first-hand what an advantage the Union North had enjoyed in terms of industrial production, technological development and advanced equipment, and he wanted the South to follow suit.

But he also wanted to imbue the young men in his charge with a sense of Christian sacrifice and duty. To Lee, the spiritual welfare of his students was as important as their physical or professional welfare, so he constantly lectured them on the benefits of discipline, selflessness and charity.

Most of all, however, Lee passed on a lesson to his students that he himself had learned at great cost. Lee had fought for the Confederacy because he considered himself a Virginian first and an American second, but in the war's wake he realized that the country's future depended on its citizens thinking of themselves as Americans above all. Thus when a southern woman implored Lee to convince her two sons not to move to the North, he replied, "Madam, forget your animosities and make your sons Americans."

When Lee died he was buried in the chapel of the college that had become the embodiment of his principles, dedication and spirit. And — most appropriately — the name of the college was immediately changed to Washington and Lee.

And Washington and Lee it remains today.

© Kauffmann 2008

Bruce's History Lessons:
The Olympic Black Power Salute

This week (Oct. 16) in 1968 at the Summer Olympic Games in Mexico City, two black American sprinters staged a political protest that galvanized the country and produced one of the most memorable photos ever taken at an athletic contest anywhere. While standing on the podium during the ceremony to award medals for the 200-meter dash, gold medalist Tommie Smith and bronze medalist John Carlos both raised a black-gloved fist in the air as a gesture of solidarity to the Black Power movement and — as they later explained — to protest against the institutional racism and poverty that black Americans suffered in the United States. (The photo, by the way, can be viewed by doing a simple Website search using either man's name.)

In response, the International Olympic Committee (IOC) stripped both men of their medals and supported the actions of the United States Olympic Committee, which suspended Smith and Carlos from the U.S. Olympic team and sent them home.

The IOC took this action because, as the committee explained at the time, "The basic principle of the Olympic Games is that politics plays no part whatsoever in them." When Carlos and Smith "advertised domestic political views," the committee added, they "violated this universally accepted principle."

Carlos and Smith would certainly agree with the charge that they had "advertised domestic political views." In fact, earlier in the summer they had planned to join an all-black-athlete boycott of the Mexico City games, which a young sociologist named Harry Edwards was trying to organize in the hopes that it would call attention to the lack of progress the Civil Rights movement was making in job discrimination, anti-poverty programs, voting rights and the like. But the boycott fell through, so Smith and Carlos, who had been friends and teammates since college, decided to take matters into their own fists.

Back home in America replays of the defiant gesture dominated the evening news and the photo was published in newspapers nationwide. Given that both Martin Luther King and Bobby Kennedy had been murdered earlier in the year, racial tensions were high in America, and while some applauded the courage that Carlos and Smith had shown, most Americans considered their action a disgrace. Carlos and Smith faced death threats, and for years both men had trouble finding lasting employment.

As an interesting aside, at the recent 2004 Summer Olympic Games in Greece, an Iranian judo wrestler refused to wrestle an Israeli wrestler because his country, Iran, does not recognize Israel's right to exist. It is difficult to imagine a more blatantly political gesture, yet the IOC did nothing. Apparently the principle that "politics plays no part whatsoever" at the Olympics depends on who is doing the playing.

© Kauffmann 2008

Bruce's History Lessons:
Agincourt

"We few, we happy few, we band of brothers."

– Shakespeare's Henry V addressing his troops before the
Battle of Agincourt

The Battle of Agincourt, among the most famous "David vs. Goliath" battles in all of war, occurred this week (Oct. 25) in 1415. The battle pitted "David," a weary and depleted 7,000-man British army led by the young King Henry V, against "Goliath," an army of 20,000 French noblemen, both cavalry and infantry, who were well rested, well equipped and were fighting on their home turf.

Claiming his right to the French throne, Henry had invaded France two months earlier and had been fighting ever since. As a result he had lost nearly half of his army either in battle or from disease, which prompted his decision to return to England to re-supply. But while marching to Calais, where he planned to rendezvous with an English fleet and sail home, he was met at Agincourt by the French force led by Charles d'Albret. The battle lines were drawn.

As most students of English history know, against overwhelming odds, Henry's forces carried the day, destroying the much larger French force, although there is still some debate over the chief causes of victory.

But some things are agreed upon. Weeks of heavy rains had made the battlefield a muddy mess, which not only weighed down further the heavy armor the French wore, but also made it virtually impossible for them to maneuver. Both French cavalry and the heavily armored French infantry repeatedly sank into the muddy fields and had difficulty moving, which made them sitting ducks for the English archers and highly mobile foot soldiers with their swords, spears, hatchets and billhooks (knives).

Further, the English changed the course of the battlefield by planting sharp wooden stakes that both protected their archers from French cavalry charges and served as a wedge, pushing French troops closer together in an increasingly narrow space that made maneuverability that much harder, and French vulnerability that much greater.

The result was a rout. Much of the French leadership was killed, including d'Albret, and the demoralized French troops soon surrendered. When the mud had settled, French casualties exceeded 5,000. English losses numbered around 300.

As a result of his victory, Henry was recognized as heir to the French throne, but his untimely death two years later of "camp fever" (probably dysentery) ended his dreams of combined rule. Still, England had the better of France for the next 14 years until the tide of battle was turned by a French military victory at least as miraculous as Agincourt.

That would be the French victory at Orleans in 1429, which was led by a French teenage girl named Joan of Arc.

© Kauffmann 2008

Bruce's History Lessons:
The Earl of Sandwich

John Montague, the 4th Earl of Sandwich, was born this week (Nov. 3) in 1718 and before he died in 1792 he traveled the world and served as a naval officer, a secretary of state, a First Lord of the Admiralty — twice — and a politician.

Yet he became famous — or so the story goes — for being such an avid gambler that once, while riding a hot streak, he instructed his servants to bring him roasted meat and cheese placed between two slices of bread so that he could hold his supper in one hand and his playing cards in the other, and never have to leave the card table. Montague's time-saving nourishment idea quickly caught on and soon a common refrain around British ale houses and pubs was "I'll have the same as Sandwich," which was shortened to, "I'll have a sandwich." And so the sandwich was born, which today is arguably the most commonly used eponym in the world. Every day millions of people order sandwiches at meal times, meaning the Earl of Sandwich earned fame for a vice rather than a virtue.

Or did he? In the 18th century, especially in the gastronomic world, British claims about inventing a new culinary delicacy were quite naturally refuted by the French, and the "sandwich" was no exception. The French claimed that, *mais non*, they invented the sandwich and as proof pointed out that in France, unlike in England, landowners were responsible by law for providing their field hands with a noontime meal. The sandwich was invented because it was so convenient. One could slap a sausage or piece of salted meat between two pieces of bread and — *Voila!* — produce a meal that was portable and would last the hours between the beginning of the workday and noon.

The truth about how the sandwich was really invented may never be known, but many historians believe some combination of both stories may be most likely. It is known that the Earl of Sandwich visited France and might well have been impressed with the convenience of the French "sandwich" enough to order a similar meal for his own field workers. Thus he may have earned the sandwich eponym without ever having eaten one, which has a ring of plausibility to it because in reality the Earl of Sandwich had a very bad gastrointestinal disorder that would have made it very difficult for him to eat a sandwich. His diet mostly consisted of liquids.

In any case, whether the British or the French invented the "sandwich" is not important. What's important is which country perfected it. And we all know to which country that honor belongs.

Waitress, I'll have a "Triple-Decker Club" on Rye, extra mayo.

© Kauffmann 2008

Bruce's History Lessons:
The Weird Attempt to Kill Hitler

Of the many assassination attempts on Adolf Hitler's life, including the most famous — the attempt in 1944 to detonate a bomb at his Wolf's Lair headquarters near Rastenburg, Germany (foiled by a thick conference table that absorbed the blast) — the attempt with the least likelihood of success may have come the closest to succeeding, this week (Nov. 8) in 1939.

Recall that several of Hitler's generals had, by 1939, become convinced that the *Fuhrer* was leading Germany to disaster, and therefore must be eliminated, but they hesitated to act, either unsure of success or unsure of one another. George Elser, however, had no such qualms. A loner with few friends and no family, his motivation for killing Hitler was economic. Under Nazi rule, laborers such as Elser had seen working conditions deteriorate sharply and he felt Hitler's removal would improve things.

Elser read that every November, on the anniversary of Hitler's failed Beer Hall Putsch, the Nazi leader addressed the party faithful at the *Burgerbraukeller* in Munich. Traveling there in April, Elser reconnoitered the area and decided that a time-bomb hidden inside a pillar near the dais where Hitler would stand had the best chance of success.

And so he taught himself bomb-making, stealing explosives from the armaments factory where he worked, and doing repeated tests of a crude exploding mechanism that he designed himself. Finally satisfied with his handiwork, he traveled back to Munich, where, for more than a month, he spent his evenings surreptitiously carving out a hole in the pillar that would hold his makeshift bomb. On November 6th he hid the bomb in the pillar and after checking it the next day — even pressing his ear to the pillar to hear the bomb ticking — he left Munich for Switzerland.

But once again, Hitler's uncanny luck saved his life. Pressed for time by the demands of his war planning, Hitler abruptly changed the scheduled time of the speech and shortened the ceremony, which usually lasted from 8:30 p.m. to 10 p.m. Instead, he began his speech at 8 p.m. and finished around 9 p.m., and rather than stay to mingle with his fellow Putsch veterans, he promptly left for Berlin.

The bomb exploded 10 minutes later, killing 8 people and wounding 60. Had Hitler been there he would have been blown to bits.

But he wasn't, further convincing the superstitious Hitler that a "higher power" watched over him so that he could fulfill his destiny — creating a German Empire. Equally unfortunate, Elser's failure further weakened the resolve of those generals around Hitler who had entertained thoughts of removing him.

Further proof that the only "law" still on the books in lawless Nazi Germany was the law of unintended consequences.

© Kauffmann 2008

Bruce's History Lessons:
The Teddy Bear

Did your little ones sleep with their Teddy Bears last night? If so, there is a reason why they slept with a Teddy Bear instead of, say, a Joey Bear or Billy Bear. It has to do with a hunting trip that President Theodore "Teddy" Roosevelt took near the banks of the Little Sunflower River in Mississippi in 1902.

Roosevelt had traveled to Mississippi for political reasons, but while he was there he decided to engage in his abiding passion for sport hunting. An expert marksman, Roosevelt was — alas — plagued by terrible luck on this particular hunting trip. For some reason the black bears that frequented the banks of the Little Sunflower River had disappeared. And doubly unfortunate for "TR" — as he was known — he had invited reporters to visit base camp each day to be apprised of his adventures. When day after day they reported in their newspapers that the president had returned from his hunting empty handed it became something of a national joke, which TR did not at all find amusing.

Sensing their boss's growing frustration, members of his party took the hunting dogs on a non-stop search for bears and finally they found and cornered one in a pond. The party's veteran hunter, Holt Collier, then lassoed the bear and, after cracking its skull with his gun, tied it to a tree.

Word went back to camp that a bear had been found and that the president should immediately ride out to kill it. Roosevelt galloped to the site only to find that his quarry was a small black bear, bloodied, semi-conscious, and lashed to a tree. Disgusted, TR refused to shoot the bear and returned to camp.

Another hunting calamity but a political windfall because the story of his "sporting" refusal to kill a defenseless bear soon got national headlines, which prompted the political cartoonist for *The Washington Post*, Cliff Berryman, to draw a cartoon commenting on TR's liberal (for those times) views on race relations. This week (Nov 16) in 1902 Berryman drew a very black bear — symbolizing oppressed African-Americans — being roped by a white man, while TR turned away in disgust.

The general public may or may not have gotten Berryman's political point, but they loved the bear and demanded more "Teddy Bear" cartoons, which Berryman, sensing he'd hit political pay dirt, obligingly gave them, drawing the bear rounder and cuddlier with each successive cartoon.

The rest is history. Toy manufacturers began churning out cuddly "Teddy Bears" and children the world over began getting them as presents. Today the bear is more famous than the president, which may be because while the president is only on Mt. Rushmore, the bear is in your neighborhood toy store.

Bruce's History Lessons:
The Lesson of The Hollywood 10

This week (Nov. 24) in 1947 the U.S. House of Representatives voted contempt charges against 10 of Hollywood's most famous writers, directors and actors for their refusal to answer questions posed to them by the House Un-American Activities Committee (HUAC) regarding their membership in the Communist Party. It was the beginning of the anti-communist "Red Scare" period of our history and all 10 men eventually were sentenced to one year in jail, their First Amendment right to free political affiliation notwithstanding.

HUAC's original purpose had been to investigate whether Communists had infiltrated Hollywood's labor unions, in particular the Screen Actors Guild, and whether that infiltration had resulted in subversive, pro-communist, anti-American messages in the films being made. As a result, immediately after the "Hollywood 10" (as they were dubbed) were cited for contempt all major Hollywood studios blacklisted them, announcing that they would no longer be allowed to work on Hollywood films until they admitted, and recanted, their Communist Party membership. For the "Hollywood 10" neither their careers nor their lives would ever be the same.

In point of fact, most of the accused were Communists, but in 1947 membership in the Communist Party was not against the law. Further, the evidence is slim at best that Hollywood screenwriters and producers were putting subversive, anti-American or pro-Soviet messages into their films, and in cases in which movies had a pro-Soviet slant it was often supported by the government. In the early 1940s the Soviet Union was America's ally, so when the unabashedly pro-Soviet film *Mission to Moscow* was made in 1943, Jack Warner, the head of Warner Brothers studio, considered it a patriotic act.

Indeed, overlooked in the controversy over the "Hollywood 10" is that the Hollywood studio system in the 1940s was so tightly controlled by omnipotent bosses such as Jack Warner and Sam Goldwyn that no "Leftist" screenwriter or actor could easily have slipped an anti-American message past them. Not only were studio bosses involved in every phase of a movie's production, from casting to the final cut, but also they often controlled the very lives of their talent, telling actors and writers how to dress and even whom to date. It's hard to imagine that a screenwriter could get an anti-American message past a control freak such as Sam Goldwyn, whose views about movies that mix entertainment with politics were summed up nicely by his famous quote, "If you want to send a message, hire Western Union."

Fast-forward to today where, more than ever, Hollywood is dominated by the Left, and many movies are little more than political diatribes. But it is the moviegoer, not a Congressional committee, who sits in judgment, which seems to me to be a marked improvement.

© Kauffmann 2008

Bruce's History Lessons: The "Premature" Birth of Winston Churchill

This week (Nov. 30) in 1874, Winston Spencer Churchill, Great Britain's greatest prime minister and — in historian William Manchester's immortal phrase — the 20th century's "last lion" was born in Blenheim Palace, the historic Churchill family home. He was product of the marriage between Lord Randolph Churchill, the son of the Duke and Duchess of Marlborough, and Jeanette ("Jennie") Jerome, the daughter of an American financier and his wife.

It had been a whirlwind courtship. Randolph and Jennie were engaged less than a week after they met, and although Jennie's father, Leonard Jerome, had serious misgivings about the relationship, he was eventually brought around and even looked forward to the marriage.

Not so the Duke and Duchess, who were appalled at the thought of their son marrying a commoner, and an *American* at that. Yet, as was often the case in Victorian England, the main quarrel over the marriage soon came down to dollars, or in this case pounds. The Duke wanted Randolph to have sole control over the family finances, while the Jeromes — who would be supporting the young couple to the tune of two thousand pounds a year (about twice what the Duke would contribute) — wanted Jennie to have a say in how the money was to be used.

All this bickering and delay by their parents caused the young couple great anguish, and not solely because they longed to put an official imprimatur on their undying love. As subsequent events would strongly hint, by the time they finally prevailed upon their parents to allow their marriage, Jennie was probably six weeks pregnant. Indeed, counting backward from Winston's birth — this week — to his parents' marriage on April 15th, 1874, one arrives at a total of just over seven months. What's more, it was not a small, sickly, premature babe that sprang from his mother's womb, but a fat, cherubic, vocal and exceedingly healthy young lion cub.

Jennie and Randolph, of course, claimed that their son *was* born premature, but practically no one believed it, and years later even Churchill himself had his doubts. Typically, however, Churchill was more amused than ashamed over the possibility, and with his customary wit would respond to all inquiries on the subject by saying, "Although present on the occasion, I have no clear memory of events leading up to it."

But for a change, his was not the last word. That, in my mind, comes from Churchill's best biographer, William Manchester, who clearly believes Jennie was pregnant before her marriage, but is willing to entertain the *possibility* that Winston was born premature. "It would have been just like him," Manchester writes in *The Last Lion: Visions of Glory.* "He never could wait his turn."

© Kauffmann 2008

Bruce's History Lessons: President Adams Goes Back to Congress

This week (Dec. 5) in 1831, John Quincy Adams, who had served as an ambassador, a U.S. senator, a secretary of state — under James Monroe, he wrote the Monroe Doctrine — and our 6th president, took his seat in Congress as a representative from Massachusetts. He is one of just two former presidents to serve in Congress.

His admirers had opposed him running for Congress, thinking it too "humbling" for a man who had once occupied the White House, but Adams, whose father, John, had helped create the government under which Congress functioned, knew better. He knew that the House of Representatives, with its frequent elections, power to initiate legislation and control of the nation's finances, was the government branch designed to be closest to "the people," so he was honored to serve.

And he wanted to serve because by the 1830s Adams was convinced that the institution of slavery was corrupting the nation's soul, and that it was his responsibility to help abolish it. That is why he voted against the annexation of Texas in 1836. He feared the Texas territory would become at least one slave-holding state and possibly several.

He also worked tirelessly to end the so-called "gag rule," which allowed members of Congress to "table" — that is, to put aside without debate or vote — the many petitions Congress was receiving demanding that slavery be abolished. By 1836 the abolitionist movement had gained considerable strength in America, but in Congress there was still an uneasy balance of power between free states and slave states, so most members wanted to duck the issue. The gag rule gave them political cover.

Adams believed the gag rule violated the constitutional right to petition and his many impassioned speeches against both the gag rule and slavery earned him the nickname "Old Man Eloquent." Finally in 1844 he succeeded in repealing the rule.

Adams was even involved in one of history's most famous slavery trials, the trial of the *Amistad* Africans, who had been illegally sold as slaves and put on the slave ship *Amistad* where they rebelled, killed the captain and commandeered the ship. After they inadvertently sailed into American waters, they were captured, put on trial and accused of murder, but when their case finally reached the Supreme Court, Adams helped successfully defend them and they were set free.

Adams spent 17 years in Congress — he suffered the stroke that finally killed him on the House floor — and today he is more honored for his Congressional service than for his presidency. Indeed, it has been said that if Adams' presidency had been as effective as his public service both before and after holding that office, he might well be on Mt. Rushmore.

© Kauffmann 2008

Bruce's History Lessons:
Bush v. Gore

Really? It's only been five years?!

Yep. Just five years ago this week (Dec. 12), the U.S. Supreme Court handed down its opinion in *Bush v. Gore,* overturning a ruling by Florida's Supreme Court that had extended the deadline for a statewide recount of Florida's votes for president. As a result, George W. Bush and not Albert Gore became America's 43rd president.

To begin at the beginning, when Election Day 2000 was over Gore had 267 electoral votes to Bush's 246, but needed 270 for victory. As a result, all eyes were on Florida, which had 25 electoral votes, but whose final vote was so close — Bush leading Gore by just 1,784 votes — that it triggered an automatic recount. But after that recount the vote was even closer. Bush now led Gore by just 327 votes!

Another recount was in order, especially since there had been voting "irregularities" thanks to Florida's rather outdated voting machinery. Many thousands of Florida's punch-card ballots, when processed by the voting machines, produced the now-infamous "chads," "hanging chads," "dimpled chads" or "pregnant chads," and determining what the voter intended by the positioning of these tiny slips of paper was a nightmare. In fact, depending on how these chads hung from the ballot, every recount promised to produce a different result than the one before it.

Which, to the U.S. Supreme Court, meant that the recount then being conducted in Florida lacked a consistent standard and therefore was unconstitutional. The court ruled that the Constitution's Equal Protection Clause guarantees individuals that their ballots cannot be devalued by "later arbitrary and disparate treatment," which the majority of the Supreme Court justices felt was clearly the case in Florida. After all, different standards were being applied not only from precinct to precinct, but also — thanks to the chads — from ballot to ballot.

For this reason the court said that no recount that would pass constitutional muster could possibly be fashioned in time to meet Florida's deadline for certifying electors. And in a separate opinion, Justices Rehnquist, Scalia and Thomas ruled that the Florida court's recount scheme was also unconstitutional because it created a new election law, which only the legislature may do.

For their part, the court's liberal wing, in particular Justices Souter and Stevens, agreed that Florida's recount violated the Equal Protection Clause, but argued that a constitutional remedy could be found given enough time. To them, an arbitrary deadline should never take precedence over proper resolution of a constitutional issue.

But in the end, a 5-4 majority — essentially representing the court's 5-4 conservative-liberal split — ruled for Bush over Gore. As a result, George Bush beat Al Gore by 537 votes — *out of six million cast* by Florida's residents.

© *Kauffmann 2008*

Bruce's History Lessons: The Christmas Bombings

It was not exactly in keeping with the spirit of the season when, this week (Dec. 19) in 1972, President Richard Nixon again escalated the Vietnam War by ordering the massive bombing of key targets in North Vietnam. Dubbed the "Christmas Bombings," the tonnage of bombs dropped by American B-52s in the next 12 days of that December exceeded the tonnage of the previous three years, and many thousands of North Vietnamese were killed.

Nixon's reasons for ordering the bombing were many but included the fact that he had recently won re-election in a landslide. Invigorated by what he perceived was a "mandate" to end the war as he saw fit, Nixon pressed both the North and South for a settlement. He pressured the South Vietnamese government under Nguyen Van Thieu to accept a deal in which a number of North Vietnamese troops would be allowed to remain in the South and any future South Vietnamese government would include North Vietnamese representation. As for the North, Nixon pressured its leaders into agreeing to keep Thieu as head of the South's future "coalition" government, while demanding a drastic reduction of North Vietnamese troops in the South.

When the North balked, Nixon ordered the Christmas bombings, and while most North Vietnamese, being Buddhists, were unaware of the irony of such massive destruction during one of the Christian world's most important religious holidays, the non-Buddhist world — including much of Europe and most of America — *was* aware, and was uniformly aghast. In fact, speaking of irony, the same election that returned Nixon to the White House put many new anti-war Democrats in Congress, and they were so appalled by the brutality of the Christmas bombings that they threatened to cut off all funds for military operations in Indochina.

Suddenly Nixon faced a revolt in Congress, which — coupled with his escalating problems because of the Watergate scandal — forced him back to the negotiating table, this time in a weakened position, where he eventually worked out a deal that became the Paris Peace Accords of 1973. On paper (adding insult to irony) this peace agreement was no different than the Geneva Accords that had proved so unworkable in 1954, and that had ultimately led to America's intervention in Vietnam.

But the reality was even worse. With Nixon increasingly impotent because of Watergate and the rest of America fed up with the war, North Vietnam ignored the Paris peace agreement, escalated its attack on the South, and eventually overran it. Soon after, America withdrew, ensuring the death of an independent South Vietnam.

And in the final irony, withdrawal came just after conclusion of the Christian world's *other* most important religious holiday, Easter, which is supposed to celebrate a resurrection.

© Kauffmann 2008

Bruce's History Lessons:
Manifest Destiny!

Some people coin phrases. Journalist John L. O'Sullivan minted one this week (Dec. 27) in 1845 when he wrote in The Democratic Review that it was America's "manifest destiny to overspread and to possess the whole of the continent, which Providence has given us."

O'Sullivan's phrase quickly caught on, and "manifest destiny" was soon invoked by countless politicians to justify America's inexorable expansion west and inevitable appropriation of the North American continent from the Atlantic to the Pacific. The fact that, at the time, significant parts of that continent — in particular the California and Oregon territories — belonged to other nations was considered a minor irritant. "Our multiplying millions," O'Sullivan also wrote, needed more land for "free development" and also to spread our "great experiment of liberty."

Mexico, to which California was then attached, had a somewhat less mellifluous phrase for America's "manifest destiny." Mexicans called it "Yanqui imperialism," which they had seen firsthand over the fight for Texas, once a part of Mexico, but as of 1845 a part of America thanks to America's superior military might. To most Mexicans, whose country had outlawed slavery, losing Texas to slaveholding Yankees who spoke of the "great experiment of liberty" was the height of hypocrisy.

And they had a point. Manifest destiny was high sounding, but self-interest was the chief motivation. The American population was growing by leaps and bounds, Americans needed room to grow and that room was westward. By 1845 the Santa Fe and Oregon trails were crowded with white settlers looking for new lands to settle, and they didn't much care whether those lands had previous, or current, occupants — as Mexico would discover once again in 1848 when another U.S.-initiated war, the Mexican-American war, cost it the aforementioned California and much of what is today America's Southwest. (Mexicans have an apt saying: "Poor Mexico, so far from God, so close to the United States.")

But to be fair, the hypocrisy of slavery notwithstanding, most Americans did have a missionary faith that the expansion of democracy — both westward and worldwide — was a good thing and that America had been chosen by Providence to spread the blessings of liberty, self-government and natural rights to as many of the un-enlightened as possible.

In fact, the phrase "manifest destiny" nicely encapsulated two quintessentially American attributes — self-interest and political idealism. For America to become a rich, but also a great and powerful nation, it needed to encompass the continent "from sea to shining sea." And with those riches and power it would best be able to defend, and spread, a political system that had the greatest chance of ensuring human freedom, happiness and progress.

Small wonder the phrase "manifest destiny" is a part of the American lexicon.

© Kauffmann 2008

Bruce's History Lessons: FDR's Four Freedoms

Arguably the most important "State of the Union" address ever given by a U.S. president was given this week (Jan. 6) in 1941 by President Franklin Roosevelt. It also became the most famous, earning its own stand-alone title, "The Four Freedoms Speech."

In it, Roosevelt told Congress and the American people that the state of the Union was perilous indeed and that, contrary to the wishes of the large and growing isolationist movement in America, the rise of Nazism, fascism and iron-fisted dictatorships that had occurred recently in Europe and East Asia was a grave threat to America's future and the future of democratic loving countries everywhere. Because of that threat, Roosevelt continued, America would dramatically increase both its defense budget and weapons production, and we would sell those weapons to any country currently fighting against these forces of evil. What's more, even if those countries could not pay, we would "share" with them any weapons or war materials they required. After all, Roosevelt said, support of those countries fighting totalitarianism and dictatorial rule was tantamount to defending America because if the forces threatening Europe and Asia prevailed, they would soon turn their sights on the Western Hemisphere.

"As a nation we may take pride in the fact that we are soft-hearted," Roosevelt intoned, "but we cannot afford to be soft-headed." A world war involving America was entirely possible the president hinted, and it would not be a fight merely for territory, but a global clash over what was to be mankind's dominant ideology.

But having issued the warning, Roosevelt, whose genius as a speaker has been matched by few in our history, ended his address on a note of hope.

Anticipating the eventual triumph of freedom-loving peoples over those seeking to destroy them, Roosevelt imagined "a world founded upon four essential freedoms."

"The first is freedom of speech — everywhere in the world," Roosevelt said. "The second is freedom of every person to worship God in his own way — everywhere in the world.

"The third is freedom from want," Roosevelt continued, which would "secure to every nation a healthy peacetime life for its inhabitants."

And the fourth was "Freedom from fear," Roosevelt concluded, "in which no nation will be in a position to commit an act of physical aggression against any neighbor."

Of course, in the years since, the world has fallen somewhat short of those noble goals, but Roosevelt's speech did lay the foundation for America's post-war foreign policy — one in which preserving American democracy would be inextricably linked with furthering and protecting democracy worldwide. For better or worse, from the Cold War containment of communism to the current war against terrorism, that has been our overall policy ever since.

© Kauffmann 2008

Bruce's History Lesson:
Broadway Joe's "Guarantee"

Lately it has become commonplace for athletes to "guarantee" victory in athletic contests, but easily the most famous such "guarantee" was uttered in 1969 by Joe Namath, the star quarterback of the New York Jets, prior to Super Bowl III against the Baltimore Colts. At a dinner three days before the game, Namath said, "We're going to win on Sunday. I guarantee it."

Namath's guarantee quickly made headlines, especially since the American Football League (AFL) champions, the Jets, were 19-point underdogs against the National Football League (NFL) champions, the mighty Baltimore Colts. In 1969, the two leagues had not yet merged for the simple reason that the NFL was so superior it had little incentive to do so.

Namath would change that, first because coming out of college he had inspired such a bidding war between the two leagues that the NFL began to see a merger as one way to save money, and second because — in Super Bowl III, which was played this week (Jan. 12) in 1969 — Namath would deliver on his guarantee. In a performance that earned him MVP honors, Namath completed 17-of-28 passes for 206 yards, and the Jets defeated the Colts by a score of 16-7.

Still considered the greatest upset in Super Bowl history, it made Namath a legend and earned the upstart AFL a new respect — a respect that furthered the momentum for a merger with the NFL. More than any other football player, Namath is the reason there is one football league today.

And he was a star off the field as well as on. With his long hair, drooping mustache, fur coats and gaudy white shoes, Namath, whose nickname was "Broadway Joe," was the perfect anti-hero at a time — the late '60s — when anti-heroes were in fashion. He dated gorgeous women and partied until all hours in America's most famous party town, New York City. Namath also made a fortune in endorsements, even wearing panty hose and shaving off his mustache in two famous television commercials.

However, for all his outlandish behavior, he was a consummate professional on the field. The only quarterback ever to throw for 4,000 yards in a 14-game season, he was selected as the quarterback for the all-time AFL team, and in 1985 he was inducted into pro football's Hall of Fame.

But there is an interesting postscript to this story. On the flight down to the Super Bowl, while examining a diamond brooch he had bought his mother, Namath noticed that it had 12 diamonds. He also noticed that the game was being played on January 12, and that his jersey number was 12. "It was an omen," he said, one that inspired him to utter his famous guarantee.

© *Kauffmann 2008*

Made in the USA
Lexington, KY
27 November 2009